AQUINAS
ON THE
EMOTIONS

MORAL TRADITIONS SERIES
James F. Keenan, Series Editor

AQUINAS
ON THE
EMOTIONS

A

Religious-Ethical

Inquiry

Diana Fritz Cates

Georgetown University Press/Washington, D.C.

Georgetown University Press, Washington, D.C. www.press.georgetown.edu

Portions of "The Religious Dimension of Ordinary Human Emotions," *Journal of the Society of Christian Ethics* 25, no. 1 (2005): 35–53, are reprinted here as part of chapter 2 with permission from the Society of Christian Ethics.

Portions of "Conceiving Emotions: Martha Nussbaum's 'Upheavals of Thought,'" *Journal of Religious Ethics* 31, no. 2 (2003): 325–41, are reprinted here as part of chapter 3 with the permission of Wiley-Blackwell.

Cover image: Mei, Bernadino (1615–1676), *Saint Thomas Aquinas*. Scala / Art Resource, NY.

Library of Congress Cataloging-in-Publication Data

Cates, Diana Fritz.
   Aquinas on the emotions : a religious-ethical inquiry / Diana Fritz Cates.
       p. cm. — (Moral traditions series)
   Includes bibliographical references (p.   ) and index.
   ISBN 978-1-58901-505-0 (pbk. : alk. paper)
  1. Thomas, Aquinas, Saint, 1225?–1274.   2. Christian ethics—Catholic authors.
  3. Emotions—Religious aspects—Catholic Church.   I. Title.
   BJ255.T5C38 2009
   241'.042092—dc22

                                          2009006666

15 14 13 12 11 10 09   9 8 7 6 5 4 3 2
First printing

Printed in the United States of America

With love for Rick, Ben, and Hannah
And in memory of J. Giles Milhaven

Contents

Acknowledgments

My first exposure to the philosophical study of emotion was long ago in a course taught by Karen J. Warren, then of St. Olaf College. She taught with such skill and passion that I continue to feel the power of her mind after all these years. Very few scholars at the time were taking the emotions seriously as a topic of philosophical study. Karen was a trail blazer. In graduate school at Brown, I had the good fortune to study with several teachers who encouraged me to pursue this neglected area of study. I am grateful to J. Giles Milhaven, my mentor and friend, who taught me to love—and to argue lovingly—with Thomas Aquinas. Giles passed away while I was writing this book. I am also grateful to John P. Reeder Jr., who has been a faithful and astute commenter on my scholarship for many years; to Sumner B. Twiss, who continues to contribute to my intellectual and professional development in countless ways; and to Martha C. Nussbaum, who deepened my appreciation for the remarkable things that ancient philosophers can teach us about the emotions and, indeed, about life. It was Martha who urged me to write this book.

Specifically with regard to this project, I am indebted to many people, for many different things. Jock Reeder and Edward Vacek offered extensive, penetrating comments on every chapter of an earlier draft. Keith Green brought to the project a keen mind and the heart of friendship. Jonathan Schofer provided remarkable perspective on the project as a whole and on matters of method. Many other colleagues read and offered helpful comments on a full draft of the manuscript, including Stephen Pope, William McDonough, Nancy Menning, Michele Petersen, Abbylynn Helgevold, Christine Darr, and Nancy Hauserman. Other colleagues who assisted me with various parts of this project, through conversation or the gift of their scholarship, include Jean Porter, Christopher Mount, Thomas Lewis, James Gubbins, Howard Rhodes, Jordan Copeland, Richard McCarty, and Ezra Plank. Many of the ideas in this book were developed through conversations with additional colleagues in the Society of Christian Ethics and graduate students in my Aquinas seminars. For the spiritual, emotional, and bodily support that kept me (more or less) in one piece, I extend thanks to Sara Pamela Star, Angelika Kieffer, Wendelin Guentner, Rachel Gordon, Lori Baldwin, and my mother, Donna Fritz.

I have received generous institutional support from the University of Iowa. I am grateful to my colleague and the chair of my department, Raymond Mentzer; to Dean Linda Maxson and Executive Associate Dean Raúl Curto of the College of Liberal Arts and Sciences; and to Jay Semel and the staff of the Obermann Center for Advanced Studies. I benefited greatly from being an Obermann Scholar. This book was supported by a Career Development Award from the Office of the Provost and an Arts and Humanities Initiative Grant from the Office of the Vice President for Research.

Parts of chapter 1 were presented in the form of a keynote address, "The Religious-Ethical Study of Emotion," for the Fourth Annual Graduate Symposium in Religious Studies, Florida State University (2005). Chapter 2 has its basis in "The Religious Dimension of Ordinary Human Emotions," originally presented at the 2004 annual meeting of the Society of Christian Ethics and later published in the *Journal of the Society of Christian Ethics*. A portion of chapter 3 was drawn from my article, "Conceiving Emotions: Martha Nussbaum's *Upheavals of Thought*," published in the *Journal of Religious Ethics*.

I am thankful for everyone at Georgetown University Press who worked on this book, especially Richard Brown, the director of the press, who provided astute advice and enthusiastic support at every stage, and to James Keenan, who agreed to include the book in his Moral Traditions series.

Finally, my husband, Rick Borchard, has been loving, encouraging, and patient beyond belief during the long time it took to write and revise this project. He has seen me through many challenges and kept me from losing sight of my goal. My children, Ben and Hannah, have lifted me up with their affection and trust and provided many unspoken assurances of the fundamental goodness of life, even in the face of tragedy. From these remarkable people, and from the rest of my family and friends, I have learned much about love. If Aquinas's thought did not illuminate, deepen, and extend this love, I would not have continued my long conversation with him.

Introduction

All of us want to live happily and well. We want this not only for ourselves but also for others who are part of us or closely connected to us. When something happens that appears to bear notably on our own or a loved one's well-being, a situation forms and holds our attention. We receive impressions and make judgments about what is happening and about how it concerns us. More than this, we are *moved* by what we apprehend. We might not be moved outwardly, in the form of physical movement, but we are moved inwardly.

Imagine that the phone rings. You answer and hear the voice of a friend with whom you have not had the chance to talk for months. She sounds happy and you feel elevated. As the conversation unfolds, you have the sense that you are drawing close to her and she is drawing close to you. You resonate with pleasure in the simple goodness of this relationship—in the way that you are poised to unite with her and she with you, in thought, by phone, or in person. When the conversation ends, your friend is drawn away from you into other aspects of her life. You are drawn back into your previous activities. Yet your friend remains vaguely present to you. You rehearse parts of the conversation, smiling.

Imagine that five minutes later the phone rings again, and you answer cheerfully. This time, however, it is a person with whom you have a difficult relationship. At the sound of his voice you experience a kind of dissonance. You recoil inside and your defenses go up. Every time you talk to this person he says something insulting. You replay a set of his past comments as you listen (and fail to listen) to what he is saying now. One part of you tends *away from* the person as you suffer the pain of old and new injuries. Another part of you tends *toward* the person as you fantasize about "knocking him off his high horse." When you hang up the phone, you go on and on, in your mind, about how awful this person is. You begin to attack *yourself* for not saying something to put him in his place, but you withdraw your attack as you recollect past attempts that have only made matters worse.

Then you hear a knock at the door. Startled, you become aware that you have been lost in a dark reverie for nearly half an hour. "Come in!" The door drifts open and a colleague appears, looking pale. She says, "I'm afraid I have some bad news." You learn that another, valued colleague has been in a car accident and is undergoing emergency surgery. Instantly, the situation that had preoccupied you since that last phone call is gone from your mind. As you picture your colleague lying on an operating table, bleeding, surrounded by bustling people in scrubs, connected to beeping monitors, you are initially stunned. You feel pinned, unable to move inside. Then you begin to extend yourself in his direction. By the power of your imagination you encircle him with your concern. You think of his wife and child and draw them into the circle as well. You are buoyed by the thought that your friend has made it thus far, and he is surely in good hands. A few moments later, your imagination drifts back to the gravity of the situation. You stiffen and shudder. The threat of death is creeping in like low-lying fog.

Many of us flow into and out of such states throughout the course of a day. Our responses to similar situations might take different forms. The details of our lives, such as our upbringing, cultural context, education, gender, social location, and the history of our relationships, all make a difference. Yet there are patterns that we can recognize. What are these patterns? What *are* the interior motions that many of us call "emotions"? How ought we to understand them? This book analyzes the writings of medieval theologian Thomas Aquinas in order to elucidate one powerful way of thinking about our emotions. I will explain shortly why I turn to Aquinas. Consider first why it is important to seek greater understanding of our emotions.

THE INFLUENCE OF EMOTION

When we are under the influence of an intense emotion, it is as though we enter a different world. A situation that appears to bear on our own or another's well-being commands our attention. Other things happen to us and around us, but many of them escape our notice. The things we *do* notice, we tend to construe in a particular way, in terms of the scenario that is playing out before us. Seeing things from this viewpoint, and being moved by what we see, we tend to act in predictable ways.

Imagine once again the first situation above. The emotion you experience when you hear your friend's voice, and picture her on the other end of the phone, will likely dispose you to treat her kindly. She might tell you that she has realized a difficult goal. At hearing this news, you tend toward her, in your imagination, as though you were rushing up to her and giving her a hug or a high-five. You praise her. When she tells you of a personal loss, you receive some of the weight of her sadness and hold it for a moment. Then you are drawn toward her, as if to her side. You express concern and offer your help. Your friend asks how *you* are doing. Within the context of your drawing near to her—and her tending toward you—many of your problems seem insignificant. Those that are serious feel less weighty than they did before you picked up the phone. When the conversation ends, you turn to the rest of the day with a positive attitude. You are prone to show kindness to the next person who crosses your path, unless it is someone whom you habitually regard in a negative light.

Now recall the second conversation with the person who says insulting things. The emotion that is aroused by *his* voice, by the image of *him* on the other end of the phone, will likely dispose you to act somewhat differently. For example, it might make it difficult for you to do your work. So much of your mental energy is invested in picturing the other's distorted face, rehearsing his words, developing a story line that makes you look like the victim in the situation, fantasizing about payback, and so on, that you cannot concentrate on the material you are to read. Your productivity drops, and this has an impact on the people who rely on you. Behaving like a stormy center of power pushing back on another center of power, you might rush down the hall oblivious to a third person whose eyes are searching yours for recognition.

For good or for ill, an emotion can affect the way we function as moral agents. It can affect our thoughts, perceptions, desires, judgments, deliberations, decisions, actions, and interactions. Particularly if an emotion is intense, arises with great frequency, or lingers for long periods of time, it can affect the quality of our lives and our relationships. It is thus important to understand our emotions and bring ethical reflection to bear on them.

THE MORALITY OF EMOTION

Our emotions can have an effect on our moral lives, but can we, as moral agents, have an effect on our emotions? Are our emotions the sorts of things over which we have any choice? Are they the sorts of things for which we can be held responsible? There are definitely limits to our capacity to influence the ways in which we are moved by the situations we confront. Some of our interior motions and the behaviors to which they give rise are quite automatic. Humans seem to have evolved to respond immediately to certain stimuli before there is time to think. Yet most emotions are more than knee-jerk responses. They are relatively intelligent responses that unfold over time, partly in response to ongoing thinking. There are points in the unfolding of an emotion at which it becomes possible for us to subject our emotions to the power of choice. Inasmuch as an emotion affects our own or another's well-being, and we have some choice in its regard, the emotion is something for which we have a degree of moral responsibility.

First, we are ordinarily responsible for the way we *act* while under the influence of an emotion. I am not referring here to bodily reactions and behaviors over which we (or some of us) have no control, such as letting out a shriek and jumping on the nearest chair at the sight of a mouse running across the floor. I refer to actions that we commit, which most of us believe we have the freedom not to commit, such as staying up on the chair for a long time or getting down and setting a trap. If we feel impelled to act on an emotion, such as fear or anger, the ideals of virtue require that we be aware of ourselves feeling so impelled and that we judge whether it would be fitting to act as our emotion impels us to act. We are required to make choices we can justify to other reasonable people.

Second, we are responsible, to some extent, for the way we *feel* our emotions. With most emotions—even those that arise under the influence of higher-level thinking about the significance of a situation—we cannot help our initial, interior movement. A situation captures our attention and triggers a response before we know what is happening. However, we can help whether we *consent* to this initial movement. That is, we can exercise some influence, in subsequent moments, over whether we continue to feel the emotion in the way we currently feel it. The very act of observing our emotion and asking the *question* of whether it is appropriate to the situation—or whether we are overreacting—changes the emotion in subtle ways. When we observe and wonder about our emotion, the object of our emotion (namely, the situation of concern, as we perceive or imagine it) is less capable of commanding our attention in a narrow and exclusive way. We put the object in broader perspective, which allows us to view it from more than one angle. Our interior tending with respect to the object is more flexible, less programmed.

We are responsible, in effect, for creating some mental space around our emotion. Moreover, we are responsible for trying to direct the course of our emotion, as needed, so that it reflects the light of reason. In other words, we are responsible for trying to feel our emotion in a way that exhibits good human functioning.[1] It is not a simple matter to determine whether our own or another person's way of experiencing a particular emotion is appropriate to a situation. We humans have different ideas about what is good for us and for other humans. Yet many of us can probably think of cases in which we would say that a person's emotion is fitting, and the way in which the person directs the course of his or her emotion is praiseworthy, while we can think of other cases in which we would say that a person's emotion is unfitting, and the way in which the person indulges that emotion, feeds it, or fails to give it direction is blameworthy.

Consider, for example, a middle-aged man who realizes that he no longer feels the emotion of love he used to feel toward his wife. There are still moments when he feels it, but these moments occur rather infrequently. When he does feel love, the feeling is not as intense as he would like it to be. The man cannot honestly say that his wife has become less lovable. It is his own attitude that has changed, for reasons he does not fully understand. Motivated to improve the quality of his life and marriage, he sets out to cultivate his love for his wife. In particular, he sets out to feel the *emotion* of love for her more frequently and intensely. Let us say that after much creative effort he begins to feel such love arising more often and ardently, in a way that rejuvenates his life and marriage. I would regard such love (in principle) as morally good, and the man as praiseworthy for feeling it as he does. His emotion is a fitting response to his wife and their marriage, an important moment within the rhythm of a good marital friendship, and he has had a hand in shaping that response.

Consider another example. A woman is consumed with the emotion of ethnic hatred for her new neighbor. Her hatred reflects a lifelong pattern of demonizing a group of people and refusing to consider the possibility that "those people" have any redeeming qualities. Once in a while, as the woman is experiencing this hatred, she has an inkling that there is something unfair about it. She senses that the neighbor could be more than he appears (as the object of her hatred) to be. However, the woman lets this intuition be drowned out by the noise of her hatred, and she fails to return to the intuition in quieter moments. Her interior act of consenting to her hatred when it arises—the act of continuing to feel the way she feels and allowing her hatred to swell, without taking the opportunity to examine whether her emotion is appropriate to the situation—is morally bad and worthy of blame. Assuming that the neighbor is not a serious threat to her way of life, the woman's hatred is unfitting. It is inconsistent with her own proper functioning and she is corrupted as she indulges it.

Many of us have heard the phrase "emotions are not good or bad; they just *are*." It can make psychological sense to say this under certain circumstances—for example, when a person judges that his or her present emotion is bad and he or she is a terrible person for feeling it, to the point that guilt or shame effectively holds the original emotion in place, not allowing it to dissipate. However, this therapeutic strategy is best considered relative to an ethical perspective that acknowledges (with compassion) that certain emotions, felt in certain ways, are good for us: they are modes of recognition, discernment, or enjoyment that we could not and would not want to do without, whereas other emotions are bad for us: they are ways of misapprehending what is happening and inappropriately being moved. According to the Aristotelian-Thomistic tradition, no emotion is morally neutral inasmuch as it is subject to reason and choice. An emotion is either suitable to a situation or it is not. When considering what is meant by "suitable," it is best to imagine a large target that includes a range of responses that are consistent with good human functioning, rather than focusing too intently on the bull's-eye and seeking one correct response. What is most to be avoided is missing the target completely.

Finally, there are some emotions that incorporate explicit moral judgments into their structure. For example, we might hear on the radio about a government's violent repression of its own people or its oppression of a geographical neighbor. As we picture acts of brutality, as described by the reporter, we undergo an interior motion of dissonance and recoil. We might also feel the impulse to rise up and defend the victims and punish the offenders. We might judge that what the offenders are doing is morally wrong. We might judge, further, that the offenders are evil. Our emotion thus becomes, in part, a hatred *of* certain actions and the people who are committing them. This is not simply an emotion that sits alongside a moral judgment; it is a moral emotion. To call an emotion a moral emotion is not to say that it is good. Rather, it is to say that the emotion has as its defining focus an object of perception or imagination (such as a person or a situation) that we judge to be morally good or bad. Moral judgments can be wrong, and the emotions that are informed by them can be misguided. For example, many of us hold that it is morally wrong to assume that a person is evil through and through. We hold that it is thus problematic to indulge an emotion in which we experience only dissonance and recoil, with no accompanying resonance with the basic humanity of the other.

I introduce the morality of emotion not because I am concerned in this book about evaluating the goodness or badness of particular emotional states. I am not. However, an interest in ethical self-cultivation lies in the background of this project. I take it that many of us would like to arrive at a better understanding of the emotions partly because we would like to alter some of our emotional habits. We would like to experience more love or joy, or decrease the frequency with which we experience self-lacerating emotions. Yet if we wish to encourage certain emotional states and discourage others, we must understand the sorts of states with which we are dealing. *How are we to understand our emotions such that it makes sense to say that we can shape them, even as we are shaped by the objects that enter our awareness and cause us a stir?* Until we can answer this question, any attempt to shape our emotions in a particular way, in light of our moral values, will come up short. We might get lucky and find a technique that allows us to have a desired effect on our emotions, but the ideal is to find a technique that makes sense to us so that we can apply it intelligently. In this book, I seek to answer the question high-lighted above by examining Aquinas's understanding of the structure of emo-tion and by considering, in the process, the relationship between emotions and the powers by which we exercise our moral agency.

THE RELIGIOUS SIGNIFICANCE OF EMOTION

Just as our emotions can be of moral significance, they can also be of religious significance. As we will discuss in chapter 1, the religious has to do with what humans regard as "really real"[2] and of the utmost importance in life. It has to do with what humans regard as the "elements and processes within and beneath ordinary experience."[3] Something is of religious significance if it bears on the way one construes the underlying nature of things, or it bears on what one does to order one's life and community in relation to what one takes to be the deepest or currently most salient source of one's well-being.

Emotions play a notable role in the lives of many people who participate in religion. Ordinary observation indicates that emotions such as fear and love draw many people into the heart of a community's religion. Moreover, a re-ligion functions, in turn, to shape these emotions so that they reflect, as far as possible, what the people believe or intuit to be the sacred order of things. Thus, a religion might enable adherents to experience certain emotions in relation to religious objects. For example, it might enable people to experi-ence an intense love for God (when God is encountered, say, in the words of a rousing sermon) or a fear of ancestral spirits (when the spirits are encoun-tered, say, in a family member's illness). A religion might also enable adher-ents to alter emotions that concern more ordinary objects, but objects that are viewed in religious perspective. For example, it might enable people to call into question and thus diminish the intensity of a sexual love that they expe-rience for someone else's partner, or it might help people to be more patient when encountering a neighbor's contrary will. By enabling people to redi-rect the course of certain emotions, especially socially disruptive emotions, religions function to uphold a particular morality.

What is an emotion that it can be directed toward a religious object or toward an ordinary object that appears against a religious horizon? How are we constituted, as humans, that we can be moved by such objects, and we can also have an influence over how we are moved? When we ask these questions in light of the study of religion they appear especially complex, for they suggest the possibility that as humans we are sometimes moved—or think we are moved—by powers or truths that are present to us in some way yet are beyond our intellectual grasp. We might think it is important

to be well moved in relation to the source of all being, the power of life, a
manifestation of limitless compassion, or a message from the spirit world.
Yet we might also be unsure what to make of such emotions, partly because
of the mysterious nature of their objects. In this book I focus primarily on
Aquinas's account of ordinary human emotions. I pay attention, however, to
some of the implications of his account for understanding the relationship
between religion and emotion. Specifically, I examine how objects of perception or imagination that appear to bear on our well-being can also appear to be religious or of religious significance, such that we are moved not
simply with emotion but with religious emotion or emotion that has a religious dimension.

When we hear the term "religious emotion," we might think of what
some Christians call "religious affections." Jonathan Edwards, who wrote an
influential treatise on the religious affections, defines an "affection" as a "lively
and vigorous exercise of the inclination" by which "the soul is carried out
towards . . . things in view of approving them, being pleased with and inclined to them"—or an inclination by which "the soul opposes the things in
view, in disapproving them; and in being displeased with, averse from, and
rejecting them."[4] Affections are "religious" when they are directed to "God
and divine things."[5] Thus, one might have a "lively and vigorous" love for God
and a similar hatred for sin. Edwards distinguishes, further, between "true"
and "counterfeit" religious affections. "Truly gracious" religious affections
reveal "the saving influences of the Spirit of God";[6] "false and delusive" religious affections do not.[7]

Aquinas does not employ the term "religious affection" as an analytical
category. He does refer to affections (*affectus*) or interior motions of the intellectual appetite (the will) or (less frequently) the superior appetite (*appetitus superior*) with the understanding that these appetitive motions can take
various objects. He also refers, of course, to love for God, hope in God, and
the like, which *we* might wish to call "religious affections." Sometimes
Aquinas uses the term "affections" to refer to a broad range of inclinations,
including inclinations that engage the intellectual appetite and those that engage the lower, sensory appetite.[8] However, he most often uses the term to
refer specifically to motions of the will relative to objects that we apprehend
as good or bad by the power of our intellect (which can be extended by a gift
of grace). He refers to "simple acts of the will" that occur "without passion
or commotion of the soul."[9]

I am interested in emotions, rather than affections. I analyze *as* emotions
what Aquinas calls passions (*passiones*), which are mediated by the body and
do involve a "commotion of the soul."[10] With respect to religion and emo-

tion, I seek to show how an emotion can arise in relation to a sensible object that appears to disclose a religious truth, mediate sacred power, provoke religious questions, or the like. I show, that is, how an emotion can have or acquire a religious dimension. I do not deny the significance of "affections of the will" for Aquinas. I discuss some of these in later chapters. However, I consider these motions as they relate to emotions. I leave the focused study of the will to others.[11] In my view, what Aquinas says about the affections that we experience as embodied beings is best understood by starting with the emotions and then considering how the emotions function in relation to motions of the will.[12]

I do not seek to distinguish in this book between true and false religious emotions—between emotions that are true in their religious dimension and those that are false—or between emotions that are caused in a special way by God and those that are not. Making such distinctions in anything but the most formal terms would require articulating and defending a view of the truth of reality, in relation to what I take to be Aquinas's view of the truth. That would require a work of metaphysics or theology. I am more interested in common religious questions and longings, which tend to accompany religious beliefs and are important in their own right. Asking religious questions in relation to various objects of experience can arouse what I take to be religious emotions or emotions with a religious dimension. By the same token, asking a broader range of religious and other questions *about* such emotions can create some mental space around them, which can put us in a better position to give them direction.

THE STUDY OF AQUINAS ON THE EMOTIONS

The emotions ought to be studied by anyone who has a serious interest in ethical or religious self-understanding and the cultivation of virtue. But why study Aquinas on this topic? What makes his way of thinking about the emotions so special? Let me introduce some notable features of his account.

First, Aquinas holds that emotions are modes of tending in relation to objects of perception or imagination that we assess to be significant for our own or another's well-being. Emotions are interior motions that are aroused by and oriented with respect to certain objects of "cognition." Accordingly, Aquinas's account allows us to attend, as any compelling account of the emotions must, to the cognitive dimension of emotion. Yet he interprets this dimension with flexibility. He includes within its realm not only propositional states, such as states of believing-that and judging-that, but also (and most importantly for the initial formation of many emotions) nonpropositional states, such as states of having in mind a sensory image or impression that we have not yet put into words—or have only begun to characterize for ourselves through the use of higher-order intellectual powers.

Second, Aquinas attends to the cognitive while also attending to the appetitive dimension of emotion. He holds that emotions are forms of object-oriented appetitive motion. They include forms of being-attracted-to, tending-away-from, rising-up-against, being-crushed-by, being-at-rest-in, being-ill-at-ease-with, and the like. Unfortunately, when many people who study the emotions hear the term "appetite," they think "hunger" or "sex," and at that point they stop thinking clearly and creatively about the relationship between appetite and emotion. One of my main goals in presenting Aquinas's view is to show that it is meaningful and fruitful to think of emotions as forms of appetitive motion.

Third, partly because of the way he analyzes the concept of appetite, Aquinas allows us to notice significant structural similarities between the object-oriented appetitive motions of humans and the object-oriented appetitive motions of other, nonhuman animals. He allows us to see ourselves in continuity with other animals, even as we suppose that there are differences in experience, which relate to the fact that most humans exercise advanced powers of thought and decision making that are unavailable to other animals. More than this, Aquinas allows us to see ourselves and our emotions in relation to other modes of tending that are evident in the natural world. He allows us to see (and experience) that we are part of a complex, interactive whole that is remarkably well ordered and exquisitely beautiful, even as the world is also (and feels to us) in many respects chaotic, destructive, and painful.

On the matter of reason and emotion, Aquinas allows us to put crude dualisms to rest and move on. Emotions are not simply thoughts or evaluative judgments or other acts of a "rational part," nor are they simply motions of a "nonrational or animal part." They are interior motions that have a complex relationship to a set of powers or capabilities by which we receive and process information about ourselves and our world. On the matter of emotions and the body, Aquinas's view is again complex, and understanding it requires patience on the part of readers who are prone to dismiss talk of the soul. In his perspective, an emotion is a mode of tending on the part of an embodied soul. It is a motion of the soul that is mediated by certain changes in the body. Aquinas avoids reducing an emotion to a purely mental state, a brain state, a bodily state of some other kind, or a bodily feeling. Aspects of his approach will likely appeal to readers who are unsatisfied with intellectualist accounts that neglect the body, on the one hand, and reductionist scientific-materialist accounts, on the other.

Finally, Aquinas's account of emotion, when placed within the context of his systematic theology, has remarkable metaphysical depth. Entertaining his conception of the nature of reality, as a thought experiment or an act of intellectual creativity, can be awe-inspiring. For me, it has been life-transforming. The world no longer appears quite the same as it did before I began this study, and I no longer feel quite the same in relation to what I see. There are aspects of Aquinas's metaphysics that I do not yet understand, aspects with which I disagree, and aspects about which I am undecided. With respect to his account of emotion, in particular, there are details that I have not yet had the chance to probe, and connections to other parts of his thought that I might never have the chance to explore, given the volume of Aquinas's writings and the way his writings presuppose an engagement with the work of his many peers and predecessors. Moreover, there are parts of Aquinas's account that need to be corrected or supplemented. For example, one would want to reconsider his understanding of the role that "vital spirits" and "humors" play in the arousal of anger. One would want to supplement his account with more accurate information regarding the physiology of emotion. Yet no part of the account is unworthy of serious study and meditation.

INTERPRETING AQUINAS IN LIGHT OF RECENT STUDIES OF EMOTION

Within academia, scholars from many disciplines are engaged in the study of emotion. Of special interest to the present inquiry are normative studies written from the perspectives of religious ethics, Christian ethics, or Catholic moral theology.[13] Also of interest are studies that are more historical and interpretive in kind, set within the broader context of religious studies.[14] This project has affinities with all such approaches, yet it has perhaps greater affinity to certain analyses in philosophy and, more specifically, philosophical and moral psychology.[15] I do not develop my own, constructive view of the emotions, but I try to present Aquinas's account as I think it must be presented if it is to stand up to other, excellent philosophical accounts.

I have learned much from philosophical studies of emotion. One thing I have learned is that there are significant differences in philosophers' ways of describing or representing emotions. Differences in interpretation probably reflect the ways in which philosophical commitments and other interests are brought to bear on the interpretation of the same or similar experiences. They might also reflect differences in experience. That is, differences in interpretation might concern somewhat different experiences that we have come to call by the same names, such as "love" and "hatred." When I read a philosophical account of emotion that does not fit my experience well, or fits some aspects of it but not others, I presume that the author's concepts illuminate his or her own experience, yet I am not always sure what to make of the fact that those concepts fail to do the same for my own experience.

I do not expect that philosophers will one day agree on a single best account of emotion. I doubt this is a worthwhile goal to seek. More worthwhile is the elucidation of multiple philosophical accounts, each of which has important insights to contribute to our understanding of certain aspects of our interior and relational lives, but none of which can hope to integrate all of the best insights that have been gleaned over the history of human thought. I confine myself mostly to a close reading of Aquinas. I expect that his account will ring true for some readers and not for others—because of limits in the account, limits in my interpretation of it, limits in readers' abilities to relate Aquinas's concepts to their own experience, differences in philosophical and religious perspective, and the like, but also because of differences in the way various people experience life.

Also of interest to the present inquiry are recent studies in neuroscience and experimental psychology that seek to demonstrate relationships among various phenomena that have to do with emotions, such as select stimuli, measurable changes in the brain, changes in other parts of the body, observable behaviors (including facial expressions), and the self-reports of experimental subjects. Of particular interest is the way in which some scientists who study the emotions recognize the need to be conscious of the philosophical assumptions they bring to their studies, including assumptions about the nature of consciousness and about the states of consciousness or awareness that it makes sense to call "emotions," while calling other states by other names, such as "feelings."[16] Choices must be made, and the more self-consciously they are made, the better. Yet it is difficult to know how to interpret a researcher's interpretations of his or her experiments when the latter interpretations are filtered through a philosophical framework and a way of dividing up the mental landscape that one does not share. In any case, we cannot go into the study of emotion thinking simply that there are facts about the brain and behavior that any good philosophical account must fit. There are such facts, but all facts must be interpreted, and some facts are open to quite different interpretations. Differences in interpretation can have different implications for understanding human experience.[17]

Also intriguing to keep in mind, as one approaches the study of Aquinas, are the anthropological accounts of emotion that have been published in recent decades. Some of these accounts seek to show the significant extent to which emotions are socially constructed. They emphasize differences in the emotions of people who are situated in different cultures.[18] Other accounts challenge radical forms of social constructionism. They proceed on the assumption that, yes, there are differences in experiences of emotion across cultures, but there are also notable similarities; if there were not, we would be unable to understand others' experiences to the extent that we can.[19] Most anthropologists who study people's emotions recognize the need to define what an emotion is before trying to study and report on the emotions of their subjects. Yet it is not easy to specify a working definition of emotion in the face of significant philosophical disagreement. One anthropologist, Catherine Lutz, sets her conception of emotion up against the foil of "Western thinking about the emotions," as if Western thinking were unified.[20] Again, it is difficult to know what to make of empirical evidence that is interpreted in light of concepts that are unclear, misleading, or defined in ways that beg important philosophical questions.

There is much to be gained through empirical studies of emotion. There is also much to be gained by pursuing greater conceptual clarity about the objects and the terms of one's study. I hope to contribute to the discussion about how best to define the emotions. Yet I do not attempt to situate Aquinas's account relative to all of the other philosophical contenders. There are too many other, fine accounts that are worth studies of their own. Each of them is marked by subtle distinctions, the discussion of which requires delving into major philosophical issues. I focus on presenting Aquinas's view in light of a couple other options, and I offer his view especially for readers who seek new possibilities for self-understanding, and not simply conceptual clarity and simplicity.

CHAPTER OUTLINE

This book is fundamentally a work of religious ethics. Because the defining features of religious ethics are a matter of some debate, I begin with a brief methodological chapter. Chapter 1 develops a working definition of religious ethics. It clarifies what is intended by the term "religious," and what I take to be religious about religious ethics. More specifically, it identifies religion and religious moralities as objects of religious-ethical study, and it indicates how religious-ethical inquiry approaches these objects. Chapter 1 prepares readers to think broadly about the religious as a factor in various emotional states. It encourages readers to reflect on the religious questions and concerns they might profitably bring to the study of emotion—and to their reflection on their own emotions.

Chapter 2 sets the stage for a religious-ethical inquiry into Aquinas by attending to some recent scholarship on ethics and the emotions. The work of James Gustafson provides a way of thinking about the relationship between religious faith and the elements of moral character, including a person's characteristic ways of being moved. What Gustafson says about faith and the affections (including the religious affections) allows us to sharpen the questions we need to bring to our reading of Aquinas. What is an affection? What makes a given affection religious? How does an affection relate to an emotion? What *is* an emotion? Can an emotion also be religious or have a religious dimension? How far can Aquinas's theory of emotion take us in accounting for the many ways in which humans are affected by objects of experience, some of which appear to be ordinary and some of which appear to have religious significance?

The work of Martha Nussbaum provides a way of thinking more specifically about the structure of emotion. In her view, emotions are forms of thought or cognition. Her account differs from that of Aquinas's, for he holds that emotions are forms of interior appetitive motion. Yet Aquinas holds that the appetitive motions that compose emotions are object-oriented. Experiencing an emotion involves having something in mind and making certain sorts of judgments in its regard. Nussbaum's way of characterizing cognition and the role it plays in evoking emotions is probing and subtle. Her analysis prepares us to look for similar subtlety in Aquinas's account of the cognitive dimension of emotion. Her analysis prepares us also to appreciate the central difference between Aquinas's account of emotion and cognitivist accounts that reduce emotions to their cognitive dimension.

Aquinas defines *passio*, or what I refer to as emotion, as an object-oriented motion of the sensory appetite that occurs within a soul-body composite. Chapters 3 and 4 begin to break this definition down into its component parts. These chapters anticipate obstacles to understanding and lay a foundation for subsequent chapters. In particular, chapter 3 distinguishes the power of apprehension (i.e., the power by which sentient beings acquire and process information) from the power of appetite (i.e., the power by which sentient beings are moved interiorly or—in some cases—move themselves, relative to objects of apprehension). Nussbaum appears in chapter 3 as well as in chapter 2. While she argues that emotions are forms of thought (which Aquinas associates with the power of apprehension), Aquinas argues that emotions are best construed as object-oriented acts of the appetitive power. Chapter 3 offers some reasons why one might want to make a distinction between the powers of apprehension and appetite, and why one might want to associate emotions fundamentally with the power of appetite.

Chapter 4 continues to lay a foundation for understanding Aquinas on emotion. A Thomistic emotion is a motion of the soul that is mediated by the body. One can no longer presume that the idea of the soul makes sense to people, that their conception of the soul looks anything like Aquinas's conception, or that people will not misapprehend Aquinas's conception of the soul-body composite in light of Cartesian and other dualisms. Hence, chapter 4 elucidates what the soul is for Aquinas and how the soul relates to the body. This chapter considers some important issues concerning the bodily dimension of emotion. It considers also some implications of Aquinas's view for thinking about emotions in God and other immaterial realities, including the human soul after its separation from the body at death.

Chapters 5 and 6 approach the center of Aquinas's account of emotion. They focus on what it means to say that an emotion is a motion of the *sensory appetite*. They approach the sensory appetite of humans "from below" with reference to Aquinas's scale of being. Chapter 5 explores structural similarities between motions of the human sensory appetite and appetitive motions that occur in other animals, in other living things, and in inanimate objects. Everything that exists, in Aquinas's view, is characterized by appetitive motion, and it is by virtue of all this motion that the universe holds together as it does. Chapter 5 also examines the formal cause of a sensory-appetitive motion, which is an object of sensory apprehension. It examines various acts of sensory apprehension, appreciating how much human and nonhuman animals have in common on the sensory level, but also anticipating how acts of sensory apprehension in humans (only) are influenced by the intellect and the will.

Chapter 6 examines what is meant by a *motion* of the sensory appetite, focusing on the structure of object-oriented tending. This chapter examines the most basic forms of appetitive tending, which are distinguished with respect to the ways in which their objects are construed, and also with respect to the direction in which one tends relative to these objects. Chapter 6 includes an analysis of the three basic moments in a typical process of appetitive tending. It examines, specifically, the moments of love, desire, and delight, which occur in relation to an object that is apprehended as good or attractive, and the moments of hatred, aversion, and sorrow, which occur in relation to an object that is apprehended as bad or repugnant. It examines also the specific forms of motion that arise when one encounters obstacles in one's tending toward or away from objects that one regards as good or evil. This chapter thus includes an interpretation of all eleven emotions that Aquinas regards as fundamental, with reference to which one can define any other emotion.

Chapters 7 and 8 approach the heart of Aquinas's account of emotion from a different direction, namely, "from above" with reference to his scale of being. Aquinas holds that human emotions are appetitive motions that are, in part, reflective of our animality. Yet humans are more than animals. We are also rational beings. We are rational animals. In Aquinas's view, this means that we have intellectual souls. We can, in principle, exercise intellectual powers, which include the power of intellectual apprehension (intellect) and the power of intellectual appetite (will). Aquinas thinks that we ordinarily exercise these intellectual powers, in some form, as we undergo motions of the sensory appetite or emotions, and that the exercise of our intellectual powers influences our sensory operations. If we wish to understand his account of emotion, we must therefore investigate the ways in which the powers of intellectual apprehension and appetite relate to the powers of sensory apprehension and appetite. Much has been written about the intellect and the will in Aquinas. I do not reproduce that discussion. I treat the intellectual powers and their operations specifically in order to elucidate the influence they can and ordinarily do have on emotions.

Chapter 7 focuses primarily on the intellect. It examines in formal terms the act (the operation of the soul) by which one understands what an object is, and the act by which one judges an object to be good. Understanding what an object is and judging it to be good (relative to one's final end) are acts of intellectual apprehension that stand in an ordered relationship to acts of sensory apprehension by which one forms a sensory image of an object and judges it, on a sensory level, to be attractive. An object that one judges sensorily to be attractive often causes a motion of the sensory appetite or an emotion. Chapter 7 thus shows how certain acts of *intellectual* apprehension are capable of influencing the acts of *sensory* apprehension that provide intentional content for particular emotions. The chapter includes a brief discussion of the way in which Aquinas thinks the power of the human intellect can be extended by a gift of grace, so that certain acts of intellectual apprehension that are "above reason," most notably acts of Christian faith, become possible for humans. Aquinas holds that these extraordinary acts of the intellect can affect the sensory judgments that give rise to emotions.

Chapter 8 focuses on the intellectual appetite or will. It examines the basic forms of appetitive tending that can occur on an intellectual level, as determined by the way in which one apprehends an object's goodness (or badness) intellectually, and the direction in which one tends in relation to what one apprehends. Paralleling the analysis of chapter 6 (up to a point), chapter 8 examines three moments that can be identified in a typical process of intellectual-appetitive tending relative to an object that one judges to be good. These moments are intellectual love, desire, and joy. In Aquinas's worldview, goodness is ontologically basic. Evil is construed as a privation of good. When he discusses the structure of intellectual-appetitive tending, he therefore focuses primarily on modes of tending toward what one judges to be good. My interpretation follows his lead, but it attends briefly to modes of tending that occur relative to objects that one judges to be bad. Aquinas's account of emotion makes it possible to reproduce on the intellectual level (with necessary modifications) all eleven motions of the sensory appetite presented in chapter 6. I do not explore the *intellectual*-appetitive motions or affections that go by such names as fear, daring, anger, and despair, but I point the way for others who might wish to do so.

Chapter 8 also investigates further the relationship between the intellect and the will, showing how the intellect (so to speak) acts on the will and also how the will, in turn, acts on the intellect. If we wish to understand the influence that the intellect and the will can have on emotions, we need to understand how the intellect and the will function as a pair. This chapter attends also to the way in which Aquinas thinks the power of the intellectual appetite (like the power of intellectual apprehension) can be extended in its operations by a gift of grace, so that a human being becomes capable of extraordinary motions of the intellectual appetite, most notably Christian hope, love, and joy. Aquinas characterizes such motions as affections. Inasmuch as these affections regard a religious object, we might wish, as noted earlier, to characterize them as religious affections. I hope to show, however, that these motions can also profitably be regarded as religious emotions. Taking a religious-ethical approach, we can open the category of religious emotion to include appetitive motions that are directed toward a range of objects that one takes to be of religious import, without having to posit, as a matter of faith, a special supernatural cause of such motions. This allows us to imagine how Aquinas's work could be of use to people outside, as well as inside, Christian circles.

Chapter 9 synthesizes and extends the work of chapters 7 and 8. It traces several ways in which acts of the intellect can affect the formation of particular emotional states. It does the same thing with respect to motions of the will. The chapter considers, finally, some of the ways in which emotions can, in turn, affect certain intellectual acts—including acts that can, in turn, affect the formation and the course of one's emotions (and so on). Chapter 9 seeks to show that the emotions of humans are typically composed (for as long as they last) at the hub of several interactive operations of the embodied soul. With respect to some of these interior operations, it is difficult to apprehend oneself (as) undergoing them; one simply undergoes the changes. With respect to other of these operations, it is a bit easier to transcend, to some extent, what is happening. By virtue of certain higher-order operations, one can make other of one's interior operations objects for thought, and one can try to alter them.

Chapter 10 synthesizes and extends the book's analysis of Aquinas on the emotions. It explores further the "order" of human emotions in relation to what Aquinas takes to be the order of human nature and the order of nature as such. It also highlights some practical ethical benefits of studying Aquinas's account and studying it with broadly religious questions and concerns in mind. The religious-ethical study of Aquinas on the emotions challenges us to become more aware of and articulate about our questions concerning the nature of reality and concerning what is most important in human life. It challenges us to see how these very questions—and the answers to which we have become attached—can affect the ways in which objects appear to us, the ways in which they cause us to be moved emotionally, and the ways in which we are capable of moving ourselves relative to these and other objects, partly by choosing to cultivate more reflective habits of emotion.

I am in a kind of conversation with Aquinas. I entertain most of his ideas as *living* ideas. Being in conversation with this great thinker requires, for most of us, that we learn a new vocabulary and grammar. As this brief introduction already suggests, it can be challenging to keep relevant definitions and distinctions straight, and to see how various parts fit together into interactive wholes. I invite readers to refer, as helpful, to the appendix for an outline of selected features of Aquinas's conception of the powers or capabilities of a typical human being. One must have a basic understanding of these capabilities if one is to understand Aquinas on the emotions.

NOTES

1. I am pointing to a form of loving self-direction that is exercised within the context of recognized passivity and vulnerability. I am not intimating a form of muscular self-control.

2. Clifford Geertz, "Religion as a Cultural System," reprinted in *The Interpretation of Cultures: Selected Essays* (New York: Basic Books, 1973), 112. See chapter 1.

3. John P. Reeder Jr., personal conversation. See the discussion of Reeder's view in chapter 1.

4. Jonathan Edwards, "A Treatise Concerning Religious Affections," *The Works of Jonathan Edwards*, vol. 1 (Avon, U.K.: Bath, 1992), 237.

5. Ibid., 238.

6. Ibid., 245.

7. Ibid., the whole of part III.

8. See, for example, St. Thomas Aquinas, *Summa Theologica*, translated by Fathers of the English Dominican Province (Westminster, Md.: Christian Classics, 1981), hereafter abbreviated *ST*, *ST* I 82.5, and I-II 102.6 *ad* 8. Latin edition: S. Thomae Aquinatis, *Summa theologiae*, edited by Petri Caramello (Rome: Marietti, 1950). In reading Aquinas, I consult the Latin and often indicate Latin terms, particularly in cases where I expect standard translations of these terms to strike English-speaking readers as odd, but the translations turn out to be rather straightforward, or where certain English terms, such as "love," have many different dimensions that are signaled by different Latin terms. However, I rely on standard translations of Aquinas's works unless I think these pose specific problems for interpretation. The work of translating Aquinas, in light of all that Aquinas wrote, and all of the thinkers with whom he was in conversation, is laden with technical difficulties, and I am unwilling to enter into that forest. I focus instead on wrestling with the Aquinas who is largely available to an English-speaking audience. With respect to the *Summa theologiae*, I rely on the Christian Classics translation rather than the Blackfriars because I think the latter begs more philosophical questions when it comes to expressing in English Aquinas's views concerning human agency.

9. *ST* I 59.4 *ad* 2, 82.5 *ad* 1. However, Aquinas qualifies this view in a way that is important to our analysis, as we will explore in later chapters.

10. Chapter 3 addresses issues concerning the translation of the term *passio*.

11. For an excellent start, see Frederick Crowe, "Complacency and Concern in the Thought of St. Thomas," *Theological Studies* 20 (1959); Robert Johann, *The Meaning of Love: An Essay towards the Metaphysics of Intersubjectivity* (Glen Rock, N.J.: Paulist, 1966); and (in a less Thomistic vein) Edward Collins Vacek, *Love, Human and Divine: The Heart of Christian Ethics* (Washington, DC: Georgetown University Press, 1994).

12. G. Simon Harak begins his delightful book with a chapter on the body and ends with a discussion of the passion for justice: *Virtuous Passions: The Formation of Christian Character* (Mahwah, N.J.: Paulist, 1993).

13. See the bibliography, which is not exhaustive. Most notable for situating my own work are Richard R. Baker, *The Thomistic Theory of the Passions and Their Influence upon the Will* (Ph.D. diss., University of Notre Dame, 1941); Harak, *Virtuous Passions*; and Vacek, *Love, Human and Divine*.

14. See especially John Corrigan, ed., *Religion and Emotion: Approaches and Interpretations* (Oxford: Oxford University Press, 2004), and John Corrigan, ed., *The Oxford Handbook of Religion and Emotion* (Oxford: Oxford University Press, 2008).

15. Most important for my own work are John M. Cooper, *Reason and Emotion: Essays on Ancient Moral Psychology and Ethical Theory* (Princeton, N.J.: Princeton University Press, 1999); Ronald de Sousa, *The Rationality of Emotion* (Cambridge, Mass.: MIT Press, 1987); William Lyons, *Emotion* (Cambridge: Cambridge University Press, 1980); Martha C. Nussbaum, *The Therapy of Desire: Theory and Practice in Hellenistic Ethics* (Princeton, N.J.: Princeton University Press, 1994); and *Upheavals of Thought: The Intelligence of Emotions* (Cambridge: Cambridge University Press, 2001); Robert C. Roberts, *Emotions: An Essay*

in *Aid of Moral Psychology* (Cambridge: Cambridge University Press, 2003); Robert C. Solomon, *The Passions: The Myth and Nature of Human Emotion* (Notre Dame, Ind.: University of Notre Dame Press, 1976); and Richard Sorabji, *Emotion and Peace of Mind: From Stoic Agitation to Christian Temptation* (Oxford: Oxford University Press, 2000).

16. See, for example, Antonio Damasio, *Looking for Spinoza: Joy, Sorrow, and the Feeling Brain* (Orlando, Fla.: Harcourt, 2003.)

17. For a critique of the biases that affect some of Antonio Damasio's experiments, see Daniel M. Gross, *The Secret History of Emotion: From Aristotle's Rhetoric to Modern Brain Science* (Chicago: University of Chicago Press, 2006).

18. See, for example, Michelle Z. Rosaldo, *Knowledge and Passion: Ilongot Notions of Self and Social Life* (Cambridge: Cambridge University Press, 1980), and Catherine A. Lutz, *Unnatural Emotions: Everyday Sentiments on a Micronesian Atoll and Their Challenge to Western Theory* (Chicago: University of Chicago Press, 1998).

19. See, for example, Charlotte E. Hardman, *Other Worlds: Notions of Self and Emotion among the Lohorung Rai* (Oxford: Berg, 2000). See also John Kloos, "Constructionism and Its Critics," in *The Oxford Handbook of Religion and Emotion*, ed. John Corrigan (Oxford: Oxford University Press, 2008).

20. Lutz, *Unnatural Emotions.* I agree with Robert Roberts that "anthropologists of emotion . . . could profit from greater conceptual (philosophical) clarity about their enterprise." See Robert C. Roberts, "Emotions Research and Religious Experience," in Corrigan, *Oxford Handbook of Religion and Emotion*, 497.

CHAPTER ONE

Religious Ethics

✦

There are many ways to approach the study of emotion. This book takes a religious ethics approach to the study of Aquinas on emotion. There is disagreement among scholars about how to define religious ethics. Hence, it would be good to set out a working definition. It is important to indicate what I take to be "religious" about religious ethics. It is important also to signal the openness and flexibility with which I approach the religious dimension of life and thought. In this chapter I clarify the subject matter of religious ethics and the sort of inquiry that is appropriate to that subject matter.

My conception of religious ethics takes its bearings from two markers. The first is a pair of essays in an issue of the *Journal of Religious Ethics* (*JRE*) devoted to reflecting on the brief history of the journal in a way that involved thinking about how to define the discipline. The second marker is the self-understanding I have sought over many years in an effort to define religious studies and religious ethics for various people in my professional life. These people include colleagues in religious studies departments who disagree with each other about how to define religion as an object of study; colleagues who study and teach ethics in departments of philosophy and have little interest in the relationship between ethics and religion; colleagues from religiously affiliated institutions who identify in their work as ethicists with a particular tradition (usually Christianity) and direct their writing and teaching primarily to other members of their tradition; colleagues who study religion and ethics in a comparative mode; colleagues from the sciences who believe that religious ideas are unworthy of serious academic attention; and other people who, for various reasons, are concerned about how religion and ethics are taught at institutions of higher learning in the United States, especially public ones.

THE SUBJECT MATTER OF RELIGIOUS ETHICS

In an essay for the issue of the *JRE* just mentioned, Jeffrey Stout considers how best to define religious ethics: "The phrase *religious ethics* is ambiguous, depending on what we take the adjective *religious* to modify. If we take it to modify the mode of inquiry instead of the subject matter of that inquiry, we might define religious ethics as ethical inquiry undertaken from the perspective of someone who has religious commitments. Then religious ethicists would themselves have to be religious."[1] Stout thinks we should define religious ethics instead with respect to its subject matter. He construes the subject matter of ethics, in general, as ethical discourse, which is a "social practice in which individuals give and demand reasons of one another" for their views concerning "right and wrong conduct, virtuous and vicious character, and good and bad forms of community."[2] Ethics, in this view, is the activity of reflecting critically *on* ethical discourse.[3] *Religious* ethics is the activity of reflecting on "religious varieties of ethical discourse: their historical development, the similarities and differences among them, and the similarities and differences between them and secular varieties."[4]

In an essay for the same issue of the *JRE*, John P. Reeder Jr. considers what makes religious ethics religious.[5] He identifies the subject matter of ethics, in general, as morality or moralities. In his view, a morality is a "a set of prescriptive practices that shape character and conduct and serve certain social functions, for example providing norms for the distribution of the benefits and burdens of cooperative activity."[6] Reeder would agree with Stout that a morality includes the practice of giving and demanding reasons, for it is partly in the exchange of reasons for moral beliefs and choices that communal norms are defined, tested, and refined. Reeder makes explicit that a morality includes also a "set of prescriptions" that specify how people ought to be and behave.[7] These prescriptions often take the form of a moral code.[8] In this view, ethics is the critical investigation of moralities. *Religious* ethics is the investigation of moralities that are connected to religious worldviews.

MORALITY

Let us examine more closely the idea of morality, taking up the specific idea of religious morality in the following section. It can be useful to think of ethical discourse or morality as a social practice in which the members of a community give and demand reasons of one another for their commitments regarding what is right and wrong and the like.[9] For our purposes, however, I want to make explicit some of what is implicit in this conception.

First, morality is partly a practice in which persons give and demand reasons of *one another*; yet this implies that it is also a practice in which persons give and demand reasons of *themselves* or hold themselves accountable for their own attitudes and actions. Morality is, in part, an ongoing activity of thinking about what is important in life, trying to make good choices, and taking responsibility for one's choices and for the person one is becoming partly through the choices one is making. Exercising this sort of reflective moral agency prepares one to answer to the inquiries of others; yet much of the activity of morality does not involve answering expressly to others' demands for the reasons for one's choices, particularly if most of one's choices are not obviously off the mark.

Second, to the extent that one acquires good habits of character one is likely to take many of one's moral commitments as given, not needing to be subjected to constant reflection. Just as the typical scientist does not regularly rehearse the reasons for holding to the fundamental principles of physics, so the typical moral agent does not regularly rehearse the reasons for holding to the basic principles and norms of his or her community. By a certain point in moral development, one regards most of these norms *as* basic, and one builds on that foundation.[10]

Third, the power to participate in the explicit exchange of reasons comes relatively slowly to humans, developmentally. It is realized by adults to different extents. It also takes different cultural forms. It is important that readers not overintellectualize the practice of morality, thinking of it as an exchange that necessarily takes highly articulate forms. Nearly all humans follow moral rules and aspire to moral goods, yet many of us find it difficult to explain and justify what we take to be most important in life. When asked to defend our values, we might be at a loss to do much more than to raise the volume of our voices. Yet even when we respond in this way, most of us are trying, in effect, to respond to a question that we understand and take seriously. We are participating in a morality, and our participation is a worthy subject for ethical inquiry.

Fourth, much of what counts as morality does not involve the exchange of reasons between persons who are already *committed* to certain views. When we challenge ourselves and each other to articulate our views concerning what is right or wrong, with respect to a particular issue or situation, we often do so as persons who are not yet sure what to think. Those of us who are still wondering and struggling are not in a position to express our moral commitments, let alone give reasons for them. For many of us, the practice of morality consists partly in being morally disturbed in ways that can be painfully opaque; having moral worries that we cannot fully articulate; trying to ask ethical questions that we do not yet know how to ask; and caring enough to puzzle over ethical matters slowly, even if this requires being stranded for a long time on an island of doubt and indecision. In other words, much of the moral life is not about defending particular moral views and challenging others to do the same; it is about trying to form our views in the first place and trying to figure out what to do with those views as we gain additional information and perspective.

Finally, a morality typically includes explicated or codified norms by which persons orient themselves as they seek to hold themselves and others accountable to a common way of life. A morality includes people's ways of interpreting, reinterpreting, embodying, expressing, reproducing, and encouraging adherence to these norms, not only through standard forms of argumentation but also through education, habituation, codification, cultural production, social sanction, and so forth. It includes also people's ways of wrestling with, resisting, and sometimes violating norms with which they disagree.

RELIGIOUS MORALITY

The subject matter of ethics is morality. The subject matter of religious ethics, in particular, is religious morality. What sorts of social practices count as religious moralities? Reeder urges us to think of religion and the religious more broadly than most of us are prone to do. He suggests, for example, that it is possible to characterize some forms of secular humanism and scientific materialism as religions.[11] Some versions of these seemingly nonreligious philosophies and forms of life offer people some of the same things as traditions such as Judaism and Buddhism. They offer an account of the fundamental nature of reality and a vision of what is possible for humans, in life and death, given the way things are. They offer also a vision of the good, a view of what is truly worth wanting and seeking—again, given the way things are.[12]

Reeder construes a religion partly as a worldview that concerns what is "really real"[13] and of the highest importance in life.[14] This way of approaching religion is helpful for our purposes, as long as it is interpreted with care. Note that a worldview is not simply a set of propositions, explicitly formulated, to which a person or group of people voluntary assents—something that can be captured well in the form of a creed. A worldview *includes* beliefs and intuitions about the real and the good, which can be expressed in various forms, but it includes more than this as well. Shifting the focus from the content of a worldview to the person who holds the view, we can say that a worldview includes a way of perceiving, envisioning, or construing events in the world in light of an (often partial and opaque) image or narrative of the cosmos and one's place in it.[15] A worldview can be largely implicit. It can be part of the general cultural wherewithal with which one encounters reality. A worldview can be so much a part of one's basic interpretive framework that it can be difficult to recognize it *as* a framework— as a way of looking, noticing, and finding-meaningful that is in some respects contingent.[16]

The notion of the really real is also in need of careful interpretation. As I use it, the idea presupposes the possibility or the actuality of a certain "difference." The difference can be—and is—specified in many different ways, each of which has a loose family resemblance to the others. It is sometimes specified as a difference between the way things appear to be (to the ignorant or the uninitiated) and the way things really are (the way things appear to the wise or initiated). It is sometimes specified as a difference between the relatively meaning*less* and the meaning*ful*, or the power*less* and the power*ful*. It is sometimes specified as a difference between the way things are and the way they used to be, before the fall of humanity—or the way things will be at the end of time, when the problem of suffering is resolved. Sometimes the difference is specified as a difference in the ontological (and related psychological) states of various persons or communities (saved or damned, liberated or enslaved) or as a difference in the states of objects or places (sacred or profane). Sometimes it is specified as a difference between various aspects of the self (flesh or spirit, ego or Higher Self); a difference between the way things are in "this world" (or "this life") and the way they are in the "other world" (or "the afterlife"); or a difference between the natural and the supernatural. The difference is sometimes specified as a difference between the (in principle) empirically observable properties of things and the hidden or underlying cause, nature, structure, principle, or order of things, which is not directly observable and may exceed the grasp of the human mind.[17]

Each of these is a distinct way of characterizing what is believed or imagined to be an actual or possible difference in states of being, levels of consciousness, or dimensions of reality, but it is helpful to consider that together they reflect a propensity on the part of many people to wonder and to care, at least once in a while, about what (if anything unusual) is really going on beneath the surface or the ordinary appearance of things.[18] Many humans have a propensity to believe—or to entertain the possibility—that there is more to reality than meets the eye, even when the eye is aided by scientific instruments. They want to know what, if anything, the underlying nature of things makes possible for them or demands of them with respect to the way they live. I would call this, broadly speaking, a religious propensity.[19] For many people, this propensity is mostly about trusting the worldview that currently organizes their perceptions. For other people, the religious propensity is more about questioning reality (wondering what is really happening) while standing in a questioning relationship to various views or narrative accounts of reality; it is about following such questions (for periods of time) wherever they lead.

I am especially interested in Aquinas's worldview, but I want to encourage readers with different worldviews to bring them into the conversation. When I refer to a religious worldview, I refer to a way of construing reality which considers that there are or could be certain dimensions of being, consciousness, or reality that are "more real" than others, where more real might mean (in a given case) more subtle, insightful, meaningful, actual, powerful, free, original, central, or the like. I appeal to the notion of some such difference without limiting myself to a particular interpretation or representation of the difference.[20] I refer also to a view of what is or might be possible and most worth seeking and enjoying, given the fundamental principles, laws, or intentions that are at work in the universe.

As Reeder puts it, "a religious worldview is one that answers basic metaphysical questions about the nature of things: it interprets the basic elements and causes of everything, within or beyond the cosmos, one or many, hidden or revealed, unified or fragmentary."[21] A religious *morality* is thus a "set of prescriptive practices" that functions in coordination with a view of the "fundamental constituents and powers of things."[22] Reeder holds that every defensible morality is a religious morality in this sense: "There is no limited sphere of value and fact [and thus no morality] whose content and justification can be debated independently of religious canopies of meaning."[23] I think he is right about this, although it might be better to say that every defensible morality relies on certain assumptions about the nature of reality. I have not found a compelling morality that does not appeal explicitly or implicitly to something like an account of human nature, an account of the nature of reason, or an account of the nature of law, all of which rely on assumptions about the nature of reality as such.

Many defenders of moralities choose to bracket the metaphysical questions raised by their moralities. Many people (from Buddhist teachers to pragmatic policymakers) regard certain kinds of metaphysical speculation as unproductive, for a variety of reasons. I agree that it can be helpful and even necessary at times to bracket the sorts of questions that draw us into a seemingly endless series of further questions about the nature of things. Each of us is compelled to proceed with the daily work of the moral life in the face of what we regard as unanswerable questions about the world in which we live and also in the face of substantial disagreements with other people in our communities. However, it is important to keep in mind, when considering matters of morality, that something *is* being bracketed, namely, implicit beliefs or intuitions about what is real and thus really possible for humans who wish to live good lives—impressions that must sometimes be made explicit in order to explain and justify features of a morality that otherwise appear incomprehensible or arbitrary.

Religious ethics takes as its subject matter people's ways of thinking, feeling, and acting in relation to what they regard as right or good, where their views about what is right or good are connected in some way to views about the "limits and the possibilities of the real."[24] This book concerns Aquinas's account of the emotions, which is part of a Christian Aristotelian morality according to which human emotions are matters of ethical concern and are, to a limited extent, subject to ethical formation. Aquinas's account of the emotions relates to a view of what is and is not possible for various sorts of beings. It includes, for example, a view of the capabilities of human and nonhuman animals, including the power to be moved and (in the case of humans) to move oneself. Aquinas's account is set, even more broadly, within a view of the underlying order of things—a view of the way in which every existing thing stands in relation to everything else. Our task is to understand Aquinas's account of the emotions in light of the fact that he sets it within a comprehensive view of the nature of reality. I can explore only some aspects of his larger view, but readers will, I hope, take the opportunity to explore additional aspects in their own study of Aquinas.

FURTHER REFLECTION ON THE RELIGIOUS

Many of us, when we hear the word "religion," think of various religions of the world. There are good reasons for thinking of religions primarily as organized social-historical phenomena. Many people wonder about the underlying causes of things, the meaning of suffering, the point of life, and so on, within the context of an established faith tradition. However, other people have experiences that alienate them from familiar, traditional answers to their pressing questions and concerns. They are inspired to take up more individual religious quests or paths.[25] Sometimes they move into lesser-known territories within their tradition of origin (if they have a tradition of origin). Sometimes they venture farther out and try to explore another tradition.

Sometimes they set off on more open, nontraditional journeys in search of something undefined that will bring them closer to the truth of things. Pursuing a religious path requires finding a symbolic language with which to express one's intuitions and longings, and people who repudiate traditional religious identities or forms of belonging commonly (and inescapably) borrow much from established symbolic systems; yet some people's ways of being religious are not wholly contained by historical traditions.[26]

Generally speaking, being religious involves thinking, wondering, doubting, trusting, fearing, caring, longing, and so on, relative to the underlying nature of reality or some feature of that reality that one takes to have "special prominence."[27] The underlying causes and constituents of things can be deeply mysterious to the religious imagination; they can be more a matter of puzzlement than belief. Being religious involves also trying (at least some of the time) to *live* in proper relationship to what one regards as most real and important. Attempting to relate well to what is real—and of real value—might involve, for example, submitting to it, obeying it, aligning oneself with it, loving it, honoring it, appeasing it, arguing with it, hiding from it, awakening to it, or realizing that "you *are* it."

To have a way of being religious that is worthy of study, one need not have arrived at compelling answers to questions concerning the real and the good. Reeder suggests that we would perhaps want to characterize people who are "searching and presently uncommitted" as "non-religious."[28] I would argue, however, that the very impulse to puzzle over matters of ultimate concern is well characterized as a religious impulse.[29] Most people in the contemporary world wonder and worry, now and then, about whether the things they were taught to believe about reality are true. They wonder whether the way they and others have been looking at things is the way things really are. They wonder especially when their worldview comes up short in explaining disturbing phenomena, such as the worldly success of cruel or callous people, the suffering of the innocent, their own death, or the death of a loved one. Moreover, many people are unable or unwilling to accept the whole of any version of reality—sometimes because none of the versions they have encountered speaks well enough to their concerns, and sometimes because more than one version does.[30] People who seek a meaningful and worthwhile life path and community of belonging, but are not ready and may never be ready to settle into one such path or community, can be included in the category of the religious. Their ways of being religious and expressing their religiosity are in principle a worthy subject matter for religious studies.

In a similar vein, the subject matter of religious ethics includes well-developed and widely shared moralities that are associated with traditions.

However, it includes also the moralities of people who are still "searching and presently uncommitted" to a particular account of the nature of reality, that is, people who are religiously unsettled.[31] It includes the study of people whose moralities are also, for various reasons, unsettled. The subject matter of religious ethics might include, for example, the way in which some people who identify with a traditional morality are working out important details of that morality. Consider the struggle of people who ordinarily trust their experiences of goodness but sometimes doubt their experiences with respect to their sexuality because what they are inclined to experience as good has been judged evil by people who are thought to have religious and moral authority. The subject matter of religious ethics might include the way in which some people struggle with competing moralities or parts of moralities in such a way that they are unable completely to invest in one or the other. Consider some people's inability to decide whether certain efforts among the powerful to promote the human rights of the powerless reflect moral clarity and an admirable integrity or are instead expressions of cultural imperialism.

This study concerns the religious morality of Aquinas. It focuses on the way he conceives of emotions as important elements of the religious and moral lives of humans, and the way he relates emotions to other modes of tending in humans, in other sorts of beings, and in the universe at large. Aquinas's religious morality (a strand of the Catholic moral tradition) is well-established; in one form or another, it has informed the lives of billions of people. Yet as we seek to understand Aquinas, it is important to consider his way of construing things as one way among many. We do well to read his theologically and metaphysically rich account of emotion in light of comparable, but different accounts, such as those of Seneca,[32] other ancient Stoics,[33] Buddhists,[34] religiously significant Chinese thinkers,[35] rabbinic authors,[36] and others.[37] In addition, we do well to keep in mind that Aquinas's account of emotion is part of a living tradition of discourse in which many people participate and to which they contribute in different ways. Some people participate from the center of the Catholic tradition, some from the margins, and some from outside the tradition. Some people participate from settled viewpoints, and some from perspectives that are still being worked out.

THINKING RELIGIOUSLY

Stout holds that "a religious ethicist need be no more religious than a molecular biologist is molecular or than a criminal psychologist is criminal." The modifier in the term "religious ethics" applies "to the subject matter, not to the scholar."[38] I want to qualify this view.[39] Many people think of being religious as a matter of being a confessing Christian, a practicing Muslim, or the like. Yet being religious can also be a matter of reflecting on religious concerns from positions outside "institutional settings officially designated as religious."[40] As I have suggested, being religious is partly a matter of wondering and caring about "the fundamental constituents and powers of things,"[41] and about what is finally worth pursuing in life, given the way things are. One can exercise this sort of curiosity and concern inside an established tradition, and one can exercise it while standing or wandering outside the parameters of a recognized religious identity. If this is the case, then we would expect most people who study their own and others' ways of being religious—even people who do not identify with a particular religion or faith community or identify only to a limited extent—to study their subject matter "religiously."

If we hope to understand a religious tradition, person, or idea, we *must* bring to our investigations some of our own working assumptions and questions about the nature of reality. Many of us are deeply attached to our current ways of construing things; we are reluctant to entertain the possibility that there are other, equally intelligible ways of perceiving and interpreting the world. Some of us transcend our emotion-laden interpretive habits only with difficulty and diligence, if we are even willing to try. Others of us might be more suspicious of our perceptions and the worldviews that organize our perceptions. Perhaps there are some phenomena that our current interpretive frameworks seem ill equipped to handle; perhaps there are parts of these frameworks to which we feel rationally bound (as elements of a systematic whole or a complete story), but which we nevertheless do not fully accept.

In any case, if we hope to understand another person's view of reality, we must bring with us some of the convictions and questions to which our own life experiences have led us. We must consider what we believe and why we believe it—how we were raised as children into certain impressions or convictions about what is real—or how we have made inferences from experience to the underlying order of things. We must ask meaningful questions of the traditions, persons, or ideas we seek to understand, and this inevitably involves turning the light on our own traditions or ways of being religious—or, perhaps, on our lack of interest in things religious. In short, we must think religiously, unless we choose to turn away from the task of understanding the other.

Considering the related question of whether people are bound to study ethical discourse or morality *morally*, Stout argues in the affirmative: "We cannot attend to normative commitments reflectively [we cannot study people's moralities] without relying on normative commitments all the while. . . . Some normative commitments are bound to be in play all along, lending significance to one's selection of examples and generating criteria of relevance and success by which one's handling of examples may be judged."[42] I agree. Thinking well about a proposed morality requires considering that morality (or parts of it) in relation to our own. This requires bringing elements of our morality into explicit consciousness—thinking about what we take to be our rights, duties, and responsibilities, about what it means to be happy or liberated, about the character traits or virtues that are evident in the best human lives—and thinking about why we think these things. Thinking well about a proposed morality involves also becoming more aware of unsettled features of our current moral practices—nagging questions, possible inconsistencies, and inclinations to reject parts of the packaged morality in which we were raised. It requires making comparisons and assessments all along with an eye toward determining which moral point of view, if any, is the more compelling.[43]

A similar point must be made with respect to religious commitments or (more inclusively) beliefs, assumptions, intuitions, questions, and the like, concerning what is most real and of the highest importance. To encounter another's worldview in a way that permits understanding, we must encounter it as a meaningful possibility relative to our own way of viewing things. This requires having our own view in mind all along *as* a view but also as an object for thought. It requires trying to articulate our view, at least to ourselves, asking ourselves why we continue to hold it and how it shapes our experiences of reality. We will perforce make many judgments of a comparative nature as we approach another's way of seeing things—judgments about whether this alternative possibility makes sense, whether it has better or worse explanatory power than ours, whether it can meaningfully be lived, and so on. Making a series of such judgments requires what I would call thinking religiously.

One need not be committed to a particular religious worldview in order to study that or another worldview. However, those of us who study religious moralities need to be broadly religious in the sense that, during times of study, we are eager to engage in forms of thinking that include (among other things) imagining, questioning, wondering, reasoning, and wrestling, as well as believing and trusting in regard to what is really real and important. Moreover, we cannot engage well in such thinking without caring about the fruits of our thinking—without having a personal interest in approaching the truth of life partly through our thinking or in the process of open-ended questioning. Successful religious-ethical inquiry will be religious in the sense that it will involve the exercise of religious curiosity *and* concern. People who are simply not interested in pursuing religious questions are not in a good position to understand a morality that is rooted in a religious worldview.

RELIGIOUS ETHICS AND CHRISTIAN ETHICS

I recommend that readers approach Aquinas's ideas in the mode of religious as well as ethical thinking. For some readers, this will involve engaging in Christian ethics. As I understand it, Christian ethics is usually undertaken by people who identify as Christians and whose thinking about religious and moral matters is framed in significant ways by Christian convictions.[44] Christian ethics ordinarily seeks to engage the moral concerns of other Christians, although it sometimes reaches out to people outside the tradition, in the mode of religious dialogue. Christian ethics is a form of discourse that usually seeks from inside Christianity (or a particular denomination) to define the (or a) Christian moral tradition and to influence the practice of Christian morality.

Religious ethics is like Christian ethics in that it seeks to speak to Christians, most notably Christians who are interested in putting their tradition in perspective relative to other ways of being religious. More than most Christian ethics, religious ethics seeks to address people of other faiths as well; people of unconventional, unsettled, or undefined religiosities; and people who regard themselves as secular but have broadly philosophical interests in religious ways of construing reality. Religious ethics seeks to promote critical thinking about the ways in which various moralities reflect religious or metaphysical views, some of which are expressed in explicit belief systems, and some of which are only implicit in the sense that they have an evident impact on people's lives, but they go largely unnoticed and unexamined. Religious ethics is eager to approach virtually any religious morality in search of genuine understanding. It is eager to step out again into the space of another morality, or into the spaces between well-defined moralities, in order to put moralities into comparative perspective.[45] Religious ethics seeks thereby to contribute responsibly to forms of religious and ethical discourse in which diverse persons and communities participate.

Religious ethics is most effective in promoting critical understanding when it is practiced by people who are religious in the sense that they share some of the curiosity and concern (which is not to say the convictions) of the people they study—or they have a personal interest in religious and moral ideas. Religious ethics, like Christian ethics, is thus a kind of insider inquiry. However, the insiders of religious ethics are mostly people who wish to engage in critical discourse about matters of religious morality in ways that are not necessarily constrained by confessional obligations that are thought to be incumbent on people (especially scholars and teachers) who identify with a particular faith community. My approach in this book is one of religious ethics. Of necessity, I bring many commitments to this inquiry. For example, I bring a conviction that there is an ultimate principle of order in the universe to which it is meaningful to relate both personally and abstractly. I bring a conviction that religious wonder is an integral part of a flourishing life. I encourage readers to bring their own commitments—including traditional faith commitments—to this study. There is every reason to expect a variety of approaches to converge in interesting ways, as long as we encounter Aquinas with loving and questioning minds. A loving mind is one that tends toward the good of understanding and uses this understanding to honor and improve human lives.

SUMMARY

Religious ethics is religious in at least two senses. First, it takes as its subject matter something religious. Its subject matter can be characterized as religious varieties of ethical discourse (Stout) or religious moralities (Reeder) that are connected to historical traditions or worldviews. Its subject matter can be characterized also as views and related practices concerning what is good, right, justifiable, and the like, where these views and practices can be fully explicated only with reference to a person's thoughts, intuitions, or impressions about the ultimate or underlying ground, source, telos, principle, power, order, or structure of reality.

The religious-ethical study of Aquinas on the emotions is the study of ideas about emotion that can be explicated and understood only by exploring their metaphysical or theological underpinnings. Aquinas's account of emotion is best studied with a genuine interest in the details of his worldview and with an accompanying awareness that his Christian Aristotelian worldview is only *one* well-developed view of the nature of reality. We do well to wonder whether certain elements of Aquinas's account could be made intelligible to people outside the Christian tradition or transported to other worlds of meaning.[46] However, drawing explicit comparisons with other religious accounts is beyond the scope of this book. Our central concern will be to interpret Aquinas, even as we consider that that the study of other accounts of emotion could alter our interpretation of Aquinas.

Second, religious ethics is religious also in the sense that it involves thinking religiously. Specifically, it involves bringing to explicit awareness some of our own assumptions, curiosity, and concern about the nature of things and about what is most important in life. For many of us, these assumptions and concerns will reflect the fact that we have adopted—or have been adopted by—a particular tradition.[47] For others, there will not be a single tradition that captures well our way of construing the world around us and within us.

My goal in this project is to display Aquinas's highly articulate account of what the emotions "are" and how they "work." The study of his account, accompanied by thoughtful experimentation with his ideas, can be useful for readers who wish to arrive at greater self-understanding and more responsible interactions with others—even if readers do not, in the end, agree with Aquinas's account, or they agree with only parts of it. The study of Aquinas, in the mode of religious ethics, can also inspire creativity in thinking about the religious dimension of life and culture. It can foster religious curiosity and wonder.

NOTES

1. Jeffrey Stout, "Commitments and Traditions in the Study of Religious Ethics," *Journal of Religious Ethics* 25, no. 3 (1998): 25.

2. Ibid., 24.

3. Ibid., 23.

4. Ibid., 25.

5. John P. Reeder Jr., "What Is a Religious Ethic?" *Journal of Religious Ethics* 25, no. 3 (1998): 157–75.

6. Ibid., 161, note 11.

7. John P. Reeder Jr., *Source, Sanction, and Salvation: Religion and Morality in Judaic and Christian Traditions* (Englewood Cliffs, N.J.: Prentice Hall, 1988), 2.

8. This is my term, not Reeder's. For our purposes, we can think of a moral code as a set of norms that govern (individual, communal, and/or institutional) character and conduct. A moral code might be conceptualized as a summary principle (such as "the Golden Rule"), a collection of rules (such as "the Ten Commandments"), a narrative that upholds an exemplar (such as the life story of the Buddha or Mohammed), a vision of the good (which might include an account of complete virtue), or a combination of such things. In practice, what people identify as moral codes sometimes overlap with what could be called legal, purity, and professional codes. We need not worry here about these distinctions.

9. Stout, "Commitments and Traditions," 24.

10. To the extent that one is an accomplished moral agent, one is ready and able to provide reasons for one's commitments if and when one is asked to do so. When perennial moral issues come to the fore of public awareness or new issues arise in response to changes in culture, virtuous moral agents play an important role in being able to recollect, rehearse, and re-examine the moral commitments they and others have come to take for granted.

11. Reeder recommends a broad conception of religion for heuristic reasons: "Conceptualizing religion in the way that I suggest accents what those who are often called nonreligious or secular share with those who are usually called religious, allowing us to see the unexpected and to focus our attention on what we might not otherwise grasp. It points to a deep similarity that unites not only various traditions usually called religious, but those traditions and others often excluded from the religious camp" ("What Is a Religious Ethic?" 168). The point is not to force people to identify as religious who do not wish to identify that way. The point is rather to invite people to think more deeply and less defensively about common human longings for meaning, connection, purpose, order, freedom, and happiness. Regarding forms of scientific materialism that function as religions, see Stephen J. Pope, *Human Evolution and Christian Ethics* (Cambridge: Cambridge University Press, 2007), 18–21; Dorothy Nelkin and M. Susan Lindee, *The DNA Mystique: The Gene as a Cultural Icon* (New York: W. H. Freeman, 1995); and Lisa Sowle Cahill, *Theological Bioethics: Participation, Justice, and Change* (Washington, DC: Georgetown University Press, 2005), which reflects on science as a "symbol system of ultimacy, morality, and meaning" and a "thick tradition" (28–34).

12. Reeder, "What Is a Religious Ethic?" 160–61.

13. Ibid., 163. The term "really real" comes from Clifford Geertz, "Religion as a Cultural System," 112. Reeder draws on the anthropological scholarship of Geertz with qualifications. See especially Reeder, 166, notes 6 and 24. The use of the symbol "really real" by Reeder or by me does not imply agreement with Geertz's theory of religion. For a critique of Geertz's theory, see Nancy K. Frankenberry and Hans H. Penner, "Clifford Geertz's Long-Lasting Moods, Motivations, and Metaphysical Conceptions," *Journal of Religion* 79, no. 4 (1999): 617–40.

14. David Little and Sumner B. Twiss urge against "[building] a condition of ultimacy or primacy into what constitutes a religious object" (Little and Twiss, *Comparative Religious Ethics: A New Method* [San Francisco: Harper & Row, 1961], 60). They note that there are many religious objects that are "not considered 'ultimate' . . . (as [Paul] Tillich would require) and they are not considered 'more important than anything else in the universe' (as [William] Christian would seem to require)" (61). Indeed, a particular religious object, such as an ancestral spirit or an angel, might not be regarded as *the* ultimate power or principle of reality; it might not be regarded as more important in the universe than any other such object; it might instead be regarded as especially prominent or more salient than other religious objects for one's present needs, say, for healing or protection from harm. However, when one regards ancestral spirits or angels as objects of concern, one usually *implies* a scale or range of related objects or a principle of organization of some kind. After all, one has to determine where in a hierarchy or panoply to direct specific sorts of requests. Thus, one *implicitly* makes reference to whatever is or might be at the high end of the scale relative to the realities of mundane human life, or at the center or the foundation of a cosmic order. In my view, it is thus acceptable to use the language of highest, deepest, utmost, most fundamental, and the like, when speaking generally about the religious; it helps to dramatize the differences to which I point in the following paragraph.

15. Robin Lovin and Frank Reynolds refer to religious worldviews as "cosmogonies" ("In the Beginning," in *Cosmogony and Ethical Order: New Studies in Comparative Ethics*, eds. Robin W. Lovin and Frank E. Reynolds [Chicago: University of Chicago Press, 1985]). Cosmogonies are "attempts to find a pattern for human choice and action that stands outside the flux of change and yet within the bounds of human knowing" (5). Cosmogonies have the "function of bestowing on certain actions a significance that is not proportioned to their empirical effects or to the individual goals of their agents, but derives from their relation to an order of the world that begins with the beginning of the world as we know it" (6).

16. Thanks to Keith Green for helping me avoid pitfalls in the use of the term "worldview."

17. When I note a difference or a distinction in each case, I do not necessarily refer to a simple duality; many social practices that I would call religions suppose that there are more than two levels of reality or levels of wisdom or insight concerning the nature of reality.

18. Lee H. Yearley writes, "The word 'religious' refers, of course, to many phenomena, but most important here is the reference to an orientation that differs from and judges many features of the ordinary world of activity, even if it also undergirds other features of that world. Such an orientation, whatever false fixities it enshrines, will call into question other generally accepted ones" ("Selves, Virtues, Odd Genres, and Alien Guides," *Journal of Religious Ethics* 25, no.3 [1998]: 132).

19. Just as I do not want to overintellectualize morality, I do not want to overintellectualize religion. None of my language is meant to imply that the average religious person participates skillfully in the discourse of metaphysics or systematic theology. The impulse to know or to wonder about what is real and good usually involves something very basic and common, such as conceiving a question that one hardly knows what to do with: "Why is this [bad thing] happening to me?" or "What did I do to deserve this?" or "Is this all there is to life?" or "What will happen to me when I die?" Such questions imply underlying metaphysical assumptions and additional questions, even if the person doing the wondering has not had the opportunity or is not particularly interested in uncovering those assumptions and questions and making them explicit.

20. This is important to keep in mind, as it is impossible for me to speak of this difference throughout the book in such a way that I explicitly include every form the difference can take. By signaling one version of the difference, I do not thereby mean to exclude other versions.

21. Reeder, "What Is a Religious Ethic?" 163. For Reeder, "metaphysical" refers to that which concerns "the fundamental elements and processes that set the limits and the possibilities of the real" (personal correspondence). In his more recent writings he has dropped the term (see John P. Reeder Jr., "Religion and Morality," in *Oxford Handbook of the Sociology of Religion*, ed. Peter Clarke (Oxford: Oxford University Press, 2009), 336–59. I cannot engage the controversies surrounding the term "metaphysical" or "metaphysics," yet I am also not interested in dropping the term. I am in a friendly working relationship with the Aristotelian-Thomistic tradition of metaphysics or nat-

ural theology, even as I recognize many of the puzzles to which this tradition has given rise. For me, metaphysics or natural theology refers centrally to the study of being *qua* being; the study of the fundamental causes and constituents of things; the study of the nature of reality as such. Metaphysical or theological inquiry takes place in culture-specific or tradition-specific terms, yet various accounts of the real ought not, for that reason, to be presumed mutually unintelligible. On a related note, Reeder wants to "refrain from referring to the nature of things or the fundamental nature of reality as 'ultimate reality' [Tillich] because the distinction between ultimate and penultimate may suggest the metaphor or model of a contingent or 'phenomenal' layer of things beyond or beneath which there is some noncontingent or 'noumenal' reality" ("What Is a Religious Ethic?" 160, note #6). This is an important caution to consider when seeking to define religion or religious in an inclusive way. Some religious people make this sort of distinction between the "phenomenal" and the "noumenal," and some do not. However, for many people the term "ultimate reality" does *not* suggest this particular metaphor or model; it simply signals what is first, final, highest, deepest, most central, most powerful, most definitive, or the like. I use the term "ultimate" to suggest these various possibilities. See chapter 2.

22. Ibid., 164.

23. Ibid., 175. This does not mean that a group of people cannot have a discussion regarding common political goals, such as the need for new laws, policies, or practices that will affect the community as a whole, while bracketing out of the conversation certain contentious differences of religious conviction. What it means is that participants *do* bring to such conversations certain convictions, intuitions, and assumptions about what is most real and of the highest importance in life, even if they hold their tongue in expressing these thoughts, and even if they find it difficult to get very far in articulating such thoughts when invited to do so. These thoughts will be part of what the participants employ as they try to envision what would be best for themselves and their community, and as they try to determine, finally, whether they or their community will be able to live, with integrity, with a particular change.

24. Ibid., 160.

25. Some readers might prefer the term "spiritual" over the term "religious" when referring to individuals who seek the truth of life largely outside the context of organized religion. I choose not to make this distinction, but to use the term "religion" in a way that is broad and flexible enough to *include* what others might call "spirituality." I do not want to feed inadvertently into popular stereotypes. I often hear self-identified "spiritual" people imply that "religious" people are two-dimensional figures who participate unthinkingly in social practices that perpetuate oppression. For many "spiritual" people, "spiritual" is synonymous with "authentic," which implies that "religious" people are not actually involved in seeking or trying to live in truth. Similarly, I often hear self-identified "religious" people imply that "spiritual" people who reject organized religion are self-absorbed, uncritical consumers of fads who are unwilling to commit themselves to the work of building and sustaining community. For many "religious" people, "religious" is synonymous with "committed and stable," which implies that non-traditional spiritual seekers are

rootless, flaky, and socially irrelevant. It is part of the function of religious studies (but beyond the scope of this project) to expose religious stereotyping and to examine the purposes that are served by various definitions and distinctions. For a discussion of "spirituality" that is relevant to the study of emotion, see William C. Spohn, "Spirituality and Its Discontents: Practices in Jonathan Edwards's *Charity and Its Fruits*," *Journal of Religious Ethics* 31, no.2 (2003): 253–76.

26. I thus agree with Stout that "there are . . . differences that set off individuals from the communities in which they were raised or with which at some point they became affiliated. Respect for individuals involves sensitivity to the ways in which they can resist conformity to type" (*Democracy and Tradition* [Princeton, N.J.: Princeton University Press, 2004], 74).

27. Little and Twiss, *Comparative Religious Ethics*, 60.

28. Reeder, "What Is a Religious Ethic?" 168.

29. While I sometimes use the image of ultimate concern, this does not imply wholesale agreement with Paul Tillich's philosophical theology. For the latter, see Paul Tillich, *Systematic Theology*, vol. 1 (Chicago: University of Chicago Press 1951).

30. See Lee H. Yearley, "New Religious Virtues and the Study of Religion," reprinted in *Ways of Being Religious*, ed. Gary E. Kessler (Mountain View, Calif: Mayfield, 2000), 7–16.

31. As Keith Green puts it, part of the work of religious ethics is to examine critically the relationship between religion and morality, considering the possibility that much "religion" or many "ways of being religious" are not part of "*a* religion" or a culturally recognized "religious identity" (personal correspondence). Similarly, religious ethics considers that there is much going on "morally" that cannot be contained by a society's moral codes or recognized moral traditions.

32. Consider Seneca's theory of emotion in light of his theory of nature as expressed, for example in "On Providence," in *Seneca: Moral Essays*, vol. 1, trans. John W. Basore (Cambridge, Mass.: Harvard University Press, 2003), 2–47.

33. See Brad Inwood, *Ethics and Human Action in Early Stoicism* (Oxford: Clarendon, 1985).

34. For an introduction to this literature, see Maria Heim, "Buddhism," in Corrigan, *Oxford Handbook of Religion and Emotion*, 17–34.

35. Consider, for example, Lee H. Yearley, *Mencius and Aquinas: Theories of Virtue and Conceptions of Courage* (Albany: State University of New York Press, 1990) and Aaron Stalnaker, *Overcoming Our Evil: Human Nature and Spiritual Exercises in Xunzi and Augustine* (Washington, DC: Georgetown University Press, 2006).

36. Consider Jonathan Wyn Schofer, *The Making of a Sage* (Madison: University of Wisconsin Press, 2005).

37. See Joel Gereboff, Keith Green, Diana Fritz Cates, and Maria Heim, "The Nature of the Beast: Hatred in Cross-Traditional Religious and Philosophical Perspective," *Journal of the Society of Christian Ethics* 29, no. 2 (fall/winter 2009), which lays some groundwork for a comparative religious-ethical study of emotion.

38. Stout, "Commitments and Traditions," 28.

39. Stout himself qualifies this view. He reflects briefly on how to characterize Emerson and other American thinkers who "[discoursed] on ethical topics from a religious point of view," but did so in a way that was not "closely tied to institutions or traditions of the kind typically known as religions" (ibid., 52).

40. Ibid.

41. Reeder, "What Is a Religious Ethic?" 164.

42. Stout, "Commitments and Traditions," 25.

43. Charles Taylor writes of "inescapable [interpretive] frameworks" that involve "strong evaluation"; these frameworks are necessarily employed in acts of moral understanding and evaluation: "Moral argument and exploration go on only within a world shaped by our deepest moral responses. . . . If you want to discriminate more finely what it is about human beings that makes them worthy of respect, you have to call to mind what it is to feel the claim of human suffering, or what is repugnant about injustice, or the awe you feel at the fact of human life" (*Sources of the Self: The Making of the Modern Identity* [Cambridge, Mass.: Harvard University Press, 1989], 8). Hans Georg Gadamer writes of the "hermeneutical circle" that is involved in all interpretation. Understanding requires approaching "things themselves" by "working" continually with our "fore-projections" of meaning, which are "constantly revised in terms of what emerges as [one] penetrates into the meaning." (*Truth and Method*, 2nd rev. ed. [New York: Crossroads, 1992], 267).

44. There are interesting counterexamples, including Jewish thinkers who had few options decades ago of pursuing the academic study of Jewish ethics outside the context of graduate programs in Christian ethics.

45. Darrell J. Fasching calls attention to the alienation that is involved in doing religious ethics. "When we pass over [into another person's tradition] (whether through travel, friendship, or disciplined study and imagination) we become 'strangers in a strange land' as well as strangers to ourselves, seeing ourselves through the eyes of another. Assuming the perspective of a stranger is an occasion for insight and the sharing of insight. Such cross-cultural interactions build bridges of understanding and action between persons and cultures that make cooperation possible and conquest unnecessary" (*Narrative Theology after Auschwitz: From Alienation to Ethics* [Minneapolis, Minn.: Fortress, 1992], 3).

46. Thanks to John P. Reeder Jr. for the image of being transportable. In some ways "transportable" is preferable to "translatable" because the former suggests better than the latter "useful" in the daily moral lives of people who construe the nature of reality in different ways, but can find meaningful connections with Aquinas's perspective.

47. On the notion of being adopted by a tradition, see Stanley Hauerwas, *Truthfulness and Tragedy: Further Investigations in Christian Ethics* (Notre Dame, Ind.: University of Notre Dame Press, 1977).

CHAPTER TWO

Religious Ethics and the Study of Emotion

◆

A religious-ethical approach to the study of emotion recognizes that there is a complex relationship between religion and emotion. In particular, there is a relationship between a person's religious worldview—the way in which the world appears to have a mysterious kind of depth—and the way in which a person is moved, emotionally, by various objects in that world. One way to elucidate this relationship is to consider the connection between religious thought and imagination, on the one hand, and the cognitive dimension of emotion, on the other.

Emotions clearly involve some form of cognition. Feeling an emotion involves having something in mind. An emotion is *about* something. It involves "seeing" an object, such as a thing, a person, a relationship, an event, or a situation, in a certain way as bearing on one's happiness.[1] Feeling the emotion of hope, for example, involves apprehending an object (a future possibility) and construing it *as* attractive, worth seeking, difficult to realize, but not beyond one's reach. Feeling the emotion of daring involves apprehending an object (a threat to one's own or another's well-being) and construing it *as* hurtful, worth confronting and overcoming, difficult to overcome, but not beyond one's capabilities.

Just as an emotion has a cognitive dimension, so does religion. The practice of religion usually involves having an object in mind. It involves apprehending something that appears in many respects to be quite ordinary but appears in other respects to be laden with unusual meaning or revelatory of an underlying power or truth.[2] Religion involves "seeing" certain things or situations as involving or *possibly* involving something more or other than meets the eye of the inattentive, unenlightened, or unimaginative observer.

Consider, for example, the way the biblical story of the Exodus (the liberation of the people of God from slavery in Egypt) informed the consciousness of many African American slaves. Many slaves who (over)heard Christian sermons on this story turned to each other and said, "We, too, are the people of God, and God will free us from our bondage!" Groups of slaves shared this story, linked it to stories about Jesus, who for them became a second Moses, expressed biblical themes in song, enacted the Exodus in dance, interpreted various events as signs of God's liberating activity, and so on.[3] Viewing the world through this interpretive lens changed the way the world appeared to them. The slaves imagined the future good of their liberation (this-worldly and/or other-worldly), and they construed this good as difficult but not impossible to attain—by the grace of God. They apprehended their enslavement, and they construed this evil as challenging, but not utterly beyond their power to confront and overcome in some way (in this life and/or in the transition to the life to come)—again, with the help of God. The emotions of hope and daring thus gained an edge over the emotions of despair and fear.

Aquinas's account of the emotions sheds light on the relationship between various forms of cognition, including acts of religious imagination, and people's ways of being moved. Yet it is easy to misread him. It is easy to read that human emotions are motions of the sensory appetite that resemble the appetitive motions of other, nonhuman animals and at that point assume that Thomistic emotions can have little to do with the religious and moral lives of persons, other than to serve as distractions or causes of misdirection. In fact, Thomistic emotions can orient humans toward a wide range of objects, including objects that are of religious and moral significance. Emotions are interior motions that can reflect religious and moral concern, even as they reflect the fact that, as humans, we experience the world through the use of our sensory powers. Here I prepare the ground a bit for interpreting Aquinas by examining some recent discussions of religion, ethics, and emotion. These discussions can help us articulate important features that we would want to find in any account of emotion that is of use for religious ethics. We are most likely to find such features in Aquinas's account (or make a place for them) if we are looking for them.

RECENT DISCUSSIONS

For the sake of brevity, I focus on two scholars. The first is James Gustafson.[4] Gustafson is a Christian ethicist who has written extensively on the way in which Christians ought to construe the relationship between God's purposes and human goals, especially in light of current scientific knowledge. He has explored with insight and patience the conceptual relationships between religious belief and imagination, the affective dimension of human experience, and the elements of moral character that define the sort of person one is.

Gustafson identifies with the Reformed tradition. He orients himself primarily with respect to the writings of Augustine, Calvin, Edwards, and Schleiermacher.[5] One of Gustafson's central ethical concerns is with the affections. He follows Edwards in associating the affections with the "will" and "inclination," terms that refer, as a pair, to the basic capacity humans have to tend toward or away from objects of "understanding" and "perception."[6] Aquinas makes a formal distinction between motions of the will or the *intellectual* appetite, on the one hand, and motions of the *sensory* appetite, on the other. Usually, he treats affections (*affectus*) as cases of the former and passions (*passiones*) as cases of the latter. Nonetheless, Gustafson's analysis of the affections, as *he* conceives them, is of value for our study, for two reasons. First, his analysis reflects an affection-centered discourse on the emotions that many Christians will find familiar. It allows us to acknowledge this discourse and then shift explicitly to an emotion-centered discourse that has its basis in an interpretation of Thomistic passions. We will not be in a position to appreciate fully the way Aquinas distinguishes passions or emotions from affections or motions of the will—and the way he conceives the relationship between the two—until we have completed our analysis.

Second, Gustafson has interesting things to say about the cognitive dimension of emotion. He examines some religious affections, and he argues that what makes them religious is the objects toward which they are directed. What he says about Christian affections allows us to anticipate that emotions, too, can be directed toward situations of perceived religious significance. Because emotions can have this sort of orientation, it makes sense to say that emotions can sometimes be religious or have a religious dimension. Our main concern in this study is to interpret Aquinas's account of the emotions as such. However, I want to anticipate some of what lies at the other end of this analysis, namely, some new possibilities for thinking about the relationship between religion and emotion.

The second author to whom we will turn is Martha Nussbaum. Nussbaum is a classicist and a moral philosopher who has written extensively on ancient theories of emotion.[7] She has also developed her own theory of the emotions.[8] With respect to the *structure* of emotion, her theory is Neo-Stoic: Emotions are forms of thought. This is the aspect of Nussbaum's theory with which we are most concerned in this book. It should be noted, however, that with respect to the *morality* of emotion, Nussbaum's theory is Neo-Aristotelian. According to most Stoics, emotions always constitute inappropriate reactions to what is happening in one's world. They have no place in a good human life. Yet for Nussbaum, as for Aristotle, emotions can be appropriate or inappropriate to a situation. Moreover, appropriate emotions are an indispensable part of a flourishing life.

On the matter of structure, there are differences between Stoic and Aristotelian accounts of emotion. Nussbaum downplays these differences, and there are ambiguities in Aristotle that allow her to do so.[9] Aquinas develops (and perhaps alters) Aristotle's view, in terms of a more detailed moral psychology. In doing so, he allows us to bring to light an important distinction between Nussbaum's Neo-Stoic view and his own Aristotelian view. For Nussbaum, emotions are forms of thought; for Aquinas, they are forms of appetitive motion. Yet Nussbaum does not serve as a simple foil for Aquinas. Aquinas's appetitive motions are object-oriented— they cannot be constituted apart from particular acts of cognition. In addition, some of Nussbaum's emotion-thoughts exhibit a kind of motion. The difference between the two accounts is thus subtle and, for that reason, interesting. In chapter 3 I examine the central difference. In the present chapter I focus on the way in which Nussbaum's account of cognition can deepen our discussion of the different kinds of objects that emotions can take.

JAMES GUSTAFSON ON THE AFFECTIONS

In an important little book, *Can Ethics Be Christian?*, Gustafson argues that having faith in God is likely to have an impact on a person's moral character, including his or her characteristic ways of being moved by objects of thought, perception, and imagination.[10] In Gustafson's view, faith is not simply a matter of believing certain propositions to be true. It is a matter of experiencing what one takes to be the reality of God, as mediated through the symbols and stories of a particular historical community. Experiencing the reality of God is partly a matter of cognition. It is also a matter of affection.[11] Faith, in this view, is an "emotional, passionate assent" and "commitment" to certain truths about God.[12] Faith is linked to various "sensibilities," most notably "a sense of radical dependence, a sense of gratitude, a sense of repentance, a sense of obligation, a sense of possibility, and a sense of direction."[13] These senses are linked, in turn, to religious affections, such as love for God, gratitude to God, and hope in God.[14] Religious affections are evidently connected to other, ordinary affections that people experience in relation to finite objects of experience. Gustafson only begins to explore these connections, but his efforts are instructive for readers who wish to explore them further.

Reflecting on what an affection (of any kind) might be, Gustafson notes that it is notoriously difficult to arrive at an adequate definition of "affection" or "emotion."[15] These words, he says, are "so uncertain in terms of their references that it might be well not to use [them]."[16] Yet he must use some such word if he is to elucidate what happens to a person when he or she is moved by the thought or perception of certain objects, and when such movements take on predictable patterns in the person's life. In need of a working definition of affection, Gustafson turns to Edwards: "Edwards uses the term 'affections' to refer to what exercises the will or inclinations; they move the person from a state of indifference to a state of caring, and to action. They are 'vigorous' and 'sensible.'"[17] For Gustafson, as for Edwards, affections "exercise not only the will to act but also the mind."[18] In seeking to define affections, Gustafson thus indicates some of their properties and some of what they "do." He says that affections "affect one's fundamental inclinations and one's desires," but he does not say whether they are themselves forms of inclination or desire. He says that affections "exercise the mind," but he does not say whether they are themselves forms of thought. He says that affections are "sensible"—which implies that they are connected to bodily changes or sensations—but he does not specify the nature of this connection.[19]

Edwards himself says that affections are "vigorous and sensible exercises of . . . the heart," where the heart is conceived as a power "by which the soul is [in] some way *inclined* with respect to the things it views or considers."[20] More specifically, affections are "lively actings of the will or inclination" by which a person is attracted to what he or she beholds approvingly and repulsed by what he or she beholds disapprovingly. Affections are modes of being inclined toward, seeking, and enjoying what one regards as likeable; they are modes of being disinclined toward, avoiding, and being displeased by what one takes to be unlikable. Affections are "lively" in that they cause—although they are not themselves composed of—notable bodily changes or sensations.[21]

Edwards says that the "motions of the animal spirits, and fluids of the body" that accompany human affections do not belong "to the *nature* of the affections," for the latter are essentially inclinations of the soul or mind, and these inclinations could just as easily occur in an "unembodied spirit."[22] Edwards appears to hold the same view with respect to the passions, for he regards the passions as a subset of the affections. He distinguishes passions from affections by saying that the former are "more sudden, and [their] effects on the animal spirits are more violent, the mind being more overpowered, and less in its own command."[23] As we will see, there are similarities and differences in the way Aquinas conceives of passions and affections. For him, affections are "simple acts of the will" that are "in one's own command." An act of the will can be "vigorous" or intense, in his view, but it cannot be "sensible." That is, an act of the will is not itself the sort of thing one can "sense." An act of the will can, however, cause a related motion of the sensory appetite, which *can* be "sensed." Passions or emotions are motions of the sensory appetite. They are always constituted, in part, by bodily changes. They are subject to the power of the will but are not always obedient.[24]

Gustafson uses the term "affectivity" to refer to a set of responses that include "'senses,' attitudes, dispositions, and more particular affections or emotions."[25] He does not attempt to define affections relative to the other members of this set. He does say that affections are situational. They are "evoked by particular events, others, and occasions; they do not have the same settledness that attitudes and dispositions have. Yet to some degree they are governed by our senses, our attitudes, and our dispositions."[26] Gustafson acknowledges the value of efforts within philosophical and moral psychology to distinguish affections or emotions from related phenomena, but he does not pursue these distinctions.[27] He is more interested in exploring the affective dimension of experience, broadly construed, in ways that reflect the unity of experience:[28] "Distinctions can be drawn and for purposes of understanding are necessary, but experience is prior to refined distinctions and to some extent resists the imposition of categories we develop."[29]

WHAT MAKES AN AFFECTION RELIGIOUS?

Working with a deliberately "loose" definition of affection, Gustafson seeks to distinguish religious affections from other sorts of affections.[30] He argues that what makes an affection religious is its "ultimate object," which is God.[31] He implies that God is the ultimate object of a religious affection in the sense that God is its metaphysical cause. A religious affection "is evoked by the powers of God."[32] As Edwards says, a *true* religious affection is evoked by the Holy Spirit dwelling in the heart as "a principle or spring of a new nature and life."[33] This thesis raises some difficult questions, including the question of how a person could know whether it is God or something other than God that evokes a particular affection (within himself or herself, or within someone else). Edwards wrestles with this issue; Gustafson does not.[34]

Gustafson also implies a weaker thesis: What makes an affection religious is that it is evoked by what one *perceives* to be the power of God (setting aside the question of whether one's perceptions are accurate). He also implies that what makes an affection religious is that it is aroused by *thoughts* about God or divine things (setting aside the question of whether these thoughts are caused by God in a way that other thoughts are not and setting aside the question of whether these thoughts reflect the way things really are). As Gustafson puts it, a person's affectivity "becomes" religious when the person brings a "religious consciousness" *to* objects and events, so that these objects and events "are perceived [by the person] to be ultimately related to the powers that sustain us and bear down upon us, to the Ultimate Power on which all of life depends."[35]

On this view, certain affections are religious in that they are "about God." It is only by noting some sort of cognitive orientation toward the divine— usually thoughts or images concerning a particular feature of the divine— that one can identify what a person is feeling *as* a religious affection, and one can determine *which* religious affection it is. Gustafson holds that "a sense of gratitude," for example, and the affection of gratitude to which it is linked can be identified in a Christian context only with reference to thoughts or images of God's goodness and beneficence.[36] Similarly, "a sense of possibility" and the related affection of hope can be identified only with reference to thoughts or images of the ultimate source of creativity and renewal.[37]

Religious affections are about God. Yet saying this is problematic, in Gustafson's view. God is not a reality that can be encountered as a "distinct and isolated object" of experience.[38] Gustafson agrees with John E. Smith, who argues that "every alleged experience of God [is also an] experience of something else at the same time."[39] In Gustafson's words, "The ultimate power that sustains us and bears down upon us is experienced through the particular objects, events, and powers that sustain us, threaten our interests, create conditions for human action, or evoke awe and respect."[40] God is encountered only in and through finite "media of disclosure."[41] As we will see, Aquinas holds a similar view.[42] How, then, can one characterize the object of a religious affection in a way that distinguishes such an affection from other, ordinary affections that take the same finite items as their objects? How, for example, can one distinguish between one's gratitude toward one's mother for her unconditional love and one's gratitude toward God, whose unconditional love one encounters in the presence of one's mother?

As I understand Gustafson, a religious affection takes God as its object in the sense that, in feeling such an affection, a person's attention is focused on a particular object, such as a person or a situation; yet it is focused at the same time and even more so on what the object discloses about "the ultimate power and orderer of all of the creation."[43] Feeling a religious affection involves being affected by the perception of an object or by the thought of one's relationship to that object; yet it involves at the same time and even more so being affected by the impression that this object and the self stand in relationship to the "purposes of the divine governance."[44] With a religious affection, such as gratitude toward God, thoughts or images concerning the divine reality become central and defining elements of the affection.

THE RELIGIOUS DIMENSION OF ORDINARY HUMAN EMOTIONS

Gustafson discusses affections that are linked to Christian faith. He refers to other, ordinary affections, but discusses them mainly as they relate to specifically Christian affections. For example, he offers an insightful analysis of the way in which a person's hope in supportive and reliable persons, especially during childhood development, relates to the possibility of hope in God's goodness and power.[45] Yet his analysis suggests that many ordinary affections can open up, in particular moments, to religious considerations or questions. As Gustafson says, "ordinary human affectivities evoked by ordinary human events [can] be at the same time religious affectivities."[46] I want to consider briefly the way in which some seemingly ordinary emotions can take religious objects or objects that appear to be of religious significance, such that one is moved by a religious emotion or an emotion that has a religious dimension. I anticipate a religious-ethical use of Aquinas's account of emotion, but without presupposing specific knowledge of that account.

First, within many worlds of religious meaning, people feel emotions that are in many respects ordinary or *feel* ordinary, except that these emotions are directed toward objects that are perceived as other-than-ordinary or more-than-ordinary. For example, some people feel anger toward the way things are going in their lives, while believing that—or wondering whether—the way things are going is due to something more than mere accident and the laws of nature as understood by the physical sciences. The intuition is that there is—or could be—a deeper principle of order in the universe that is somehow causing things to unfold in a certain way. This sort of anger is typically evoked by and focused, to some extent, on an ordinary object of experience. For example, one's anger might be focused on the way a family member's mental illness is affecting the rest of the family. One's anger might be focused primarily on something hurtful the ill person just did, and on the way another family member reacted. It might be focused also on the possibility of punishing the ill person for his or her thoughtlessness. Yet many people experience this sort of anger, in this sort of situation, while wondering whether the person is even responsible for his or her actions, and thus whether he or she is properly an object of anger rather than, say, compassion.[47] If there is ambiguity in the situation, a person might vacillate between anger and compassion.

Some people who experience this sort of anger or vacillation entertain thoughts, raise questions, and make accusations of a religious nature: "Why does [the ill person] have to suffer in this way? What did [he or she] ever do to deserve this? It's not fair. And it's not fair that my life and the lives of so many others are now marked by what has become, in effect, a family illness." At this point, the anger is directed not simply at the ill person but at "the whole situation," and in the angry person's perspective the situation is of religious significance. The angry one has the impression that there is—or ought to be—a power or principle at work in the universe that is somehow, on some level, responsible for what is happening. The angry person might go on to ponder, "Maybe there is a reason for all of this sickness and suffering. Maybe there is a purpose for it." The person might vacillate between anger at God or the order of things, hope in the discovery of a hidden meaning, and sadness over a cosmic process that is painful and over which he or she has no power. In any case, the person experiences an emotion that is of religious significance. He or she experiences a religious emotion inasmuch as his or her focus is primarily on the "mysterious beyond," or the person experiences an emotion that has a religious dimension inasmuch as his or her focus is primarily on a medium of disclosure or an *opening* to the "mysterious beyond." We would expect the focus of such a person, and thus the emotion itself, to shift frequently, so we do not want to overdraw this distinction.

Consider another example. Some people, on occasion, feel the emotion of love toward another person in such a way that the intentionality of their love (what they have in mind as the object of their love) extends to include thoughts or intuitions concerning the awesomeness of the other's life and the unfathomable depth of her reality as a person. Upon seeing the other, the lover (the one who loves) is sometimes drawn out of himself and toward the other. Moreover, the lover is drawn beyond the surface reality of the beloved. He is invited and perhaps compelled to look (as it were) behind the beloved's eyes.[48] When the lover tends toward the beloved in this way, the lover has the impression that he is approaching something surprisingly, profoundly real, in comparison to which much of what he encounters in everyday life pales in significance and might even appear illusory.

The lover's emotion orients him toward the other, but in such a way that the other appears against a religious horizon, or as a window to the sacred. Beholding the other, the lover is captivated by something more than he ordinarily apprehends in the other—something amazing that presents itself in the guise of the other but cannot be fully contained by her. The lover who encounters this "uncontainable something" might go on to think that he has just received a glimpse of eternity, at which point a love for God might displace the love for the beloved. In a nontheistic context, the lover might think that he has just gained insight into the interconnectedness of all things, at which point he might be captivated by the joy of beholding this truth. In either case, the lover experiences a religious emotion inasmuch as his attention is focused primarily on something incredible or wonderful that takes him beyond the other; or the lover experiences an emotion that has a religious dimension inasmuch as the focus is primarily on the other, but on a person who functions as a kind of symbol, pointing beyond herself to something higher, deeper, or the like.[49] Again, for the duration of such an emotion we would expect the particularity of the other to come into and out of focus as the lover searches for a way to grasp or appreciate what is really happening. Hence, the distinction ought not to be overdrawn.

The more active and developed a person's religious consciousness is, the more likely he or she is to experience emotions of this sort, namely, emotions that cannot be described adequately without identifying some of the religious beliefs or intuitions that condition the way certain situations appear. Some people have relatively little religious consciousness or imagination; they do not often intuit that (or even wonder whether) there is a difference between the way things appear to be and the way things really are, or between ordinary experience and that which lies beneath or beyond the ordinary. Nonreligious people can be expected to experience mostly nonreligious or ordinary emotions. Many other people have religious world views that are symbolically rich, but their religious imagination is not such as to shape every experience of emotion in a notable way. In a given situation, a person's emotion might be more a function of his or her sensory powers than a function of his or her religiosity, in which case the person experiences a rather ordinary emotion.[50] Yet I take it that many people, some of the time, encounter situations that appear to bear on their well-being *as* beings who are oriented by religious concerns. When people are moved by such objects, they experience religious emotions or emotions that have a religious dimension.

A religious emotion thus arises when one has an object in mind or in view *and* one's interest and attention are drawn beyond the object's surface toward the hidden source of its power, toward the ultimate cause or reason for its being, or toward a horizon of meaning (only partly visible) against which the object takes on a significance that it would not otherwise have. Most people find it difficult to express what happens to them when they think they encounter a sacred depth through a finite medium that might otherwise appear ordinary, profane, or flat. Nevertheless, it is clear that many people are sometimes captivated or charged, in their encounters with a particular object, by

what strikes them on some level of awareness as lying at the heart of the object, transcending it on all sides, or cradling it with extraordinary meaning.
They are sometimes gripped by the notion or an inarticulate impression that
they are (or some dimension of them is) related in some way to this ineffable
ground, power, or structure.

If we are to analyze the sorts of experiences to which I have pointed, we
need an account of emotion that is up to the task. We need to be able to say
what emotions are—or how we do well to think of them—relative to other
kinds of mental states. We need to be able to specify the sorts of objects that
emotions can take and the way in which different objects elicit different emotions. We need to be able to specify the elements of which emotions are composed (for example, thoughts, perceptions, appetites, bodily changes,
awareness of bodily changes) so emotions can be analyzed, where helpful, in
terms of their elements. This is particularly important if we wish to alter certain of our emotions. We need to know where "we" can step into a complex
experience of emotion and make a difference to the way it unfolds. Aquinas's
account of emotion addresses these needs. Before we turn to his view, however, I want to consider the work of a second contemporary scholar.

MARTHA NUSSBAUM ON EMOTION

Gustafson's analysis of faith and the moral life reflects a subtle way of thinking about the object-orientedness of human affectivity. Nussbaum addresses
explicitly what she takes to be the cognitive dimension of emotion: She considers what ought to be included in the category of "cognition" or "thought,"
and she specifies the relationship between "thought" and "emotion." Her scholarship can thus help us to extend and sharpen our thinking about the role cognition plays in the formation of emotional states. It can help us also to
understand better the way an object of perceived religious significance can
elicit a religious emotion—or an emotion that has a religious dimension.

Most philosophers who study the emotions agree that some form of cognition plays a role in evoking emotions. Many hold that emotions are not
only *caused* psychologically or mentally by thoughts; they are also (at least
partly) *composed* of thoughts. Emotions are composed of thoughts about some
person, event, situation, or the like—commonly thoughts about what has
happened, is happening, or is likely to happen; about *how* that situation matters to the self or to others who are important to the self; and about *how
much* that situation matters relative to other things that also matter.[51]

Nussbaum argues in a Stoic vein that emotions are composed not only
partly but entirely of thoughts. For her, "thought" is a category that includes

a wide range of mental acts or activities. It includes, for example, entertaining an initial appearance, assenting to an appearance as "the way things *are*," pondering one's goals and projects, and assessing what is happening with a particular object that bears on one's goals and projects.[52] "Thought" includes picturing an event in one's imagination; it also includes apprehending formal musical structures that embody "ideas" of urgent need.[53] Emotions are thoughts about "how things are with respect to the external (i.e., uncontrolled) items that we view as salient for our well-being."[54] They are "judgments in which the mind of the judge is projected unstably outward," like a "geological upheaval," into a world full of value.[55]

Typically, in this account, a given emotion embodies a complex set of related thoughts. Some of the thoughts that make up emotions are *conscious*. Some are less than fully conscious or are *unconscious*. They become evident to the mind only as one considers possible psychological causes for otherwise unaccountable mental phenomena and behavior.[56] Some emotion-thoughts are *general* in kind. They refer to generalizable features or abstractable properties of persons, situations, or the like.[57] Other emotion-thoughts are more *concrete*. They refer in imaginative and perceptive detail to what is specific to a person or situation.[58] Some emotion-thoughts, whether general or concrete, are *background* in nature. They "persist through situations of numerous kinds."[59] They can be characterized as "ongoing," even if the person who has them is not always aware of having them (just as a person who has the background belief that he or she will die someday is not always thinking about death).[60] Some emotion-thoughts are *situational*. They arise only in the context of a particular situation, and they change as features of the situation change or the person's way of construing the situation changes.[61] All of these distinctions suggest differences of degree, rather than sharp divisions of kind.

In Nussbaum's account, all emotions include some form of the thought that one's own well-being and the well-being of others to whom one is attached are important.[62] All emotions also include some form of the thought that "the well-being of this thing or person is not fully under one's own control."[63] All emotions include something like the tumultuous thought that one is vulnerable to loss and to the pain of loss because one's happiness depends, to some extent, on external goods—especially on other persons whose lives and flourishing one cannot secure.[64] Such thoughts about value and vulnerability ordinarily remain in the background of one's awareness. They come to the fore when one encounters an event in the world or in one's imagination that gives rise to the thought that a valued object is at issue in some way. An object might appear to be at issue inasmuch as it is now close at hand, terribly far away, gone forever, threatened, or itself a threat. As one conceives such an object, many background thoughts about value and vulnerability come forward, they join thoughts that are specific to the situation, and all of these thoughts together thrust themselves toward the object—at which point, Nussbaum says, one feels an emotion.[65]

Consider the example of grief. Nussbaum argues that grief over the death of a loved one is composed of a dense web of thoughts, including thoughts about who the person was and how important that person has been to one's life. Grief includes the thought that the person is dead and that one is therefore cut off from him or her forever.[66] Grief includes picturing, in imagination, and thus remembering the person prior to his or her death.[67] It includes thoughts about how incomplete one's life will be without this person and thoughts about how vulnerable one is to additional loss because one's life and happiness are tied to other loved ones as well. Grief includes thoughts about one's own mortality.[68] Some grief-composing thoughts, such as the thought that one has been orphaned or abandoned, might be unconscious in that they can be accessed only through honest and courageous self-examination, usually with the help of others. Some grief-thoughts are better construed as conscious, but background thoughts in that they come to the fore relatively easily at the occurrence of an ordinary event, such as a question from a friend about how one is doing. Some grief-thoughts are general; they are about life, death, and love. Some are concrete and situational; they are about this person, in all of his or her relevant detail.

RELIGIOUS THOUGHT AND EMOTION

Although I want to articulate and affirm Aquinas's understanding of emotion as a form of appetitive motion, Nussbaum's discussion of thought and its role in arousing emotion is instructive. She makes manifest the large number and many different kinds of cognition—general and concrete, linguistic and nonlinguistic, entertained on different levels of consciousness—that can enter into the composition of an emotional state. In her view, emotions are thoughts that are naturally followed in an active mind by additional thoughts. As more thoughts arise, they might call forth additional visual images, which might trigger additional memories, which might arouse additional judgments, causing a shift in one's interpretation of what is happening. As this occurs, a person's experience changes. A given emotion might mutate into what feels like another emotion if there is a significant enough change in the way the central object is construed. The emotion might, instead, dissipate. It might change in more subtle ways, taking on a somewhat different felt quality because of the way a few new thoughts alter how the central object appears. There is a lot of insight here that we will look for also in Aquinas's account of emotion, specifically in his account of the different acts of (the power of) apprehension that provide intentional content for particular emotions.

Nussbaum's analysis is helpful to us in another respect as well. It makes clear that emotions such as fear, anger, love, and grief all include ways of construing what is happening in one's world or one's life and how much it matters. More than this, her analysis suggests that some of these seemingly ordinary emotions include (perhaps only incipient or inarticulate) beliefs, assumptions, intuitions, or questions about the nature of reality—about the ultimate causes of events, about whether humans are free in any significant sense, about how important certain things really are, about the ultimate import of one's choices, and so on. Thoughts such as these, which are broadly religious, are in the background of many emotional states. These thoughts are likely to influence how certain emotions form and how they feel, whether the person is explicitly aware of the thoughts or not. When such thoughts *are* explicit—when religious curiosity and concern become part of the conscious wherewithal with which one assesses what is happening with respect to a valued object—the impact on how one feels is likely to be notable. This impact is worth investigating.

Upheavals of Thought opens the door to this sort of inquiry with a discussion of the socially conditioned nature of much human emotion. Nussbaum notes that a person's emotions can be affected by his or her metaphysical, religious, or cosmological beliefs.[69] The fear of death, for example—which appears to be very common across cultures—is nevertheless "powerfully shaped by what one thinks death is, and whether one believes there is an afterlife."[70] Experiences of grief are also affected by such beliefs: "Although people who have a confident belief in an afterlife still grieve for the deaths of loved ones, they usually grieve differently, and their grief is linked to hope."[71] The door to religious inquiry opens further when it becomes evident, in Nussbaum's analysis, that differences in people's emotional lives are present not only across cultures but also within cultures that include different views of what is ultimately real and really valuable. Much of the latter half of *Upheavals of Thought* is an inquiry into a particular form of erotic love as a constituent of human flourishing. This inquiry raises important questions about the highest good for humans and the deepest meanings of inevitable loss.

Nussbaum does not discuss the idea of religious emotion per se, nor does she seek to distinguish religious from nonreligious emotions. Rather, she defines emotions as layered networks of thought and evaluative judgment, and she offers examples of such networks that include or imply what many students of religion would regard as religious elements, including ways of construing things in light of the possible "difference" we discussed in chapter 1. Earlier in the present chapter, we considered some ways in which a person with a religious imagination can sometimes experience an emotion, such as anger or love, such that his or her attention lights on a particular person or situation but also extends beyond it, to the heart of it, or around it, toward a horizon of meaning against which the person or situation takes on special significance. Nussbaum's account allows us to say that an implicit or explicit religious consciousness can condition a person's emotions by contributing to the thought-networks that (at least partly) compose these emotions.

THE RELIGIOUS DIMENSION OF ANGER

Let us return to the emotion of anger to explore briefly some additional significance that Nussbaum's analysis has for religious ethics. We will be examining in later chapters the specific cognitive content of anger.[72] For now we can perhaps agree that anger typically involves the thought that one has been treated with deliberate or callous disregard and one has been injured by this disregard. It involves the thought of rising up and striking back at the one who committed the injury. It involves the thought of restoring one's power in relation to the offender. As such, anger involves thoughts about the *self*. Arguably, it involves thoughts about the *nature* of the self that are likely to be implicit or in the background of a person's awareness unless or until these thoughts are brought to explicit consciousness, say, by a spiritual counselor or a teacher.

According to many Buddhist teachers, anger typically involves the (mistaken) assumption that one is or has a self.[73] It involves the impression that there is something substantial and permanent about who or what one is, when the truth is that one is simply a cluster of mental and physical factors that are part of an endless sea of change. Even as anger involves the impression that there is something solid about the self, it involves the (also mistaken) impression that one must reinforce this solidity and defend it. Anger involves the (mistaken) notion that another person's disrespect—and its public visibility—constitute assaults on one's dignity: A self-respecting individual defends himself or herself against such assaults. I take it that these are, broadly speaking, religious thoughts (about which there has been much religious debate). If thoughts about the self and its vulnerability are in the background of a lot of anger, then a lot of anger appears to have an implicit religious dimension.

Some people who have religious imaginations might, at times, become aware of this dimension of their anger; they might make their religious thoughts explicit. Perhaps they have grown tired of the frequency and intensity with which they experience anger, and they have been encouraged to ponder the mental causes of their anger. Perhaps they have the impression that by changing some of the above thoughts they might be able to reduce the frequency of their anger or at least weaken and shorten particular episodes. They might wonder, for example: "Is it *true* that I am defined by other people's regard for me, such that if they ignore me or don't care about me I become less real? Is it *true* that who I am is determined partly by the power I hold in relation to others, such that if someone slights me, and I fail to respond in kind, I am literally diminished? Is it *true* that my value as a person, my dignity, rests on other people's recognition of that dignity? Who or what am I, really?" At issue within the heart of anger is not only the nature of the self but the nature of reality as such. Is *anything* in reality solid and stable? Is the thought that I can, by *any* course of action, make myself more solid and stable an illusion?

Again, a person of religious curiosity wonders periodically about what is really going on in his or her relationships. He or she might wonder specifically about the value that an emotion such as anger has to these relationships. On the one hand, anger seems to provide important information by registering (in a body-resonant way that is difficult to ignore) that something is wrong in a particular relationship: Someone is failing to show one the respect one is due or a balance of power has been upset. On the other hand, anger *could* register distorted perceptions or judgments about what is real and really important. The anger of a person who wonders about such things might be caused or composed, in a particular case, of a belief that it is good to be happy, along with a belief that to be happy one must secure the respect of certain people, combined with the impression that a particular individual just treated one as if one were of little account, and he or she did so knowingly and on purpose. Yet this anger might also include the suspicion that allowing one's happiness to hang on other people's regard makes one a slave to their changeable opinions. This anger might include the thought that the offender must not be given the power to determine the quality of one's consciousness. At issue within the anger of someone who wonders about what is really happening in a given situation—and about what his or her emotional reaction is really about—is the ultimate meaning and ground of happiness. Is happiness found in recognizing that one is a person of remarkable value and persuading others to affirm this value? Or is it found, instead, in acknowledging that this purported path to happiness leads to a dead end? Is the very thought that happiness is important and to be sought a cause of suffering? Can one live without this thought?

These examples might seem too heady. Let us say, then, that the person of religious curiosity who experiences anger has the thoughts, "How dare you treat me that way! I deserve better than that!," combined with the thought, "I'm going to make you show me the respect I deserve!," combined with the creeping suspicion that "maybe he simply doesn't care about me. Maybe the only thing my anger does is reveal how much power he has to control my state of mind. I'm such a fool!" The point is the same: Such thoughts can be analyzed to uncover metaphysical and moral assumptions to which they are attached, all of which are open to examination. Are the assumptions true or are they false? In my view, it would be a mistake to make too much of such thoughts, for nonhuman animals appear to have experiences that resemble human anger in certain respects, and we would not want to say that these animals are working with implicit metaphysical assumptions. Yet many humans experience forms of anger that occur frequently and intensely, and last for a long time. Their anger appears to incorporate a lot of high-level thinking, interpreting, assessing, and rehearsing. Some of this anger could involve assumptions about what is real (in general and with respect to the self, in particular) and what is ultimately important in life (such as "being somebody" and being treated with respect).

From the perspective of religious ethics it is important to reflect critically on the religious meanings that attach to people's emotions. Greater understanding of the emotions is needed by people who participate in organized religions, for it is part of the business of religions to evoke or redirect people's emotions to bring about desired ends. By working with the emotions, religions can affect in profound ways the quality of people's lives and the way people get along—or fail to get along. Greater understanding is needed also by people who have little to do with organized religion but are prone to wonder, care, and sometimes agonize about what is really happening in their lives and their world, and about how (or whether) a particular situation really matters in the larger scheme of things.

The challenge for religious ethics is to talk about emotions in a way that people find workable. The challenge is to use concepts that capture some of what a significant number of people would likely say, upon reflection, about what they feel when they are moved emotionally. The challenge is also to use concepts that allow people to say *more* about their emotions than they might otherwise be able to say. Indeed, the challenge is to allow people to *feel* more or differently than they might otherwise feel—by learning to encounter emotion-evoking features of reality with greater self-awareness, curiosity, creativity, and flexibility.

CONCLUSION

Our brief consideration of the work of Gustafson and Nussbaum confirms that there are good reasons for bringing a broad conception of the religious to the analysis of the moral life and to the study of emotion, in particular. Bringing such a concept to the study of emotion allows us to identify some of the ways in which certain assumptions or intuitions about the nature of reality, the fundamental order of things, the source of real power, or the meaning of human life, can affect not only the way the world appears to us but also how it feels to us. Religious thoughts, intuitions, and questions can condition a wide array of emotions. They can condition emotions that are about God or divine things. They can condition emotions that are about the way things are going in our lives, where we suspect that something unusually deep or significant is happening. They can condition emotions that are about other finite objects, where these objects appear to connect us to a sacred power or a truth that is missed or neglected by people when they are preoccupied with daily life. Feeling emotions that are religious or have a religious dimension, particularly if they are pleasing, can reinforce the habits of thought and imagination that are partly responsible for evoking these emotions. Religious ethics can help us notice some of the ways of "seeing" and being moved that have become second nature to us; it can empower us to imagine how we might feel differently if we saw the world somewhat differently.

Another reason for bringing the idea of the religious, along with methods for the study of religion, to the study of emotion is that it begins to reveal how difficult it is—and why it is so difficult—to determine how one *ought* to feel. One cannot make a good decision about how to feel about people and events in one's life (episodically or as a matter of cultivated habit) until one determines, at least to one's own satisfaction, what is really going on and what is really at stake. Yet many people, when they think about it, realize that they are unsure about the nature of reality. Many are unsure, for example, about whether there is a final guarantor of justice, so that it is morally responsible for humans to let God or the universe take care of making things right—which means that many people are unsure about what to do with some of their righteous anger. This wondering and worrying is likely to affect the composition of their anger in ways that are worth analyzing. Similarly, many people are unsure about what will happen to them when they die, and about whether and in what form they will meet up with their dead loved ones—which makes them unsure, on some level, about what to do with some of their fear and their grief, as well as their love for other people in their lives who could die at any moment. Again, this wondering and worrying is likely to affect the intentional content of their fear, grief, and love.

Gustafson says that religion is partly a matter of the affections. Analyzing the idea of religious emotion reveals that some emotions are partly a matter of religion. Nussbaum's work helps us to appreciate that some emotions are composed, at least in part, of religious beliefs, assumptions, intuitions, wonder, and concern. Some religious "thoughts" might function primarily as background beliefs until they are evoked by a situation that demands more than a surface interpretation and assessment. Some of them might be at work in composing emotion-laden meanings in ways that are barely evident to consciousness and are difficult, even upon reflection, to identify. If an important task of religious ethics is to promote self-understanding and understanding of others with whom we share the planet, we do well to continue our inquiry into religion and emotion, turning our attention now to Aquinas's account of emotion.

NOTES

1. Robert Roberts makes "construing" the center of his account of emotion, coupled with the notion of "concern." See *Emotions: An Essay in Aid of Moral Psychology*. Roberts is a philosopher who has made valuable contributions to Christian ethics and religious ethics. I might have spent more time on his perspective, in this project, were it not for the fact that I had already done significant work on Nussbaum's theory of emotion by the time I had the chance to read Roberts's book, and their views are very similar. Roberts characterizes emotions as "concern-based construals" (64). Nussbaum characterizes them as "eudaimonistic thoughts," where "thought" is a capacious category that would include (among other things) ways of construing objects that appear to bear on one's own or a loved one's well-being. See *Upheavals of Thought*, chap. 1.

2. Keep in mind the conception of "religious worldview" articulated in chapter 1.

3. See Albert J. Raboteau, *Slave Religion: The "Invisible Institution" in the Antebellum South* (New York: Oxford University Press, 1978). I recommend considering Raboteau's analysis of slave religion in light of Maya Angelou's autobiographical account of African American religion in Stamps, Arkansas. See *I Know Why the Caged Bird Sings* (New York: Random House, 1969).

4. In what follows I focus on James M. Gustafson, *Can Ethics Be Christian?* (Chicago: University of Chicago Press, 1975) and *Ethics from a Theocentric Perspective, Volume One: Theology and Ethics* (Chicago: University of Chicago Press, 1981).

5. Gustafson, *Ethics from a Theocentric Perspective*, chap. 4. Wayne Proudfoot has written on some of the same figures, attending to the relationship between religious experience and emotion. See *Religious Experience* (Berkeley: University of California Press, 1985).

6. Gustafson, *Can Ethics Be Christian?* 43. See also Jonathan Edwards, "A Treatise Concerning Religious Affections," 237.

7. Nussbaum, *Therapy of Desire*.

8. Nussbaum, *Upheavals of Thought*.

9. Nussbaum, *Therapy of Desire*, chap. 3.

10. Gustafson, *Can Ethics Be Christian?*, 42–44.

11. Ibid., 38–39, 49.

12. Ibid., 39. See also 63.

13. Ibid., 92.

14. Ibid., 43, 92. See also *Ethics from a Theocentric Perspective*, 198.

15. Gustafson, *Can Ethics Be Christian?*, 43. He uses these terms synonymously. See *Ethics from a Theocentric Perspective*, 197–99.

16. Gustafson, *Can Ethics Be Christian?*, 43.

17. Ibid.

18. Ibid.

19. Ibid.

20. Edwards, "A Treatise Concerning Religious Affections," 237.

21. Ibid.

22. Ibid.

23. Ibid.

24. *ST* I-II 24.3 *ad* 1.

25. Gustafson, *Ethics from a Theocentric Perspective*, 198.

26. Ibid., 199.

27. Gustafson, *Can Ethics Be Christian?*, 43.

28. Gustafson, *Ethics from a Theocentric Perspective*, 120. Following Julian Hartt, Gustafson is interested in reflecting the unity of experience under the impact of theology, which he describes as "a way of construing the world" that has both "affective religious elements and more cognitive or intellective elements" (158). Somewhat as Jeffrey Stout conceives of ethics as "ethical discourse gone reflective," Gustafson seems to conceive of theology as the religious-moral life (which already includes "a way of construing the world") "gone reflective" (Stout, "Commitments and Traditions in the Study of Religious Ethics," 30).

29. Gustafson, *Ethics from a Theocentric Perspective*, 120; see also 129. I agree with this point, but I would argue that the unity of experience is best captured by identifying many of its elements or dimensions and tracing the complex ways in which they are related, rather than settling for an undifferentiated whole.

30. Gustafson, *Can Ethics Be Christian?*, 43.

31. Gustafson, *Ethics from a Theocentric Perspective*, 199.

32. Ibid.

33. Edwards, "A Treatise Concerning Religious Affections," 265.
34. Gustafson, *Ethics from a Theocentric Perspective*, 172.
35. Ibid., 195.
36. Gustafson, *Can Ethics Be Christian?*, 100.
37. Ibid., 110–12.
38. Gustafson, *Ethics from a Theocentric Perspective*, 205.
39. John E. Smith, *Experience and God* (New York: Newman, 1971), 52. Quoted in Gustafson, *Can Ethics Be Christian?*, 68.
40. Gustafson, *Ethics from a Theocentric Perspective*, 208–9.
41. Gustafson, *Can Ethics Be Christian?*, 68.
42. See especially chapter 7. Aquinas conceives of religion (*religio*) as a moral virtue—a disposition to pay God the honor that God is due (*ST* II-II 81). He says that worship (*cultus*), which is an act of religion, "is paid to images . . . leading us to God incarnate. Now movement to an image as image does not stop at the image, but goes on to the thing it represents" (81.3 *ad* 3).
43. Gustafson, *Ethics from a Theocentric Perspective*, 308.
44. Ibid. See also 227.
45. *Can Ethics Be Christian?*, chap. 3. Here he draws on the work of Erik Erikson.
46. Gustafson, *Ethics from a Theocentric Perspective*, 205.
47. An option in some cultures is to presume that the person is possessed by a spirit, which is likely to evoke different sorts of emotional responses.
48. I am grateful to Rachel Gordon for this image. Poetically, it seems to say something more than "*through* the beloved's eyes."
49. Tillich, *Systematic Theology, Volume One*, 239–41.
50. As my student Abbylynn Helgevold says, "Sometimes you're just pissed!"
51. In "Emotion and Religious Ethics," *Journal of Religious Ethics* 16, no. 2 (1988): 307–24, Paul Lauritzen argues against "the traditional view" of emotions, as epitomized by William James, according to which emotions are "irrational and animal-like" and "little more than stomach aches and fatigue" (307). My own study of emotion has focused on different voices in the western philosophical and religious tradition, especially Aristotle and other ancient philosophers, and Thomas Aquinas—none of whom hold such a view.
52. Nussbaum, *Upheavals of Thought*, 23, 37.
53. Ibid., 65, 272.
54. Ibid., 4.
55. Ibid., 1–2.
56. Ibid., 71–72.
57. Ibid., 68.
58. Ibid., 65.
59. Ibid., 69.
60. Ibid., 69–70.
61. Ibid., 69.
62. Ibid., 52–55.

63. Ibid., 74.

64. Ibid., 43.

65. Ibid., 44–45.

66. Ibid., 39. This thought is especially variable in light of different religious beliefs. Many people believe, in their grief, that they have been cut off from their usual way of relating to their loved one (as embodied), but they have not been cut off in all ways or forever.

67. Ibid., 65.

68. Ibid., 70–71, 75–76.

69. Ibid., 152.

70. Ibid., 153.

71. Ibid.

72. At issue is the extent to which the following intentional content is specific to certain cultures and to persons who occupy particular social positions within the same culture. Aquinas's account of emotion allows us to say that of course the form our anger takes is determined, in part, by cultural and social particularities; but our anger is also, in part, a function of our animality: some form of anger is recognizable across cultures and even across species.

73. See, for example, Dalai Lama, *Healing Anger: The Power of Patience from a Buddhist Perspective*, trans. Geshe Thupten Jinpa (Ithaca, N.Y.: Snow Lion, 1997), and Chögyam Trungpa, *The Myth of Freedom and the Way of Meditation* (Boston: Shambhala, 1988).

CHAPTER THREE

Approaching Aquinas on the Emotions (I)

✦

To explore further how ways of being religious can affect the composition of emotional states, it is necessary to delve further into the structure of emotion. Even if we are not particularly interested in the impact that religion has on people's emotions, it is important to understand how emotions are composed if we wish to become more articulate about our interior lives, more deliberate in shaping our emotions, and more discerning about the constraints that our "nature" imposes on this sort of ethical work.

Aquinas offers a remarkable account of this structure. In outline, he argues that *passio* or an emotion is a motion of a soul-body composite.[1] It is a motion that occurs with respect to the appetitive dimension of an embodied soul. In other words, it is a motion that occurs through the exercise of one's appetitive powers.[2] An emotion occurs, in particular, through the exercise of one's sensory appetite. As such it has a material element. It is composed, in part, of patterned bodily changes that can be subtle, but are often noticeable in the form of felt bodily sensations. Yet an emotion is also intentional. It concerns some object—again, a thing, a person, a relationship, a situation—which one apprehends in a certain way, as bearing directly or indirectly on one's well-being. An emotion is evoked and defined, more precisely, by sensory judgments, images, and impressions, which are basic forms of cognition. Yet a given emotion is ordinarily informed, in a human being, by higher forms of cognition as well, which allow one to interpret on different levels the significance of an object of concern—in ways that further determine one's experience of emotion.

Aquinas's account is complex and subtle. To understand it, relevant details of the account and their most important implications must be encountered with patience, with the understanding that it is only after getting a glimpse of the whole that one is in a good position to grasp any one of its parts. In this and the next chapter, I lay some groundwork for approaching Aquinas. Specifically, I introduce the idea that an emotion is a form of *appetitive motion*, and the idea that an emotion takes place within a *soul-body composite*. These are aspects of Aquinas's account that I expect to be controversial, for various reasons. I treat them up front in the hope of clearing the path a bit—not so as to remove the controversy but to provide reasons for not getting hung up too quickly on these controversies such that one is unwilling to move forward with an investigation of Aquinas's account.

In chapters 5 and 6, I focus more specifically on the *kind* of embodied appetitive motion Aquinas intends, approaching the structure of emotion, as it were, from below, bringing into perspective the appetitive motions that characterize other sorts of things in the universe. In chapters 7 through 9, I approach the structure of emotion from the other direction, so to speak, from above, analyzing the relationship between acts of the intellect and the will, on the one hand, and emotions, on the other. The idea is to provide something like the photographic lighting (from both the front and the back) that is necessary to expose the dimension and detail of an object. In interpreting Aquinas, I seek to show that emotions can meaningfully be located along a continuum of appetitive motions within the human being, and that the appetitive motions of humans can meaningfully be thought of in relation to the appetitive motions of other sorts of entities, within the context of a cosmos that is governed by Love as the first and final principle of all appetitive motion.

EMOTION AS A FORM OF THOUGHT: NUSSBAUM, REVISITED

For Aquinas, emotions are appetitive motions that cannot be aroused or sustained apart from particular acts of cognition; yet emotions are not themselves forms of cognition. At least, Aquinas recommends that we not view them that way. Let us return briefly to Nussbaum's cognitivist account of emotion in order to bring out some of what is distinctive in Aquinas's account.

Nussbaum constructs her theory of emotion in response to an "adversary." Her adversary holds that "emotions are 'non-reasoning movements,' unthinking energies that simply push the person around, without being hooked up to the ways in which she perceives or thinks about the world."[3] Nussbaum argues in response to this adversary that emotions are better construed as forms of thought that "attempt to fit the world—both to take in the events that really do take place, and to get an appropriate view of what matters or has value."[4] As we can already recognize, Nussbaum's foil could also serve as a foil for Aquinas. Thomistic emotions are definitely not "unthinking energies" that have no relationship to the way a person "perceives or thinks about the world." Yet neither are they simply "thoughts."

Nussbaum argues that emotions "embody . . . beliefs—often very complex—about [a particular] object."[5] These beliefs are "essential to the identity of the emotion."[6] Emotions are "ways of registering how things are with respect to the external (i.e., uncontrolled) items that we view as salient for our well-being."[7] They are "forms of evaluative judgment that ascribe to certain things and persons outside a person's own control great importance for that person's own flourishing."[8] Emotions are thus ways of "seeing" an object as "invested with value or importance."[9] They are, more specifically, ways of "assenting to or embracing a way of seeing [an object], acknowledging it as true."[10]

Thought, in this view, must not be caricatured as cool, detached, and static. For Nussbaum, the kind of thought that composes an emotion is "dynamic": "Reason here moves, embraces, refuses; it can move rapidly or slowly, it can move directly or with hesitation."[11] Emotion-composing thought "[entertains] appearances"; it rushes toward appearances, opening up to take them in; it assents to them, saying, "yes, this is how things are."[12] Emotion-thoughts can have "urgency and heat."[13] Some of them are like geological upheavals "[projecting] outward like a mountain range."[14] The thoughts that Nussbaum has in mind are not mere preparation for the upheaval of emotion—they are the upheaval itself.[15] For example, Nussbaum's assent to the proposition that "my mother, an enormously valuable person and an important part of my life, is dead," was such an upheaval.[16] It was "itself a tearing of [Nussbaum's] self-sufficient condition. Knowing can be violent, given the truths that are there to be known."[17]

Nussbaum argues that thought, properly understood, is both necessary and sufficient for emotion.[18] Anticipating objections, she asks whether emotions necessarily include anything other than thoughts, taking the relevant question to be whether emotions necessarily include any "objectless feelings of pain and/or pleasure,"[19] such as "a fluttering in [the] hands" or "a trembling in [the] stomach,"[20] a "mere . . . heartleaping,"[21] a rise in blood pressure or pulse rate,[22] or a movement of the limbs.[23] In her view, some emotions might include one or another of these "unthinking movements," but they need not and often do not. Where such movements do occur, there are no consistent correlations between particular movements and particular emotions. Emotions such as grief and anger always include certain thoughts (on some level of awareness), but they feel different to different people.[24] Nussbaum maintains therefore that a "given feeling or bodily process" is not a necessary part of any emotion's "internal conditions of identity."[25]

Nussbaum considers briefly the relationship between emotions and *desires*, but she construes desires narrowly as "action-guiding" or "productive of a concrete plan of action," which allows her to conclude that emotions do not necessarily include desires.[26] She also discusses briefly the relationship between emotions and *appetites* but construes the latter as "unthinking" bodily appetites, focusing almost exclusively on hunger. This causes her to draw a sharp distinction between emotions (as "object-flexible, value-suffused pulls") and appetites (as "object-fixated, value-indifferent pushes").[27]

Nussbaum discusses more extensively the relationship between emotions and *feelings*. Again, she focuses on feelings that have no cognitive content, such as a feeling of "fatigue" or of "extra energy."[28] It is not surprising that she finds no necessary connection between objectless feelings of this sort and particular emotions. She acknowledges that there *are* "feelings with a rich intentional content—feelings of the emptiness of one's life without a certain person, feelings of unhappy love for that person, and so forth. Feelings like these," she grants, "may enter into the identity conditions for some emotion." In her view, however, "the word 'feeling' now does not contrast with our cognitive words 'perception' and 'judgment,' it is merely a terminological variant of them."[29] She would likely say the same thing about desires and other forms of appetite that have "rich intentional content"—such as the desire to spend time in someone's company (which is arguably ingredient in the emotion of love), or the appetite for revenge (which is arguably ingredient in the emotion of anger). Object-oriented attachments, longing, need, and even erotic love are all construed by Nussbaum as thoughts.[30]

APPREHENSION AND APPETITE: EMOTION AS A FORM OF MOTION

Nussbaum seeks to define thoughts in such a way that some of them appear flexible, dynamic, eruptive, and urgent enough to capture what most people, I believe, associate with the motional aspect of emotion, namely, the experience of being moved by something, captivated by it, attracted to it, repulsed by it, or pulled in different directions. However, there are good reasons not to ask thought to do all the work of emotion.

Stepping back and reflecting on the phenomenon of motion in humans, many philosophers and theologians have taken it as axiomatic that there are two basic powers or capabilities that account for motion, including bodily motion (such as motion from place to place) but also, by implication, the interior motion of an embodied soul. According to this familiar view, humans have, first, a *cognitive* power, broadly construed. We have the capability of "receiving and processing information," to use Nussbaum's words.[31] In *De*

Anima, Aristotle says that the power of cognition includes the power of both thought and sensation.[32] Similarly, in the *Summa theologiae*, Aquinas refers to the cognitive power as the power of apprehension (*apprehensio*), which includes both intellectual and sensory apprehension.[33] Readers must take care not to confuse "apprehension" or "apprehensive" with "anxiety" or "anxious"; in this project, "apprehension" refers to a power or an operation (Aquinas also calls it an "act") by which a being apprehends and/or processes intelligible and/or sensible information of some kind.

The power of sensory apprehension, for Aquinas, includes the five exterior senses and also what he calls the interior senses (*interiores sensus*). The interior senses include, for example, the power to apprehend a sensible object as having certain properties that bear on one's life and well-being ("danger!").[34] The power of intellectual apprehension makes it possible to engage in higher forms of conceiving, thinking, reasoning, and judging, which require the use of abstract ideas, such as universal concepts ("this is a wolf; wolves are dangerous; this wolf poses a threat to me").[35]

More than this, however, humans have an *appetitive* power.[36] Aquinas distinguishes two different powers of appetite (*appetitus*), namely, the power of the intellectual appetite or will and the power of the sensory appetite.[37] The intellectual appetite is the power to tend (*appetere* or *tendere*) toward a universal object, namely, "good in general";[38] it is the power also to tend toward (or away from) a particular object in light of its relationship to goodness.[39] The person who exercises his or her intellectual appetite relative to an object tends toward (or away from) the object because he or she apprehends intellectually that it is productive (or destructive) of human flourishing.[40] The sensory appetite, in distinction, is the power to tend toward (or away from) an object that one apprehends on the level of the exterior and interior senses to be suitable (or unsuitable).[41] The person who exercises his or her sensory appetite tends toward (or away from) an object because he or she apprehends that it is suitable (or unsuitable) in its particularity.[42]

Keeping the powers of both apprehension and appetite in mind, consider the motion of rational choice and action. For Aquinas, the power of apprehension originates this sort of motion in a specific sense. The power of apprehension makes it possible to find an object of thought intelligible; it allows one to regard an object *as* an object of a certain kind. The power of apprehension also makes it possible to find an object of sensation sensible; it allows one to pick something out as a sensible object and recognize its sensible properties. In short, the power of apprehension makes it possible to entertain something *as* an object of consciousness or awareness.

The power of *intellectual* apprehension, in particular, makes it possible to identify the sort of object something is. It also allows one to discern (where relevant) that the object is of moral significance. It allows one to judge the object good or bad relative to a standard of goodness, such as an ideal of human flourishing. However, unless one also experiences an appetitive motion in relation to the object—unless one is moved, or one moves oneself, to approach the object interiorly, to withdraw from it, or to engage in some other form of interior motion—there arises no choice with respect to the object and thus no action. As Aristotle says, "mind is never found producing movement without appetite."[43] Similarly, Aquinas says that "the apprehensive power presents the object to the appetite," but it is by virtue of the appetite that one tends toward or away from an object: "Wherefore choice is substantially not an act of the reason but of the will: for choice is accomplished in a . . . movement of the soul toward the good which is chosen. Consequently it is evidently an act of the appetitive power."[44]

Consider also the motion of emotion. Aquinas argues along similar lines that it is the coordinated exercise of the apprehensive and appetitive powers that produces such motion. By exercising the power of *sensory* apprehension, in particular, a person is able to register sensory images or impressions of an object and make some initial discriminations in the object's regard.[45] (As we will see, a person is generally able to reflect on the sensible object intellectually as well, finding it intelligible; in a rational animal the sensory powers ordinarily function in tandem with the intellectual powers.) If it were not for the power of appetite, however, the person would not be moved relative to what he or she apprehends. It is the act of being moved by an object of apprehension (which is thus also an object of appetite) that constitutes an emotion.[46]

As Aquinas conceives it, the motion of emotion orients us relative to an object of apprehension, but in such a way that we reach, in a sense, beyond our cognitive grasp of the object and toward (or away from) the object itself.[47] Rather than simply holding an object in mind, the object also gets hold of us. Technically, an emotion orients us toward an object as we construe it. Yet inasmuch as the object or some of its features are really there, our apprehension of the object relates us to something outside ourselves. Our apprehension of the object is caused, in part, by the object being there and having the properties it has. With an object of memory or imagination, we usually have the impression that the object has a kind of reality: It has an impact on us that is similar to the impact it would have if it were actually present to us. In any case, with an emotion that regards an attractive object, the object seems to draw us out of ourselves; it compels us to attend to it, to resonate with it, perhaps to approach it inwardly, to dwell within it, and to enjoy the pleasure of being with it. Sometimes an interior reaching finds expression in the extension of arms, in the movement of the body as a whole toward the attractive object, or in speech that is intended to "reach" someone's ears—which is why it makes sense to identify a causally prior, interior reaching *as* a form of interior motion. When an interior motion finds exterior, bodily expression, there is usually continuity in experience between how the motion feels *before* it finds expression and how it feels *as* it finds expression.

The power of appetite makes it possible for a person to be gripped by an object in a way that apprehension alone does not. Aquinas says that "the operation of the apprehensive power is completed in the very fact that the thing apprehended is in the one that apprehends: while the operation of the appetitive power is completed in the fact that he who desires is borne toward the thing desirable."[48] Again, an act of apprehension is implicated in the act of "being borne," for the person is borne toward (or away from) an object as conceived or perceived, but it is the power of appetite that makes it possible for one to go beyond the state of merely having something in mind to the state of being moved in relation to it as something that is more than merely mental or behaves as though it were.

APPREHENSION AND APPETITE: A COLLAPSE OF THE DISTINCTION?

For Aquinas, the activities of apprehension are thus formally distinct from the activities of being reoriented, desiring or loathing, resisting or surrendering, seeking or avoiding, enjoying or suffering. It must be acknowledged, however, that the activities of apprehension and appetite function in such a tight and seamless relationship with respect to each other that it can be difficult to pry them apart conceptually. Sometimes when we apprehend an object, we do not simply apprehend it *as* something in particular. We also apprehend it *as* good or bad, advantageous or disadvantageous, attractive or repulsive. In experience, it might seem that when we apprehend something as attractive (or repulsive) we just are attracted to it (or repulsed by it). It can therefore seem that there is no formal distinction between making an assessment of an object's value and undergoing an interior motion in its regard.[49] If there is no such distinction, then we might as well define an emotion as an evaluative judgment.

It is possible, however, to judge something attractive in the sense of judging it to be something toward which one might, under certain circumstances, be drawn, but toward which one is not currently drawn because one is preoccupied with something else. It is possible also to judge something worthy of our attraction—to think that we *ought* to be attracted to it because of its good and objectively pleasing qualities—but not feel attracted to it. Similarly, it is possible to judge something unworthy of our attraction—to think that we *ought not* to be (so) attracted to it because it is not good for us and, perhaps, it is not even pleasing to us (anymore)—but nonetheless feel drawn toward it. Some addictions fit this description. To acknowledge the possibility of such cases is not to deny that most of the time, when we judge an object to be good and attractive (or bad and unattractive or repulsive), we are also attracted to it (or unattracted or repulsed)—in some way, on some level of awareness, to some degree. Nor is it to deny that we are constituted, as biological organisms, in such a way that certain perceptions automatically trigger corresponding appetitive motions. The point is that, strictly speaking, being attracted to an object is something more than apprehending it and judging it to have good or attractive properties. If we are actually attracted to an object that we judge to be good, it must be because the powers of both apprehension and appetite are engaged.

For Aquinas, the power of apprehension never functions apart from the power of appetite, which makes it difficult to test this conceptual distinction in relation to our experience. Appetite operates not only in the immediate wake of thought, such that certain objects of thought ordinarily cause appetitive motions toward (or away from) the objects that are represented by thought. Appetite operates also prior to and along with thought, as that which helps to drive a particular process of thinking or deliberating. Even the act of holding an object in mind, for a period of time, implies a desire to hold it in mind, which implies a prior and ongoing desire to attain and process information in order to realize some good that contributes to human happiness or the experience of sensory pleasure. Similarly, the act of judging or assessing a given object to be good presupposes a prior and ongoing act of wanting—and generally liking—to notice and focus on certain sorts of objects, namely, those that answer to appetites that relate in some way to one's desire for happiness or pleasure. When an object of thought specifies or turns an appetite in a particular direction or makes a dispositional appetite occurrent, the act of thinking about that object can perhaps feel like an "upheaval."

Aquinas says that with an interior act of choice (a motion of the intellectual appetite) two things "concur to make one," namely, an intellectual judgment that some object is good or evil and an appetitive motion toward or away from that object.[50] As we will see, he would say, by the same token, that with an interior act of emotion (a motion of the sensory appetite) two things "concur to make one," namely, a sensory impression that some object is delectable or odious, advantageous or disadvantageous, and a sensory-appetitive motion toward or away from that object. Yet choice is substantially an act of the intellectual appetite; it is an interior (and sometimes exteriorized) motion whose object is specified by an act of intellectual apprehension. Similarly, emotion is substantially an act of the sensory appetite; it is an interior (and sometimes exteriorized) motion whose object is specified by an act of sensory apprehension.

When one experiences an object-oriented motion of the appetite, certain acts of apprehension and appetite "concur," but these acts are separable in thought. Aquinas employs this distinction partly because it allows him to elucidate important connections between various forms of human motion, none of which are reducible to judgments. In particular, it allows him to make manifest how certain exterior acts (most notably actions that involve bodily movement or locomotion) are caused by prior interior acts, including acts or motions of the will (say, the choice to engage in bodily movement for a particular purpose) and acts or motions of the sensory appetite, which resemble motions of the will structurally and often function in tandem with the will to motivate human action.

APPREHENSION AND APPETITE IN CONFLICT?

Maintaining the conceptual distinction between acts of apprehension and acts or motions of appetite—and identifying emotions with forms of object-oriented appetitive motion, rather than with forms of judgment alone—is important to Aquinas also because it allows him to acknowledge conflicts between evaluative judgments, on the one hand, and emotions, on the other. As mentioned previously, thinking something to be good (judging, say, that it contributes directly or indirectly to one's flourishing as a human being) does not necessarily amount to being drawn toward it, and thinking something to be bad does not necessarily amount to finding it unattractive or being repelled by it. In common cases of *akrasia* or weakness of will, a person judges a particular activity to be bad and hurtful to his or her best interests, yet nonetheless craves the activity and the pleasure associated with it, or the reduction in pain that the activity allows. The craving becomes so intense as to overwhelm thought, in the sense that the craving makes it nearly impossible for the person to think clearly or much at all about the activity in question or its value for his or her life, to the point that the activity ceases to be in question and the person simply does it.[51]

St. Paul of the Christian New Testament wrote a letter to other followers of Jesus, trying to help them recognize the power of unruly appetites within themselves: "I find it to be a law that when I want to do right, evil lies close at hand. For I delight in the law of God, in my inmost self, but I see in my members another law at war with the law of my mind and making me captive to the law of sin which dwells in my members" (Romans 7:21–3).[52]

Aquinas takes Paul to be identifying here the power that the sensory appetite has to resist the power of thought.[53] On a related note, Aquinas quotes Augustine as saying, "My soul hath coveted to long for Thy justifications:——The intellect flies ahead, the desire follows sluggishly or not at all: we know what is good, but deeds delight us not."[54] Aquinas represents Augustine as referring here to sluggish motions of the will, but the sensory appetite can exhibit the same sort of sluggishness. Commenting on a passage in Aristotle's *Politics*, Aquinas echoes Aristotle by saying that motions of the sensory appetite are like "free subjects, who, though subject to the government of the ruler [reason], have nevertheless something of their own, by reason of which they can resist the orders of him who commands."[55]

In all of these cases it seems natural to say that a person's thoughts or judgments are in conflict with certain motions of his or her appetite: The person judges something to be good, but the object holds no real attraction; or the person judges something to be bad, but he or she is nonetheless drawn toward it. None of this implies, however, that for Aquinas the mind is a rational power capable of "thinking movements," while the appetitive power is a nonrational power that is capable of only "unthinking movements."[56] Aristotle and Aquinas do say that emotion-composing motions occur in a "nonrational part of the soul" and that these motions can cause people to act in ways that are contrary to reason.[57] Yet Aristotle and Aquinas also indicate that this "nonrational part" (specifically the sensory power) "shares" or "participates" in reason in various ways.[58] Aristotle notes, for example, that in the continent person (namely, the person who has disordered sensory appetites but manages nonetheless to follow reason's guidance) the nonrational part "obeys reason."[59] In the virtuous person (namely, the person who has well-ordered sensory appetites and thus follows reason without internal struggle) the nonrational part "listens still better to reason, since there it agrees with reason in everything."[60] Aquinas agrees with Aristotle and adds that "insofar as the [sensory] appetite obeys reason, good and evil of reason are no longer accidentally in the [emotions], but essentially."[61] The present point, however, is that there appear to be cases in which rational judgments conflict with at least some appetitive motions or emotions. Emotions can fail, to some degree, to display the influence and governance of the rational part of the self. The vehemence of a particular motion of the sensory appetite can cause a person to ignore or refuse, to some extent, the judgment of reason.[62]

Nussbaum acknowledges that there are cases in which it seems as though the "thinking" part of the self is in conflict with some other, resistant part of the self (which she characterizes as "mindless"), but she argues that it is more helpful to think of such cases as conflicts within thought itself.[63] To work with our previous example, Nussbaum would likely argue that the person who feels inner tension over the prospect of forgoing a pleasurable activity is best construed as a person who holds conflicting beliefs. On the one hand, the person believes that it is good for him or her to pursue moral excellence or true human happiness, and he or she believes that this particular activity would likely undermine that excellence or happiness (although the belief might be blurred by questions of whether this activity is *really* as bad as people say it is). On the other hand, the person judges that it would be good for him or her to enjoy the pleasure of this activity (shifting attention away from its problematic features). If the person chooses to enjoy the activity it is because he or she currently judges it more important to pursue this pleasure than to exercise continence for the sake of human flourishing (even though the person might be reluctant to admit that he or she has made this judgment). For Nussbaum, what might feel like conflicts between thought and something else are thus better construed as conflicts between thought and thought—between thoughts of various kinds, of varying degrees of generality and specificity, entertained on various levels of consciousness, with varying degrees of conviction. Emotional conflict is best conceived as "a story of reason's urgent struggles with itself concerning nothing less than how to imagine life."[64]

This is a challenging thesis. Many emotional conflicts do seem to involve conflicting judgments regarding how important something is to us. Reforming emotions that are responsible for such conflict does commonly involve becoming aware of one's evaluative judgments and changing one or more of them. When someone is unsuccessful at altering a malformed emotion or habit of emotion, one can always argue (rightly or wrongly, but meaningfully in either case) that the person is evidently not willing to admit into consciousness, examine, and surrender a judgment about how valuable some item is to him or her. At the same time, however, there also seem to be cases in which a change in thinking does not bring about the change in emotion that one desires. One can always argue that one has not yet (even after years of effort) uncovered the relevant judgment that needs to be changed in order to change a particular emotion or habit of emotion. Yet one can also argue that a change of mind is not always enough—not unless and until one changes one's mind in a way that engages one's appetite, and one thereby shifts the way one is *oriented* relative to what one has in mind.

USEFULNESS OF THE DISTINCTION

I do think that searching for conflicting judgments can be a helpful approach to understanding and resolving certain interior, emotional conflicts, and

Aquinas would agree. However, Aquinas would also want to clarify the sorts of judgments that tend to contribute to such conflicts. In his view, as reflected in his interpretation of Paul and Augustine, it is often a relatively basic form of sensory apprehension that comes into conflict with a higher-order, rational judgment. Sometimes the sensory apprehension is a basic impression that has not been subjected to much thought (for example, mmm! ugh! or danger!, which are impressions that correlate with the basic emotions of love, hatred, or fear). Some of these impressions are difficult to subject to rational reflection because they are connected to fundamental (survival-oriented) appetites for food, drink, sex, or self-defense.[65] If such appetites are aroused in intense forms, they can command one's attention and undermine one's power to make good judgments.[66] One could thus construe some internal conflicts as conflicts between a rational judgment and a recalcitrant, misleading sensory impression according to which some item appears to be better than in fact it is, but one still has to account for the recalcitrance. Aquinas can account for it by linking the impression to an appetitive motion that has a connection to (and might be a specification of) a basic human (indeed, animal) drive.

Motions of the sensory appetite *are* evoked by sensory impressions and involve holding those impressions in mind, on some level of awareness. Hence, it is sometimes helpful, in a case of interior conflict, to focus on the conflict between a particular higher-order evaluative judgment and a competing sensory impression. In such a case, one would be dealing with two acts of apprehension rather than an act of apprehension and an act of appetite. By the same token, however, there is no reason why one could not productively focus on the conflict between competing motions of the appetite. Consider once again the person who judges that engaging in some activity would be a bad thing to do but is inclined to engage in it anyway. From one angle, the person experiences a conflict between the judgment that it is good to be a person who behaves according to a certain standard, and the judgment that it is good to enjoy this particular pleasure. From a different angle, the same person experiences a conflict between the desire to be good and to act rightly and the desire to enjoy this particular pleasure.[67]

It can be helpful in situations of inner turmoil to search out both sorts of conflict, namely, conflicts between one thought (or set of thoughts) and another, contrary thought (or set of thoughts), and conflicts between one appetite (or set of appetites) and another, contrary appetite (or set of appetites). With the conceptual distinction between thought and appetite in mind, one can move deftly between the dimension of thought and the dimension of appetite until one finds the most effective interpretive key. It can also be helpful to identify and reflect upon a conflict between thought and appetite, understanding that thought and appetite are, in certain respects, like apples and oranges yet are also, in other respects, like two sides of a coin. Reflecting on a conflict between thought and appetite can be helpful especially where the relevant thought is a relatively high-level or abstract thought, such as a judgment about an object's moral value, and the relevant appetitive motion is a relatively basic, sensory motion that resists the influence of thought because it is associated with a consciousness-captivating drive or instinct. Yet a high-level judgment of this kind can also be considered in light of the related appetite for goodness or happiness, and the basic, sensory motion can be considered in light of the sensory images or impressions that have evoked it. Questions thus naturally arise: Is seeking (or avoiding) this sensible object *really* what I want? Is there another way I can look at this object, which will cause this painful conflict to shift? Is there a way that I can seek (or avoid) this object that is consistent with the demands of my rational as well as my animal nature?

Nussbaum seeks to provide people with a theory of emotion that has "superior power to explain experience."[68] Readers must decide whether her account of emotion as thought has more or less explanatory power than other accounts, including Aquinas's. Of course, we have only begun to explore Aquinas's account, so it would be premature to judge *its* adequacy. I hope simply to have provided some reasons for taking seriously the possibility that emotion is something more than thought, perception, or judgment. Those who are interested in the problem of *akrasia* can delve more deeply than I am able to do here into the nature of various internal conflicts.[69]

One of the most compelling features of Aquinas's account is its flexibility. It allows us to attend to the cognitive dimension of emotion, if we choose. It allows us to attend also to the appetitive and, by extension, the motive dimensions. It allows us to isolate different apprehensions (from intellectual and general to sensory and particular), and it allows us to conceive their relationships to different kinds of appetitive motion (from those whose objects are intelligible and general to those whose objects are sensible and particular). We will see the possibilities that this flexibility opens up when we examine in more depth what it means to say that an emotion is, more specifically, a motion of the sensory appetite—yet a motion that occurs in a human being with intellectual powers.

NOTES

1. There has been some controversy over how to translate *passio* in Aquinas. For example, Shawn Floyd argues that Aquinas's conception of *passio* differs considerably

from "our" contemporary understanding of emotion (Shawn D. Floyd, "Aquinas on Emotion: A Response to Some Recent Interpretations," *History of Philosophy Quarterly* 15, no. 2 (1998): 161). He argues that Thomistic *passio* lacks a cognitive component; it *must* lack a cognitive component because Aquinas distinguishes between apprehension and appetite and locates *passio* in the (sensory) appetite. Almost everyone today agrees that emotion has a cognitive dimension. Hence, Floyd thinks we need to define emotion as an act of apprehension plus *passio*. In my interpretation of Aquinas, *passio* is indeed a motion of the sensory appetite, but it is inherently object-oriented. A situation is apprehended in a certain way; this act of apprehension causes a *passio*; it also enters into the composition of the *passio* because it defines the form of the *passio*, as long as the *passio* persists. In the absence of a defining object of apprehension, what might look like a *passio* of the soul is reduced to something else, namely, a physical change or a felt sensation that is not *about* anything. Moreover, without knowing the object that someone has in mind, it is impossible to identify which *passio* the person is feeling. For further reflection on the relationship between *passio* and emotion, see chapter 4. The larger point of this book is to show that, if we give Aquinas the benefit of the doubt, the realm of *passio* can be seen to reflect all kinds of basic and more subtle forms of intelligence.

2. Aquinas speaks of diverse human "powers" that have particular "operations" or "acts," including "motions." As we will see, every existing thing, in his view, has powers of some kind, and at least some of its powers must be, to some extent, in act, or the thing ceases to exist. With respect to human beings, we can think of a power as a capability or an ability to do something, to perform a function, or to undergo a change, under certain conditions. One can have a power in potentiality, and one can have it in act, which is to say that one can have a capability, and one can also exercise it or actualize it—or, in the case of a passive power, one's capability can be actualized (that is, one can be acted upon and changed) by the act of another. "Act" refers broadly to the actualization of an active or a passive potency of any kind. See Peter King, "Aquinas on the Passions," in *Aquinas's Moral Theory: Essays in Honor of Norman Kretzmann*, ed. Scott MacDonald and Eleonore Stump (Ithaca, N.Y.: Cornell University Press, 1999), 101–32. Thus, with respect to a human being, Aquinas can refer to the act of smelling an object, the act of judging the object to be edible, the act of being drawn toward the object interiorly, the act of consenting to the way in which one is being drawn, the act of choosing to eat the object, the act of chewing it, the act of digesting it, the act of being nourished by it, the act of feeling satiated, and so on. Using the term "act" with respect to everything on this list might seem strange at first, but I think it is meaningful and helpful. It allows us to appreciate that each of these items has something in common: It is a function of a particular entity—in this case, a human being. Each item is something of which a person is capable, and each is a way in which he or she is, at a particular moment, in act, rather than merely in potentiality, with respect to one or more of his or her capabilities. Sometimes Aquinas speaks as if particular powers, rather than persons themselves, were the agents or the patients of particular acts. I think he does so partly because different powers are connected in different ways to the powers of

the intellect and the will, which Aquinas associates closely with the subject of experience and the agent of choice, and he wants to keep these differences in view. For example, a healthy man has the power to digest food that enters his digestive system, but
he is not ordinarily aware of exercising this power, and the act of this power is not
under his command. A man also has the power (so to speak) to "digest" information.
He is usually aware of this act, but it can be more or less subject to his command. The
"digestion" of information involved in what Aquinas calls sensory apprehension is less
in the man's command than the "digestion" involved in intellectual apprehension. All
of this being said, however, it is still the man as a whole who engages in or undergoes
his own processes of "digestion." Throughout this book I remain flexible in referring to
the subject of an act, but I try to keep the whole being in view.

3. Nussbaum, *Upheavals of Thought*, 24–25.

4. Ibid., 48, 56–57.

5. Ibid., 28.

6. Ibid., 29.

7. Ibid., 4.

8. Ibid.

9. Ibid., 30.

10. Ibid., 38.

11. Ibid., 45.

12. Ibid., 45–46. It is with this point especially that Robert Roberts takes issue in
responding to Nussbaum's account. He argues that "it is better to think of emotions as
a kind of appearance or *phantasia* or construal than as a kind of judgment, because emotions do have the character of appearance and often occur in the absence of assent to
that appearance. . . . Emotions do typically 'assert' something about a situation, about
its character (what kind of situation it is), and about its importance to the subject. But
what the emotion 'says' is not always agreed to by the subject of the emotion, and it is
that agreement that would be required for the emotion to be a judgment *of the subject*"
(*Emotions*, 89).

13. Nussbaum, *Upheavals of Thought*, 27.

14. Ibid., 1.

15. Ibid., 45.

16. Ibid., 76

17. Ibid., 45.

18. Even as Nussbaum packs all of this and more into the thoughts that compose
emotions, she wants to lower the bar for what can count as an emotion-cognition in
order to allow that infants and some animals have emotions. On her view, emotions "always involve thought of an object combined with thought of the object's salience or importance," but this does not imply "the presence of elaborate calculation, of computation,
or even of reflexive self-awareness" (23). In addition, the cognitive appraisals of some animals, human infants, and young children are "linguistically formulable in a way, since
we characterize their cognitive content by choosing the nearest plausible verbal for-
mula." However, "this does not mean . . . that the content actually uses linguistic sym-

bolism, or is formulable in language without a degree of distortion. Nor does it mean that it is formulable, even with distortion, by the subject of the emotion" (127). Finally, Nussbaum holds that there are emotion-composing forms of "seeing-as," including "pictorial imaginings, musical imaginings, the kinetic forms of imagining involved in the dance, and others," that are "not all reducible to or straightforwardly translatable into linguistic symbolism, nor should we suppose that linguistic representing has pride of place as either the most sophisticated or the most basic mode" (128).

19. Ibid., 35.

20. Ibid., 44.

21. Ibid., 27.

22. Ibid., 57–58.

23. Ibid., 45.

24. Ibid., 60–61.

25. Ibid., 57.

26. Ibid., 135–36.

27. Ibid., 129–32.

28. Ibid., 60.

29. Ibid.

30. In part III of *Upheavals of Thought*, which concerns erotic love, Nussbaum agrees with Adam Smith that (in her words) "love is an intense response to perceptions of the particularity, and the particularly high value, of another person's body and mind" (465). Her analysis in part III includes innumerable references to desire, wish, and longing, but I take it that these are to be understood as much as possible in a manner that is consistent with part I, as forms of thought: "love itself is in the upheaval of mind" (476).

31. Ibid., 23.

32. Aristotle, *De Anima*, trans. J. A. Smith, in *The Basic Works of Aristotle*, ed. Richard McKeon (New York: Random House, 1941), 432a15.

33. *ST* I 81.1 and 64.2.

34. *ST* I 78.3 and 78.4. I will discuss the interior senses in more detail in future chapters. By way of introduction, these senses include the common sense (the power to synchronize impressions that are received via multiple exterior senses); the imaginative power (the power to store and employ the sensible forms of objects, namely, sensory images and impressions that are formed via the exterior senses and the common sense, and the power to create "imaginary forms"); the cogitative power (the power to "know many things which the [exterior] senses cannot perceive" directly, by discovering and "[comparing] individual intentions," such as the "properties" of being useful and friendly); and the memorative power (the power to store and employ "intentions" formed via the cogitative power) (*ST* I 78.4). It is helpful at this point to think of the interior senses as powers of sensory apprehension that allow one to engage in forms of cognition that resemble, to some extent, the cognition of relatively intelligent but nonrational animals.

35. *ST* I 79.

36. St. Thomas Aquinas, *Commentary on Aristotle's "De Anima,"* trans. Kenelm Foster and Silvester Humphries (Notre Dame, Ind.: Dumb Ox, 1994), sect. 795. Latin edition: S. Thomae de Aquino, *Sentencia libri De anima. Opera Omnia* (Fundación Tomás de Aquino, 2006), http://www.corpusthomisticum.org/iopera.html. See also Aristotle, *De Anima*, 432a19.

37. Aquinas thinks he finds a concept of the will in Aristotle (St. Thomas Aquinas, *Truth*, vol. 3, trans. Robert W. Schmidt (Indianapolis, Ind.: Hackett, 1994), 22.4 *sc* 1). Compare Aristotle, *De Anima*, 432b5. See also Terrence H. Irwin, "Who Discovered the Will?" *Philosophical Perspectives* 6 (1992): 453–73. Note that volume 3 of *Truth* covers questions 21–29. Volume 2 of this three-volume publication, which I also cite in this book, is translated by James V. McGlynn. It covers questions 10–20. I cite both, hereafter, as *Truth*. Latin edition: S. Thomae Aquinatis, *Quaestiones disputatae de veritate*, ed. Raymundi Spiazzi (Rome: Marietti, 1949).

38. *ST* I-II 9.1.

39. *ST* I 80.2 *ad* 2.

40. Ibid.; see also *ST* I 82.5 and I-II 13.5 *ad* 1.

41. *ST* I-II 30.1 *ad* 3.

42. *ST* I 81.2 *ad* 2.

43. Aristotle, *De Anima*, 433a23. Consider the practical syllogism as another representation of the need for both appetite and apprehension in the generation of motion. See Nancy Sherman, *The Fabric of Character: Aristotle's Theory of Virtue* (New York: Oxford University Press, 1989), chap. 3. Regarding Aquinas's appropriation of the practical syllogism, see Daniel Westberg, *Right Practical Reason* (Oxford: Clarendon, 1994), and Michael S. Sherwin, *By Knowledge and By Love: Charity and Knowledge in the Moral Theology of St. Thomas Aquinas* (Washington, DC: Catholic University of America Press, 2005).

44. *ST* I-II 13.1. It is possible to have this sort of interior motion yet be incapable of physical movement, as when a person is paralyzed. Aquinas therefore follows Aristotle in insisting that an additional motive power is necessary for carrying out actual bodily movements (*ST* I 78.1 *ad* 4).

45. *ST* I 78.4.

46. *ST* I 80.1. As Aquinas says elsewhere, "Neither sense nor any other apprehensive power moves immediately, but only mediately through the appetitive. Consequently, upon the operation of the sense apprehensive power, the body is changed in its material dispositions only if the motion of the appetitive power supervenes. For the alteration of the body disposing itself to obey follows immediately upon this movement" (*Truth* 26.3 *ad* 11).

47. *ST* I 81.1.

48. Ibid.

49. Some interpreters of Aquinas use the term "pro attitude" to speak of the motion of the sensory appetite. See, for example, Claudia E. Murphy, "Aquinas on Our Responsibility for Our Emotions," *Medieval Philosophy and Theology* 8 (1999): 168. As I use the term, an "attitude" is a cognitive state. Inasmuch as a pro attitude (or a con attitude)

implies interior (and perhaps also exterior) motion toward (or away from) a situation, something more than cognition is involved. I think this "something more" is occluded by the term "attitude."

50. *ST* I-II 13.1.

51. *ST* I-II 10.3.

52. On Paul's rhetorical strategy in this passage, see Krister Stendahl, "The Apostle Paul and the Introspective Conscience of the West," in *The Writings of St. Paul*, ed. Wayne A. Meeks (New York: W. W. Norton, 1972), 422–34.

53. *ST* I 81.3 *ad* 2.

54. *ST* I-II 9.1 (objection 1).

55. *ST* I 81.3 *ad* 2.

56. Nussbaum, *Upheavals of Thought*, 24.

57. Aristotle, *Nicomachean Ethics*, trans. Terence Irwin (Indianapolis, Ind.: Hackett, 1985) (hereafter *NE*), 1102b13–25. See also St. Thomas Aquinas, *Commentary on Aristotle's "Nicomachean Ethics,"* trans. C. I. Litzinger (Notre Dame, Ind.: Dumb Ox, 1993), sect. 237. Latin edition: S. Thomae de Aquino, *Sententia libri Ethicorum. Opera Omnia* (Fundación Tomás de Aquino, 2006), http://www.corpusthomisticum.org/iopera.html.

58. *NE* 1102b30. See also Aquinas, *Commentary on Aristotle's "Nicomachean Ethics,"* sect. 237, and *Truth*, 25.4.

59. *NE* 1102b25.

60. Ibid.

61. *ST* I-II 24.4 *ad* 1.

62. *ST* I-II 46.4 *ad* 3.

63. Nussbaum, *Upheavals of Thought*, 24, 85–88.

64. Ibid., 86.

65. *ST* II-II 141.4.

66. *ST* I-II 24.3 *ad* 1.

67. *ST* I-II 9.2 *ad* 3.

68. Nussbaum, *Upheavals of Thought*, 40.

69. Michael Sherwin offers a fine interpretation of Aquinas on weakness of will that highlights the ways in which competing mental constructions of an event can elicit competing intentional appetites. See *By Knowledge and By Love*, chap. 2.

CHAPTER FOUR

Approaching Aquinas on the Emotions (II)

✦

In order to approach Aquinas's account of emotion, we must appreciate the distinction between apprehension and appetite. "Apprehension" refers very broadly to the power (or set of powers) to acquire and process information. It includes the power to receive sensory impressions, to form and manipulate sensory images through the use of the imagination, to make sensory judgments, to make higher, intellectual judgments, to think, to engage in reasoning, and the like. "Appetite" refers very broadly to the power (or set of powers) to be moved or to move oneself interiorly, and perhaps also exteriorly, in relation to objects of apprehension. It includes the power to *tend* in relation to mental representations that typically have a connection to actual things, persons, or situations in the world. In chapter 3, I provided some reasons for thinking that the conceptual distinction between apprehension and appetite is meaningful, and that it can be useful for sorting through some complexities of one's interior life. I did so with an awareness that Nussbaum is not the only philosopher who wishes to define emotions as forms of thought, judgment, perception, or the like, while neglecting their appetitive dimension.

There is another matter that must be addressed as we approach Aquinas, namely, his conception of the sort of being who experiences emotion. Aquinas says that emotion is a kind of motion (*quidam motus*).[1] He refers to it as a motion of the soul (*motus animi*). He refers to it also and more precisely as a motion of the soul-body composite (*compositum*) or (in the case of a human) the human being as a whole.[2] I anticipate that many readers will stumble, at the start, over this language. What does Aquinas intend by the term "soul," and how does he conceive the relationship between the soul and the body? Has his conception of the self not been discredited by modern

philosophy and science? I will not seek to defend Aquinas's conception of
the self as a soul-body composite (although I find it compelling in many respects), but I do want to present this conception in outline, specifically as it
bears on his conception of emotion.[3] We must familiarize ourselves with the
Thomistic self if we wish to understand the sorts of interior motions of which
that self is capable.

EMOTION AND THE SOUL-BODY COMPOSITE

Aquinas holds that a human being is composed of a soul and a body. The idea
is *not* that a human being is essentially a soul that happens (for a time) to in-
habit a body, such that the body is an accidental property of the human,
inessential to the human's being. As Aquinas puts it, it is *not* that "the entire
nature of [a human being] is seated in the soul, so that the soul makes use of
the body as an instrument, or as a sailor uses his ship."[4] Rather, a human being
is essentially an embodied soul.[5]

Aquinas agrees with Aristotle that a soul (*anima*) is the form of a living
body.[6] This means at least three things. First, the soul is the principle or cause
of life in a living thing—in a plant, a nonhuman animal, or a human being.[7]
The soul is what makes a material entity a living entity; it is what distinguishes a living material entity from a corpse.[8] Second, the soul is the defining principle of a living entity. It is that by virtue of which an entity is
regarded as an entity of a specific kind, namely, a plant, a nonhuman animal,
or a human being. Having an intellectual or rational soul[9] is what defines an
entity as a human being or a rational animal.[10] Third, the soul is a principle
of ordered operation; it is that by virtue of which an entity is capable of functioning in a characteristic way.[11] The intellectual soul of a human being, in
particular, is that by virtue of which a being is capable of functioning, in the
present life, as a subject of both intellectual and sensory experience who has
a typical bodily form.[12]

To say that emotion is a motion of the *soul* is to say that emotion occurs
in and through the coordinated exercise of various powers or capabilities.
To say that emotion is a motion of the *soul-body composite* is to say that the main
powers or capabilities that are involved in the production of an emotion are
exercised directly by means of the body. For Aquinas, "[*passio*] . . . is not
found in the soul, except accidentally: but the composite, which is corruptible, admits of it by reason of its own nature."[13] An emotion is aroused, in
part, by an act of sensory apprehension. Experiencing an emotion involves
having a sensible object in mind, on some level of awareness. An act (or
process) of sensory apprehension might involve, for example, receiving and

entertaining sensory impressions, making basic judgments of the significance
of the impressions, associating these impressions with similar impressions
from the past, and/or creating sensory images by the power of imagination.[14]
According to Aquinas, all such acts take place by means of bodily organs.[15]
In some cases, they take place by means of the organs of exterior sense, such
as the eyes or the ears. In all cases they take place by means of the chief organ
of interior sense, which Aquinas identifies with "the middle part of the
head."[16] Today we would say that acts of sensory apprehension take place by
means of the brain and the rest of the nervous system, which extends
throughout the body.[17]

Aquinas argues that anger, for example, is caused and constituted partly
by the apprehension that someone has committed a slight against one's excellence.[18] This sort of apprehension is basically sensory in nature. One sees
or hears (of) a person and his or her action. One has the impression that this
person has treated one as if one were of no account—that one has been reduced in stature or one is being viewed by others as insignificant. One imagines doing something to regain one's stature and put the offender in his or
her place. As anger is aroused, higher powers of intellectual apprehension operate in coordination with the powers of sensory apprehension. The powers
of intellectual apprehension allow one to make judgments that are more abstract and refer more explicitly to a reflective moral ideal—for example,
one judges that the slight committed by the other was unmerited, that one
deserves better; and one judges that, in the interest of asserting one's dignity
and, perhaps, restoring justice, the slight must be denounced and avenged.[19]
Nonetheless, for Aquinas, these reflective judgments are rooted in the sensory impression that one has been brought low by someone. This impression and the impression that one must defend or assert oneself are primarily
a function of the exterior and interior senses.[20]

Just as acts of sensory *apprehension* involve changes in bodily organs, so
do motions of the sensory *appetite*. Aquinas holds that "in the passions of the
soul, the formal element is the movement of the appetitive power, while the
bodily transmutation is the material element. Both of these are mutually proportionate; and consequently the bodily transmutation assumes a resemblance to and the very nature of the appetitive movement."[21] To stay with
our example, anger is fundamentally a motion of the sensory appetite. In
other words, it is an experience of the person that has its basis primarily in
the capacity to be moved in one way or another with respect to certain objects of sensory apprehension. Anger is an interior motion that is actually
composed of contrary motions. It is partly a motion of dissonance and recoil
relative to the apprehension that some object has caused one to be or to ap-

pear diminished. It is also a motion of resonance and desire relative to the prospect of asserting oneself and getting even.[22] Each of these motions is embodied, and together they generate a kind of "commotion." Aquinas describes the material element of anger as a "fervor of the blood and vital spirits around the heart, which is the instrument of the soul's passions."[23] This fervor is not always intense, but it *can* be. Aquinas quotes Gregory as saying, "*The heart that is inflamed with the stings of its own anger beats quick, the body trembles, the tongue stammers, the countenance takes fire, the eyes grow fierce, they that are well known are not recognized. With the mouth indeed he shapes a sound, but the understanding knows not what it says.*"[24]

EMOTION AND THE BODY

The form-matter connection between a motion of the (object-oriented) sensory appetite and a corresponding bodily change implies that if one recoils interiorly from a perceived slight and, at the same time, one responds defensively or goes on the offensive (if only in one's mind) against the person who committed the slight, one's body enters a state that differs from the state it was in prior to the perception of insult and the arousal of appetite. As one replays the emotion-evoking scene, one's body is likely to remain in a state of relative commotion. However, if one recounts the scene, and one judges that one's impressions were off the mark—if one judges, for example, that the person did not say what one thought he or she said; or that the person did not intend disrespect; or that the slight was small and is thus easily forgotten—then one's pain over being injured is likely to subside, as is one's appetite to strike back. If the appetite for revenge subsides, one's body will likely undergo predictable changes, such as a slowing of heart rate, a lowering of blood pressure, and a shrinking of dilated blood vessels.[25]

It makes sense to say that emotion necessarily involves bodily changes if we think emotion occurs by virtue of the brain and [the rest of the] the nervous system—particularly if we recognize that "the brain and the body are indissociably integrated by mutually targeted biochemical and neural circuits."[26] It makes sense to say also that at least some emotions have a characteristic brain-body signature—that there is a patterned way in which the brain and the rest of the body tend to be altered when a person is moved by certain objects of apprehension.[27] Neuroscientific research has begun to reveal patterns that link particular stimuli (such as objects of perception) to measurable neural activity in particular regions of the brain.

The initial triggering of fear and anger, for example, has been mapped especially to the amygdala; the initial triggering of social emotions such as embarrassment and guilt has been mapped especially to the frontal lobe (ventromedial prefrontal region).[28] Neuro-evolutionary research postulates that the brain—in relation to the rest of the body—is "hard-wired" to exhibit some of these patterns in reliable ways. When evolutionarily old regions of the brain are stimulated by particular objects of perception, these regions can initiate bodily responses quicker than the time it takes one to make a conscious judgment (for example, "providing increased blood flow to arteries in the legs so that muscles receive extra oxygen and glucose, in the case of a flight reaction, or changing heart and breathing rhythms, in the case of freezing on the spot").[29] This can be an advantageous arrangement in a situation of mortal danger.

At the same time, however, brain-body patterns can be difficult to isolate and specify, and whether a given person exhibits a specified pattern is a matter of degree. It is reasonable to expect that different people, even within the same culture—and also the same person, under different conditions— will undergo somewhat different brain-body changes in conjunction with what they report to be the same emotions.[30] One would expect such differences, given differences in brains and bodies and countless factors of experience. Aquinas holds that with many emotions the basic material correlations (for example, changes in heart rate and facial expression) are relatively common and well known.[31] However, he tends to speak in a flexible manner about an emotion's material element as "a certain bodily change."[32] He seems to expect that there will not in every case be a one-to-one correspondence between a particular emotion and a highly specific set of bodily changes. Some differences will exist between individuals or within the same individual over time.[33]

It is relatively uncontroversial today to hold that all emotion involves changes in the brain-body complex of the person experiencing the emotion. It is quite controversial, however, to hold that all (or nearly all) emotion involves undergoing patterned bodily changes that are *noticeable* by the subject—and, moreover, that all (or nearly all) emotion involves actually *noticing* or *feeling* these changes, to some extent. Some people report being in an emotional state while being unaware that anything unusual is happening in their bodies.[34] Other people deny being in an emotional state because they are unaware of any bodily resonance or dissonance, but they later come to believe that they must have been in an emotional state; they just did not realize it at the time. A person might make this judgment in order to account for his or her behavior—as when one acts in a way that is typical of fear, and one judges that one must, therefore, have been afraid. Scholars who identify emotions with forms of cognition tend to argue that persons can have emotion-composing thoughts and thus emotions without experiencing anything out of the ordinary in their bodies.[35]

Other scholars argue to the contrary that if a person's thoughts are not accompanied by any unusual bodily feelings—particularly feelings that are tied, in the thinker's experience, to a situation that is represented in his or her mind—then it is inappropriate to say that the person is in an emotional state. The person's thoughts might have the same basic content as the thoughts that are typical of a particular emotion, but thoughts are not themselves emotions or ought not to be regarded as such.[36] Some scholars go so far in this direction as to say that an emotion just is (or is most fundamentally) the feeling of certain bodily changes, so that these changes effectively become the central intentional object of the emotion.[37] In such a view, it makes no sense to speak of emotion apart from the awareness of unusual bodily changes.

Aquinas's view is that the central object of an emotion is typically a perceived or imagined situation that appears to bear on one's well-being or the well-being of someone for whom one cares. The object is *not* one's own body or how one's body feels, unless one's emotion is about one's body or a particular bodily state, as when one is worried about the significance of one's expanding waistline or the pain in one's chest. For Aquinas, having a particular situation in one's awareness sometimes causes a motion of the sensory appetite. It causes one to resonate with the situation, recoil from it, rear up against it, come to a painful repose in it, or the like. As one undergoes this sort of interior motion, one is moved or changed bodily. A healthy, well-integrated person who is "in touch" with his or her body is usually aware of such changes. To be sure, there are times when such a person lacks explicit awareness of certain features of his or her own mental or physical state—times, for example, when emotion-defining apprehensions slip out of the person's conscious awareness or when the person is distracted (say, in study or play) from the material element of his or her appetitive state. There can be good reasons for saying that such a person is in an emotional state all along, whether or not he or she is aware of being and feeling changed in relation to an object of apprehension and appetite. In addition, many movements of the soul-body composite (especially in the virtuous) are subtle and might not be noticeable in the form of specific, localized bodily changes; they might involve changes such as a slight rising or lowering of energy level.

Nevertheless, I take it that for Aquinas most emotions register to some degree—for most people—as familiar patterns of feeling enlivened, agitated, lifted up, weighed down, constricted, relaxed, or the like. This is presumably why most people speak of "feeling" an emotion: We feel an interior motion or a tending in relation to an object of apprehension (for example, we have the experience of rising to meet a challenge—or resting, subsequently, in a goal attained), and we feel a related change in the body (for example, an increase in energy level—or a subsequent sense of euphoria or relaxation). It is the first sort of feeling (the imaginative experience of tending or coming to rest) that is most definitive of emotion, but this feeling has a material dimension. It occurs by means of changes in the body. If one becomes aware of these bodily changes, one experiences the second sort of feeling. In a typical experience of emotion, the second sort of feeling concurs with the first; one does not separate the two mentally. In any case, some people might, for various reasons, be less aware than others of the material dimension of their emotional states, but the norm is to be "sensitive" to such changes—capable of sensing or feeling them.

EMOTION AND THE SOUL

Aquinas constructs his account of emotion primarily with reference to the sensory powers of the soul, namely, the powers of sensory apprehension and appetite. We will explore these powers in more detail in subsequent chapters. Nonhuman animals exercise sensory powers in ways that reflect that they have *sensory souls*. To say that an animal has a sensory soul is to say that it is a living entity whose highest principle of operation is sensory. Humans have sensory powers that are in many respects like the powers of other animals. Yet humans exercise their sensory powers—and all of their other powers, as well—in ways that reflect a higher principle of operation, namely, an *intellectual soul*. To understand Aquinas's account of emotion, we must try to understand his conception of the intellectual soul. We must delve into some metaphysical issues that challenged him and continue to challenge people today.

A human being has one soul, one principle of life and functioning, but he or she has many different powers of soul. For Aquinas, the intellectual soul is what makes it possible for a human to exercise the powers of intellect, namely, intellectual apprehension and appetite, while exercising the sensory and other powers that are characteristic of human functioning.[38] As we have seen, the sensory powers operate by means of bodily organs. The intellectual soul is thus, in part, a principle that makes it possible to engage in forms of apprehension and appetite that are mediated directly by the body. Yet the intellectual soul is also a principle that makes it possible to engage in higher, intellectual operations. In Aquinas's view, the latter operations are "performed without a corporeal organ."[39] Acts of intellectual apprehension and appetite "belong to the soul alone as their subject," rather than to the soul-body composite.[40]

This is a difficult thesis that is easily misunderstood. Aquinas holds that all human knowing or understanding in the present life—and thus all willing—is dependent on the coordinated operation of the senses, and the exterior and interior senses *do* engage the brain (and nervous system) directly.[41] In outline, the function of the intellect or the power of intellectual apprehension is to make it possible to understand one's world.[42] To understand something is basically to find it intelligible; it is to apprehend the "universal nature existing in the individual."[43] In Aquinas's view, one finds something intelligible by forming a "phantasm" (*phantasma*) of it, which requires the use of one's interior sensory powers. A phantasm is a sensory image; it is a "likeness of an individual thing."[44] With a phantasm in mind, one uses one's intellect to "light up" the phantasm.[45] Lighting up a phantasm involves identifying the sort of thing one has in mind. It involves "abstracting" the form of an individual thing.[46] It involves grasping the thing's essence—its "whatness."[47]

Aquinas holds that it is with reference to sensible things that incorporeal things, too, are known:

> Incorporeal things, of which there are no phantasms, are known to us by comparison with sensible bodies of which there are phantasms. Thus we understand truth by considering a thing of which we possess the truth; and God, as Dionysius says (*Div. Nom.* i), we know as cause, by way of excess and by way of remotion. Other incorporeal substances we know, in the present state of life, only by way of remotion or by some comparison to corporeal things. And, therefore, when we understand something about these things, we need to turn to phantasms of bodies, although there are no phantasms of the things themselves.[48]

Whether the object of knowledge is sensible, incorporeal, or conceptual, Aquinas holds that knowing an object and applying one's knowledge of it requires having recourse to phantasms or sensory images.[49] As Robert Pasnau explains, "Even once the mind has grasped some fact [or, one might add, some idea], the intellect constantly returns to the phantasms, reinforcing its knowledge through further sensory data, reminding itself of what it already knows, supplementing its always shaky understanding with the confirming and reassuring evidence that the senses, memory, and imagination can provide."[50] The intellect of a human is thus dependent on the sensory powers. It cannot enable one to acquire knowledge or understanding without the cooperation of the senses. Yet Aquinas insists that the intellect or the power of intellectual apprehension is itself, strictly speaking, immaterial. It does not operate directly by means of the brain or other bodily organs.

What is true for the power of intellectual apprehension is true, by extension, for the power of intellectual appetite or will. Whereas the power of intellectual apprehension allows one to understand an object as having the form of goodness, as contributing to the end or *telos* of human flourishing, the power of intellectual appetite allows one to be inclined with respect to such an object of understanding; it allows one to be moved, and to move oneself, relative to the end of human flourishing and relative to a means that one judges good by virtue of its contribution to this end.[51] Like the power of intellectual apprehension, the power of intellectual appetite is immaterial. It is "not exercised by means of a corporeal organ."[52] Yet operations of the intellectual appetite are dependent on the senses, and thus on the brain and body, inasmuch as related operations of the intellect are dependent on the senses. An act of the intellectual appetite is always about something that one has in mind as the result of an act of intellectual apprehension, and understanding an object by means of the latter sort of act requires turning to phantasms.

For Aquinas, it is *proper* for the intellectual soul of a human being to be united to a body. A human being is thus different from an angel for whom it is proper to be and to function as an immaterial intellect or, more precisely, as a created being that has certain powers of intellectual apprehension and appetite but no body.[53] As long as a human being is alive—as long as his or her intellectual soul functions as the form of his or her body—all of his or her intellectual operations will engage the brain-body complex in one way or another, directly or indirectly. It is thus a mistake to think of the intellectual acts of humans, such as conceiving, understanding, analyzing, choosing, and experiencing affections, as if they were acts of a spirit that inhabits a body but does not really use it—or uses it but in a way that is not determined (to some extent) by the body itself, such that one could engage in intellectual acts in much the same way if one were to slip free of the body. Nonetheless, it is important to Aquinas to assert that the powers of the intellectual soul are immaterial.

THE IMMATERIALITY OF THE INTELLECTUAL POWERS

Aquinas argues that these powers could not function as they do—they could not enable one to do what one is able to do, on an intellectual level—if they were mediated directly by bodily organs.[54] Consider first the power of intellectual apprehension. It is impossible for this power to be a function of the brain and nervous system because this power is what makes it possible for one to know the nature of a particular body, to know the nature of *any* given body, to know the nature of one's own embodiment, and to conceive the nature of embodiment as such. Aquinas holds that, if the power of intellectual apprehension operated by means of a bodily organ, it would be "just one particular sensible nature among many."[55] It would not enable one to comprehend all sensible natures. It would not enable one to "think" the idea of corporeality itself.[56]

Consider also the power of the will. The will is what makes it possible for one to be attracted to—or repulsed by—an object in light of that object's contribution to goodness as such. The will is thus what makes it possible for one to consent—or not consent—to motions of one's sensory appetite, as promoting or diminishing one's well-being. Whereas Aquinas thinks that the sensory appetite operates directly by means of the heart,[57] he thinks that it is impossible for the will to operate in this way. He specifies the material dimension of a few emotions: For example, anger includes a "fervor of the blood and vital spirits around the heart";[58] joy includes a "*dilation* of the heart";[59] and fear includes a "[cooling] off and [tightening] up" of the heart.[60] If the will were a power that is exercised directly by means of the heart, the will would not make it possible for one to determine oneself with respect to these other changes of the heart. But the will does makes this possible, to some degree. One has *some* power, for example, to calm one's own anger (by changing the way one construes a situation), to the point of lowering one's heart rate —just as one has some power to intensify one's anger, such that the rate of one's circulation increases. In Aquinas's view, "a rational nature . . . so has its inclination within its own power that it does not necessarily incline to anything appetible which is apprehended, but can incline or not incline. And so its inclination is not determined for it by anything else but by itself. This belongs to it inasmuch as it does not use a bodily organ."[61]

Many people today believe, to the contrary, that all intellectual activities are mediated directly by the brain. We know a lot about the brain that Aquinas could not have known, even though the study of the brain is in many respects still in its infancy. Neuroscientists are creating maps of the brain that seek to correlate intellectual activities—such as contemplating the divine and making moral decisions—with specific brain states. In addition, there is considerable evidence that damaging the brain or introducing certain chemicals into it can damage and even destroy higher-order intellectual functions. Aquinas acknowledges that an injury to the brain can hinder or destroy the exercise of the human intellect and will: "Wherefore it is clear that for the intellect to understand actually, not only when it acquires fresh knowledge, but also when it applies knowledge already acquired, there is need for the act of the imagination and of the other [interior sensory] powers. For when the act of the imagination is hindered by a lesion of the corporeal organ, for instance, in a case of frenzy; or when the act of the memory is hindered, as in the case of lethargy, we see that a [person] is hindered from actually understanding things of which he had a previous knowledge."[62]

Aquinas's point, however, is that such an injury, strictly speaking, disables the internal sensory powers upon which the intellect and the will continually depend (and without which the intellect and the will cannot perform their specific acts in the present state of life). Such an injury does not disable the intellect or the will directly, for these powers are in themselves incorruptible.[63] Some readers might wish to depart from Aquinas on this point. Yet some of us might wish to affirm the view that acts of the intellect and the will are not completely reducible to operations of the brain. We might wish to affirm that such acts surpass the material operations of the brain-body complex in some respect and to some extent. Why might a person be attracted to such a view?

THE INTELLECTUAL POWERS IN THE ABSENCE OF A BODY

This brings us to a second thing that the powers of the intellectual soul could not do if they were directly dependent on the brain and body: They could not continue to operate after death. Aquinas thinks that, if one were to cause a person serious brain damage, one would destroy his or her capacity to think as a human being; if the damage were serious enough, one would destroy the human being as such. Yet one would not destroy the intellectual soul of the human being.[64] One would not destroy the seat of personal identity that was shaped by the human's earthly experiences, and one would not destroy the human's power to engage in certain intellectual operations. Nor would one destroy his or her power to engage in the other operations of embodied human life when the human is reunited with his or her body—a "glorified" form of that body—in the resurrection.[65]

What sort of intellectual operations does Aquinas have in mind as possible for (what is left of) the human being between death and resurrection? Aquinas struggles to describe them. He refers to a mode of knowing "by means of participated species arising from the influence of the Divine light."[66] He suggests that, for a human being, this mode of knowing is "only . . . general and confused."[67] It is different from and inferior to the knowing that is possible for a human in his or her normal, embodied state. Again, it is proper for a human to know by turning to phantasms, and a separated intellect cannot entertain phantasms because it no longer operates in coordination with a human's sensory powers.[68] The mode of knowing of a separated human intellect is similar to that of an angel, but much inferior; unlike an angel, a human being is not made for a purely intellectual existence.[69]

It is hard to imagine life as a seat of intellectual power that does not function in and through a body. Most of us cannot picture ourselves understanding anything in the absence of all sensory powers, for all of our understanding (including our understanding of our current mode of understanding) is mediated by our sensory powers in one way or another.[70] Yet the fact that we cannot understand or even imagine what it would be like to function as a separated intellectual soul does not mean that such an existence is impossible or nonsensical. Millions of intelligent people of many religious faiths and philosophies— including many scientists—believe that something of who they are (beyond the products of their labor, the memory of their lives in other people's minds, and so on) will survive their physical death, even though they cannot say exactly what that "something" is. Many more people at least *wonder* whether some sort of life after death is possible, especially in light of countless reports of near-death experiences and human interactions (across many cultures) with ghosts and the spirits of dead relatives.[71] Some people posit that something of their personal consciousness survives the death of the body, but (unlike Aquinas) they want to say that this consciousness is material in a sense that cannot yet be specified or measured by physical science. They hypothesize a mode of existence that places various forms of disembodied consciousness in continuity with other existing things in a single, irreducibly "material" universe.[72]

In any case, our task is not to debate this endlessly complex issue. Our task is to try to grasp Aquinas's conception of the intellectual soul as it relates to his conception of emotion as a motion of the sensory appetite. Perhaps the most important point to take from this discussion is that, in the present life, the powers of the intellect and the will function in coordination with the sensory powers. The former powers do *not* operate in this life as they do (or might do) when they are deprived, after death, of their proper, embodied mode of operation. Thus, one ought not to think of the intellectual soul (in Aquinas's thought) as a principle that makes it possible for one to engage in immaterial operations that work the same way now as they will when one is without a body—and one ought not to imagine operations beyond this life as if they will be quite like one's present operations but without the limits of a body. In particular, one ought not to think of "simple acts of the will" or affections in a human being as if these were acts of a "spirit" that occur in much the same way whether or not one has a body. We are

concerned here with the operation of our human powers in the present, embodied form of life, but we will periodically project (as an abstraction from
ordinary experience) the possibility of appetitive motions in purely intellectual beings and in humans who are no longer capable of bodily life.

One could reject Aquinas's thesis about the immateriality of the intellectual soul and still work with many features of his account of the emotions.
One could conceive of the human being's intellectual powers as higher-order
powers that interact with lower-order sensory (and other) powers, all of
which are mediated by various parts of the brain, and none of which can operate, in any form, without a brain. However, making this move would be
costly. One would lose the ideal of complete happiness, namely, the perfect
and perfectly enjoyable exercise of one's intellectual (and glorified bodily)
powers in a life to come—in the knowing and loving of the highest principle of reality, and in the reciprocal being-known and being-loved by that
principle. For Aquinas, complete happiness is the end of human existence,
the ultimate point of all of our ordered human operations, including our
well-ordered forms of emotional tending.

My own inclination is to leave open the possibility that *something* of the
human being (namely, something of the powers of apprehension and appetite) survives the dissolution of the body and continues to function after
death, but to agree with Aquinas that it is impossible to imagine this mode
of functioning in anything but the vaguest of terms, particularly if we pos-
tulate in such a state the absence of interior sensory powers. Leaving this
possibility open allows one to contemplate a capacious universe that could
be replete with modes of tending that most humans cannot apprehend, that
we cannot at present measure with scientific instruments, but which we (or
some of us) might yet be able to encounter and learn more about in the
future.

EMOTION AND GOD

Emotions are "properly to be found where there is corporeal transmutation."[73] They are motions of the sensory appetite that are mediated by particular changes in the body. Shortly, we will examine the operations of the
sensory appetite in more detail. Before proceeding, however, I want to acknowledge an important theological implication of this interpretation of
Aquinas. Marcel Sarot frames it this way: According to Aquinas, in order to
have emotions one must have a body; God does not have a body; therefore,
God "cannot have emotions."[74] The same is true of angels, including fallen
angels or demons.

Daniel Westberg objects "sharply" to Sarot's interpretation of Aquinas and might also object to the way in which my own interpretation is unfolding.[75] Westberg argues that, according to Scripture, God experiences "emotions" such as love and anger toward human beings. If Christians were to "eliminate emotion from God," they would be "unfaithful to revelation."[76] I take it that this argument does not concern a particular term that was used in original biblical languages to refer to the appetitive motions of God; rather, it concerns the way in which the English term "emotion" is used by Christians in referring to the biblical God—particularly Christians who identify with the Thomistic tradition.

Westberg wants to maintain the theistic view that God is a "moral agent," "an intelligent being with powers to act."[77] In his view, which he associates with Aquinas, "Beings that have intellect and will (or rational appetite) have emotion; that is, they are capable of being 'moved' towards (or away from) an object by appetite."[78] Therefore, "emotions should be ascribed to God, as the Bible does."[79] Incorporated within this skeletal argument is a definition of emotion that appears to cover every form of being moved relative to an object of apprehension, from the most intellectual and universal (in God, angels, and the intellectual dimension of human beings, considered in abstraction from other operations of the soul-body composite) to the most sensible and singular (in humans). Yet this is precisely what is at issue: How ought the English term "emotion" to be used in interpreting Aquinas and developing a Thomistic theory of emotion? In my view, it is best to use this term to signify *passio*, but where *passio* is properly understood—as a motion of the soul-body composite that engages the sensory powers, but ordinarily reflects the influence of the intellectual powers (in humans) as well, in ways that I will specify in subsequent chapters. Westberg suggests that "emotion" ought to be used to signify all forms of appetitive motion within intelligent beings, irrespective of whether those beings have bodies.

Aquinas holds that there are forms of appetitive motion that do not involve "corporeal transmutation."[80] In other words, there are forms of appetitive motion that do not take place directly by means of organs such as the brain and nervous system, or the heart and circulatory system. As Westberg notes, Aquinas refers to these forms of appetitive motion as affections (*affectus*). Aquinas defines an affection as a "simple act of the will" that arises "without passion or commotion of the soul."[81] The question, then, is whether the English term "emotion" ought to be used to cover *affectus* in God, angels, and the intellectual soul of a human being, considered in abstraction from the soul's relationship to the soul-body composite, *and* what Aquinas calls *passio*—or whether "emotion" ought to be used more specifically to refer to embodied forms of being-moved in humans and, perhaps, in other animals.

Aquinas does not—and could not—anticipate exactly this question. He does note that in the ordinary language use of his time, specific *passio*-terms, such as "anger" (*ira*) and "love" (*amor*), were sometimes used to signify "simple acts of the will." Thus, "the will for revenge is called 'anger,' and the repose of the will in some object of spiritual affection is called 'love.'"[82] Aquinas also says, however, that using *passio*-terms in this way involves stretching their ordinary meanings.[83] I would say, further, that using such "figure[s] of speech"[84] involves abstracting from the sensory dimension of human experience. Engaging in such abstractions can be useful for certain purposes, but it is important to realize what is being abstracted.

Consider an example. As just noted, Aquinas says that the term "anger" is sometimes used to signify a simple act of the will. In the case of a human being, it is difficult (at least for me) to imagine such an act. One tries to picture a human being who is engaged only in the dimensions of intellect and will. One imagines a person who judges that he or she (or someone in his or her range of concern) has been the victim of an unjustified slight, which must be denounced and punished. Yet one must imagine a person who does not have a sensory image of the person or the incident in mind (is not engaged in any imaginative mental playback), and one must imagine a person who is not at all disturbed or excited at the abstract thought of an injury or the thought of what he or she will do to exact revenge for an injury. A person who has reason to be disturbed or excited—but is not—is commonly characterized as emotionally detached, which implies unemotional. If one says that such a person is "angry," one stretches the ordinary meaning of the term. If one says that the detached person is experiencing "emotion," one stretches the ordinary meaning of *that* term as well.

To approach the issue from another angle, many Christians and other religious believers think of God as a being who experiences anger. When they imagine the anger of God they tend to draw on sensory images that reflect their own experiences of anger. God in a state of anger is depicted in the Bible as wielding a weapon or raising God's hand as a weapon against those who do evil. *Psalm* 18:8–13 says of the angry God that "smoke went up from his nostrils, and devouring fire from his mouth; glowing coals flamed forth from him. . . . The Lord also thundered in the heavens, and the Most High uttered his voice, hailstones and coals of fire." As this passage shows, when humans attribute anger to God, they tend to attribute something like the emotion of anger, which most humans (I believe) associate with being heated and disturbed. A person making such attributions might believe, upon reflection, that God does not really have nostrils or breathe fire, for God is not a material entity. A person might try to abstract from his or her anthropomorphic images of God to form the idea of a simple act of the will in the divine being. Yet it is only with reference to the human experience of anger that an act of the divine will could meaningfully be identified by a human *as* an act of anger, and the human experience of anger is fundamentally a sensory experience. Similarly, it is only with reference to the human experience of emotion that an act of the divine will gets identified *as* an emotion, and for most people the experience of emotion involves feeling disturbed or excited or calmed or in some other way changed bodily while one is moved interiorly at the thought or perception of certain situations.

EMOTIONS AND THE BODY, REVISITED

For Aquinas, *passio* is a motion of the soul-body composite that engages the sensory powers. In my view, we do well to construe emotion in the same way, but where the sensory powers of a human being are understood in their remarkable range and in their intricate relationship to higher, intellectual powers. In what follows, I therefore continue to develop an account of Thomistic *passio* as an account of emotion.

Seeking to reflect the thought of Aquinas, Westberg says that "the *essence* of emotion has to do with being a moral agent, not with bodily existence."[85] The claim seems to be that emotion is *essentially* a motion of the intellectual appetite or will. As we have seen, Aquinas thinks that *passio* has *essentially* to do with bodily existence—with the way in which soul-body composites entertain and are altered by certain sensory images and impressions. The implication of Westberg's view thus seems to be that the term "emotion" corresponds most properly to what Aquinas calls *affectus* (and to other motions of the will), and it corresponds only indirectly—if at all—to what Aquinas calls *passio*. Westberg asserts that not all emotions—not even all human emotions—have a feeling component. With experiences such as anger, love, fear, and joy in mind, he says that emotions do not necessarily involve "arousal or excitement."[86] Indeed, he agrees with some philosophers who think that emotions are only "sometimes felt."[87] He says that bodily changes and the feeling of such changes are "almost a side aspect of emotion,"[88] that they are merely "incidental," "far from essential to emotion itself."[89]

Aquinas devotes twenty-six questions of the *Summa theologiae* to analyzing the nature of a related set of human experiences that go by the familiar names of love, anger, fear, sorrow, and the like. He refers to each of these as a form of *passio* and argues that *passio* involves changes in the body (especially the heart and circulatory system) that are ordinarily noticeable to an attentive self-observer. Most people today who speak English call these experiences "emotions" or, perhaps, "feelings." It might be helpful on occasion to use the word "emotion" in an extended sense to refer to certain acts of the will in God or in other purely intellectual beings, particularly if one trusts that God is (somehow) both the first principle of being, and thus beyond all beings, *and* a personal being or friend with whom one can carry out searching inquiry, and in relation to whom one can *feel* loved and transformed by love. However, I think it is best to refer to "simple acts of the will," rather than "emotions," if what one really has in mind is an interior act that has no relationship—or no noticeable relationship—to a body. Otherwise one runs the risk of neglecting the bodily dimension of human emotions; one runs the risk of neglecting the nature and the value of our embodiment. Alternatively, one could use the term "affection" for this purpose, as Aquinas does. What we need to do, however, is to keep in mind that all acts of the will, in a living human being, depend on intellectual operations that have an integral relationship to operations of the interior senses. They are not operations of a "spiritual being" that take the same basic form whether or not one has a body.

CONCLUSION

At this point one can perhaps begin to appreciate that, in order to say anything significant about the emotions, one has to say a lot about a lot of other things. If one wishes to say that an emotion is a kind of motion, then it is important to say that not everything humans do or undergo counts as a motion in the same sense. Cognition or apprehension, in particular, does not count as a motion in the same sense that appetition does. For Aquinas, an act of apprehension is not parallel, in its formal structure, to a motion of the intellectual appetite, a motion of the sensory appetite, or a bodily motion, including (in some cases) motion from place to place; yet all of the latter *are* importantly similar in structure. The conceptual distinction between apprehension and appetitive motion is admittedly difficult to hold on to, especially when one encounters a view in which thought itself is sometimes characterized by motion and heat. But I try, in this project, to hold on to that distinction.

If one wishes to say that emotion is a kind of appetitive motion, then one needs to say, more specifically, what kind of appetitive motion it is—in Aquinas's case, one needs to distinguish between motions of the sensory appetite and motions of the intellectual appetite, and one needs to clarify the relationship between the two. One needs further to reflect on the personal subject or the agent who undergoes and/or causes within himself or herself different sorts of appetitive motion—and is ordinarily aware of doing so or is at least capable of being aware. For Aquinas, this requires reflecting on the soul and the body, and on the relationship between them. A discussion of the intellectual soul of a human being requires reference to the idea of an immaterial substance. It requires discussion of the puzzling relationship between immateriality and materiality, which invites discussion of the divine and its relationship to the human.

At every point in this inquiry, people of broadly religious curiosity and concern will have much to query and perhaps much with which to quarrel in Aquinas's account. Yet the impressive thing is that his account has so much depth and volume—there are so many aspects of his account that are worth pondering. In my view, a compelling theory of emotion will, at some point, challenge readers to ask and pursue questions about the fundamental nature of reality and about what is finally worth pursuing in life, given the way things are. How could a compelling account of love, grief, or anger, for example, not arouse at least some reflection about the true object of one's longing, about whether there is a point to loving what one will inevitably lose, about the real object of one's frustration or aggression? A compelling theory of emotion will try to relate emotions to other, related phenomena that mark the interior lives of humans. It will also gesture beyond human experience to what is or might be going on elsewhere in reality, looking for other forms of tending that resemble, in structure, the interior motions of humans.

I understand that many people are tempted to cut this sort of inquiry short, partly because such questioning seems only to raise more questions— the kinds of questions that many of us feel incompetent to answer and even to frame very well. Many people would rather treat emotions in ways that are less speculative, more subject to empirical investigation and proof, more subject to the constraints of rational philosophical inquiry, rather narrowly construed, and more amenable to secular clinical settings. Yet it is valuable for human beings to ask broadly religious questions and to be borne by such questions—to be curious, yet patient in so being borne. Being in a state of patient curiosity regarding the nature of reality is intrinsically valuable. It also has practical implications for the investigation of emotion. Most notably, it can make one more receptive and discerning in approaching the interior and relational lives of humans and imagining what is possible for them. It can make one more capable of accepting—indeed, loving—a good deal of the complexity and mystery that one finds within the human.

NOTES

1. *ST* I-II 23.2.
2. *ST* I-II 22.1.
3. For a brief, accessible discussion of Aquinas's conception of the soul-body composite in light of recent neuroscience, see Nancey Murphy, *Bodies and Souls, or Spirited Bodies?* (Cambridge: Cambridge University Press, 2006).
4. *ST* Suppl. 75.1.
5. *ST* I 76.1 *ad* 5. As we will see, an implication of this view is that, at death, the human being, as such, ceases to exist. That is, the embodied soul ceases to exist. Yet a dimension of the human being survives, namely, the intellectual soul. This soul does not change species; it does not cease to be "human" in some sense. Yet it is capable of only limited "human" operations until it is reunited, at the resurrection, with (a glorified version of) its body. Embodiment *of some kind* is essential to the normal operations of a human being. In thinking about the human soul and its relationship to the body, I have benefited from Robert Pasnau, *Thomas Aquinas on Human Nature* (Cambridge: Cambridge University Press, 2002). See especially chapter 12.
6. Aristotle, *De Anima*, 412a1–413a10. See also Aquinas, *Commentary on Aristotle's "De Anima,"* sects. 211–234.
7. "Principle" in this project ordinarily refers to one or more of the four Aristotelian causes of a thing (material, formal, efficient, or final).
8. *ST* I 75.1.
9. When referring to a human being, I will use "intellectual soul" and "rational soul" interchangeably. Technically, "rational" activities are associated especially with the activities of discursive reasoning, which are only a subset of "intellectual" activities.
10. *ST* I 76.1. In Aquinas's view, whether a being is properly regarded as a rational animal depends on it powers or capabilities. As we would expect, Aquinas correlates the powers of rational animality with members of the human species, and the powers of nonrational animality with members of other species. He thinks that, generally speaking, humans and certain other animals have many similar powers, not only within the sensory and vegetative domains but also with respect to basic intelligence. Yet he thinks that a typical human being is capable of many intellectual activities of which no other animals are capable. This thesis raises many questions that are important for ethics. For example, do we want to say that there is a basic difference in kind between rational and nonrational powers (of apprehension and appetite)? How, exactly, would we define these powers and the differences between them? Would it make more sense to talk of differences in degree, rather than kind? We would still need to be able to define the relevant powers and place them on a scale. Is it misleading to try to place these powers on a single scale? Is it justifiable to correlate differences in powers with different species, given that many nonhuman animals, such as dolphins and chimpanzees, have powers of apprehension and appetite that are more advanced (more like those of a typical, adult human) than the powers of many (other) humans? I cannot address these important questions here. I simply ask readers to consider that most healthy, adult humans have

many intellectual powers that allow them to do remarkable things that no other animals can do (as far as we can tell), such as contemplate their lives five years from now, as they also reflect on how they were doing five years ago, engage in complex processes of moral reasoning and decision making, reason from the observation of the natural world to the idea of a first principle of being, and recollect or invent stories. Because most healthy humans have such capabilities, they are likely to construe situations and experience emotions in ways that other animals do not. For philosophical and ethical reflection on the relationship between humans and other animals, see Alasdair MacIntyre, *Dependent Rational Animals: Why Human Beings Need the Virtues* (Chicago: Open Court, 1999), and Mary Midgley, *Beast and Man* (London: Routledge, 1995).

11. *ST* 76.1, 76.3. See also Aquinas, *Commentary on Aristotle's "De Anima,"* lect. XIV.

12. *ST* I 76.1 *ad* 5, 76.2 *ad* 2. Aquinas holds that the center of intellectual activity in a human being is an immaterial substance. I will discuss this challenging point later in the chapter.

13. *ST* I-II 22.1 *ad* 3. See also *Truth* 26.2.

14. *ST* I 78.4. Chapters 5 and 7 include more extensive discussion of the interior sensory powers.

15. *ST* I 77.5.

16. *ST* I 78.4.

17. Notice that, for Aquinas, these acts are not simply acts or functions of a brain but they are functions of a brain that correlate with the consciousness or the awareness of a situation on the part of a personal subject. This is partly what the language of "soul" allows Aquinas to capture.

18. *ST* I-II 47.2, including *ad* 3.

19. *ST* I-II 46.4.

20. Ibid., including *ad* 1.

21. *ST* I-II 44.1. In the simplest case, the bodily change prepares one for a specific behavior or action that is motivated, in part, by the emotion.

22. *ST* I-II 46.2.

23. *ST* I-II 48.2.

24. Ibid.

25. One's appetite might remain stubborn in the face of reinterpretation, say, if one is intoxicated by the energy of anger. Persons who are attached to this energy commonly look for reasons and motives to be and to remain angry, feeling agitated all the while.

26. Antonio R. Damasio, *Descartes' Error: Emotion, Reason, and the Human Brain* (New York: Avon, 1994), 87.

27. Harak discusses an emotion's "bodily signature" in *Virtuous Passions*, 12.

28. Damasio, *Looking for Spinoza*, 60–61.

29. Ibid. See also Antonio R. Damasio, *The Feeling of What Happens: Body and Emotion in the Making of Consciousness* (New York: Harcourt Brace, 1999), 53–56.

30. The President's Council on Bioethics, Session Five: Neuroscience, Brain, and Behavior, IV: Brain Imaging (Case Study), June 25, 2004, http://www.bioethics.gov/transcripts/june04/session5.html (accessed March 7, 2006).

31. See, for example, *ST* I-II 28.5. According to Paul Ekman, several facial expressions of emotion are universal and thus recognizable across cultures. See "Facial Expressions of Emotion: New Findings, New Questions," *Psychological Science* 3, no. 1 (1992): 34–38.

32. *ST* I-II 28.5.

33. *ST* I-II 46.5.

34. See Lyons, *Emotion*, 118–19, for a helpful discussion of the sense in which the physiological changes associated with emotion are "unusual."

35. See, for example, Nussbaum, *Upheavals of Thought*, 56–64, and Roberts, *Emotions*, 151–55.

36. Damasio, *Looking for Spinoza*, 86–87.

37. William James, *The Principles of Psychology*, vol. 2 (New York: Dover, 1950).

38. Aquinas generally uses the term "intellect" (*intellectus*) to refer specifically to the power or powers that make it possible to engage in such acts as understanding and reasoning (*ST* I 79). However, he also includes in the subsistent intellectual soul the power of intellectual appetite or will (*ST* I 77.5). He *must* include the latter if he is to hold that perfect human happiness is found not only in knowing God (as perfect truth), but also in loving God (as perfect goodness). In this project, I use the term "intellect" (or "power of the intellect" or "act of the intellect" or the like) to refer to any or all powers or acts that Aquinas includes under the category of the intellect in *ST* I 79. I use the term "intellectual apprehension" (or "power of intellectual apprehension" or "act of intellectual apprehension" or the like) as *synonymous* with "intellect" (and related formulations). I use the term "intellectual powers" (and related formulations) to refer more inclusively to the power of intellectual apprehension *and* the power of intellectual appetite (i.e., intellect *and* will). The phrase "intellectual apprehension" can be awkward, and it can occlude fine distinctions between various acts of the intellect; but I use it because I want to keep in view the structural relationship between acts of apprehension (acquiring *and* processing information) and acts of appetite (being moved and—in the case of the intellectual appetite—also moving oneself). This distinction obtains on both intellectual and sensory levels of human functioning. On the "order" of the various powers of the human, see *ST* I 77.4 and 77.7. See also the appendix.

39. *ST* I 77.5.

40. *ST* I 77.8.

41. *ST* I 84.7. See especially chapters 7–9 of this book.

42. See Pasnau, *Thomas Aquinas on Human Nature*, part III.

43. *ST* I 84.7.

44. *ST* I 84.7 *ad* 2.

45. *ST* I 79.4, 84.7.

46. *ST* I 84.6.

47. *ST* I 84.7.

48. *ST* I 84.7 *ad* 3.

49. *ST* I 84.7, 85.1 *ad* 5.

50. Pasnau, *Thomas Aquinas on Human Nature*, 289. It is fascinating to ponder the possibility that, within the realm of quantum physics, it is impossible to form images or examples to help one conceive the nature of subatomic reality. According to some physicists, the only way to know things in this realm is in the form of mathematical formulas that have no evident correlation to human experience. See Gary Zukov, *The Dancing Wu Li Masters: An Overview of the New Physics* (New York: Bantam, 1980). I am not competent to comment on the precise nature of the challenge this might pose to Aquinas's thought.

51. *ST* I 82.4, 83.4.

52. *ST* I-II 22.3.

53. *ST* I 50.1.

54. *ST* I 75.2.

55. Aquinas, *Commentary on Aristotle's "De Anima,"* sect. 684.

56. Further argument on Aquinas's part takes the form of arguments from analogy. He considers what the determinate nature of the power of sight (associated with the eyes) and the power of taste (associated with the tongue) imply about how the mind would have to be similarly determinate if it were directly a function of the brain. I find these arguments unconvincing and do not wish to defend them here.

57. *Truth* 26.3; *ST* I-II 24.2 *ad* 2. Today, we might think of the whole circulatory system as an "organ" of emotion. Damasio says that there are "two routes of transmission" of sensory signals that are available to the brain in the generation of emotions and feelings: "humoral *(in which, for example, chemical molecules conveyed by the bloodstream directly activate neural sensors in the hypothalamus or in circumventricular organs such as the area postrema);* and neural *(in which electrochemical signals are transmitted in neural pathways by the axons of neurons firing upon the cell body of other neurons, across synapses)*" (*Looking for Spinoza*, 107).

58. *ST* I-II 48.2.

59. *ST* I-II 31.3 *ad* 3.

60. *Truth* 26.3.

61. *Truth* 22.4.

62. *ST* I 84.7.

63. Ibid.

64. As Pasnau notes, Aquinas says that the natural state of the intellectual soul of a human being is to exist in matter (as the form of a body), but the intellectual soul "[does] not exist in matter in such a way that [its] existence ultimately depends on matter" (Pasnau, *Thomas Aquinas on Human Nature*, 49, quoting *Summa contra Gentiles* II.51.1268).

65. *ST* I 76.5, 77.8; Suppl. 79.

66. *ST* I 89.1 *ad* 3.

67. *ST* I 89.3.

68. *ST* I 89.6.

69. *ST* I 75.6 *ad* 3, 89.1.

70. *Truth* 19.1.

71. See Michael Potts, "Sensory Experiences in Near Death Experiences and the Thomistic View of the Soul," *International Journal for Philosophy of Religion* 49 (2001): 85–100. I have not studied the scholarly literature on the latter sorts of experiences, but I am aware of a growing body of popular literature on the topic.

72. At issue is the nature of "materiality," and the relationship between "matter" and "energy."

73. *ST* I-II 22.3.

74. Marcel Sarot, "God, Emotion, and Corporeality: A Thomist Perspective," *The Thomist* 58 (January 1994): 64.

75. Daniel Westberg, "Emotion and God: A reply to Marcel Sarot," *The Thomist* 60 (January 1996): 109–21.

76. Ibid., 109.

77. Ibid., 110.

78. Ibid.

79. Ibid. Westberg says that such ascriptions are not merely "metaphorical" but "real." "The love of God (or the joy or the anger) is a real quality, and stands in the same relation to its symbolic representations (such as an embrace for love, or inflamed countenance for anger) as the power of God does to the expression of God's 'scepter' or 'right hand.' The emotions ascribed to God refer to the attitudes of a moral agent" (111). It is beyond the scope of this project to delve into analogical predication. See book 1 of Thomas Aquinas, *Summa contra Gentiles*, trans. English Dominican Fathers (New York: Burns, Oates, and Washbourne, 1924) (hereafter *SCG*), http://library.nlx.com/display.cfm?&clientID=79640633&depth=2&infobase=pmaquinas.nfo&softpage=GetClient42&titleCategory=0&view=browse. Latin edition: S. Thomae de Aquino, *Summa contra Gentiles*, *Opera Omnia* (Fundación Tomás de Aquino, 2006) http://www.corpusthomisticum.org/iopera.html. See also related portions of the *prima pars* of the *ST*.

80. *ST* I-II 22.3.

81. *ST* I-II 22.3 *ad* 3; I 82.5 *ad* 1.

82. *Truth* 25.3.

83. Ibid.; see also *ST* I 82.5 *ad* 1.

84. *Truth* 25.3.

85. Westberg, "Emotion and God," 110. My emphasis.

86. Ibid., 118.

87. Ibid., 117.

88. Ibid.

89. Ibid.

CHAPTER FIVE

Approaching the Human Sensory Appetite from Below (I)

✦

Human beings are embodied souls. We have begun to explore some of the implications of this thesis for understanding the way in which emotions are composed. I want to step back now and put humans in some perspective. Aquinas holds that everything that exists can be characterized relative to a scale of being. The principle of his scale is that "the nobler a form is, the more it rises above corporeal matter, the less it is merged in matter, and the more it excels matter by its power and its operation."[1] At the top of the scale is God, namely, the perfect operation of immaterial intellectual power.[2] At the bottom of the scale is elementary matter, which is "altogether material" and "capable of no operation except such as comes within the compass of the qualities which are the dispositions of matter, for instance heat, cold, moisture and dryness, rarity, density, gravity and levity."[3] Humans are situated between the two ends of the scale. We are situated, more specifically, between the angels (purely intellectual beings who are created to function without bodies) and nonhuman animals (embodied beings whose highest principle of operation is a sensory soul).[4] Humans are embodied beings with sensory and other powers, but our highest principle of operation is an intellectual soul. We are created to function with bodies, but we are destined, finally, to function with resurrected bodies in a life to come.

This continuum stretches above and below the human. As we have seen, it also stretches right through the human, such that some powers of the human approximate the powers of angelic beings[5] and some approximate more closely the powers of nonhuman animals.[6] Accordingly, some acts of humans resemble the acts of purely intellectual beings, while other human acts resemble more closely the acts of sensory beings that are without intellectual

powers.[7] For example, acts of the immaterial intellect and will (such as deliberating and choosing) are relatively high on the scale of being, relatively
angel-like, even as these acts are qualified, in a human being, by corporeality
and the exercise of sensory powers. Emotions, which are a function of the
sensory powers and thus have a material dimension, are lower on the scale of
being, more animal-like, even as they are qualified, in a human being, by the
exercise of intellectual powers. Because the intentional content of some emotions (what one has in mind while experiencing the emotions) reflects more
input from the intellect than the content of other emotions, some emotions
are themselves higher on the scale than others.[8] Anger toward a friend who
has violated a trust is higher on the scale than anger toward the fly buzzing
around one's head or the car that will not start.[9]

　　Some of us might recoil at the idea of a scale of being whose end points
are defined as Aquinas defines them. We might object to the idea on theological grounds, arguing for example that this model does not allow one to
capture well the notion that God is the principle of being itself, and not simply a being (albeit a perfect one) among other beings. We might object on
other, metaphysical grounds, arguing for example that the notion that the
same person's intellectual powers could function at one point (during the
present life) in a body and at another point (after death) without a body is incredible and perhaps unintelligible. We might object to the idea on scientific
grounds, arguing that various features of the scale of being are untenable in
light of certain experimental findings or the best models of biology and
physics.[10] We might object to the idea on ethical grounds, noting for example the ways in which the scale has been used by people in positions of power
to define other people (such as women and racial or ethnic minorities) as
naturally inferior specimens of the human kind. We might object also from
the perspective of environmental ethics, noting the way in which the scale
has created the mistaken impression among many humans that everything
below them on the scale exists simply to serve their interests.[11]

　　There is something to be said for all of these objections and for many
more objections that have been and could be raised in response to the particulars of Aquinas's worldview. There is also much that could be done, by
way of creative counterresponse, to reinterpret the symbol of the scale of
being, say, in terms of degrees of complexity, which are linked to capabilities that are appropriately valued by humans. Moreover, there is much that
could be done to subvert some of the ideological and immoral purposes to
which the symbol has been put. It is not my intention, however, to rehabili-
tate this symbol. My intention, rather, is to present some features of
Aquinas's well-ordered universe in a spirit of generous-mindedness and cu-

riosity so that we can begin to appreciate how an emotion can be located within the structure of that universe.

It is impossible to understand and fully appreciate Aquinas's theory of emotion without examining it through the lens of his worldview. However, it is not necessary to affirm the whole of his view of reality in order to affirm what he says about the emotions. For example, it would be possible to challenge the thesis that the human intellect is immaterial, or the thesis that there is a difference in kind between the intellectual capabilities of humans, as such, and those of other animals, while still retaining the core of Aquinas's theory of emotion. It is also possible to seek analogues, within different worldviews, to elements of Aquinas's metaphysically rich theory of emotion. First, however, one must entertain some of Aquinas's worldview, ask questions of it, and allow it to ask questions of oneself, in an effort to imagine emotion as a meaningful part of a larger whole.

Here I approach the structure of emotion from a point far below the human on Aquinas's ontological scale, namely, that occupied by nonliving, material entities. Rising gradually to a point on the scale that is occupied by sensory beings, I examine briefly the power such beings have to entertain objects of sensory apprehension. In chapter 6, I analyze several forms of appetitive motion that are caused by and directed toward objects of sensory apprehension. I attend, for the most part, to appetitive motions that are common to human and many other, nonhuman animals, but in a way that points to what is distinctive about human emotions.

In chapters 7 through 9, I take a different tack, approaching the structure of emotion from a point on Aquinas's scale above the sensory per se. I do not begin with an analysis of the intellectual powers of God or the angels. Such an analysis would be interesting, but I leave that work to others. Rather, I begin with the human intellect and will, considering these powers in relation to the powers of sensory apprehension and appetite. I explore, more specifically, some of the contributions that the intellect and will can and do make to the formation and re-formation of emotional states. Taking this two-directional approach should provide us with some different ways of conceiving what is going on inside of us and between ourselves and others; it should allow us to apprehend some of the structural similarities between emotions and other sorts of goings-on within and, perhaps, beyond "this world."

THE NATURAL APPETITE: STONES AND OTHER EXISTING THINGS

For Aquinas, an emotion is an act of an appetitive power. It is an actualization of the potential one has to *tend* in relation to certain objects of apprehension.

Following Aristotle, Aquinas holds that humans have three basic powers of appetite, namely, natural, sensory, and intellectual.[12] Taken together, these powers make humans capable of (passively) undergoing and, in some cases, (actively) bringing about various sorts of interior and exterior motion or change. Aquinas characterizes emotion specifically as a motion of the *sensory* appetite, but it is instructive to approach this appetite with the other forms of appetite in view, beginning with the natural appetite.

In Aquinas's view, everything that exists has a natural appetite in the following specific sense: Every existing thing tends by its own natural principles toward its proper end or good.[13] It tends to be what it is and to behave in ways that are consonant with its nature.[14] It tends "to obtain what is suited and favorable to [its] nature, and to gain, as it were, a victory over whatever is opposed to it."[15] Every existing thing tends to do all of this in constant interaction with other things, which have their own tendencies.[16] The tendency of each thing to keep being itself in the face of other things—things that sometimes function as agents of change—derives from each thing's internal principles, but these principles derive ultimately from the first principle of being itself.[17] Aquinas holds that this principle—this Agent—determines that everything is oriented as part of a whole toward the good of its own being and toward the good of the whole.[18]

Aquinas sometimes uses the term "love" (*amor*) to refer to natural appetites.[19] Depending on the context, "love" can refer to the tendency an entity has to be itself and thus to resist being reduced to something other than what it is. By implication, "love" can refer to the tendency a thing has to actualize the potential that is inherent in its being. "Love" can thus refer to the tendency that an object has to actualize its potential by uniting with other objects that are suitable for this purpose. "Love" can refer, that is, to the way in which one thing is oriented (by virtue of the sort of thing it is) to interact (under certain conditions) with other things (by virtue of the sorts of things *they* are) in ways that are beneficial, at least to the first thing. Sometimes Aquinas uses the term "love" to refer not only to this basic tendency or orientation but also to more active, directional forms of tending, such as desiring or seeking;[20] however, "love" is technically a form of tending that is prior to these other forms of appetitive motion. It is basically a being-oriented-toward or a being-poised-to-interact-with objects that are suitable for oneself. In Aquinas's world, every entity exhibits "love" in this sense. In what follows, I usually employ the language of "appetite" or "tendency," but I sometimes use the language of "love" to signal the way in which, for Aquinas, the first principle and final end of all tending to be what one is in relation to others is God, often characterized within Christianity, and in the context of other paths, as Love.[21]

Every existing thing has appetitive tendencies, broadly construed. Consider, for example, an earthbound stone. A stone has a tendency to be and to remain a stone, and it resists becoming something other than a stone. In accordance with its nature, it tends also toward a state of being-at-rest on the surface of the planet. Ordinarily a stone achieves such a state unless it is kept from doing so. What Aquinas says about the element of earth (*terra*) applies also to a stone: "In the element earth there is a certain nature by which being in the center is characteristic of it, and consequent upon this nature there is an inclination to the center according to which earth naturally tends to such a place even when it is violently kept away from it; and so when the obstacle is removed it always moves downward."[22]

In this perspective, a human being has quite a lot in common with a stone. For example, both entities have the tendency to be and to remain something in particular (albeit something different). Both entities have the tendency to be and to remain entities that are characterized by materiality, and both entities can be considered with respect to their materiality. Considered materially, a stone and a human being (a human body) are composed to some extent of similar elements. Both have weight. By virtue of having weight, both entities have the tendency to fall to the earth if they are lifted and dropped. Both have the tendency to break if they are dropped in certain ways, under certain conditions.

Some tendencies that are characteristic of both human bodies and stones are tendencies that bodies and stones exhibit in relation to each other. For example, a cold human body has the tendency to gain heat when it comes into contact with a warm stone, and a cold stone has the tendency to gain heat when it comes into contact with a warm body. Some tendencies of human bodies and stones are exhibited, under certain conditions, at each other's expense. For example, if a stone is large and heavy, and it is dropped above a human body, the stone will exhibit the tendency to crush the body en route to the surface of the earth. Similarly, if a stone is small and fragile, and it is placed beneath a heavy human body (fortified, say, by hard-soled boots), the body will exhibit the tendency to crush the stone under its weight.

Aquinas holds that all actions and interactions of material things are governed, fundamentally, by the principle of love, even in cases where one thing happens to destroy another, for each thing acts and is acted upon by others in accordance with its own natural principles, the principles that govern nature generally, and the first principle of order in the universe. Employing explicitly theological and teleological language, Aquinas says that each thing is "directed by God" to "love God."[23] He elaborates: "To love God above all things is natural to [the human] and to every nature, not only rational but irrational, and even to inanimate nature according to the manner of love [*amoris*] which can belong to each creature. And the reason of this is that it is natural to all to seek [*appetat*] and love [*amet*] things according as they are naturally fit (to be sought and loved) *since all things act according as they are naturally fit* as stated in Phys. ii. 8."[24] In tending toward what is suitable to it, an inanimate entity is said to love its own being, to love that which is suitable to it, to love God as the principle of all being and goodness, and thus to love "the common good of the whole universe, which is God. Hence Dionysius says (*Div. Nom*. iv) that *God leads everything to love of Himself.*"[25]

A human being and a stone are alike in many respects, but they are also different. While a human body, considered materially, has a natural appetite or a tendency to have and to retain a certain physical form and to exhibit properties that are characteristic of that form, a human *being* has the tendency to have and to retain the more specific form of a *living* material entity. Indeed, a human being has the tendency to seek what is suitable to him or her, not only as a living being but also as a being with sensory and intellectual powers. Nevertheless, it is valuable to attend to what a human being and a stone have in common. Like a stone, an embodied human being is oriented by the principles of his or her nature, and by the principles of nature generally, to act on other things—and to be acted upon—in ways that are mediated, directly or indirectly, by materiality.

THE NATURAL APPETITE: PLANTS AND OTHER LIVING THINGS

When Aquinas discusses objects that are characterized by natural appetite alone, he often uses the example of an inanimate object, such as a stone. Another object that has a natural appetite, but lacks a sensory or intellectual appetite, is a plant.[26] Plants are like stones in many respects. Both have a natural appetite or tendency to be what they are and to behave in ways that accord with their nature; both have the tendency to "conquer" what is contrary to their being and their good.[27] Considered in their material dimension, both plants and stones are composed of some of the same elements of nature. Both also have weight. Both therefore have the tendency to fall to the ground when lifted and released.

Yet a plant is more than a material entity. It is a material entity that has a principle of life and organic operation. A plant is a living organism that has the innate tendency to carry out the functions that define planthood, which are nutrition (the taking in and processing of nutrients), growth, and reproduction.[28] By virtue of its tendency to be alive and to behave specifically as a plant, a plant is said by Aquinas (as by Aristotle) to have a soul—a vegetative soul.[29]

Just as human beings have a lot in common with stones, so humans have as much and more in common with plants.[30] Notably, humans and plants are characterized not only by materiality but also by life.[31] Considering humans and plants simply as living organisms, they both exhibit vegetative appetites or tendencies. Both have the tendency to perform a range of nutritive and other life functions, for a limited period of time. Both have the tendency to grow to a certain size and then to stop growing. In general, both have the tendency to generate more of their kind.

Humans and plants exhibit some of their tendencies in relation to each other. For example, a human being, considered as a living organism, has the tendency to digest certain plants that enter its digestive system. The digestion of these plants often builds the human organism and serves its proper functioning. Similarly, a plant has the tendency to assimilate elements of human waste (say, feces or, in the case of death, a decaying corpse) as nutrients that contribute to the physical makeup and well-being of the plant. Some tendencies of humans and plants are exhibited, under certain conditions, at each other's expense. A human body tends to destroy the life of a plant when the plant enters the body's digestive system. Similarly, some (say, poisonous or highly allergenic) plants tend to injure or destroy some humans when those humans are brought into physical contact with the plants.

Again, Aquinas holds that the principle of love orders all of these acts and interactions, even in cases where one living organism happens, through its own proper activity, to destroy another living organism. Each organism, on this basic level, is simply following its own internal principles in ways that are consistent with the principles that govern nature as such. Each organism is thus following the underlying principle of being and order in the universe, under given circumstances. This principle determines that both life and death are integral parts of a larger cosmic process.[32]

Humans are in many respects like plants, but they are also notably different. Because humans have powers of sensation, thought, will, and action, they possess the powers of nutrition, growth, and generation in a unique way. They have the power or the ability, under certain circumstances and to a limited extent, to change the natural course of their physical development. For example, by manipulating their diet they can accelerate or stunt their growth or alter their bone or muscle mass. By changing other conditions and behaviors many humans can influence whether, when, and how often they reproduce. Nevertheless, it is valuable to reflect on what humans and plants have in common as biological organisms. Each sort of entity tends by the principles of its own nature and by the principles of nature generally to be drawn toward and to seek what is suitable to it—including the continuation of its life, up to a point—in ways that affect and are affected by other living things, which tend similarly to be drawn toward and to seek what is suitable for themselves. Both sorts of entities are vulnerable to injury, disease, and death.

SENSORY BEINGS: FROM PLANTS TO ANIMALS

In Aquinas's worldview, a plant has the appetite to be and to behave as the sort of being it is, namely, a living material entity. More specifically, it has the appetite or the tendency to exercise the power of "nutrition." It has the tendency to unite with the nutrients and water that it needs to live and grow. Human and nonhuman animals are somewhat like plants in this respect. The body of an animal, considered simply as a living organism, has the tendency to take in the nutrients and water that are necessary for life and functioning. More specifically, a living animal's body tends to absorb, process, and distribute goods that are directly available to its relevant organ systems.

Much of the activity of nutrition and hydration in animals takes place in ways that do not register—and do not need to register—in the animal's sensory awareness. Just as a plant does not feel H_2O and other chemicals traveling up its stem, an animal does not feel chemicals being absorbed into and flowing through its bloodstream. Yet some of the activities of nutrition and hydration *do* register in the sensory awareness of an animal.[33] For example, a relatively complex animal sees, smells, and tastes what it ingests. It feels solids and liquids entering its mouth and going down its throat. It feels pain when it is hungry and pleasure when its hunger is sated. It feels pain when it ingests a substance (or a particular amount of a substance) that is not suitable to its nature, and if it has good judgment it will avoid that substance (or ingest a different amount of it) in the future. If an animal did not have these and other sensory powers, it would not be inclined to eat or drink at all. If it did eat or drink, it would not be inclined to eat or drink what is good for it, and it would not be inclined to eat or drink the right amount of what is good for it. The animal would likely not survive. The question would arise as to whether the entity in question were an animal at all.[34]

Whereas a plant is oriented by its natural principles to absorb the nutrients and water that are necessary for its life—and parts of an animal's body are oriented in analogous ways—an animal, considered in a more complete way, as a sensory being, is oriented to pursue nutrition and hydration (and to perform other vital functions) via the exercise of sensory as well as vegetative powers. An animal has a natural appetite or tendency to be drawn toward what it apprehends via the senses to be suitable, and it has a tendency to avoid or attack what it apprehends to be unsuitable. In other words, an animal has a sensory appetite or sensory appetites. Aquinas says, "To tend [*ap-*

petere], which is in a way common to all things . . . becomes in a way special for animate beings, or rather animals, inasmuch as there are found in them appetite [*appetitus*] and what moves the appetite."[35] Here "appetite" implies sensory awareness and thus refers specifically to sensory appetite.

Again, Aquinas employs the language of soul, saying that, just as a plant has a vegetative soul, an animal has a sensory soul.[36] Specifically, a *nonhuman* animal has a sensory soul. As we have seen, a human animal has an intellectual soul that qualifies the sensory powers that it otherwise shares with nonhuman animals. To say of a nonhuman animal that it has a sensory soul is to say that the animal has a principle of life and operation that causes it to be specifically an animal. It has an innate tendency to perform the functions that are definitive of animality. These functions include but surpass the functions that are characteristic of plants.[37]

Just as a stone can be said to love the (center of the) earth, in accordance with the nature of the stone, and a plant can be said to love what is required for its life and proper functioning as a plant (even as the plant also loves the earth), so an animal can be said to love what is suitable to its nature as an animal. Considered with respect to its materiality, an animal (like a stone and a plant) loves the earth. Considered as a living material entity with vegetative powers, an animal (like a plant, but unlike a stone) loves the sources of nutrition and hydration that are necessary for its life and well-being. Considered more specifically as a sensory being, an animal (unlike a stone or a plant) loves the objects it apprehends through the use of its sensory powers to be suitable for it as an animal.

As we can anticipate, Aquinas holds that, when an animal tends toward an object as suitable for it, the animal not only loves that object but the animal also loves its own actualization or perfection as a sensory being. The animal also (thereby) loves the first principle or cause of its perfection, which is the principle of all perfection, which is to say that the animal loves God or the good.[38] Indeed, the animal can be said to love God inasmuch as it is oriented to operate in well-ordered ways as a material entity and a living organism; yet the animal loves God in a more perfect (albeit still implicit) manner inasmuch as it is oriented to exercise its sensory powers in relation to objects of experience—inasmuch as the animal tends, by nature, to actualize some of its defining potential by interacting with sensible objects.[39]

THE POWERS OF SENSORY APPREHENSION: NONHUMAN AND HUMAN ANIMALS

What is most definitive of animals (relative to plants and nonliving things) is their sensory powers. It is on account of these powers that animals are

capable of being moved by objects in ways that are determined, not simply
by the objects as such (and by the internal principles that determine the animals' relations to those objects) but also by the ways in which those objects
are *apprehended* by the animals.[40] Let us delve further into the way in which
sensory objects are experienced by animals—first, how animals are capable of having certain objects in mind or in sensory awareness, and then (in
the following chapter) how animals are capable of being *moved* by what is
thus represented in mind or awareness.

In describing acts of sensory apprehension, Aquinas tends to focus more
on nonhuman than on human animals. One reason for this focus is probably
that acts of sensory apprehension in nonhuman animals are not, in his view,
complicated by acts of the intellect and will, as acts of sensory apprehension
in humans ordinarily are. It makes sense for Aquinas to move from the seemingly simpler case of nonhuman animals to the more complex case of the
human, although one could argue that Aquinas proceeds also in the opposite
direction, having no choice but to project what is going on in the minds of
animals partly on the basis of reflection on and abstraction from what he
takes to be going on in the minds of humans.

In any case, an interpreter of Aquinas must piece together an analysis of
the powers of sensory apprehension in humans from what Aquinas says about
both nonhuman and human animals. When Aquinas focuses on nonhuman
animals without explicit mention of the human, the implication is usually
that nonhuman and human animals are much the same in the respect under
consideration, within the realm of the sensory. When Aquinas turns explicitly to the human, he usually calls attention to the way in which the intellectual powers condition human sensory apprehension. In the rest of this and
the following chapter, I focus on what nonhuman and human animals have in
common, in Aquinas's perspective, but I do so with an eye toward some of
the ways in which the intellect and the will are bound to have an effect on
the sensory experiences of humans.[41]

As noted in chapter 3, the power of sensory apprehension is what makes
it possible for a sensory being to acquire and process sensible information.
The power of sensory apprehension takes the form of the exterior and interior senses, both of which Aquinas takes to be "exercised by means of a corporeal organ."[42] The exterior senses include the powers of sight, hearing,
touch, smell, and taste.[43] The interior senses include some version of "the
common sense, the imagination, and the estimative and memorative powers,"
all of which are exercised by means of the brain (and nervous system).[44] The
interior senses are of special significance for our inquiry. In conjunction with
the exterior senses, they enable a sensory being to entertain various sensory

images and impressions, and make sensory judgments. These forms of sensory apprehension make it possible for a being to undergo object-oriented, sensory-appetitive motions.

The first interior sense is the common sense (*sensus communis*). It is "the common root and principle of the exterior senses."[45] It is also their "common term."[46] The common sense is the power that makes it possible for an animal—whether nonhuman or human—to have relatively complex sensory impressions. Whereas a power of exterior sense, such as sight, makes it possible to discern a particular visible quality and to discriminate (by sense) one visible quality from another, say, "white from black or green," the common sense makes it possible to discern sensible qualities of multiple kinds so that an object can appear as white, sweet, soft, and fragrant, all at the same time.[47] The common sense makes it possible to have a unified sensory experience of an object that has many sensible properties,[48] and to be aware that one is having such an experience.[49]

The second interior sense is the imagination (*imaginatio*). It is the power that makes it possible for an animal—whether nonhuman or human—to retain and make use of the sensible forms of objects (i.e., to work with sensory images).[50] More specifically, the imagination includes the power to create "a storehouse of forms received through the [exterior] senses."[51] It includes also the power to "represent . . . again to understanding" the forms that have been received and retained.[52] By the power of imagination an animal can thus apprehend a sensible object, "not only at the actual time of sensation, but also when it is absent."[53] By virtue of this power, an animal can seek the likeness of a sensory image in the actual world—it can look for an object that is not (yet) present to its exterior senses. In humans alone (among the animals) the power of imagination makes it possible also to form images of sensible objects that one has never seen, "as when from the imaginary form of gold, and the imaginary form of a mountain, we compose the one form of a golden mountain."[54]

THE ESTIMATIVE AND COGITATIVE POWERS

With regard to the third interior sense identified by Aquinas, the differences between the nonhuman and the human are more notable. In a nonhuman animal, this sense or power is called the estimative (*aestimativa*). The estimative power makes it possible to "perceive . . . intentions, which the exterior sense does not perceive."[55] Aquinas focuses in his (few) examples of such "intentions" on the properties of "threatening" and "useful." As he uses the term, "intention" (*intentio*) does not seem to refer to a sensory image of an object, which an animal apprehends as having such a property. It seems to refer, instead, to a sensory impression of the property itself. Yet the property the animal apprehends is a property *of* the object, which the animal must also apprehend. Evidently, the estimative power operates in conjunction with the common sense and the imagination, so that the animal has an image of something before or in its mind, and it is struck by certain properties of that image. For the sake of simplicity, I will be referring in this project to the estimative—and cogitative—powers allowing one to apprehend a sensible object and certain of its properties at the same time.

Aquinas offers the following two examples of how the estimative power works—examples to which he regularly returns. He says, "an animal needs to seek or to avoid certain things, not only because they are pleasing or otherwise to the senses, but also on account of other advantages and uses, or disadvantages: just as the sheep runs away when it sees a wolf, not on account of its color or shape, but as a natural enemy: and again a bird gathers together straws, not because they are pleasant to the senses, but because they are useful for building its nest."[56]

To take one of these examples, a bird has a sensory impression of an item that is yellow, short, and rather stiff. Under certain circumstances, the bird apprehends this item to be useful. One could say that the bird simply apprehends the item, picks it up, and puts it to use in building a nest because the bird has natural principles that cause it to do just this.[57] However, Aquinas says that a nonhuman animal can and often does make a "well-regulated judgment *[iudicium]* . . . about certain things."[58] In his perspective, animals make judgments "from a natural estimate, not from any deliberation, since they are ignorant of the basis of their judgment."[59] Nevertheless, they make basic sensory judgments.

Human beings are like nonhuman animals in that sometimes humans make judgments that involve little more than registering in their awareness certain properties of sensible objects, specifically properties that are not directly available to the five senses.[60] Shifting from the property of "useful" to that of "threatening," it is common for humans to judge a long, thin object moving quickly through the grass at their feet to be a threat of some kind, even before they have time to think, "this is a snake, and some snakes are dangerous." As noted previously, neuroscientific studies indicate that certain preorganized neural circuits in humans effectively determine that certain sensory inputs will sometimes cause activity within evolutionarily older parts of the brain (and particular physiological responses) before related activity occurs within evolutionarily newer parts of the brain, which are involved in higher cognitive functions.[61] In the present case, we are considering a sensory input that takes the form of seeing an object and thus being aware of it. Sometimes humans "judge" an object to be dangerous before they have time to think about it.

Aquinas says that, unlike a sheep or a bird, which perceives "intentions" by a kind of "natural instinct," a human being perceives "intentions" by "some sort of collation" or by "a coalition of ideas."[62] The precise nature of this difference in modes of perceiving and judging is unclear. Nonhuman animals make sensory judgments (the notion of "instinct" can be misleading here, suggesting a behavior that does not rise to the level of awareness); yet Aquinas believes that, even on a sensory level, humans are capable of more complex judgments than other sorts of animals. Humans have a version of the estimative power that he calls the cogitative (*cogitiva*). The cogitative power enables them to "[compare] individual intentions, just as the intellectual reason compares universal intentions."[63] Like other animals, humans have a power that enables them to apprehend sensible properties beyond those that are available to the five senses, but unlike other animals, humans can apprehend multiple such properties in complex combinations within the same object and within different objects at the same time. For example, the cogitative power allows a human to apprehend sensible objects with regard to their dangerousness, usefulness, *and* natural beauty.[64] It allows one to judge, say, the relative danger, usefulness, and beauty of one's current path, which features a snake, a rather direct route, and a pleasant view, relative to an alternative path, away from the snake, but less direct, and less delightful to the senses. Because these sorts of "comparing, adding and dividing" with respect to particulars resemble (and also, as we will see, tend to function in coordination with) the activities of "universal reason," Aquinas sometimes refers to the cogitative power as the power of "particular reason."[65]

With the cogitative power, we have not yet arrived at the (more advanced) power to engage in acts of understanding or practical reasoning. We have not yet arrived at the power to conceptualize a thing or its properties, to think about a thing's properties *as* properties, to name them, or to compare them in terms of their contributions to a desired end of which we also have a concept. All of these cognitive activities rely on the intellect. With the cogitative power, we are still on the level of the sensory and the particular. Yet it is significant that even on this level a human can perceive or imagine a "sensible good or evil," namely, an object with sensible properties that appear to be relevant to the human's efforts to go on living and doing what he or she wishes to do. By virtue of the cogitative power, a human can form impressions of many different objects and their suitability or unsuitability with respect to his or her basic concerns.

Unfortunately, Aquinas's comments on the cogitative power are few and formulaic. It is difficult, on the basis of what he says, to specify, except in the most general terms, what the cogitative power or the power of particular reason makes possible in distinction from what the intellect make possible, where the intellect includes the power of universal reason (and the latter includes the power of practical reason). This difficulty is due, in part, to the fact that, in a being who is intellectual by nature, intellectual apprehension always informs and qualifies the sensory apprehension of particulars, to some extent. For most of us, most of the time, sensory and intellectual judgments function seamlessly in relation to each other.[66] I perceive an object outside my window, and I judge it to be dark red, to have a distinctive shape, to be a brick, to be part of a building that has a particular name and function, and so on, all at the same time.

Taking the sensory dimension of human cognition seriously, Aquinas identifies a power of perception and judgment that functions within the sensory domain. It is helpful to identify such a power, if only in concept, partly because doing so enables us to keep in mind what humans share with other animals. Humans often behave more like nonrational animals than like rational animals, especially when we have the impression that our lives or safety, or the lives or safety of our kin, are at stake—or food, sex, or other tangible pleasures are involved. Often, in such situations, humans do not act in the absence of judgment; rather, we act on the basis of sensory judgments that have not been informed by rational reflection. It is helpful to be able to say what these lower-order judgments are like—how they are judgments about objects and their properties, and judgments about how these objects are significant for one's well-being—but also how they differ from higher-order intellectual judgments that presuppose a reflective view of what is good for a human being and for oneself *as* a human being.

Aquinas wants to say that a human being is by nature a rational animal and that "the sensitive power at its highest—in [a human being], in whom sensitivity is joined to intelligence—has some share in the life of intellect."[67] Even the basic sensory judgments of humans ordinarily reflect the influence of the intellect to some degree. The cogitative power owes its excellence "not to that which is proper to the sensitive part; but to a certain affinity and proximity to the universal reason, which, so to speak, overflows into [it]."[68] It is thus not possible to draw a sharp line between the (relatively high-level) sensory and the (relatively low-level) intellectual, but it is also unhelpful to not make any distinction at all.

To conclude our survey of the interior senses, the fourth power identified by Aquinas is the memorative (*memorativa*). This is a power that makes it possible for a sensory being to make use of a "storehouse" of "intentions" that are perceived via the exercise of the estimative power (in nonhuman animals) or the cogitative power (in human animals). The memorative power, or the power of memory, makes it possible to have a "sudden recollection" of a sensory judgment that one made in the past,[69] and to associate this judgment with certain features of the present situation.[70] For example, this power makes it possible for a bird to judge, partly in recollecting past experience, that a given sensible item (a piece of straw) is too large for it to carry.[71] The power of memory (in coordination with the other interior senses) would make it possible for a human to judge that the object in the grass is like something he or she has encountered before, which could come closer before it slithers away. With a human, the power of memory includes the power of "reminiscence" (reminiscentia). By virtue of the latter, it is possible for one actively to *seek out* a range of sensory judgments that one made in the past so that one can judge the suitableness or unsuitableness of a particular item, in the present, in light of this "storehouse" of impressions.[72]

THE ROLE OF THE COGITATIVE POWER IN CONCEIVING AN OBJECT OF EMOTION

An emotion is caused by an object of sensory apprehension. Now that we have familiarized ourselves with the powers of sensory apprehension, it would be good if we could say, more specifically, which of these powers is engaged when one conceives the object of an emotion. With an object that is available to the exterior senses, the exterior senses and the common sense (at least) will be engaged. With objects that are not immediately present to the exterior senses, the imaginative power will be engaged in a way that presupposes prior acts of the exterior senses and common sense. But what about the cogitative power? It would be helpful if we could say whether, for Aquinas, the cogitative power is engaged in conceiving an object of emotion (and thus undergoing an emotion).

Aquinas does say explicitly that the cogitative power is involved in the arousal of one type of emotion, which he calls irascible.[73] An irascible emotion takes as its object a sensible good or evil that is perceived or imagined under the aspect of *difficulty*. Such an emotion arises when one apprehends an obstacle to attaining what one wants, or avoiding what one wants to avoid. It involves a kind of spiritedness or struggle.[74] Fear is an example of an irascible emotion. Again, Aquinas turns to nonhuman animals for insight. He notices that, when a sheep sees a big hairy object with sharp teeth (a wolf) that is moving in a particular way, the sheep judges the object to be threatening, is immediately alarmed, and (if possible) flees.[75] The sheep is alarmed and flees not because looking at the object is painful to its senses—not or not only because the object is disturbing to the eyes, smells bad, is painful to the touch, or the like. Rather, the sheep is alarmed and flees because it makes a sensory judgment of "danger!" with respect to the object. Such a judgment is informed by the exterior senses and common sense, but it involves more than these senses can deliver on their own.[76]

Similarly, I do not gasp when I see the skinny green object moving at my feet simply because my senses are displeased by its color, shape, movement, or what have you. I gasp because I judge this object to be a threat to my well-being. Making this judgment does not require abstract thoughts about what constitutes human well-being or related thoughts about whether this object is really a threat—although such thoughts might follow quickly on the arousal of the fear as I apprehend that this is, after all, only a garter snake, and I am a coward for (still) being afraid of it. The initial judgment that the object is a threat is sensory and particular. Yet this judgment is more than what the exterior senses and common sense alone make possible. Accordingly, we can say that, for Aquinas, at least some emotions take as their objects sensible items that a human judges, by means of the cogitative power, to have properties beyond those that are immediately available to the five senses.[77]

What is not as clear, in Aquinas's writings, is whether he thinks the cogitative power is typically involved in the arousal of the other major type of emotion, which he calls concupiscible. He says that a concupiscible emotion takes as its object "sensible good or evil, simply apprehended as such, which causes pleasure or pain."[78] A concupiscible emotion has as its object "what is suitable [or unsuitable], according to the senses."[79] Aquinas says, again, that "the concupiscible power is moved to enjoyment upon the mere apprehension of the pleasurable object."[80] At times, Aquinas associates the concupiscible appetite with objects of five-sensory apprehension; he seems to contrast the concupiscible and the irascible in ways that suggest that only irascible emotions require the engagement of the cogitative power.[81]

One example of a concupiscible emotion is delight (delectatio). Speaking broadly about the concupiscible, Aquinas suggests that there are forms of delight that arise when a human being apprehends an object as simply pleasing to the senses.[82] Consider the delight of seeing and hearing a hummingbird move from flower to flower. When one apprehends such an object, one does not ordinarily make a judgment that the object is suitable for looking at or listening to. Indeed, one might go on to make such a judgment, a moment later, when one must elect to continue watching the bird or get back to one's gardening, or when one notices, with some concern, that one does not delight in birds as much as one used to, and one wonders why that is. However, when one first apprehends the bird, one simply apprehends it as pleasing to the senses, and one enjoys it as such.[83]

A more complicated example offered by Aquinas concerns hunger, namely, a motion of the sensory appetite in relation to a particular item of food. Such a motion arises when a sensory being apprehends an object, not only as suitable to the senses for sensing but also as "suitable to the animal"[84] or suitable "for the very existence of the one sensing."[85] At first glance, it might seem that looking at, smelling, and tasting an object and finding it pleasant is sufficient to elicit an appetite to go ahead and eat it—there is no need to judge that the object is "suitable for nourishment."[86] Yet just because an object is pleasing to the exterior senses does not guarantee that it is edible or nourishing. Some objects that look, smell, and taste delectable are not, in fact, fitting to eat. It is thus doubtful that the property "suitable for eating" is given immediately with the five senses and common sense. Apprehending this property requires the exercise of the estimative or cogitative power (and, in some cases, the exercise of higher intellectual powers as well). The apprehension that an object is suitable not simply for sensing but also for ingesting (and thus for "the very existence of the one sensing") is similar in kind to the apprehension that an object poses a threat to the one sensing, is useful for building a shelter, or—to use another example offered by Aquinas—is useful for the self-defense of the one sensing, all of which engage the estimative or cogitative power.[87]

As with hunger, so with many other appetitive motions of the concupiscible type, including motions that most of us are more prone to call emotions.[88] The objects that elicit emotions are sometimes apprehended as suitable or unsuitable to the senses, but usually they are also judged suitable or unsuitable to one's being—where one is aware, on a basic sensory level, of having a life and wanting it to go pleasantly or well. Most sensory beings have an appetite to engage in countless activities beyond five-sensory experiences, and it is against the backdrop of this appetitive tending that they construe the significance of particular sensible objects.

Loving a human being, for example, involves judging his or her company to be good or attractive in some respect.[89] On a sensory level, the judgment that someone's company is good for one does not involve recourse to a universal, such as "the contributions of friendship to a good human life," although it is common for a human to engage in higher-order intellectual operations when sensory love is aroused, and one would expect such operations to influence the intentional content of the emotion. One must also take seriously the way in which intellectual reflection on the nature of happiness, or the point of life, can precede and condition an intellectual being's sensory perceptions and judgments. Nevertheless, the sorts of judgments that arouse sensory love are principally sensory and particular: This person has many attractive qualities; he or she is fun to be with. Yet these judgments involve

more than undergoing (and being aware that one is undergoing) enjoyable
five-sensory impressions: It is not simply that he or she is pleasing to the eye
or smells good. Emotions such as love must ordinarily involve the exercise of
the cognitive power.[90]

In a discussion of concupiscence or sensory desire in the *Summa theologiae*, Aquinas says that sometimes when one judges an object to be suitable
for oneself—especially when one apprehends an object that is not in an immediate way necessary for one's life (such as food or drink) but one judges
that the object has attractive properties—one engages in a form of judging
that is sensory but also uniquely human.[91] In judging that an object is inessential but nevertheless worth seeking (and more worth seeking than other available objects), a human exercises sensory "apprehension together with
deliberation."[92] Aquinas gives as an example the "desire to be rich, not up to
a certain limit, but to be simply as rich as possible."[93] Such a desire presupposes the exercise of the cogitative power, as well as the imagination.[94]

Aquinas's view thus seems to be that the cogitative power is engaged in
the formation of the intentional content of many, if not most, concupiscible
emotions. When Aquinas says that some emotions take as their objects "sensible good or evil, simply apprehended as such,"[95] he might, in some cases,
have in mind objects that simply strike one or more of the exterior senses as
attractive or repulsive, but he must also have in mind objects that a subject
perceives or judges via the cogitative power to be suitable or unsuitable with
respect to one or more of the subject's purposes—with respect to appetites
for more than pleasing sensations per se.

Here as elsewhere, with Aquinas, it is best to think in terms of a scale or
range. With respect to the examples at hand, the range might extend from
a simple impression that an object is attractive to the eye (which might not
engage the cogitative power)—to a judgment that an attractive object is suitable for eating (which appears to engage the cogitative power on a basic
level)—to a judgment that an object (such as a fellow human being) is suitable company (which engages the cogitative power to a greater degree)—
to a judgment that "this person qua moral agent is good, and is also good for
me" (which takes us well beyond the cogitative power and requires the engagement of the intellect).[96]

REGAINING PERSPECTIVE

The phenomena that Aquinas describes as acts of sensory apprehension are
phenomena that I would expect most of us to recognize, even if we would
label or analyze them differently. The phenomena to which he points are

complex and constantly in interactive motion. In humans, these phenomena tend to be tied up in intricate ways with higher cognitive functions. Hence, these phenomena are difficult to isolate and describe in anything but the most formal terms. What is important for understanding Aquinas on emotion is not that readers assent to his particular descriptions of the powers of sensory apprehension. Rather, what is needful is that readers be willing to imagine with him, in general terms, a range of capabilities that seem, in some ways, to be like the perceptual and cognitive capabilities of many nonhuman animals, yet also seem, in other ways, to stretch beyond the limits of these capabilities, without stretching all the way to the capabilities that most of us associate with the intellect (such as the capability of thinking about human well-being and reasoning that this or that response to a situation is choice-worthy because it is most likely to contribute to human well-being). This is admittedly a rather loosely defined mid range of capabilities, but it is a range that we must try to recall when we consider, in the analysis that follows, what it means to have a sensible object in mind.[97]

Aquinas's thesis is that an emotion is elicited by sensory images, impressions, associations, and judgments regarding the suitability or unsuitability of a particular object for one's life or well-being. Given the parallels to nonhuman animal experience that have been drawn in this chapter, it should be clear that, in humans, on a sensory level, the judgment that an object is "suitable for one's life or well-being" is not necessarily conceptualized as such. Just as nonhuman animals have sensory impressions and make sensory judgments that certain things or situations are beneficial, harmful, or useful to them, so humans sometimes have such impressions and make such judgments without thinking to themselves explicitly or in so many words, "Ah, this object would be a good thing for me to unite with in order to actualize some of my potential" or "Yes, this object would likely serve my purposes better than any of the others." As we proceed to discuss particular emotions, we will identify in formal terms the intentional content of these emotions, but it is important that we try to imagine what it is to apprehend objects on the basis of our sensory powers (without reducing the sensory to the five senses). The sensory domain should appear quite large at this point, given that nonhuman animals are limited to this domain, and many of them possess considerable intelligence.

Let us recollect, finally, how we began this chapter. We noted that, for Aquinas, an emotion is a kind of appetitive motion. As such, it has intriguing structural similarities to other kinds of appetitive motion or tendencies that can be said (albeit with what I would call religious imagination) to characterize nonliving things, plants, and nonhuman animals. We continue now to approach the human sensory appetite from below, heeding the sensory dimension of the human partly by attending to what humans appear to have in common with other sensory beings. Viewing the human relative to non-human animals is a valuable exercise because it discourages us from separating the intellectual too sharply from the sensory within the human. It keeps us from supposing that the intellectual powers can be exercised in relative isolation from the sensory.

I suspect that some of us downplay the sensory dimension of human life and are quick to identify the human with the intellectual because we want to recognize and celebrate the peculiar dignity of the human relative to other sorts of beings. This impulse is understandable, and it can serve good purposes. However, when we focus too intently on the human *qua* intellectual, we neglect the dignity that is ours, as humans, by virtue of the fact that we are also sensory beings akin to other animals; we are living beings akin to other living things, such as plants; and we are (partly) material entities akin to other material entities, such as stones. When we recognize and celebrate the dignity that is ours on account of our sensibility, our vegetative powers, and our beautifully ordered material composition, as well as our intellectual capabilities, we put ourselves in a better position to appreciate the dignity of other existing things, all of which in their own ways reflect and glorify the first principle of being.

NOTES

1. *ST* I 76.1; see also *ST* I 14.1, and *SCG*, bk. 2, chap. 68.

2. *ST* I 2.3, 14.1–2.

3. *SCG*, bk. 2, chap. 68; see also *ST* I 14.4, 16.5, 18.3.

4. *ST* I 51.1.

5. *ST* I 50.1 *ad* 1, 54.5.

6. *ST* I 78.4.

7. Keep in mind that "act" refers simply to the actualization of a potency. When I refer to an act of a human being or a particular power, I could be referring to any operation of which a human being or an embodied human organism is capable.

8. *Truth* 25.2.

9. Aquinas argues that the object of anger is a person who has committed an unmerited slight against our excellence. I agree that this is the paradigm. However, I think we can and ought to consider that any time someone frustrates our being or our activity, this frustration can be interpreted as a slight on the part of another. For example, the stranger who is driving slowly in front of us, keeping us from getting to work on time, can become an object of anger; in the moment of anger, the driver appears to be someone who fails to give us the regard we think we are due. By extension, an object such

as a toaster that fails to operate properly and thus fails to cooperate with us, can become an object of anger. Such anger reflects an underlying attitude that I take to be quite common, namely, the attitude that everyone and everything in the world ought, in effect, to take notice of us, revolve around us, stay out of our way when we are in a hurry, and so on (*ST* I-II 47.2).

10. Nancy Ellen Abrams and Joel R. Primack make an interesting case for thinking of subsequent cosmologies as "encompassing" rather than "overthrowing" earlier cosmologies, including the medieval ("Scientific Revolutions in Cosmology: Overthrowing vs. Encompassing," http://physics.ucsc.edu/cosmo/primack_abrams/htmlformat/SciRevolutionsinCosm.html (accesed on May 13, 2009).

11. See, for example, Lynn White Jr., "The Historical Roots of our Ecological Crisis," *Science*, 155 (March 10, 1969), 1203–7. See also an environmental ethical defense of a broadly Thomistic conception of the rational order of nature by Willis Jenkins, "Biodiversity and Salvation: Thomistic Roots for Environmental Ethics," *Journal of Religion* 83, no. 3 (2003): 401–20.

12. *ST* I 80.1; *Truth* 25.1.

13. *Truth* 22.1. Aquinas uses the terms *appetere* and *tendere* very broadly to indicate the forms of tending that characterize any and all existing things.

14. *Truth* 21.2.

15. *Truth* 25.2. To say that a thing *tends* to obtain what is suitable does not necessarily mean that the thing is likely, in fact, to obtain what is suitable; it simply means that the thing is *oriented* in a certain way, to behave in a certain fashion, under certain conditions.

16. Every existing thing exists with reference to other existing things in a fundamentally interactive cosmos: "Inasmuch as it is characteristic of any being, whether material or immaterial, to have some reference to something else, it accordingly follows that it pertains to everything whatever to have an appetite, natural or animal or rational (that is, intellectual); but in different beings it is found in different ways" (*Truth* 23.1). As Richard Baker notes, "the constant movement which characterizes this world of *ens mobile* is a sign of the initial lack of full perfection suffered by each creature. . . . The creature is given the perfection of existence and is endowed with various powers; but it must exercise these powers to secure from outside itself those things which can actualize its natural capacities" (*The Thomistic Theory of the Passions and Their Influence upon the Will*, 3).

17. *Truth* 22.1.

18. In Aquinas's view, human beings have internal principles that order them toward their own perfection. However, humans also possess inherited and acquired tendencies to act in ways that are inconsistent with these principles. Aquinas recognizes and wrestles with the problem of evil. What he says about goodness and order must be qualified by reflection on the destructive power of natural evil, moral evil, and sin. However, I must leave it to others to explore the implication of his doctrine of sin for his theory of emotion.

19. *ST* I-II 25–28.

20. Aquinas notes that the presence of love is most evident when it finds expression in *desire* (*ST* I-II 25.2 *ad* 1).

21. *ST* I 20.1 *sc* and *ad* 3.

22. *Truth* 27.2.

23. *Truth* 22.1.

24. *ST* I-II 109.3. *Appetere* can also be translated "to tend." For our purposes, tending does not necessarily involve actively desiring and seeking, although it can. See chapter 6.

25. Ibid. See also *ST* I 60.5 *ad* 1.

26. *ST* I 59.1.

27. *Truth* 25.2.

28. Aquinas, *Commentary on Aristotle's "De Anima,"* sect. 347.

29. In Aquinas's view, plant souls and animal souls (unlike the intellectual souls of humans, following death) cannot exist apart from the matter they inform. They are simply the principles by virtue of which certain bodies are alive and have the form (and thus the capabilities) they have. See part II of Aquinas's *Commentary on Aristotle's "De Anima."*

30. A human being and a banana share about half of the same genes, which drives home how many of the life-sustaining processes of humans and plants involve the same biochemical pathways.

31. Technically, for Aquinas, a dead plant is no longer a plant, just as a human body after death is no longer a human being, but rather a corpse that used to be a human being. See chapter 4.

32. *ST* I 22.2, 49.2.

33. Aquinas, *Commentary on Aristotle's "De Anima,"* sects. 289–91.

34. Hence, we commonly say that a person who is in a coma, who can be fed and hydrated only via tubes, is in a vegetative state.

35. *Truth* 22.3.

36. According to Aquinas, an animal begins (in its earliest stages of development) with a vegetative soul—a principle of vegetative life. A sensory soul "supplants" the vegetative soul when the organism develops physiologically to the point that its body can support the activities or capabilities that are definitive of sensory life. "When a more perfect form supervenes," he says, "the previous form is corrupted: yet so that the supervening form contains the perfection of the previous form, and something in addition" (*ST* I 118.2 *ad* 2; see also *ST* I 76.3 *ad* 3, and Aquinas, *Commentary on Aristotle's "De Anima,"* sect. 262).

37. Aquinas, *Commentary on Aristotle's "De Anima,"* sect. 255.

38. *Truth* 22.1–22.2, 22.4.

39. A sensible object is simply an object that is capable of being sensed by an entity with sensory powers.

40. *Truth* 25.1.

41. Aquinas wrote at a time when there was no disciplinary distinction between philosophy (*qua* humanistic inquiry) and psychology (*qua* science). It is important for

our purposes to keep in mind that he is engaged primarily in what we would call philosophical inquiry, and so are we. One could try to map his interior senses to the perceptual and cognitive powers that have been identified and labeled in different ways by scientists who work experimentally with humans or other animals. This would be a valuable thing to do, but it would take us beyond the limits of our present inquiry. The point here is mainly to identify generally (albeit with Aquinas's labels) some ways of acquiring and processing sensory information, some of which Aquinas, and most of us today, would take to be common to human and at least some nonhuman animals, and some of which most of us would presume to be peculiar to mature and healthy humans. Aquinas and we could be wrong in our thinking about what humans and other animals do and do not have in common. Some people seem to sell certain nonhuman animals short, presuming for example that cows do not feel sorrow when they are forcibly separated from their calves; other people perhaps overestimate what is going on in the minds of certain nonhuman animals in ways that resemble the projection of celebrity human voices onto animal characters in children's movies. The main point, however, is that most of the animals that Aquinas, and most of us today, would identify as "human" have (or are likely to acquire) powers that Aquinas associates with the intellect, including the power to conceive the ideas of individual and communal flourishing, the power to desire what promotes both sorts of flourishing, and the power to deliberate and choose to act in ways that are likely to promote such flourishing. Most of the animals that we would identify as "nonhuman" lack these powers.

42. *ST* I-II 22.3. See also *Truth* 26.3.
43. *ST* I 78.3.
44. *ST* I 78.4.
45. *ST* I 78.4 *ad* 1.
46. *ST* I 78.4 *ad* 2.
47. Ibid.
48. Aquinas, *Commentary on Aristotle's "De Anima,"* Lecture III.
49. *ST* I 78.4 *ad* 2.
50. *Truth* 15.2 *ad* 7.
51. *ST* I 78.4.
52. *Truth* 15.2 *ad* 7.
53. *ST* I 78.4.
54. Ibid.
55. Ibid.
56. Ibid.
57. See Aquinas, *Commentary on Aristotle's "De Anima,"* sect. 398.
58. *Truth* 24.2. Notably, Aquinas uses the same term "judgment" (*iudicium*) to refer to acts of both intellectual and sensory judgment. I think this is fitting. Ordinary observation suggests that many animals make judgments that resemble basic human judgments (e.g., "danger!" when a car is speeding by), even if those animals do not also make intellectual judgments that involve an appeal to universals ("I'll be run over by that car if I don't get off the road!"). At issue, of course, is where one draws the line

regarding the sorts of judgments of which various animals are capable. It is difficult to characterize any nonhuman animal judgment without putting it into human language, which naturally creates the impression that the judgment involves an appeal to universals. For good discussions of the sorts of judgments of which various nonhuman animals are capable, with reference to the issue of language, see MacIntyre, *Dependent Rational Animals*, and Midgley, *Beast and Man*.

59. *Truth* 24.2. See also *ST* I 78.4, and Aquinas, *Commentary on Aristotle's "De Anima*,*"* sect. 397.

60. Damasio, *Descartes' Error*, 114–18.

61. Damasio, *Looking for Spinoza*, 60.

62. *ST* I 78.4.

63. Ibid.

64. There are many dimensions to the power to apprehend natural beauty, including some that are intellectual. Yet I take it that a simple apprehension of "proportion" among the parts of a sensible object constitutes a way of apprehending its beauty.

65. *ST* I 78.4, including *ad* 5. See chapter 7.

66. *ST* I 81.3. See Pasnau, *Thomas Aquinas on Human Nature*, 253–57.

67. Aquinas, *Commentary on Aristotle's "De Anima*,*"* sect. 397; see also *ST* 81.3.

68. *ST* I 78.4 *ad* 5.

69. *ST* I 78.4.

70. *Truth* 10.2.

71. *ST* I 78.4.

72. Aquinas says that a human being "has not only memory . . . but also 'reminiscence' by syllogistically, as it were, seeking for a recollection of the past by the application of individual intentions" (*ST* I 78.4). For further study of the interior senses see Aquinas's *Commentary on Aristotle's "De Anima."* See also Pasnau, *Thomas Aquinas on Human Nature*.

73. See *ST* I 81.2 *ad* 2; *Truth* 25.2. We will analyze the irascible and the other major form of emotion, the concupiscible, in chapter 6.

74. *ST* I 81.2; I-II 23.1.

75. *ST* I 78.4.

76. *ST* 81.2 *ad* 2.

77. *ST* I 81.2.

78. *ST* I-II 23.1.

79. *ST* I 81.2.

80. *Truth* 25.6 *ad* 3.

81. *ST* I 81.2 *ad* 2; *Truth* 25.2.

82. *Truth* 25.1.

83. See, for example, *ST* I 81.2 *ad* 2.

84. *ST* I 80.1 *ad* 3.

85. *Truth* 25.1.

86. *ST* II-II 141.5 *ad* 1.

87. *ST* I 81.2 *ad* 2.

88. Aquinas does not appear to distinguish between an act of the sensory appetite, such as hunger for food, and a passion of the soul (usually *passio animae*). He does distinguish at *Truth* 26.2 between a passion of the body (*passio corporalis*) and a passion of the soul (here *passio animalis*). It might seem odd to characterize hunger, thirst, or the desire for sexual pleasure as a passion or, in terms of our analysis, an emotion. Keep in mind, however, that an act of the sensory appetite is, by definition, intentional. In order for hunger, thirst, or the desire for sexual pleasure to count as an act of the sensor appetite or an emotion it must be more than a bodily feeling. It must be an interior motion that is directed toward an object that one judges, on a sensory level, to be suitable for one's being. Ordinary observation suggests that hunger, thirst, or the desire for sexual pleasure often has a physiological basis that many emotions lack: Often (but not always), one first becomes aware of a sensation, such as a soreness in one's stomach, and one then imagines something edible, which allows a sensory-appetitive motion for food to arise. With most emotions, one first imagines or becomes aware of a situation of concern, and this apprehension causes an interior motion that has a material element. Nonetheless, once a sensory-appetitive motion for food arises, it appears to be quite similar in structure to an emotion, especially in cases where the appetite for food is not really dependent on particular physiological causes, as when one desires to eat, and all one can think about is food, even though one does not have the familiar sensation in one's stomach that would indicate a need to eat. Love, desire, and delight are three emotions that are analyzed by Aquinas; I will focus on them in chapter 6. For now, using our current understandings of these terms, let us consider that, for some people, the sensory "love" of chocolate, the "desire" to eat it, and the "delight" one experiences in tasting it and feeling it melt in one's mouth are not different in kind from the sensory "love" for another's affection, the "desire" to receive tangible signs of that affection, and the "delight" one experiences in being smiled at, hugged warmly, and told how wonderful one is. I am more interested in highlighting these sorts of similarities than in determining the precise point at which, say, the longing for food or sexual intimacy is not appropriately regarded as an emotion. Unless otherwise indicated, I treat "acts or motions of the sensory appetite" and "emotions" as equivalent.

89. *ST* I-II 28.1 *ad* 2.

90. Aquinas says explicitly that perceiving the "intentions" of friendship and hostility requires an act of the estimative or cogitative power (*Truth* 25.2). These "intentions" can contribute to the objects of concupiscible emotions, such as love and hatred.

91. *ST* I-II 30.3.

92. *ST* I-II 30.3 *ad* 2.

93. *ST* I-II 31.4.

94. *ST* I-II 30.3 *ad* 3. See also I 81.3. Compare *Commentary on Aristotle's "De Anima,"* sect. 825. Aquinas appears in this commentary to agree with Aristotle that "unlike the irascible, [the concupiscible] has no admixture of rationality."

95. *ST* I-II 23.1.

96. *Truth* 25.1; *ST* I 78.4.

97. The difference between the cogitative power in the typical human being and the estimative power in very intelligent nonhuman animals, such as chimpanzees, dolphins, and certain birds, such as parrots, is arguably negligible. I do not see that anything significant is lost with respect to Aquinas's theory of emotion by keeping soft the line of demarcation between the powers of sensory apprehension in rational and in nonrational animals.

CHAPTER SIX

Approaching the Human Sensory Appetite from Below (II)

◆

In Aquinas's view, the sensory appetite "stands midway between [the] natural appetite and the higher, rational appetite, which is called the will."[1] By virtue of the *natural* appetite, an entity "tends to [an] appetible thing without any apprehension of the reason for [the thing's] appetibility; for natural appetite is nothing but an inclination and ordination of the thing to something else which is in keeping with it, like the ordination of a stone to a place below."[2] By virtue of the *will*, a being that has intellectual powers "tends directly to the very reason for appetibility itself in an absolute way. Thus the will tends primarily and principally to goodness itself, or utility, or something like that."[3] By virtue of the will an intellectual being tends, secondarily, "to this or that appetible thing . . . inasmuch as [the thing] shares in the above-mentioned reason."[4] For example, the will orients a human being to seek complete happiness and to do so, in a given situation, partly through the exercise of virtue.

The *sensory* appetite is unique relative to the natural and intellectual appetites. It "tends to the appetible thing itself as containing that which constitutes the reason for its appetibility."[5] Aquinas explains: "[The sensory appetite] does not tend to the reason for the appetibility in itself because the lower appetite does not tend to goodness or utility or pleasure itself, but to *this particular useful or pleasurable thing*. In this respect the [sensory] appetite is lower than the rational appetite. But because [the sensory appetite also] does not tend only to this or only to that thing [irrespective of an apprehension of the thing's appetibility], but to every being which is [apprehended as] useful or pleasurable to it, it is higher than the natural appetite."[6] The sensory appetite orients a being to interact with particular objects that strike it, on a sensory level, as suitable to its being. For example, it orients a being to seek pleasing companions.

A being with both intellectual and sensory powers tends to interact with a given object with regard to the object's intelligibility (its capability of being apprehended by virtue of the intellect) as well as its sensibility (its capability of being apprehended by virtue of the exterior and/or interior senses). A human tends, for example, to judge (on an intellectual level) that it is morally fine to act kindly toward one's companions and toward *this* companion, in particular, even as the human judges (on a sensory level) that this companion is pleasing company. One tends, accordingly, to exercise one's intellectual and sensory appetites at the same time. One is attracted to the goodness of being kind and thus promoting the well-being of self and others, including this particular other, even as one is attracted to sensible features of the particular other and to particular sorts of interactions with him or her. Yet Aquinas identifies emotions fundamentally with motions of the sensory appetite that are evoked by acts of sensory apprehension, and this is where we must begin. Our concern is to explore in greater detail what it means to say that an emotion is a motion of the sensory appetite. Our more specific concern is to analyze a core set of sensory-appetitive motions or emotions identified by Aquinas.

PRELIMINARY POINTS

Three points need to be made before proceeding. First, a sensory-appetitive motion cannot be "in act" if it does not have an object, which is supplied by an act of sensory apprehension. By the same token, a particular sensory-appetitive motion cannot be identified and distinguished from other such motions without reference to its object. It bears emphasizing that a motion of the sensory appetite—and thus an emotion—is *irreducibly* intentional.[7] It is thus misleading to argue, as Shawn Floyd does, that for Aquinas, "'passion' denotes an act of sense appetite which takes place through a bodily change. Emotion, on the other hand, appears [to us] to have a cognitive component— a belief or judgment about some object or state of affairs. . . . I will suggest that what we call emotion consists, for Aquinas, in two separate acts: an act of cognition and a passion."[8] This representation does not capture the fact that a Thomistic passion is intrinsically object-oriented. One might not be fully or explicitly aware of the object of one's emotion, but if one is experiencing an emotion, one has an object of concern in mind.

Similarly, it is misleading to say, as Claudia E. Murphy does, that for Aquinas, "passions are not themselves cognitive states, they are responses to cognitive states. They are attitudes for or against objects that have been perceived and construed as good or bad by cognition. Now most contemporary philosophers interested in the emotions have argued, and I tend to agree, that 'emotions,' whatever else they involve, involve at least cognitive states. So Aquinas's passions don't, on their own, constitute emotions."[9] As I interpret Aquinas, *passiones* and thus emotions are "on their own" intentional.[10] It is true that an emotion is not itself an act of sensory apprehension, but an emotion relies on an act (or process) of sensory apprehension *at all times* in order to be what it is, namely, an appetitive motion that is about something in particular. One could say that an emotion includes, but is not reducible to, an act of sensory apprehension. In any case, if one loses the defining apprehension, one loses the emotion itself.

Second, an emotion is a mode of tending. With respect to the sensory appetite, tending is construed by Aquinas as a *passive* act or operation of the embodied soul. It is passive partly because it involves suffering bodily changes.[11] It is passive also because it involves being acted upon by an "agent" of change.[12] The agent or formal cause of an emotion is an object of sensory apprehension. A given object could simply be a product of one's imagination. (Even when one deliberately conjures up an object, one is technically passive with respect to the way that object affects one's appetite.) Yet the objects of most emotions are situations in one's life that involve persons and things that have some objective reality. In other words, what one has in mind while undergoing an emotion is usually something that is caused, in part, by actual objects with properties that are capable of being sensed.[13]

Given that acts of emotional tending are caused by objects in one's mind that generally relate to situations in one's extramental world, it is to be expected that Aquinas would characterize such acts in passive terms: A sensory being is drawn toward an object that appears to be good or repulsed by an object that appears to be evil. Yet Aquinas characterizes such acts also in active terms: A sensory being reaches out toward a good object or recoils or turns away from an evil object. This use of active language might appear inconsistent, but it is unavoidable and appropriate. Many emotions involve feeling that one is reaching out toward something interiorly or turning away from it. Aquinas recognizes this. However, he holds that one is made to feel that one is moving in one direction or another by the object of one's apprehension. Again, remove the object from one's mind, and one loses the emotion.

With respect to the intellectual domain, humans have some power to consent to an emotion or to withhold consent. We have some power to direct our imagination so as to view a particular object from a different angle and reconsider its significance for us. We can redirect our imagination in ways that we know, from experience, are likely to make us feel one way or another. We thus have the power to become active, in certain respects, in determining how we are moved. Nonetheless, it is an object of sensory apprehension that evokes and defines the interior motions about which we can and must make choices. I do not want to get bogged down at this point with a discussion of the factors, beyond particular acts of sensory apprehension, that cause an emotion to form and unfold as it does. I simply want to follow Aquinas's lead in using both passive and active language to describe acts of sensory-appetitive tending. When I speak of "active, directional tending," I have in mind acts of the sensory appetite that feel like actively reaching out toward, actively turning from, or the like, even though such acts are technically passive.

Third, even as we recognize that Aquinas often uses active language to refer to acts of the sensory appetite, we need to understand that not all acts of sensory-appetitive tending involve (what feels like) actively reaching or recoiling or even being attracted or repulsed. Often we stand in relationships of tending with objects that are already present to us, either because they are, in some respect, part of us or because we have sought and achieved a desired union with them. I use the term "tending" in a broad and flexible way to refer to appetitive tendencies of any kind, including the tendency to be a certain sort of entity that typically behaves in certain ways, and the activation of a specific tendency in a particular situation. Thus a sensory being has the tendency to enjoy interacting with objects that help it to actualize its potential, and it actually enjoys beneficial interactions.

Finally, in many texts of Aquinas concerning motions of the sensory appetite, *passiones*, or emotions, Aquinas implies that these object-oriented motions are common to nonhuman and human animals.[14] In his most mature and detailed analysis of particular emotions, in the *prima secundae* of the *Summa theologiae*, the subject of the emotion is frequently not specified. One simply reads in the text about how the sensory appetite (itself) is moved in one way or another, irrespective of the sort of being in which the appetite operates. Aquinas's examples do become more human-centered in this part of the *Summa*. This makes sense, given that his analysis of emotion follows a discussion of the structure of human action and precedes a discussion of habits and virtues—and given that the audience of the *Summa* is most interested in emotions as they bear on the exercise of virtue and the realization of human happiness.

Here I continue to represent the subject of a sensory-appetitive motion as a sensory being, sometimes nonhuman and sometimes human. As we turn to analyses of specific emotions, it is good to keep in view the forms these emotions appear to take in many nonhuman animals. Yet it is also important to have our own and each other's human emotions in perspective as we interpret and consider the merits of Aquinas's analysis. While nonhuman and human versions of basic emotions have much the same structure (which is why they can be and often are called by the same names), we should expect the level of detail and complexity in the intentional content of these emotions to differ considerably, depending on whether an object is apprehended by a nonhuman animal or by a human animal. Most humans do not function simply on the sensory level, and even on that level they are ordinarily influenced by the power of the intellect, as Aquinas tries to capture with reference to the cogitative power.

MODES OF TENDING

Aquinas holds that the "common act of the appetitive power" is "to tend."[15] The "common act" of the sensory appetite, in particular, is to tend in relation to an object of sensory apprehension.

There are two other specific powers of the sensory appetite that make sensory-appetitive tending possible. An animal has one power by which it "is simply inclined to seek what is suitable, according to the senses, and to fly from what is hurtful, and this is called the concupiscible."[16] The concupiscible power makes it possible for an animal to undergo concupiscible emotions. An animal also has a second power, which comes into play when it encounters difficulties or obstacles in tending toward what is suitable and away from what is hurtful. This is the irascible power, which makes it possible for an animal to resist, attack, or overcome what hinders it.[17] This power makes it possible for an animal to undergo irascible emotions. Concupiscible and irascible emotions are distinguished chiefly with respect to the formal objects that evoke and define them. The object of a concupiscible motion is a "sensible good or evil, simply apprehended as such," and the object of an irascible motion is "this very good or evil, inasmuch as it is of an arduous or difficult nature."[18]

By virtue of the concupiscible power, an animal tends *toward* what it apprehends as good and pleasant and *away from* what it apprehends as evil and painful.[19] Aquinas notes that nonhuman animals are ordinarily on target in their sensory judgments about what is, in fact, good or bad for them.[20] For example, if a nonhuman animal apprehends that an object is suitable for eating, it usually *is* suitable for eating. Humans have similar powers of discrimination, and these usually serve us well. If they did not, we would not survive for long. At the same time, however, humans have the tendency to misjudge the suitability of some objects. For example, some of us judge, on a sensory level, that it is suitable to continue eating large quantities of unhealthy food, even though doing so makes us fat or sick. How is it that we come to such distorted judgments? How is it that we sometimes seek to clarify the truth of the matter, through the use of reason, but even after we recognize intellectually that something is bad for us, we continue to judge it attractive on a sensory level, and we continue to tend toward it? I touched on this issue in chapter 3 and will explore it a bit further in later chapters, but I cannot do it justice in this book. For now, let us simply note that it is possible for humans to tend by virtue of the sensory appetite toward what is, in fact, bad for us. Yet the point remains that within the sensory domain we tend toward what we *apprehend* (rightly or wrongly) to be good or suitable for us and away from what we *apprehend* (rightly or wrongly) to be evil or unsuitable.[21]

Motions of the concupiscible appetite are distinguished in terms of "the contrariety of [their] objects," namely, with respect to whether the motion regards (what the animal takes to be) a good or an evil, and thus whether the motion is a tending-toward or a tending-away-from.[22] Various concupiscible appetitive motions are distinguished also inasmuch as they are "referred in different ways to the same object, or in other words according to the different stages that can be considered in the course of an appetitive movement."[23] Aquinas identifies three stages or moments of tending that can occur with a concupiscible motion. More specifically, he identifies three moments that can occur in the course of tending toward an object that is apprehended as suitable, and three moments that can occur in the course of tending away from an object that is apprehended as unsuitable. He associates each of these moments—in regard to both the suitable and the unsuitable—with a particular motion, and gives it its own name. This yields six distinct but related concupiscible emotions. I want to examine these emotions and some of their relationships, focusing first on emotions that concern what one judges to be straightforwardly good or suitable, and second on emotions that concern what one judges to be straightforwardly evil or unsuitable. Finally, I turn to the irascible power and the more complex emotions that *it* makes possible.

CONCUPISCIBLE EMOTION: DESIRE

Aquinas says that when an animal apprehends a sensible object that it takes to be suitable to it in some respect,

> the pleasurable object is first united [in some way, *aliqualiter*] with the [one] who seeks it, by being apprehended as like him or agreeable to him. From this there follows the passion of love, which is nothing but the specifica-

tion of the appetite by the form of the appetible object. For that reason love is said to be a sort of union of the lover with the beloved. But what has . . . been united [in this way] is sought further with a view to its being united [in reality], so that the lover enjoys the possession of the beloved. Thus is born the passion of desire, which, when the object has been obtained in reality, begets joy.[24]

This description appears to call attention to a three-fold motion as it occurs in humans, but the same three-fold structure is present in the concupiscible motions of nonhuman animals.

The moment in this process with which it is most fruitful to begin is the middle one, namely, desire (*desiderium*).[25] This is the moment of active, directional tending in relation to something from which one is separated.[26] When a nonhuman or human animal apprehends a sensible object as suitable for it in some respect, the animal is typically drawn toward the object interiorly.[27] In some cases, the animal also approaches the object exteriorly or bodily (if the animal is mobile) by moving in the object's direction. When one notices an animal moving intently toward an object, one usually posits an interior cause of the motion. One posits a desire that can explain why the animal is approaching this object, at this time, in this manner. For Aquinas, a desire is thus defined partly with reference to its typical outward expression.[28] It is defined with reference to what the desire motivates an animal to do. As Aristotle says, "whatever a thing chiefly desires this it will do."[29] Often when Aquinas refers to the motion of an animal, it is unclear whether he has in mind the exterior motion of the body (the motion of the limbs or locomotion) or the interior motion of desire. The ambiguity reveals the intimate connection between these forms of motion, each of which is best understood in relation to the other.

For Aquinas, as for Aristotle, a sensory desire is an interior principle that sometimes imparts exterior motion.[30] It is more specifically a principle that sometimes imparts motion or action *for an end*. On a sensory level, acting for an end does not imply acting *for a reason* as determined by an operation of the intellect, for that sort of action is reserved for a being in respect of his or her intellectual appetite. On a sensory level, acting for an end simply implies acting because one apprehends as attractive the prospect of uniting or interacting in some way with a sensible object. Ordinarily, an animal seeks to unite with an object by acting on the object and/or allowing itself to be acted upon, such that the animal is perfected in some respect.[31]

Notice that the intentional object of a sensory desire can be specified in more or less specific ways. One is attracted to a particular object because it appears to be good or attractive. More specifically, one is attracted to particular *properties* of the object. More specifically yet, one is attracted to the prospect of *uniting* with that object in respect of its attractive properties. For example, one might be attracted to one's friend, attracted to the prospect of being with one's friend, attracted to the pleasantness of the friend's company, and attracted to the end of enjoying the friend's company in a particular shared activity. We can continue to be flexible in referring to an object of a sensory-appetitive motion.

A sensory desire sometimes functions as a principle of animal behavior; yet a sensory desire is more than a causal principle. It is also, for Aquinas, a state of the soul. It is an interior motion that is ordinarily experienced by a subject of awareness. One can characterize a sensory desire as a psychological state as long as one keeps in mind that it is fundamentally sensory. Experiencing a sensory desire usually involves having before one's mind an object that is present to one's exterior senses, or having in mind an object that is present to one's imagination, but has a relationship to something outside one's mind. It usually involves judging that it would be good to unite with that object in a more tangible way and feeling an interior pull toward that union. If one imagines a more tangible union, one might also imagine the outward motion required to bring it about. Yet a sensory desire does not necessarily give rise to outward motion. It can be helpful to approach a desire from the perspective of its typical outward expression, but a desire is itself a form of interior motion.

A sensory desire is a state of the soul, but it is more precisely a state of the soul-body composite.[32] As we know, Aquinas holds that acts of sensory apprehension and appetite both involve "bodily transmutation."[33] When we think of a sensory desire as a state of being and feeling drawn toward an object interiorly, we must therefore think of it partly as a matter of undergoing corresponding physiological changes. These changes can be considered with respect to the way that they prepare an animal's body for action or outward motion. They can be considered also with respect to the way they feel from the inside. Relatively significant and unusual physiological changes will be noticeable in the form of bodily sensations or a generalized feeling of bodily pleasure (or the reduction of pain).

What, more precisely, is the relationship between the feeling of being attracted to a suitable object—being attracted to a suitable union with a particular agent of change—and the bodily changes that compose the material element of that attraction? I interpret Aquinas to hold that a sensory desire cannot be reduced in definition to a change in the subject's body, nor can it be reduced to the feeling of a bodily change (a bodily sensation) or the feeling of pleasure that attends a bodily change. If a desire were simply a *change in the body*, the desire would not be *about* anything. Yet a desire *is* about something; it is directed toward an object or an end that is apprehended in a certain way. If a sensory desire were simply the *feeling* of a bodily change or the *pleasure* of such a change, one would expect an animal's focus during an episode of desire to be on its own body or sensations, rather than on the object, the apprehension of which evoked the bodily changes and sensations. This is not ordinarily what happens. A sensory desire is usually *accompanied* by an awareness of corresponding bodily changes, and the awareness of these changes becomes part of the experience of a desire; yet the intentional focus of a sensory desire is on an apparent good, the apprehension of which elicited the desire in the first place and continues to direct one's appetite.[34] The pleasure that one experiences, as one is drawn toward this good, is principally that—the pleasure of being drawn toward what one takes to be a suitable union.[35]

Some of us might find it strange to characterize sensory desire as an emotion. In my view it is a positive feature of Aquinas's account that it displays the structural similarity and also the similarity in experience, on a sensory level, between, say, desiring a cold glass of water on a hot summer day and desiring the physical company of one's partner in life (whom one also desires on an intellectual level, in a way that involves wishing the other well for his or her own sake). Some readers might want to limit the sorts of unions that can count as objects of emotion, so that one can be moved, emotionally, by the prospect of indulging one's thirst for good company, but one cannot be moved, emotionally, by the prospect of quenching one's thirst for water, but at this point it is instructive to keep the range open.[36]

Some of us might wish to call the emotion of sensory desire, as described above, by the name "love." As we are about to see, however, Aquinas intends something more specific by the emotion of love. Whereas desire is a mode of tending in relation to an object that is apprehended as separate from us, love is a mode of tending in relation to something that is, in a sense, present to us from the start, as soon as it engages our awareness and our appetite. It is easy to confuse desire and love because love is most evident when it gives rise to the experience of (what we are calling) active, directional tending.[37] Yet we need to grasp the distinction between these two forms of interior motion and reflect on their relationship.

CONCUPISCIBLE EMOTION: LOVE

Sensory desire is the second moment in the course of tending toward an object that one apprehends to be good or suitable. As such, it presupposes a

prior act of the sensory appetite. Aquinas says that when an animal apprehends an object as suitable, the object "introduces itself, as it were, into [the
animal's] intention,"[38] and this introduction "causes [first], in the appetitive
power, a certain inclination, aptitude or connaturalness in respect of [that
object]."[39] Before the object arouses a desire—an appetitive motion of reaching out toward the object interiorly (and perhaps also outwardly or behav-
iorally)—the object causes a simple "aptitude to tend to the [object]."[40]
Aquinas says that this "first change wrought in the appetite by the appetible
object is called love [amor], and is nothing else than complacency [compla-
centia] in that object."[41] He also says that "every movement towards something, or rest in something, arises from some kinship or aptness to that thing;
and in this does love consist."[42] Again, "whatever tends to an end has, in the
first place, an aptitude or proportion to that end, for nothing tends to a dis-
proportionate end. . . . And this very aptitude or proportion of the appetite
to good is love, which is complacency in good."[43]

What does it mean to say that an animal's sensory appetite acquires an
"aptitude" or "proportion" to an object of sensory apprehension? What is it
for an animal's appetitive power to be "complacent" in an object? As we have
seen, every existing entity has the tendency to interact with other entities in
ways that are suitable to its nature. Recall the example of the stone. When
a stone is lifted off the ground, we can say (metaphorically) that it has the desire to return to the earth. If the stone is released, and nothing else inter-
feres, the stone will return to its (relative) resting place. In Aquinas's view,
this desiring and physical moving presuppose something about the nature of
the stone. They presuppose that the stone has a tendency or aptitude, by
virtue of its own principles (considered in relation to the principles of the
earth and of nature generally) to relate to the earth as its home. This aptitude defines the being and the behavior of the stone at all times, whether it
happens to be at home or is separated from its home. By virtue of this aptitude, the stone is said to love the earth.

An animal, in respect of its materiality, also has a natural appetite for the
earth. Moreover, as a sensory being it has an appetite for what it apprehends
via the use of its sensory powers to be suitable for it. Consider a sensory-
appetitive act of hunger. An animal desires to unite with a particular object—
say, a piece of meat—when the object is present to the animal's sensory
awareness, and the animal is drawn inwardly toward the object and perhaps
also engages in outward motion aimed at eating the object. Yet for Aquinas,
the animal desires this object in this way because it has internal principles
that make it fit for uniting with objects of this kind. The object, in turn, has
its own principles that make it fit for functioning as a source of nutrition for

certain animals. An animal (such as a wolf) is by nature fitted to specific sorts of sensible objects (such as sheep) as predator to prey, in a way that other animals (such as bluebirds) are not fitted to the same objects, and in a way that the first animal (the wolf) is not fitted to other objects (such as stones). We can say, accordingly, that a wolf has a natural love for sheep (*qua* prey), and that the being and the behavior of the wolf are determined by this love at all times, whether or not it has a particular sheep in mind.

However, when a wolf becomes aware of a particular sheep, the sheep makes it possible for the wolf to have a specific sensory-appetitive motion of love in relation to that sheep. The wolf's apprehension of the sheep causes the wolf's appetite to become tuned to the possibility of a suitable union with the sheep. The object of apprehension does not yet cause the wolf to approach the sheep in desire or action; it simply makes that motion possible by making the sheep appear to the wolf as something in relation to which an attractive union (namely, pleasant eating and the satiation of hunger) is possible. Aquinas says that love is "nothing but the specification of the appetite by the form of the appetible object."[44]

What more can we say about this "specification" of the sensory appetite, this "being made fit" to tend toward a particular union with another, this "aptitude" that is more precisely a "being made apt" in one's appetitive dimension to relate to a sensible object in a particular way? This specification must involve something more than having an object in mind, for the latter is technically an act of apprehension, not appetite. This specification must also be more than an abstract appetitive "change" that functions as a "principle" for the motion of desire.[45] Indeed, these are terms that Aquinas uses to refer to love; yet he also notes that love is a sensory-appetitive motion in its own right.[46] Can we identify anything in experience that corresponds to this motion or emotion? It is easy to identify in experience the interior motion of desire, but what about this prior motion of love?

We can begin by characterizing sensory love as a state of the soul in which we have an impression that that there is a "likeness of proportion" (a fitting relationship) between a sensible object and ourselves.[47] In love, we apprehend that some object of experience is such that we are capable of acting on it, being acted upon by it, or interacting with it, in ways that allow us to be ourselves and to actualize some of our potential. In this sort of love we feel, moreover, comfortable in relation to the object. We appreciate the way in which it stands in relation to us. Consider, for example, the sensory love that one might experience in apprehending one's child. Sometimes, when the child comes to one's awareness, one experiences an appetitive change, but this change does not (yet) amount to a desire to do anything in particular; it is not (yet) a tending toward some sort of (further) union. It is simply the feeling of recognizing and appreciating the way in which the child is already, in a sense, part of oneself. In being who he or she is, the child allows one to be and to become more fully one's own (relational) self.[48]

We commonly say we love another person even when we are not undergoing a particular appetitive motion of (in this case) sensory love. In Thomistic terms, we naturally love any person who is like us (with respect to things about ourselves that we like) and also persons who are unlike us (but in ways that bring out the best in us). A particular emotion of love is an activation of this basic tendency. It is an interior change that we typically experience as a change or, more specifically, as a being-changed. Aquinas says that love "denotes that movement whereby the appetite is changed by the appetible object, so as to have complacency therein."[49] Complacency or *complacentia* implies a state of being in agreement with an object in some respect, but it also implies a state of being pleased in the apprehension of this agreement. *Complacentia* has the connotation of resonating pleasantly with an object in its suitability.[50] Love includes the experience of being notably at ease and pleased in the apprehension of a suitable object.[51]

Aquinas says that "love does *not* denote the movement of the appetite in *tending* towards the appetible object," for this is specifically the motion of desire.[52] Yet love is, nonetheless, a form of appetitive motion. I want to characterize it as a mode of tending in its own right, so that it can appear as one among many modes of tending that allow objects to be what thay are and to interact with other objects in relatively well-ordered ways. An emotion of sensory love is a tending in the sense that it is an activation or expression of a tendency to be changed with respect to one's sensory appetite when one apprehends certain objects of apprehension, under certain conditions. In love, the tendency to undergo responsive appetitive motion takes the initial form of resting in the awareness that a perceived object is suitable to oneself. It takes the form of appreciating the object's attractive properties. It takes the form of resonating with pleasure in the presence of an object to which one is already united by a sensible suitability ("connaturalness") and by the apprehension of this suitability.[53]

CONCUPISCIBLE EMOTION: DELIGHT

That the emotion of love is a state of being-pleased-with is evident if one considers the third moment or stage in the course of tending toward a sensible object as a simple good. Just as love can be understood in its relationship to desire, as that which makes a particular motion of desire possible, so love can be understood also from the other side of desire, as it were, in its likeness to the term of desire, which is the joy or sensory delight that accompanies the achievement of a desired union.[54]

Aquinas says that when animals attain an object that they apprehend as suitable to themselves, they perfect themselves in some way; they are thereby "established in [a] state becoming their nature."[55] When this happens, animals tend to be *aware* that they are in a becoming state, "[a]nd from this perception there arises a certain movement of the soul in the sensitive appetite; which movement is called delight [*delectatio*]."[56] In a way, "delight" would seem to name the *cessation* of movement. Aquinas considers the objection that "delight does not consist in being moved, but in having been moved; for it arises from good already gained." His response is that in one sense (execution) motion has ceased in delight, but in another sense (intention) it continues: "For though delight is a certain repose of the appetite, if we consider the presence of the pleasurable good that satisfies the appetite, nevertheless there remains the impression made on the appetite by its object, by reason of which delight is a kind of movement."[57] Although delight would seem to be the end of tending or the coming-to-an-end of an active-tending-toward, it is more precisely the "end" of such tending in the sense of its culmination and completion. In this completion there is still a tending in the sense of an embracing and an enjoying of this completion.

One could say that the "impression made on the appetite by its object" is present not only in the motion of delight, and in the prior motion of desire, but also in the initial motion of love. In love, this impression made on the appetite is a pleasing resonance that occurs when one apprehends an object's suitability relative to oneself (or to another who is part of oneself). The delight that follows desire arises most fully in the "complete establishment" of a suitable union.[58] It arises when one becomes aware of the "real presence of [a] pleasing good."[59] Yet a form of delight or pleasure can accompany the initial impression of an object's fittingness, just as it can accompany the impression that one is borne, in desire, toward a fitting end.[60]

Aquinas speaks of a metaphorical "expansion of the soul," which occurs when a being perceives that it has actualized some potential or "attained a certain perfection."[61] He says that the appetitive power "acquiesces in the pleasurable object, and rests therein, offering, as it were, to enfold [the object] within itself. And thus [one's] affection is expanded by pleasure, as though it surrendered itself to hold within itself the object of its pleasure."[62] I would argue that something like this holding and expanding takes place not only in the motion of delight but also in the initial motion of love. When an animal apprehends an object as suitable for uniting with, the animal rests with pleasure in this apprehension.[63] The soul of the animal (most notably its power to engage objects of sensory experience) becomes "more ample" and "more capacious," and this expanding makes the animal more "[fit] to receive the good which is loved."[64] One can say, then, that love is the activation of one's tendency, as a sensory being, to expand interiorly in relation to an object that is, in certain respects, already active within.

Love and delight are motions of the soul, but they are more specifically motions of the soul-body composite.[65] Again, if the bodily changes that mediate these appetitive motions are relatively out of the ordinary, the changes will be noticeable, and they will likely be noticed by the subject of the changes in the form of bodily sensations or feelings. I take it that these bodily feelings are usually pleasurable; they might take the form of a generalized physical euphoria, a surge in energy, or something more specific. If the bodily sensation is connected in the animal's experience to the apprehension of a possible or actual union with a suitable object, then the sensation will be included in the experience of sensory love or delight. Yet love and delight are not simply bodily sensations. They are body-resonant feelings of being moved interiorly in relation to an object of apprehension.

In summary, love, desire, and delight are three moments that commonly occur in the course of tending toward what one apprehends as suitable for oneself or for those to whom one is attached. Aquinas construes these moments, respectively, as (1) an initial motion of being at ease with, opening to, and being pleased at the impression that a particular object is such that it is possible for one to interact with it in a way that is suitable for oneself; (2) a subsequent motion of actively tending or being drawn toward a union that usually goes beyond mental union; (3) a motion of resting with pleasure and being expanded in the union effected.

Regarding the relations between these moments, an animal can love an object in the sense of enjoying complacency in it, without going on to desire a further sort of union with it. One might, for example, be satisfied simply to hold another being in one's awareness and take pleasure in the perceived proportionality that marks the relationship between the other and oneself. Indeed, animals are oriented to notice and resonate momentarily with many, many sensible objects in their environment that are in a position to perfect them in one way or another, yet animals conceive a much more limited number of desires. A motion of love does not necessarily give rise to a desire, but a desire always presupposes a motion of love. A desire presupposes love at every moment that the desire is in act, such that a desire effectively includes the prior motion of love. An animal does not desire a particular union, on a sensory level, unless the animal recognizes—and continues to recognize—

that the union is suitable, where "recognition" is partly a matter of sensory judgment and partly a matter of appetite (feeling comfortable or pleased in relation to the object).[66] Finally, one can desire a particular union (say, a more tangible union) without doing anything to attain it; moreover, even if one attempts a tangible union, one can fail to achieve it. Complete union with what is truly good for one is necessary for the fullness of sensory delight, but the very apprehension of that union as a possibility and the sense of being drawn toward something good can both yield a kind of delight.

CONCUPISCIBLE EMOTION: AVERSION

Aquinas posits a three-fold structure that is evident, not only with respect to the motions of love, desire, and delight, but also with respect to other appetitive motions, all of which are, in one way or another, related to love, desire, or delight. Specifically, with respect to the concupiscible motions that regard an *evil* simply apprehended as such, he identifies the parallel motions of hatred (*odium*), aversion (*fuga*), and sorrow (*tristitia*).[67] In introducing the triad of love, desire, and delight, we began with the second moment or motion. This is the most fruitful way to approach the second triad as well.

Aquinas does not devote a section of the *Summa theologiae* or *Quaestiones disputatae de veritate* to a discussion of sensory aversion. He simply constructs this form of appetitive motion as the contrary of sensory desire.[68] Given this construction, we can say that an aversion is a motion of tending away from a sensible object that one apprehends to be bad or unsuitable for oneself. More specifically, it is a motion of being repelled by, or withdrawing from, the prospect of uniting with an object in a hurtful way and thus being hurt or otherwise diminished. Within the realm of the concupiscible, the object of an appetitive motion is regarded by the subject of the motion as good or evil "simply," rather than as posing a difficulty that requires a spirited response.[69] Hence, in the motion of aversion, the hurtful union is regarded as not being "more than our animal nature can easily . . . avoid."[70] An animal apprehends that some object is present to it in the sense of being near at hand and poised to unite with it in a way that is detrimental to the animal's life, well-being, or pleasure.[71] Under this impression, the animal tends away from the object and the prospect of hurtful union.[72]

An aversion is structurally similar to a desire (as defined above), except that an aversion regards an evil, rather than a good, and it thus involves tending away from the object, rather than toward it. Given this similarity, we can say that an aversion, like a desire, commonly serves as a principle of acting for an end. An aversion commonly causes an animal to act for the end of avoiding a tangible union that is unsuitable for the animal and thus painful. Suppose an animal apprehends an object that appears initially to be edible but, on closer examination, smells rancid. The animal apprehends that uniting with this object (further) by ingesting it would be unsuitable, and the animal is repulsed—it turns its nose and walks away. Or suppose one apprehends another human being to be unpleasant, and the prospect of uniting with the other in face-to-face conversation to be unsuitable. At the sight of the other along the path, one is repulsed, so one takes the long way to one's destination, avoiding contact.

An aversion commonly functions as a principle of aversive action, but one can undergo an aversion without fleeing or showing other external signs of the aversion. An aversion is, more fundamentally, a state of the soul. It is an interior appetitive motion of which an animal is typically aware. Aquinas suggests that an interior motion sometimes *feels* like an interior version of a corresponding exterior act. It is common for a human being, in particular, to construct a pictorial image of his or her own, interior self. It is common to imagine that this self has its own, virtual body, and to imagine this virtual body doing things like beaming and jumping for joy, raising the arms high to the theme from *Rocky*, or cringing and turning away. One would expect a human being who undergoes an interior appetitive motion and imagines this interior self to be engaged in a kind of virtual-bodily expression of that motion to feel somewhat like he or she would feel (or has felt in the past) in exteriorizing that motion or expressing it in act. When speaking of sorrow, for example, Aquinas says that "if the evil which is the cause of sorrow be not so strong as to deprive one of the hope of avoiding it . . . [the soul] retains the movement whereby to repulse that evil. If, on the other hand, the strength of the evil be such as to exclude the hope of evasion, then even the interior movement of the afflicted soul is absolutely hindered, so that it cannot turn aside either this way or that. Sometimes even the external movement of the body is paralyzed, so that [one] becomes completely stupefied."[73] It is as if the sensory powers themselves—or what one experiences to be the seat of those powers—turn this way or that in an attempt to avoid further injury.

CONCUPISCIBLE EMOTION: HATRED

Aquinas has a bit more to say about the prior motion of hatred, which parallels the first moment of the first triad, namely, love. Recall that sensory love is an initial change wrought in the appetite by an object that is apprehended to be good or suitable for the animal. In love, an attractive object "introduces itself" (or the prospect of union with it) into the animal's awareness and gives the animal's appetite, "first, a certain adaptation to [the object or the prospect of union], which consists in complacency . . . ; and from this follows movement toward the appetible object" in the form of desire.[74] Similarly, sensory hatred is an initial change wrought in the appetite by a object that is apprehended to be evil and hurtful. In hatred, a hurtful object (or the prospect of union with it) "introduces itself" into the animal's sensory awareness and causes a "dissonance of the appetite."[75] Commonly, from this dissonance follows an interior motion of tending away from the object.[76]

Hatred is thus a principle of aversion (just as love is a principle of desire). It is a specification of the sensory appetite that we must presuppose if we are to account for the subsequent motion of withdrawing from what is hurtful (which amounts to withdrawing from what is hateful). To have one's appetite specified in the form of hatred is to stand in relation to an object in the mode of disagreement or disharmony: "Now, with regard to the natural appetite, it is evident that just as each thing is naturally attuned and adapted to that which is suitable to it, wherein consists natural love; so it has a natural dissonance from that which opposes and destroys it; and this is natural hatred. So, therefore, in the animal appetite . . . love is a certain harmony [consonantis] of the appetite with that which is suitable; while hatred is dissonance [dissonantia] of the appetite from that which is apprehended as repugnant and hurtful."[77] This disharmony or dissonance is not simply an objective state of affairs in which one entity's appetite to be and to actualize its potential is opposed in a specific respect to another entity's appetite to be and to actualize its own potential. This dissonance is also a state of the soul or a psychological state in which the animal is aware of the unsuitability or ill-fittedness and is uncomfortable with it.[78]

Aquinas notes that animals are usually more aware of being in a state of hatred than they are of being in a state of love: "The unbecomingness of that which is hated is felt more keenly than the becomingness of that which is loved."[79] This is partly because sensory love (as Aquinas defines it) is such a common appetitive motion. An animal is ordered by its interior principles to resonate, to some extent, with most of the objects that it apprehends as suitable. In a world that is fundamentally good and full of attractive possibilities, love tends to become something familiar that is easily taken for granted. When a particular motion of sensory love does come to an animal's awareness, it tends to pass quickly unless the animal undergoes a further motion of desire.[80] By contrast, when an animal apprehends an object as disagreeable, such that being united with the object would hurt or otherwise diminish the animal, the animal readily notices the object and its disagreeableness and feels disturbed.[81]

Consider again the animal that apprehends the rancid food. In spotting the object initially, the animal apprehends it as a possible food item. If the animal did not apprehend the possibility of a fitting union with the item, the animal would not approach it. Yet when the animal actually smells the food, it apprehends that the food is unsuitable for eating, and it is pained at the apprehension. Notice that hatred presupposes love, for "nothing is hated, save through being contrary to a suitable thing which is loved. And hence it is that every hatred is caused by love."[82] In a way, the nasty item has already united with the animal by causing the animal to apprehend it (via the senses of sight and smell) and by becoming an object of the animal's sensory appetite. The animal has been changed interiorly by this initial union, and this change generates (on some level of awareness) a feeling of dissonance. Ordinarily the change also generates a motion of withdrawal or repulsion (and corresponding aversive action), and this sort of motion can dominate the animal's sensory awareness. However, hatred is structurally prior to aversion, and it can be experienced as a appetitive motion in its own right. Even though hatred is not an active-tending-away-from, it is nonetheless a form of tending. It is an activation of a defining tendency that we have as sensory beings to recognize and be pained by objects that are capable of hurting us. In hatred, we are disturbed by what appears to be an unsuitable prospect.

Consider also the human being who imagines meeting up with a disagreeable neighbor and shudders at the scenario. He or she undergoes an appetitive motion of dissonance at the apprehension that the neighbor is a human being with whom he or she is fitted by nature and by circumstance to interact (*qua* human being)—yet this interaction promises to be hurtful. In working with Aquinas's account of emotion, some of us might want to stretch the meaning of hatred to include the subsequent motion of aversion. We might also want to include under the category of hatred some of what Aquinas places under the category of anger.[83] For our purposes, however, it is important to grasp that, in Aquinas's scheme, sensory hatred does not technically describe the interior motion of recoiling from an evil object, or turning toward the object and wanting to destroy it, but rather the simple act of being pained at the apprehension that one stands (in a particular respect) in relation to an object that is poised to actualize (more of) its potential at one's expense—and one is thus poised to be (further) hurt.

Like every other emotion, hatred is a state of the soul-body composite. Aquinas notes that hatred usually involves a stifling of the vital energies of the body. The very act of being pained by a hurtful prospect hinders one's activity to some extent. It hinders one from doing what one would rather be doing, which is resting in and opening to what one judges to be suitable, actively tending toward and pursuing what is suitable, and enjoying that attainment.[84] Yet there are times when sensory hatred, although painful, is a fitting response, in Aquinas's ethical view, namely, when one correctly apprehends a possibility of being acted upon (further) in a notably hurtful way.

CONCUPISCIBLE EMOTION: SORROW

Just as love can be elucidated with reference to the third moment of the first triad, which is delight, so hatred can be elucidated with reference to the third moment of the second triad, which is sorrow. Aquinas says, "Just as two things are requisite for pleasure; namely, conjunction with good and perception of this conjunction; so also two things are requisite for pain; namely, conjunction with some evil (which is [evil insofar as] it deprives one of some good), and perception of this conjunction."[85] As we have seen, there is a relationship that exists between the animal and a given sensible object, whether the animal is aware of the relationship or not, namely, the aptitude of the animal and the object to act on each other—and to be acted upon— in determinate ways. With respect to certain interactions, the aptitude is a negative one for the animal. That is, in some instances the animal stands in relation to an object that has the ability to unite with the animal in ways that injure the animal or deprive it of a good. In hatred, the animal notices the possibility of a hurtful union and is pained by it. In aversion, the animal withdraws from the hurtful prospect interiorly, and it may also be motivated to avoid the prospective union (especially a tangible union) through aversive action. If the "evil conjunction" of an actual union occurs anyway, and the animal is deprived of a good, the animal experiences (more) pain at the awareness of this deprivation.[86] It experiences sorrow.

Aquinas describes this third moment as "like a violent repose."[87] Like delight, sorrow is partly a coming-to-rest or a being-at-rest. Sorrow is a cessation of the motion of withdrawing from and trying to avoid an unsuitable union (if indeed the animal had the opportunity to avoid the union). Yet sorrow is a coming-to-rest that is marked by the impression of an evil that is painfully present in the sense of being fully upon one and not simply close at hand.[88] Sorrow is, in other words, a motion of being-weighed-down, crushed, or "depressed."[89] It is the activation of a tendency, typical of most sensory beings, to be and to feel closed down and dispirited under the impact of something that has injured one. Aquinas explains that "in movements of the appetite pleasure is to sorrow, what, in [animal] bodies, repose is to weariness, which is due to a non-natural transmutation; for sorrow itself implies a certain weariness or ailing of the appetitive faculty."[90]

Sorrow is a painful motion of the soul. As Aquinas says, "We speak of pain of the body, because [or in cases where] the cause of pain is in the body: as when we suffer something hurtful to the body. But the movement of pain is always in the soul; since *the body cannot feel pain unless the soul feel[s] it*, as Augustine says (*Super Psalm*. lxxxvii.4)."[91] In the case of a human being, the sensory awareness of the loss of an important good can so affect the soul that one can become disabled in the use of one's intellect—disabled in one's ability to think clearly about the loss or about anything else—and one can succumb to "melancholy or madness."[92] As a motion of the soul-body composite, sorrow has a material element. Aquinas notes that even well-ordered sorrow diminishes the "vital movement" of the body. Excessive sorrow can literally paralyze a sensory being and keep it from seeking and enjoying what is suitable.[93]

In summary, hatred, aversion, and sorrow form a triad parallel to love, desire, and delight. Hatred, aversion, and sorrow are three moments in what is commonly a seamless process of tending. The process includes (1) an initial motion of being uncomfortable with or disturbed by the sensory impression that one stands in a disharmonious or injurious relationship to an object, and one is poised to be (further) united with that object in a way that is hurtful to oneself; (2) a subsequent motion of recoiling or withdrawing interiorly, and perhaps also in the form of bodily motion, from the prospect of (further) union with the object; and (3) a motion of being (further) pained if the (further) hurtful union occurs anyway. As with the first triad, so with the second: aversion always presupposes hatred, but hatred might or might not yield the subsequent motion of aversion; aversion might or might not issue forth in aversive action; and aversive action might or might not be successful. If the union that one regards as hurtful occurs, and the union *is* hurtful, then sorrow results. One could say that there is a dimension of sorrow—a painful dissonance—present at every stage of this process. Being gripped by the prospect of a hurtful union and feeling impelled to avoid that union are themselves disturbing.[94]

There are six basic concupiscible emotions. Each of them is an object-oriented appetitive motion or a mode of appetitive tending. Relative to desire, love and delight appear as forms of being-at-rest; they appear as forms of premotion and postmotion, respectively. Yet they do involve a kind of motion. They are activations of the tendency that sensory beings have to be comfortable and to open with pleasure in relation to what appears suitable. The same applies to hatred and sorrow. They, too, involve interior motion. They are activations of the tendency to be uncomfortable, to close down, and to feel weighed down in relation to what appears unsuitable. This is an important point, for many theorists of emotion deny that emotions are appropriately construed as forms of appetite or desire because some emotions do not involve wanting or seeking anything. According to Aquinas, it is true that not all motions of the sensory appetite are specifically acts of desire or aversion, but they are nevertheless appetitive motions.

IRASCIBLE EMOTIONS: HOPE AND DESPAIR

As noted earlier, Aquinas divides the power of the sensory appetite into two parts, namely, the concupiscible and the irascible. By virtue of the concupiscible power, an animal tends "simply" toward an object (or union with an object) that the animal apprehends as suitable, and an animal tends "simply" away from an object (or union) that it apprehends as unsuitable. The moments of desire and aversion are taken as central, and the appetitive motions on either side of them are understood with reference to these central moments. By virtue of the irascible power, an animal tends in ways that are more complex. An act or motion of the irascible appetite takes as its intentional object something that an animal apprehends as suitable or unsuitable, but it takes as its object more specifically something suitable or unsuitable that the animal apprehends "under the aspect of difficulty or arduousness."[95] An irascible motion is spirited.[96] It is a motion whereby an animal "[resists] . . . corruptive and contrary agencies which are a hindrance to the acquisition of what is suitable, and are productive of harm."[97] The irascible is "the champion and defender of the concupiscible" in that the irascible power makes it possible for an animal to "overcome and rise above obstacles" in achieving what it regards as good and avoiding what it regards as evil.[98] Aquinas identifies several irascible motions or emotions. Each of them regards one or another sensible object (or union) that is apprehended to be good or evil (or both); each of them regards one or another sort of difficulty; and each of them tends in one direction or another (or both) relative to the object and/or the difficulty at issue.

One sort of irascible motion arises when an animal apprehends a sensible object (or union) as *good, but difficult to attain*. Implicit in this description is the notion that the object in question has not yet been attained, nor is it close at hand in the way that the object of a sensory desire is close at hand. The object has the property of being future (perhaps far in the future). It also has the property of being beyond the animal's usual abilities to attain.[99] Yet the object appears to the animal to be attainable—with considerable effort. Inasmuch as the animal apprehends the object in question as a good, it tends toward the object. Inasmuch as the animal apprehends the object as so good that it is worth overcoming obstacles to attain, the animal undergoes a specifically irascible motion. It becomes energized and tends toward the object despite the struggle involved. The struggle itself usually appears under the aspect of evil; it is a source of pain for the animal.[100] Yet the struggle appears also under the aspect of good inasmuch as the animal finds it invigorating to rise to a challenge.[101] The focus of the animal's attention during this sort of appetitive motion is primarily on the good to be attained, rather than on the difficulty of attaining it. Aquinas calls this irascible emotion "hope" (*spes*).

An animal's assessments of the difficulties it faces—and its ability to respond to these difficulties—make a big difference to the appetitive motions that arise in response to a sensory apprehension. A second sort of irascible motion (which Aquinas constructs as contrary to the first) arises when an animal apprehends an object (or union) as *good, but impossible to attain*. Inasmuch as an animal apprehends a good object as impossible to attain, the animal apprehends a good under the aspect of evil. It thus tends away from what one would otherwise expect it to approach.

In order for Aquinas to be consistent with his general description of the irascible, he needs to say that this interior withdrawing from an impossible good involves a kind of struggle—a "tendency to overcome and rise above obstacles."[102] I take him to have something like the following in mind. To say that an animal withdraws from a good *qua* impossible to attain implies that at some point the animal approached that good with the impression that it might be possible to attain.[103] If the animal apprehended and accepted the object's unattainability from the start, it would never have approached the object with such high energy, and it would not now be in the position of having to withdraw all of that energy.[104] Reversing the course of its appetitive tending is arduous enough. Inasmuch as the animal retains even a glimmer of hope—inasmuch as the animal is unable fully to accept that the good in question is impossible to attain—its tending-away becomes more arduous still. Hope itself becomes an obstacle that must be overcome if the animal is not to be tortured by continuing to reach out interiorly for what is impossible. Inasmuch as the animal, at any point in its withdrawing, re-apprehends the object *as* a good, without focusing on its unattainability, the animal is to some extent re-attracted to the object, and this creates a new obstacle for what might otherwise be a straightforward withdrawal.[105] Aquinas calls this irascible emotion "despair" (*desperatio*).

An animal's assessments of its chances of attaining a difficult good can shift—and shift repeatedly—due to changes in circumstance and changes in what the animal imagines to be possible. An animal can thus fluctuate between corresponding sorts of irascible motions, namely, motions that regard the object as good, possible, but difficult to attain (by which the animal tends primarily toward the object) and motions that regard the object as good, but impossible to attain and thus bad in this impossibility (by which the animal tends primarily away from the object). It is especially in cases of shifting circumstance and judgment that the emotion of despair has the quality of being arduous and involving struggle, rather than simple resignation.

IRASCIBLE EMOTIONS: DARING, FEAR, AND ANGER

A third sort of irascible motion arises when an animal apprehends an object (or union) as *bad, difficult to avert, but worth trying to avert*. Included in this description is the notion that a relatively powerful object is poised to injure the animal by keeping the animal from attaining some good or avoiding some evil. The object has the property of being future; it has not yet caused the animal injury. Yet the object cannot be ignored; it poses a serious threat. The animal has the impression that averting injury will be difficult, but not impossible. The animal assesses that it has enough power relative to the evil object to challenge the object directly—to fend it off or to overcome it. Inasmuch as the animal is drawn toward, rather than repulsed by, the prospect of "attempting something arduous," the animal tends toward the evil object under the aspect of good.[106] Aquinas calls this irascible emotion "daring" (*audacia*).[107]

Again, it makes a difference how the animal assesses its ability to respond to various difficulties. A fourth sort of irascible motion (constructed by Aquinas as contrary to the third) arises when an animal apprehends an object (or union) as *bad and virtually impossible to avert*.[108] Included in this description is the notion that, again, a relatively powerful object threatens to cause the animal injury. The object is future in the sense that it has not yet caused the injury, but the injury appears to the animal to be imminent. It also appears to be irresistible. The animal apprehends that the object's power to cause it injury exceeds the animal's power to resist the object directly. Hence, the animal tends away from the evil object.

If Aquinas is to be consistent with his general description of the irascible, he needs to say that there is an element of resistance or struggle in this tending-away. He implies something like the following. When an animal encounters an evil object that appears to be superior in power, the animal has only one direction in which it can tend, which is away from the object. Yet the object is so imposing that it seems to the animal that even this tending away is all but impossible. The animal withdraws into itself in an attempt to create some distance between itself and the evil object. Yet when it tries to pull back interiorly, it apprehends (so to speak) that its back is up against the wall. If the animal manages under this sort of internal pressure to flee, it seems to the animal that the evil object is right at its heels. The animal experiences this being pinned or hemmed-in to be terribly arduous. Aquinas calls this irascible emotion "fear" (*timor*).

An animal can experience frequent shifts in its assessments of the power
an evil object has to cause it injury—and the power it has to avert the object
and the injury. In one moment, escape might seem possible; in the next moment, the animal's impression might be proven wrong. In a subsequent moment, the evil object might expose its flank, and capitalizing on its weakness
appears possible. In the next moment, the evil object's superior force bowls
the animal over, and all the animal can do is try to shrink into itself or otherwise become invisible. Accordingly, an animal can fluctuate in its experience of irascible emotions that are oriented toward a future evil.

A final sort of irascible motion arises when an animal apprehends a sensible object (or union) as *bad and impossible to avert, but worth trying (after the
fact) to overcome.*[109] Implicit in this description is the notion that the evil object is present in the sense of being fully upon the animal. The evil object has
already deprived the animal of a good and caused it pain. Yet the animal has
not been totally crushed; a spirited response to the object or injury is still
possible. Inasmuch as the animal apprehends that it has indeed been injured
by the object, the animal tends away from the object as evil. If this is all that
happens, the simple concupiscible motion of sorrow results.[110] Yet if the animal has a strong impulse to defend its life and well-being, and it apprehends
as good the possibility of striking back at the evil object, the animal tends toward the evil object under the aspect of good. The animal tends toward the
good of asserting its power and driving the other off or putting it in its place.
Aquinas calls this irascible emotion "anger" (*ira*).

This tending toward evil under the aspect of good is arduous, for the
evil other is a powerful foe that could cause the animal further injury; the foe
is not easily vanquished.[111] It is arduous also because the animal must rise up
under the weight of an injury that has already caused the animal some diminishment. With respect to this sort of tending, too, an animal can change,
over time, some of the assessments that enter into its description of the evil
object and the animal's relationship to that object. The animal can thus experience shifts in its tending—between what is predominantly a concupiscible motion of simple withdrawal and what is predominantly an irascible
motion of spirited approach and counterattack.

Like all other sensory-appetitive motions, irascible emotions are embodied. Aquinas does not specify the material elements of all the irascible
emotions. He does take particular note of the physiological changes that
occur with fear and anger. He says that fear is an appetitive motion that is accompanied by a kind of "contraction": "Thus we observe in one who is dying
that nature withdraws inwardly, on account of the lack of power: and again
we see the inhabitants of a city, when seized with fear, leave the outskirts,

and, as far as possible, make for the inner quarters. It is in resemblance to this contraction, which pertains to the appetite of the soul, that in fear a similar contraction of heat and vital spirits toward the inner parts takes place in regard to the body."[112] In fear, the heat and vital spirits of the outer parts (limbs) contract and gather relatively low in the torso. The vital spirits of the heart also flow toward this part of the body, leaving the heart smaller, colder, weaker.[113] In anger, too, the vital spirits contract from the outer to the inner parts of the body, but instead of gathering low in the torso, they concentrate around the heart, causing it to dilate and blood circulation to increase. Aquinas says that "because the movement of anger is not one of recoil, which corresponds to the action of cold, but one of prosecution, which corresponds to the action of heat, the result is that the movement of anger produces fervor of the blood and vital spirits around the heart, which is the instrument of the soul's passions."[114]

Getting "cold feet" and hands, having one's "blood run cold," and trembling are common in experiences of fear, as are becoming flushed and heated in one's upper torso, neck, and face in experiences of anger. Yet we have seen that no sensory-appetitive motion is reducible in definition to bodily changes or to the feeling of such changes. One could become—and feel — cold or hot due to material causes, such as a drop or rise in room temperature. Embodied sensory-appetitive motions are caused primarily by situations that are apprehended as bearing on one's well-being.

RELATIONSHIPS AMONG THE ELEVEN BASIC EMOTIONS

Aquinas summarizes the emotions that we have considered in this chapter, noting the way in which each emotion is either simple or arduous, regards a good or an evil (or both), involves tending in one way or another (or both) relative to the object, and can be identified with one stage or another in what is commonly the unfolding of a process. With respect to the concupiscible appetite,

> good has, as it were, a force of attraction, while evil has a force of repulsion. In the first place, therefore, good causes . . . a certain inclination, aptitude or connaturalness in respect of good: and this belongs to the passion of *love*: the corresponding contrary of which is *hatred* in respect of evil.—Secondly, if the good be not yet possessed, it causes in the appetite a movement toward the attainment of the good [that is loved]: and this belongs to the passion of *desire* or *concupiscence*: and contrary to it, in respect of evil, is the passion of *aversion* or *dislike*.—Thirdly, when the good is obtained, it causes the appetite to rest, as it were, in the good obtained: and this belongs to the passion of *delight* or *joy*: the contrary of which, in respect of evil, is *sorrow* or *sadness*.[115]

With respect to the irascible appetite, "the aptitude, or the inclination to seek good, or to shun evil, is presupposed as arising from the concupiscible faculty, which regards good or evil absolutely."[116] However, the good desired and the evil disliked are perceived by the animal as difficult or impossible to attain or avoid: "And in respect of good not yet obtained, we have *hope* and *despair*. In respect of evil not yet present we have *fear* and *daring*. . . . In respect of good obtained there is no irascible passion: because it is no longer considered in the light of something arduous. . . . But evil already present gives rise to the passion of *anger*."[117] Aquinas thus names eleven emotions that can be organized, for the most part, in pairs: "In the concupiscible faculty there are three couples of passions; viz., love and hatred, desire and aversion, joy and sadness. In like manner there are three groups in the irascible faculty; viz., hope and despair, fear and daring, and anger which has no contrary."[118]

There are other forms of sensory-appetitive motion that humans are wont to call emotions, but Aquinas thinks they are best defined with reference to the eleven basic emotions.[119] Some appetitive motions are distinguished, in part, with regard to their intensity. Rage, for example, is defined as intense anger.[120] Other motions are defined as species of the original eleven. For example, envy and pity are identified as species of sorrow: "Envy is sadness about the prosperity of someone else in so far as it is regarded as an evil for oneself, whereas pity is sadness about the adversity of someone else in so far as it is regarded as one's own evil."[121]

Motions of the irascible appetite are basically forms of desire or aversion that incorporate an element of struggle. As such, irascible motions "arise from the passions of the concupiscible and end in them."[122] They begin in love or hatred and are completed in delight or sorrow. For example, anger "arises from sadness, and having wrought vengeance, terminates in joy."[123] More specifically, the sorrow that gives rise to anger presupposes hatred, namely, a painful dissonance caused by the apprehension that a particular object is poised to cause one injury. Hatred, in turn, presupposes love, namely, the act of appreciating a relational possibility that is in some respects suitable. If it were not for love, there would be no cause for hatred or sadness when one apprehends a relational transgression; and if it were not for love, there would be no point to the central desire of anger, which is to attain vengeance in order (somehow) to correct a transgression and restore a more suitable relationship. The rising of a spirited desire to strike back amounts to the rising of hope. If what is hoped for is achieved, this complex of interior motions culminates in delight.

Similar stories can be told about other appetitive motions.[124] This is part of what is so attractive about Aquinas's theory of emotion. This theory allows us to identify a set of key appetitive motions that can be expanded in number by specifying different intensities, by offering further specifications of the objects (and the circumstances) of the motions, and by combining the motions in different ways. This theory allows us to consider that even some of the most basic motions are complex and shifting amalgams of other motions. With any given motion, this theory allows us to account for the fact that the object of the motion can be apprehended in different ways, from different angles, to different effects, which opens up possibilities for choice in humans who wish to cultivate virtuous habits of being moved.

This theory allows us to account for the fact that many of the sensory judgments that elicit appetitive motions can be implicit. We must make them explicit if we are to understand the inner workings of a given motion or set of motions, but these judgments do not have to be explicit for one to experience the emotion. This theory allows us also to account, to some extent, for the temporality of appetitive motions—for the way in which some motions occur immediately, while others unfold in stages, such that some motions presuppose and build on prior motions. This theory allows us to refer meaningfully to all appetitive motions *as* related forms of motion, even though, relatively speaking, some of them appear to be forms of being-at-rest. In all of these ways and more, Aquinas's theory of emotion provides helpful structure, but it also allows for great flexibility.

Aquinas often characterizes appetitive motions as heading in one direction or the other, such that the motions appear to be mutually exclusive.[125] He tends, for example, to categorize fear and daring as emotions that directly oppose each other.[126] However, once the basic distinctions are grasped, the theory allows us to say with more subtlety that an animal might be moved in contrary directions at the same time or in periodic alternation, in respect of different or changing specifications of an object, and in light of changing assessments of the animal's power to attain what it desires, avoid what it loathes, or face what is on its path. Similarly, Aquinas tends to draw a sharp distinction between concupiscible and irascible emotions (associating each with a distinctive power); yet he also indicates that an appetitive motion can fall into one category or the other, depending on how one construes the difficulties that come into (and may also go out of) play during the run of that motion.[127]

MOTIONS OF THE SENSORY APPETITE: NONHUMAN ANIMALS AND HUMANS

To step back for a moment and put this chapter in perspective, recall that in Aquinas's view the same principle of being and order is at work in all existing things, and between all things—from inanimate objects—to living organisms—to nonhuman and human animals—and beyond. Each thing naturally tends toward the actualization of its potential in dynamic relation to everything else.

The appetites or tendencies of most things are not mediated by sensory powers. The lifted stone does not apprehend re-union with the earth to be a suitable thing and crave it as such, nor does the early-morning plant apprehend re-union with the sun to be a suitable thing and bend toward it as such. Nonsensory entities simply stand in certain relationships to other objects such that certain forms of union or interaction are possible and, under certain circumstances, occur. Sensory beings, however, are *aware* of standing in relation to other things. They tend to unite with what they apprehend via the senses to be suitable and pleasant; they tend to avoid union with what they apprehend to be unsuitable and painful; and they tend to resist, struggle under the weight of, or try to rise above the obstacles that get in their way.

As sensory beings, nonhuman and human animals have a lot in common: They share a set of appetites that dispose them to resonate with, to desire, to pursue, and to enjoy what contributes to their sensory well-being. They also share a set of appetites that dispose them to find disagreeable, to be repulsed by, and to resist or suffer in pain what causes them dysfunction and diminishment. To recall Aquinas's theological frame, nonhuman and human animals both participate as sensory beings in a universe ordered by Love, which is the first principle and final goal of all tending. Animals tend toward their own good inasmuch as their sensory appetites operate in ways that allow the animals to live and function well on a sensory level, as circumstances allow. In this very tending, animals implicitly tend to God, the principle of their perfection. They implicitly love God in interacting with the possibilities of their own being and with other objects in ways that actualize some of what is good within themselves.

Humans are also unlike nonhuman animals in significant ways. One important difference is that motions of the human sensory appetite (in fully formed and healthy humans) are caused by acts of sensory apprehension that are influenced by the intellect. Sensory-appetitive motions in humans thus tend to have more complex objects. For example, a nonhuman animal might apprehend that another animal is attacking the first animal's young. If the first animal judges that it has some power relative to the second, it will likely be moved interiorly and exteriorly to attack and drive the second animal off. By contrast, a human animal, say a man, might apprehend that another human has injured the man's honor and reputation by slighting him in a way that is publicly visible. If the man regards the slight as unjustified, he will likely be moved interiorly and (depending on the circumstances) in word or action to attack the offender in a way that reasserts the man's power. The same basic structure is present in the two forms of anger, but to the extent that the concepts of honor, respect, self-respect, and justice inform the man's way of apprehending the situation and its significance, his anger reflects the power of a human intellect. It reflects a moral sensibility and, indeed, a complex worldview.

Another important difference is that humans have the capacity to detach from many of their emotions and evaluate them prudentially and morally.[128] This means, in part, that humans can be aware of themselves undergoing emotions, rather than simply being "inside" the emotions as modes of encountering what is "there." Humans have the capacity not to act on emotions that function as motive principles; they have the capacity not to consent to emotions when they first arise; they have the capacity to alter the course of their emotions; and they have the capacity to alter their very propensities to be aroused to certain emotions by reconceiving certain features of their lives and environments. Humans can be said to love God implicitly (if not also explicitly), as distinctively rational animals, when they choose to do what they can to make themselves more prone to undergo, consent to, and act on appetitive motions in ways that promote their own and others' flourishing.[129]

Some of what accounts for differences between nonhuman and human animals with respect to emotion will be elucidated in subsequent chapters. The purpose of this chapter has been to highlight some of what many sensory beings appear to have in common, which is a great deal. Approaching emotions from below allows us, as humans, to take our animality seriously. It allows us to appreciate, for example, that all of our emotions have a material component. Even if some of our emotions involve significant contributions from the intellect, they also involve forms of sensory apprehension that are mediated by changes in the brain and nervous system; they also involve appetitive motions that are mediated by additional bodily organs and organ systems. Our emotions involve changes in the body that are often significant or unusual enough (even in the virtuous) to be noticed or felt by people who are attentive to their bodies. From below, it is puzzling to hear someone refer to physiological arousal as "almost . . . a side aspect of emotion."[130] In addition, emotions commonly function as causes of outward expression, bodily movement, and action. Approaching emotion from below allows us to think creatively about the relationships between emotions and other forms of interior and exterior motion.

Finally, approaching emotions from below permits us, if we wish, to exercise our religious curiosity and concern. Some people find it meaningful to "see" a structural similarity between the falling of stones, the growing of plants, the hungering of animals for food, the hungering of humans for companionship, and the hungering of humans for truth. They find meaning in the notion that everything tends, in its own ways and on multiple levels, toward God or the good as the final end or goal of appetition as such. They find it meaningful to conceive of their own interior motions as expressions of the fact that they tend, as humans, to appreciate or enjoy the good that is possible for them. Of course, *I* find this meaningful, even as I also find meaningful other ways of construing the nature of reality and the role of emotions in shaping experience and behavior (e.g., Stoic and Buddhist ways). In any case, our approach to Aquinas and emotion makes clear that one cannot construct his view without elucidating his underlying assumptions about the real and the good. Our approach raises the question of whether *any* account of emotion that seeks to be full and reasonably satisfying can escape the demand of acknowledging and elucidating its own metaphysical underpinnings.

NOTES

1. *Truth* 25.1.
2. Ibid.
3. Ibid.
4. Ibid.
5. Ibid.
6. Ibid. My emphasis and parenthetical insertions for the sake of clarification.
7. Indeed, Aquinas holds that every appetitive act or motion is in a sense intentional, such that even the appetite of the stone for the surface of the earth exhibits intentionality. The object of the earth (construed as suitable for the stone) is present, not in the mind of the stone (for the stone does not have a mind), but in the mind of God, which determines the stone to have the nature it has (*Truth* 22.1). This is a way of saying that everything that is, is characterized by appetite; appetite as such is always directed toward an object; and there is a principle of order that accounts for how all object-oriented appetites come together to compose a functioning whole.
8. Shawn Floyd, "Aquinas on Emotion," 561.
9. Claudia E. Murphy, "Aquinas on Our Responsibility for Our Emotions," 168. Although I disagree with Murphy on several points, this is an excellent article.
10. At *ST* I-II 26.2, Aquinas speaks of an object "introducing itself" into the "intention" of the "appetite" (*appetibile enim movet appetitum, faciens se quodammodo in eius intentione*).
11. *ST* I-II 22.1.
12. Peter King's analysis of *passio* as a "passive potency" is probing and illuminating. See King, "Aquinas on the Passions," 101–10.
13. *ST* I-II 22.2.
14. *ST* I-II 24.1 *ad* 1.

15. *Truth* 25.2 *ad* 8.

16. *Truth* 26.4.

17. *ST* I 81.2.

18. *ST* I-II 23.1.

19. *Truth* 26.4.

20. *Truth* 22.7; *ST* I-II 15.2.

21. *ST* I-II 9.2, 23.2.

22. *Truth* 26.4.

23. Ibid.

24. Ibid. "Ipsum enim delectabile *primo* appetenti coniungitur aliqualiter secundum quod apprehenditur ut simile vel conveniens: et ex hoc sequitur passio *amoris*, qui nihil est aliud quam formatio quaedam appetitus ab ipso appetibili: unde amor dicitur esse *quaedam* unio amantis et amati. Id autem quod sic *aliqualiter* coniunctum est, quaeritur *ulterius ut realiter* coniungatur: ut amans scilicet perfruatur amato; et sic nascitur passio *desiderii*: quod quidem cum *adeptum* fuerit in re, generat *gaudium*."

25. *ST* I-II 30.1 *ad* 2. When the desire in question is specifically a motion of the concupiscible appetite, Aquinas often refers to it as concupiscence (*concupiscentia*).

26. The reader is advised to keep in mind the qualification introduced earlier concerning the use of active language.

27. If the animal tends at all, it tends toward what it apprehends as suitable; yet it is possible to apprehend something as suitable but not desire it—for example, if one is already captivated by a desire for something else that is more attractive.

28. It can be defined also with reference to facial expression, posture, and the like, but our interest here is with the relationship between desire and exterior motion in the form of action.

29. Quoted in St. Thomas Aquinas, *Commentary on Aristotle's "Metaphysics,"* trans. John P. Rowan (Notre Dame, Ind.: Dumb Ox, 1961), 599. Latin edition: S. Thomae de Aquino, *Sententia libri Metaphysicae. Opera Omnia* (Fundación Tomás de Aquino, 2006), http://www.corpusthomisiticum.org/iopera.html. The text under analysis is Aristotle, *Metaphysics*, 1048a8–10. The adverb "chiefly" is important, for it can happen, especially with humans, that someone desires to approach an item bodily, but does not do so (ever) when the opportunity arises. This can happen, for example, when an individual consistently wants something else more, as when one exercises continence.

30. As discussed previously, a sensory desire is (on one level of explanation) passive because it is caused by an object of sensory apprehension. Yet such a desire is (on another level of explanation) the cause of other changes. In effect, we are stepping into the stream of a complex causal process, at the point of an actual desire, and considering this desire as a cause in its own right.

31. *ST* I-II 28.1, 31.1 *ad* 1.

32. *Truth* 26.3. Aquinas holds that it is one of the functions of *passio* to alter the body. The same can be said of sensory desire (which is, for Aquinas, a form of *passio*). Animals rely on sensory-appetitive motion to motivate them to act in ways that preserve their lives. See also *ST* I-II 22.1.

33. *ST* I-II 22.1 and 22.2 *ad* 3. See also *Truth* 26.2 and 26.3.

34. The distinction Aquinas draws between bodily passion (*passio corporalis*) and a passion of the soul or the soul-body composite (*passio animalis*) is perhaps helpful here. A passion of the body, such as a bodily injury, "begins with the body and ends in the soul inasmuch as it is united to the body as its form." A passion of the soul, however, "begins with the soul inasmuch as [the soul] is the mover of the body, and ends in the body. . . . Passions of this kind are aroused by the apprehension and appetency of the soul, and a bodily transformation follows upon them" (*Truth* 26.2).

35. *ST* I-II 31.1, 32.1.

36. Recall note 88 of chapter 5.

37. *ST* I-II 25.2 ad 1.

38. *ST* I-II 26.2.

39. *ST* I-II 23.4.

40. Ibid..

41. *ST* I-II 26.2.

42. *ST* I-II 27.4.

43. *ST* I-II 25.2.

44. *Truth* 26.4.

45. *ST* I-II 26.1 and 2.

46. *ST* I-II 26.2.

47. *ST* I-II 27.3 *ad* 2.

48. *ST* I-II 26.2 *ad* 2.

49. *ST* I-II 26.2 *ad* 3.

50. Michael Sherwin interprets *complacentia* as "pleasing affective affinity" or "with pleasing assent," implying "incipient enjoyment." See *By Knowledge and By Love*, 70, 78. Thanks to William McDonough for these references and for conversation on the nature of *complacentia*. See his article, which focuses on *complacentia* as a motion of the intellectual appetite, "Etty Hillesum's Learning to Live and Preparing to Die: *Complacentia Boni* as the Beginning of Acquired and Infused Virtue," *Journal of the Society of Christian Ethics* 25, no. 2 (2005), 179–202.

51. In discussing *complacentia* as an act of the will that is distinct from desire or concern, Frederick Crowe identifies a generalized experience of "consent to being, harmony with all that is, peace with the universe." In the moment of *complacentia*, one "neither rebels at necessity nor grasps at possibility." One "does not desire or seek or strive or fret or sorrow." *Complacentia* is "the human spirit at rest in relation to its object, at the end of a process" (Crowe, "Complacency and Concern in the Thought of St. Thomas," 347).

52. *ST* I-II 26.2 *ad* 3 (my emphasis).

53. *ST* I-II 26.1. I depart from Crowe who associates desire ("concern") alone with tending (Crowe, "Complacency and Concern in the Thought of St. Thomas," 3).

54. *ST* 28.1 *ad* 2. Although the opening quotation of the prior section of this chapter titled "Concupiscible Emotion: Desire" refers to the third moment as "joy" (*gaudium*), Aquinas generally refers to this moment as "delight" (*delectatio*) within the

sensory realm: "We do not speak of joy except when delight follows reason; and so we do not ascribe joy to irrational animals, but only delight" (*ST* I-II 31.3).

55. *ST* I-II 31.1.

56. Ibid.

57. *ST* I-II 31.1 *ad* 2.

58. *ST* I-II 31.1. See also *ST* I-II 32.3: "The greatest pleasure is that which arises from sensation which requires the presence of the sensible object." See also *Truth* 26.4 *ad* 5: "for sensible pleasure involves on the part of the body union with something agreeable, and on the part of the soul the feeling of this agreeableness."

59. *ST* I-II 32.3 *ad* 3.

60. ST I-II 11.4. See also *ST* I-II 32.3 *ad* 3: "Love and concupiscence also cause pleasure. For everything that is loved becomes pleasing to the lover, since love is a kind of union or connaturalness of lover and beloved. In like manner every object of desire is pleasing to the one that desires, since desire is chiefly a craving for pleasure."

61. *ST* I-II 33.1.

62. Ibid.

63. The object of sensory love (that with which one tends to unite) can be one's own actuality, in which case one resonates, in self-love, in the sensory awareness that one is in a position to actualize some of one's potential. One might go on to desire and seek this actualization, and enjoy whatever perfection one attains; but prior to the motion of desire or active seeking there is a pleasing resonance simply in the recognition that one exists and one is well suited to realize some of one's potential.

64. *ST* I-II 33.1 *ad* 1, 28.5.

65. *ST* I-II 22.1.

66. *ST* I-II 26.2.

67. *ST* I-II 23.2, 23.4. Aquinas also uses the term *abominatio* in referring to the second moment.

68. *ST* I 81.2; I-II 23.2, 23.3.

69. *ST* I 81.2; *Truth* 25.2.

70. *ST* I-II 23.1. Aquinas needs to say something like this in order to distinguish aversion (the interior motion behind the simple flight response) from fear (the interior motion behind the fright response). It is particularly when one is *unable* easily to turn away from a hurtful union that fear arises.

71. *ST* I-II 35.1 *ad* 3.

72. *ST* I 81.2.

73. *ST* I-II 37.2.

74. *ST* I-II 26.2.

75. *ST* I-II 29.1.

76. I take it that aversion presupposes hatred in the same way that desire presupposes love.

77. *ST* I-II 29.1.

78. *ST* I-II 29.3.

79. Ibid.

80. Ibid.

81. Ibid.

82. *ST* I-II 29.2.

83. Indeed, in his treatise on anger, Aquinas says that the hater "wishes evil to his enemy, as evil" (*ST* I-II 46.6). "Wishing evil" appears to involve something more than simple dissonance; it appears to involve an irascible motion, discussed below. In some cases it involves anger that is no longer tethered to the prospect of restoring a relationship with a problematic other. It also involves related motions of the intellectual appetite, such as malevolence, which can find expression in maleficence. For further reflection on the many dimensions of hatred in the thought of Aquinas (and other great thinkers) see Joel Gereboff et al., "The Nature of the Beast."

84. I draw this as an implication of *ST* I-II 37.4.

85. *ST* I-II 35.1.

86. *ST* I-II 36.1.

87. *ST* I-II 31.8 *ad* 2.

88. "Now it is evident that it is contrary to the inclination of the appetite to be united with a present evil: and whatever is contrary to a thing's inclination does not happen to it save by the action of something stronger. . . . But it must be noted that if the stronger power goes so far as to transform the contrary inclination into its own inclination, there will be no longer repugnance or violence. . . . Accordingly if some greater power prevail so as to take away from the will or the sensitive appetite their respective inclinations, pain or sorrow will not result therefrom; such is the result only when the contrary inclination of the appetite remains" (*ST* I-II 36.4). See also 31.1 *ad* 2.

89. *ST* I-II 37.2.

90. *ST* I-II 38.1.

91. *ST* I-II 35.1 *ad* 3.

92. *ST* I-II 37.4 *ad* 3.

93. *ST* I-II 37.4.

94. *ST* I-II 36.2.

95. *ST* I-II 23.2.

96. *ST* I-II 40.6.

97. *ST* I 81.2.

98. Ibid.

99. *ST* I-II 40.1.

100. *ST* I-II 23.1 *ad* 3.

101. *ST* I-II 23.2.

102. *ST* I 81.2.

103. Aquinas says that despair presupposes hope (*ST* I-II 25.3).

104. *ST* I-II 40.3.

105. *ST* I-II 40.4 *ad* 3.

106. *ST* I-II 45.2. I would argue that the animal can also be daring in planning and carrying out an escape. This involves tending away from the object as evil, but also hav-

ing spiritedness in this tending (in contrast to the lack of daring that obtains when one freezes). See the description of fear, below.

107. *ST* I-II 45.1.

108. *ST* I-II 41.2, 42.5.

109. *ST* I-II 46.2; *Truth* 26.5.

110. *ST* I-II 46.1 *ad* 2; *Truth* 26.4.

111. *ST* I-II 46.3.

112. *ST* I-II 44.1.

113. Ibid.

114. *ST* I-II 44.1, 48.2. The material element of daring is similar to that of anger. See *ST* I-II 45.3.

115. *ST* I-II 23.4.

116. Ibid.

117. Ibid.

118. Ibid.

119. Ibid.

120. *Truth* 26.4.

121. Ibid.

122. Ibid.

123. *ST* I 81.2.

124. Kevin White refers to an "order of emergence of the passions," in Aquinas's view, "which constitutes a suite or sequence that is like a narrative, of which genres of poetry such as comedy and tragedy represent portions. Knowledge of the whole story might be especially useful to one charged with care of souls, enabling him to quickly 'find his place' when dealing with a particular soul caught up in some passion" ("The Passions of the Soul," 107).

125. "Now every movement of the appetitive power is reducible to one either of pursuit or of avoidance" (*ST* I-II 45.2).

126. *ST* I-II 45.1.

127. *ST* I-II 41.2 *ad* 3.

128. *Truth* 24.2.

129. *ST* I 65.2.

130. Daniel Westberg, "Emotion and God," 117.

CHAPTER SEVEN

Approaching the Human Sensory Appetite from Above (I)

✦

When we approach the human sensory appetite from below, with reference to Aquinas's scale of being, we put ourselves in a position to imagine that all existing things are marked by appetites or tendencies of one sort or another. The tending of each part toward its own being and perfection—in relation to the tending of all other parts—reflects a principle of order according to which the cosmos as a whole is tending toward perfection.[1]

A small number of entities within this comprehensive appetitive field stand out from the rest because they have sensory powers. By virtue of their *exterior and interior senses*, some entities can apprehend particular objects as suitable or unsuitable for their well-being, considered on a sensory level. By virtue of their *sensory appetite*, some beings can tend toward objects that they apprehend as suitable for themselves and their loved ones. They can tend away from objects that they apprehend as unsuitable. They can tend in more complex and sometimes conflicted ways in relation to objects that they apprehend as suitable, but difficult to attain—or unsuitable, but difficult to avoid—due to some obstacle.

A small subset of sensory beings—namely, humans—have intellectual powers as well.[2] By virtue of the *intellect* we can apprehend (conceive) the highest end for humans and for this human, in particular. We can also apprehend the way in which various sensible objects relate to our highest end. We can reason about and judge whether a given object is likely to promote or injure our happiness or has no significant bearing on it. By virtue of the *will* we can undergo appetitive motions in response to objects of intellectual apprehension. We can tend toward the well-being of ourselves and our loved ones, as we conceive it intellectually, and we can tend toward particular objects that we judge to be productive of that well-being. Similarly, we can tend away from our diminishment, our failure to thrive as humans, and we can tend away from objects that we judge to be destructive. We can tend in more complex ways relative to objects that we judge to be productive or destructive of our well-being, but difficult to attain or avoid, due to some obstacle.[3]

Humans have many sensory powers in common with other animals. Yet the presence of intellectual powers in humans changes, to some extent, how our sensory powers operate. Most notably, having an intellect and a will allows us to engage in acts of interior sensory apprehension that surpass the related acts of other animals. It thus allows us to undergo motions of the sensory appetite or emotions that are more complex than the appetitive motions of other animals. In addition, particular acts of the intellect and the will can influence how sensible objects appear to a human. Acts of the intellect and the will can thus influence the way in which emotions form around these appearances.

The task of this chapter, along with chapters 8 and 9, is to explore further how Aquinas thinks the intellect and the will contribute to the formation of distinctively human emotions.[4] The goal is to illuminate the structure of emotion from a position on Aquinas's scale of being above the animal per se, but without going so high on the scale that we transcend animality altogether and treat humans as if we were intellectual souls whose proper intellectual operations did not depend on the coordinated exercise of our sensory powers.

PRELIMINARY POINTS

Approaching emotions from above provides a more complete picture of the intelligence of emotion. Much of the time, our appetitive tending reflects a basic sensory intelligence; it orients us toward what is in fact beneficial to us as sensory beings and away from what is harmful. Fear, for example, is usually an indication of real danger; it orients us toward self-preservation. Yet our tending can also be off target. It can be off target with respect to our sensory well-being: We can recoil from an object that is not actually a danger to us, or is not a very significant danger, and we can do so with such an intensity that our fear nearly consumes us. Our senses can fail, as a result, to register other information that is relevant to our well-being. Our tending can be off target also with respect to our flourishing as rational beings: If an interior motion of recoil is excessive, and we fail to do what we reasonably can (and can reasonably be expected to do) to alter it, we diminish ourselves morally. We exhibit cowardice. From above, we can see that while our sensory appetites often show a degree of natural intelligence, our intellectual powers are needed to help guide the formation and course of our emotions in light of an ideal of good human functioning.

Aquinas holds that if we wish to thrive as humans we must pursue the highest truths available to us and seek to live in accordance with these truths—in practical thought, action, and emotion. As a Christian, he trusts that our natural powers can, by the grace of God, be healed of various self-defeating corruptions. Our intellectual powers, in particular, can be extended so that we are able to apprehend truths about human life that transcend the limits of reason, and we are able to make moral choices in light of these transcendent truths. As we investigate the powers of intellect and will, we are going to consider them primarily as natural powers that are available to humans as such. Yet we will consider also a surprising reformation and extension of these powers that can come to humans as a gift from beyond, in Aquinas's view.

I encourage readers who are not Christian and are unfamiliar with Christian ways of talking about religious transformation to keep exploring the thought of Aquinas with curiosity. Countless people from diverse traditions and paths have had experiences that seem to carry them beyond the limits of their natural powers of understanding and loving. People who are otherwise mentally healthy have encountered what strikes them as most real and important in life or something that is more real and important than much else that they experience in the daily round of existence. In the wake of such encounters they often realize that their hearts have been changed in ways they could not have anticipated and could not have brought about by their own will. I urge readers to consider what is distinctively Christian about Aquinas's view, including his view of grace and the way it can transform people's lives, while seeking analogues to his concepts within their own worldviews.

THE INTELLECT

To understand the impact that the intellect and the will can have on sensory-appetitive motions in humans, one must understand what the intellect and the will are and how they operate. The study of the intellect and the will, in the thought of Aquinas and within the broader scope of Western philosophy and theology, has a long and distinguished history. My intention here is modest. I wish to say only what I need to say about these powers to elucidate the influence they can have on our emotions, in order to do justice to Aquinas's theory of emotion.

In working with Aquinas, it is important to consider the intellect and the will as a pair; yet the only way to proceed is to begin with one unit of the pair. For our purposes, it is most fruitful to begin with the intellect. The human intellect is a power that makes it possible for one to find intelligible the world in which one lives: "The word *intelligence* [*intelligentia*] properly signifies the intellect's very act, which is to understand [*intelligere*]."[5] Aquinas is most concerned with the apprehension of intelligible *truths*—with the apprehension of what is in fact the case. However, it suits our purposes to note that, by the power of the intellect, one can understand an object correctly or incorrectly (one can understand it or misunderstand it).[6] I want to set aside, as much as possible, the question of what it takes to perform a given intellectual operation *well*. Speaking of the intellect in this way prepares us to discuss the will. An act of the will is caused, in part, by an intellectual apprehension of an object's goodness; yet "in order that the will tend to anything, it is requisite, not that this be good in very truth, but [only] that it be apprehended as good. Wherefore the Philosopher says (*Phys.* ii.3) that *the end is a good, or an apparent good*."[7]

In Aquinas's view, one seeks to understand the world by applying the power of one's intellect to the investigation of particular material things (informed by first principles that are "known without any investigation on the part of reason,"[8] as soon as one encounters instances of them[9]). The proper object of the intellect is the essence of a thing, namely, *what the thing is*.[10] The intellect is thus a power that makes it possible to apprehend "the universal nature existing in the individual."[11] The intellect allows one to apprehend an object as an object of a certain kind that is both like and unlike other objects of the same and different kinds. By the power of the intellect one can apprehend multiple "universals," for example, that an object is an existing thing, a living being, and a particular sort of living being.

A principal act of the intellect, in this view, is that of "abstracting" universals from particulars.[12] Aquinas holds that in apprehending what an object is, one first forms a sensory image or impression of the object, which he calls a "phantasm" (*phantasma*). A phantasm is formed via the exercise of the sensory powers, including the imagination (*phantasia*), the cogitative power, and the power of memory.[13] Recall that the imagination allows one to create and draw from "a storehouse of forms received through the senses," so that one can have sensible objects in mind whether or not the objects are also present to the exterior senses. The cogitative power allows one to apprehend certain "intentions" or properties. It allows one to have, on the sensory level, an impression that an object has "advantages and uses, or disadvantages" beyond being agreeable or disagreeable with respect to the exterior senses. The power of memory allows one to create and draw from a "storehouse" of "intentions" formed via the cogitative power.[14] To proceed, Aquinas says that, in apprehending what an object is, one forms a phantasm of it and then one "light[s] up the phantasm" by considering its "intelligible species" or its "universal form."[15] By the power of the intellect, one "causes the phantasms received from the senses to be actually intelligible."[16]

Abstracting what is universal from a phantasm is more complicated than it might appear, and abstraction is, in any case, only part of a process in which one must engage if one is to acquire a good grasp of something—a sufficiently determinate apprehension of what it is. Aquinas says that "the human intellect does not acquire perfect knowledge by the first act of apprehension; but it first apprehends something about its object, such as its quiddity [essence], and this is its first and proper object; and then it understands the properties, accidents, and the various relations of the essence."[17] Suppose, for example, that one apprehends a human being. For Aquinas, to understand what this object is, one must abstract from a phantasm of the object the form of "rational animal." Yet this is a form that one learns to identify only over time, as one learns to identify related forms, including "animal" and "rational."[18] The ability to identify "animal" and "rational" implies an ability to identify these forms separately (as when one apprehends an animal that is not rational, or a rational being that is not an animal), in combination with each other (as when one apprehends a being that is both an animal and rational), and in combination with additional forms (as when one apprehends a rational animal that is specifically female).[19] To understand that something is a human being and to understand, further, what sort of human she is (for example, a woman with a just and merciful character), one must thus engage in a lot of mental "composition and division." One must also advance from one "composition and division . . . to another, which is the process of reasoning."[20]

Through a process of composition, division, and (multiple layers of) reasoning, one can progress from an "indistinct" and "confused" apprehension of the nature and properties of an object to a more distinct and determinate apprehension.[21] One can make this progress with respect to a growing number of objects, and one can increase one's ability to grasp the relationships among various objects. As one engages in further inquiry, one can "rise" from a consideration of "temporal things" to reflection on matters that are more and more abstract, culminating in the "contemplation and consultation of things eternal."[22] One can reflect on things eternal through the use of one's natural powers, which are perfected (to a degree) through learning and the exercise of virtue. In some cases, one can reflect on such things also with supernatural aid, which can take the form of divinely infused virtue.[23] As noted, Aquinas thinks that God can make it possible for one to carry out intellectual activities that are "higher" than those possible on the basis of natural human powers alone.[24] Yet no matter how high one rises above the sensible and the particular in pursuit of the immaterial and the universal, one must—as long as one is embodied—continue to be tied in one's thinking to sensory experience.[25]

THE INTELLECT'S DEPENDENCE ON THE SENSORY

Aquinas agrees with Aristotle that "in the present state of life in which the [intellectual] soul is united to a passible body" as the form of the human body, "it is impossible for our intellect to understand *anything* actually, except by turning to the phantasms."[26] In this view, the nature of "any material thing cannot be known completely and truly, except in as much as it is known as existing in the individual. Now we apprehend the individual through the senses and the imagination."[27] Accordingly, "for the intellect to understand actually its proper object, it must of necessity turn to the phantasms in order to perceive the universal nature existing in the individual."[28] One must turn to phantasms repeatedly if one wishes to arrive at a reasonably complete understanding of what an object is. Aquinas invites his readers to test his thesis with reference to their own experience:[29] "Anyone can experience . . . that when he tries to understand something, he forms certain phantasms to serve him by way of examples, in which as it were he examines what he is desirous of understanding. For this reason it is that when we wish to help someone to understand something, we lay examples before him, from which he forms phantasms for the purpose of understanding."[30] I take it that the "examples" one employs, particularly for the benefit of one's own understanding, are not necessarily clearly depicted visual images or pieces of mental video; they might simply—or in addition— be vague sensory impressions through which one runs mentally, as when one tries to understand what water is partly by flashing through clear, blue, thirst, stream, fish, liquid, solid, and so on. Aquinas holds that even after one arrives at a decent grasp of an object's essence and its properties, one must continue to turn to the phantasms if one wishes to extend one's investigations and apply what one has learned.[31]

Even in seeking to apprehend something highly abstract, such as the concept of truth, one must keep one's bearings with respect to particular matters that one takes to be true, and doing this requires periodically calling to mind "sensible bodies of which there are phantasms."[32] Aquinas agrees with Dionysius that, by the natural power of one's intellect, one can apprehend the highest reality, namely, God, only "as a cause, by way of excess and . . . re-motion"—by reasoning from what one apprehends via sensory experience.[33] Aquinas thinks that by *faith* one is able to apprehend "the invisible things of God in a higher way," but faith does not come to a person fully actualized; it is a capability that requires development.[34] Growing in faith requires learn-ing to interpret what has been revealed by God, and Aquinas holds that "God does not make any revelations to [the human intellect] except under the species of phantasms."[35] Moreover, faith does not overwhelm one's rational nature; it perfects that nature.[36] It extends one's intellectual capabilities. Hence, it is necessary for a person of faith—who is also a person of rea-son—to relate what transcends reason to what is within reason's reach, in order to have a relatively coherent view of reality, and this again requires reference to sensible images or impressions. Thus, if one wishes to under-stand any object, corporeal or incorporeal, one must "turn to phantasms of bodies, although there are no phantasms of [incorporeal] things themselves."[37]

Some of the implications of this epistemology for the study of emotion can already be anticipated. If acquiring and processing information intellec-tually requires the cooperation of our interior sensory powers, then ordi-narily when we apprehend an object intellectually we will also apprehend it (or something related to it, such as its *effects* or an *example* of it) sensorily. That is, we will have in mind one or more sensory images or impressions of the object (or something related to it). If we apprehend an object to be good or desirable intellectually—if we abstract the universal of "good" from an image or impression of it—we will likely apprehend the object (or something re-lated to it) to be good or desirable on a sensory level as well. Accordingly, we will likely tend toward the goodness of the object via motions of both the intellectual and the sensory appetite.[38]

The reverse is also true. Because we are animals who have intellectual powers, and we have a natural desire to understand the world in which we live, most of our sensory experience is accompanied by intellectualization. When we apprehend an object sensorily, we usually apprehend, at the same time, what the object is. If we apprehend that the object is pleasing to the senses or useful to us as sensory beings, then we are likely to at least ask the question of whether the object is also good for us as beings who seek a distinctively human happiness. If we answer this question "yes," then we are likely to tend toward the object via the intellectual as well as the sensory appetite.[39]

It is only if we can draw these connections—between apprehension (in-tellectual and sensory) and appetite (intellectual and sensory)—and also be-tween the intellectual (apprehension and appetite) and the sensory (apprehension and appetite)—that we can understand how the intellect and the will function in relation to the sensory powers. It is only if we can trace these lines of relationship that we can grasp, in particular, how the intellect (via its connection to the powers of interior sensory apprehension) and the will (via its connection to the intellect and also on account of its role as a motive principle) can have an impact on sensory-appetitive motions in humans. Hence, we would do well to examine some of these relationships further, beginning with the relationship between intellectual and sensory apprehension.

INTELLECTUAL AND SENSORY APPREHENSION CONJOINED

In Aquinas's scheme, the power to apprehend an object via the senses is distinct from the power to apprehend what the object is: "What the sense knows materially and concretely, which is to know the singular directly, the intellect knows immaterially and in the abstract, which is to know the universal."[40] Yet apprehending what an object is requires the exercise of both intellectual and sensory apprehension. In the final analysis, it is not the "intellect" or the "sense" that apprehends an object; it is the person who apprehends it. Moreover, it is not simply a universal nature that one apprehends. With a sensible object—or an object that one associates with something sensible—one grasps the nature *of the object*, which implies an apprehension of the object as both intelligible and sensible—or conceived with reference to something sensible.[41]

Aquinas signals the unity of the human subject who engages in various acts of apprehension, commonly in respect of the same object.[42] He also posits interior sensory powers that operate at the intersection of the intellectual and sensory domains—making sensory-dependent acts of the intellect possible, as we just noted, but also making it possible for sensory operations to benefit from closely related operations of the intellect. In particular, Aquinas posits the cogitative power, assisted by memory and imagination, as the power of interior sensory apprehension that is closest in operation to the power of the intellect.[43] We have considered the way in which the cogitative power allows one to apprehend and "distinguish individual intentions and compare them with one another" on the sensory level. We must now consider further how this power relates to the higher, intellectual power by which one apprehends, "compares and distinguishes universal intentions."[44]

The cogitative power makes it possible for one to apprehend certain "intentions." It makes one able to "collate" sensible information in such a way that one apprehends, for example, that a particular sensible object would be useful for meeting a particular need. This power also allows one to compare objects in terms of such properties and to judge on a sensory level that one object would be more useful than another for meeting a need. Aquinas locates the cogitative power in the sensory realm because something like this power is evident in nonhuman animals, which lack intellects in Aquinas's view.[45] Recall the example of the bird that is able via the estimative power (the animal version of the cogitative power) to apprehend a piece of straw, not simply as a colored shape but as something that is useful for building a nest—and more useful than other objects lying close at hand.

If this sort of cognitive activity is present in birds, then it is present in humans as well, on a sensory level. Yet this sort of apprehending, comparing, and judging, when they occur *in* humans, generally look a lot like—and intermingle with—activities that Aquinas takes to be intellectual. When it comes to building a house, for example, humans draw on a larger number and variety of sensory inputs, including inputs from memory and imagination. We form more complex images and impressions of the objects that could be useful for our purposes. We engage in more extensive considerations of relevant items and their relative usefulness than is apparent in other animals. Whereas a bird might judge between one piece of straw and other straw-like objects in the same vicinity, or the bird might need to search elsewhere for straw with an image of straw in mind, humans judge between a large number of possible building materials, some of which come to mind only as we search our memory and exercise more advanced powers of imagination.

Humans construe items *as* items of certain kinds, through the use of our interior senses but aided by concepts that are supplied by the intellect.[46] For example, we apprehend certain items, not only as useful for building but as "wood" or "sheet rock." With more substantial input from the intellect, we reflect on these and related items with reference to more general categories, such as "building material." We consider the universals by virtue of which any object counts as a building material. In assessing particular materials, we assess them with reference to additional universals, such as durability and safety. We carry out complex forms of practical reasoning—choosing, for example, to rank cost-efficiency relative to beauty in determining how useful a given material is, and then choosing materials that are most useful in the desired respect. Due to the influence of the intellect, a human's power to receive and process information on a sensory level extends beyond what is possible for other animals. In addition, acts of the cogitative power are aided and overlaid by acts that are more strictly intellectual. Yet the cogitative power remains, for Aquinas, a sensory power. It is concerned with the apprehension of sensible properties, and its operations rely directly on bodily organs, most notably the brain and nervous system.

Aquinas says relatively little about the more precise relationship between the intellect and the cogitative power. This is unfortunate, given that understanding this relationship appears to be key to understanding how distinctively human emotions are composed. Let us consider, however, what he does say. Approaching this relationship from the perspective of the intellect, he focuses on how it is possible to bridge the gap between the immaterial intellect or the mind and the particular things one seeks to apprehend or know. He says, "our mind is not able directly to know singulars, for we know singulars directly through our sensitive powers which receive [sensible] forms from things into a bodily organ. . . . Nevertheless, the mind has contact with singulars . . . in so far as it has continuity with the sensitive powers which have particulars for their object."[47] Aquinas comments briefly on the nature of this contact, saying that it "comes about in two ways." In one way, "the movement of the sensitive part terminates in the mind, as happens in the movement that goes from things to the soul. Thus, the mind knows singulars through a certain kind of reflection, as when the mind, in knowing its object, which is some universal nature, returns to knowledge of its own act, then to the species which is the principle of its act, and, finally, to the phantasm from which it has abstracted the species. In this way, it attains to some knowledge about singulars."[48] The suggestion is that, inasmuch as the intellect allows one to abstract universals from a phantasm in an effort to apprehend what an object is, and inasmuch as the intellect must continually return to the phantasm as a touchstone, the intellect seems in a way to have the phantasm (and thus the object represented by the phantasm) within its own domain, even though technically the domain of the intellect is the intelligible as such.

The domain of the intellect seems to extend to sensible particulars also when one incorporates sensory-based phantasms into pieces of practical reasoning: "In the other way, this conjunction is found in the movement from the soul to things, which begins from the mind and moves forward to the sensitive part in the mind's [governance, regit] over the lower powers. Here, the mind has contact with singulars through the mediation of particular reason, a power of the sensitive part . . . which is also known as the cogitative power."[49] Specifically in determining what is to be done in a given situation: "The mind's universal judgment . . . cannot be applied to a particular act except through the mediation of some intermediate power which perceives the singular. In this way, there is framed a kind of syllogism whose major premise is universal, the decision of the mind, and whose minor premise is singular, a perception of the particular reason. The conclusion is the choice of [a] singular work."[50] The intellect thus comes into contact with particulars, not only when one seeks to know what the particulars are, but also when one uses that knowledge to reason about what to do in relation to those particulars—when one deliberates about and decides how to act or feel, and one acts or feels in ways that bring about new forms of contact with those and additional particulars.

THE INTELLECT AND THE COGITATIVE POWER

Aquinas considers the connection between the intellect and the cogitative power also from the perspective of the cogitative power (from below), noting the way in which acts of this power resemble and function in continuity with acts of the intellect, so that it can be difficult to say where an act of the materially mediated cogitative power (e.g., an act of sensing the relative usefulness of different pieces of wood) differs from an act of the immaterial intellect (e.g., an act of understanding the nature of wood and the specific properties of wood that make it useful for building a shelter). It can be difficult to say where an act of the one power leaves off and the other begins, especially when these acts combine in joint operations (e.g., when one *senses* that one wood is harder than the others, and that hardness is useful for shelter; one *understands* what makes some woods harder than others, and *why* hardness is important; one *understands* as well that hardness is not the only important consideration in selecting a building material; and one *reasons* that one wood is better than the others in providing protection, but it is not sufficiently better to warrant the high cost of the harder wood). Aquinas says, "The cogitative power is that which is highest in the sensitive part of [the human], and, thus, sense in some way comes in contact with the intellective part so that it participates in something of that which is lower in the intellective part, namely, discursive reason."[51]

Aquinas ranks the cogitative power higher in perfection than the imagination relative to the power of the intellect. Both of these interior sensory powers are "naturally guided and moved according to the universal reason," as is the power of memory.[52] Yet the imagination is somewhat more likely than the cogitative power to mislead; it is more likely to be involved in the arousal of appetitive motions that catch "universal reason" off guard and resist its guidance.[53] Nevertheless, all of these sensory powers allow us to register and assess information in remarkable ways. Again, our interior senses include, generally speaking, what other animals are capable of and also much more, for our interior sensory operations resemble certain intellectual operations and, at a certain point, blend into them.[54] An implication of this view is that much of what readers might be used to thinking of as intellectual is actually interior-sensory or involves the interior-sensory. Aquinas says that our interior senses "owe their excellence not to that which is proper to the sensitive part; but to a certain affinity and proximity to the universal reason, which, so to speak, overflows into them."[55]

The thesis that the cogitative power is a sensory power that benefits from a close relationship to the intellect has significant implications for Aquinas's theory of emotion. Emotions that are evoked by acts of the cogitative power are, by that very fact, already influenced by the intellect.[56] Consider the example of anger. As discussed in chapter 6, anger is caused by two basic acts of sensory apprehension. It is caused by the apprehension that someone has offended one by treating one as if one were of no account. It is caused also by the apprehension that one could—and one would feel better if one did—strike back at the offender, bringing him or her down to size and regaining some of one's power and standing.[57] The visual imagery here is vivid. One pictures being knocked down, becoming heated and red in the face, rising up to defend oneself, attacking the offender, and making him or her suffer for what he or she did—making the other feel one's power and buckle under it.[58] Such images and impressions are clearly sensory, yet they are more than five-sensory. They are also more than most of us imagine taking place (via comparable interior senses) in most other animals, which seem to exhibit simpler forms of sensory judgment.

Aquinas suggests that one relies on acts of the cogitative power that resemble acts of the intellect—and on related acts of the intellect itself—as one seeks, in anger, to find intelligible certain sensory impressions ("she just treated me like a piece of dirt . . . ouch"), to interpret more fully the significance of those impressions ("does she really think so little of me and our friendship, or did I misinterpret what she just said?"), and to conceive a fitting response ("I'm going to show her that she can't treat me that way and get away with it"). Aquinas says, more specifically, that "anger is a desire for vengeance. Now vengeance implies a comparison between the punishment to be inflicted and the hurt done; wherefore the Philosopher says (*Ethics.* VII. loc. cit.) that anger, as if it had drawn the inference that it ought to quarrel with such a person, is therefore immediately exasperated. Now to compare and to draw an inference is an act of reason. Therefore anger, in a fashion, requires an act of reason."[59] The phrases "as if" and "in a fashion" indicate that Aquinas does not, in the final analysis, want to say that anger is caused by acts of intellectual apprehension, such as an understanding of what justice is and a judgment that a particular act violates the principle of justice. Saying this would imply that anger is an act of the will, rather than an emotion. Instead, anger is caused by acts of sensory apprehension, most notably acts of the cogitative power by which one receives and combines impressions of sensible properties, such as "attractive (in some respects), but hurtful," and "powerful, but not beyond the power of others." Yet when humans form impressions of this kind, we ordinarily do so in a way that is informed by—and becomes layered with—intellectual judgments: "The intellect likewise judges about the things which sense apprehends."[60] This layering yields complex judgments and processes of reasoning that are so well integrated that it is difficult to say exactly what, in a given amalgam, is an operation of practical reason (an intellectual power) and what is an operation of particular reason (a sensory power).

Given that our chief aim in this and the following two chapters is to understand the relationship between certain acts of the intellect and the will, on the one hand, and motions of the sensory appetite, on the other, it is important to appreciate the *idea* of the cogitative power as a mid-range power of apprehension—at the high end of the sensory, in contact with the low end of the intellectual—even if Aquinas's account of this power is sketchy. In the main, we want to avoid thinking of sensory apprehension in an impoverished and isolated way, as if apprehending a prospective union or interaction to be hurtful, and determining how best to respond to it, did not already involve a basic form of (body-mediated) conceptualizing, inference-drawing, and judgment-making. Similarly, we want to avoid thinking of acts of intellectual apprehension, such as understanding and deliberating, as if they were not always coordinated with various sensory operations. The sorts of judgments that typically evoke emotions are judgments that we make, not merely as sensory beings or intellectual beings but as sensory-intellectual beings who function at the mysterious intersection of the material and the immaterial, the corruptible and the incorruptible, the particular and the universal.

THE INTELLECTUAL APPREHENSION OF AN OBJECT'S GOODNESS

We will come back to the continuity between acts of intellectual and sensory apprehension, but I want to return, first, to the intellect as such. As we have noted, the intellect makes it possible for one to abstract what is universal from a phantasm so that one can apprehend the essence of a thing, along with "the properties, accidents, and the various relations of the essence."[61] The intellect makes it possible to abstract from a phantasm the universal of "good" so that one can apprehend that (and in what respects) objects of any kind are good, and one can apprehend, more specifically, that (and in what respects) *this object* is good. Given that an act of the will is caused, formally, by an intellectual apprehension of an object's goodness (just as a motion of the sensory appetite is caused, formally, by a sensory apprehension of an object's goodness), it is important to consider what is involved in the intellectual apprehension of an object's goodness.

First, let us consider what makes any object good. This will give us a better idea of what it is to apprehend an object intellectually *as* good (although one can apprehend as good an object that is only *apparently* good). For Aquinas, to say that an object is good is to say, in part, that it has being or actuality and thus a degree of perfection.[62] Yet the notion of good "adds to the concept of *being* a relationship of that which perfects."[63] To say that an object is good is thus to say that it is "capable of perfecting another after the manner of an end."[64] It is to say that the object, in being what it is or behaving as it does, allows another object to actualize some of its own potential. To say that an object is good is to say that it is something with which it would be suitable for another object to *unite* in some way. It is to say that the object is appetible in some respect: It is not only capable of being loved, desired, sought, and (in principle) attained by another in that respect; it is capable also of perfecting or completing the other, to some extent, when attained.[65] On this general level, one could meaningfully say anything from "the surface of the Earth is good for the stone" to "God is good for the human who seeks consciously and deliberately to attain God as his or her highest end."

When Aquinas refers to an object that is "capable of perfecting another after the manner of an end," one can think of the object as a human *other*, and one can think of "another" as the *self*. The other is good inasmuch as he or she is someone with whom it would be suitable for the self to unite in some way.[66] One can think of the object also as a dimension of the self. One's own being is good inasmuch as one's actuality and happiness are objects toward which one can and ordinarily does tend (if only implicitly) as ends; they are objects with which one can unite by doing certain things (for example, by acting virtuously).

One can think of the object also as something that is part of the self in a different sense. Following Aristotle, Aquinas characterizes a close friend of the self as "another oneself"—a self that is other and separate in certain respects but also composes part of one's extended self.[67] A friend is good in that he or she provides one with opportunities to actualize one's potential, some of which is distinctive to the self and some of which is shared with one's friend.[68] A friend is good also inasmuch as he or she provides one with opportunities to assist the friend in actualizing his or her own potential for his or her own sake.[69] In this perspective, one can—and a fine person often does—seek a fitting union with another self precisely by seeking to benefit the other for his or her own sake. The fact that an act of virtuous benevolence also perfects the self does not negate the fact that it is fundamentally other-regarding.

We will focus on objects that exist, to some extent, outside the self, even as these objects perfect or complete the self when a suitable union with them is attained. We are most concerned with objects of apprehension that are also objects of appetite. An object of the appetite might be a simple item toward which one tends and with which one seeks to unite in a simple way: For example, the object might be a glass of water with which one seeks to unite via drinking, or it might be the pleasure of quenching of one's thirst. An object of the appetite might also or instead be something more complex, such as an interpersonal state of affairs: The object might be a friend with whom one seeks to "live together, speak together, and be united together in other like things,"or it might be the prospect of sharing one's life with this friend over time.[70]

THE STANDARD OF GOODNESS

A given object is capable of perfecting other objects in different ways, on different levels, to different degrees. There is, however, a standard with respect to which the goodness of any object is determined. The standard is "the very essence of goodness,"[71] which Aquinas calls God.[72] God is, by definition, that which is perfectly and unambiguously good in itself and thus capable of perfecting every sort of being in every respect. The goodness of every being in the universe is determined with reference to the goodness of God.

From the perspective of humans, there appears to be only one "object" that could be completely perfective of one's being, namely, perfect goodness itself or a perfect union with perfect goodness. To realize this union is the only thing that could "so fill [one's] appetite" and cause such perfect and unending bliss "that nothing is left besides it for [one] to desire."[73] To realize this union is to become fully and perfectly actual as the sort of being one is.

The notion that humans love and desire complete happiness and can attain it (in some measure) by uniting (in some way) with the first principle of being and goodness, or by glimpsing and delighting in the true nature of reality, is something that many people apparently come to believe through the use of their natural powers. Many people seek to know "the God of the philosophers" by reasoning from features of sensory experience to the necessary first cause of those features. Aquinas acknowledges that "the sensible effects of God do not equal the power of God as their cause. Hence from the knowledge of sensible things the whole power of God cannot be known; nor therefore can [God's] essence be seen. But because [sensible things] are [God's] effects and depend on their cause, we *can* be led from them so far as to know of God whether [God] exists, and to know of [God] what must necessarily belong to [God], as the first cause of all things, exceeding all things caused by [God]."[74] To know of God that God is the ultimate cause of goodness is to know that God is in some sense the ultimate source of one's happiness. Knowing that God is the source of one's happiness makes it possible for one to tend explicitly toward God as such, even as the specific nature of God remains an open question.

Aquinas believes that some people receive from God the gift of Christian faith, namely, the ability to assent intellectually to propositions about God that are "above reason."[75] By the power of faith, one still "cannot know of God *what [God] is*," and thus one is united to God, in faith, "as to one unknown."[76] The First Truth remains a mystery. Yet by a kind of supernatural light, "the intellect's natural light is strengthened," and thus one can "know [God] more fully according as many and more excellent of [God's] effects are demonstrated to [one], and according as [one attributes] to [God] some things known by divine revelation, to which natural reason cannot reach, as for instance, that God is Three and One."[77] As we will see in the following chapter, the intentional content of Christian faith makes possible Christian forms of love, hope, and joy. For Aquinas, the latter are acts of a supernaturally elevated intellectual appetite that are directed to God—and to what belongs to God—as God is apprehended via the power of faith.[78]

In Aquinas's scheme, God or union with God is an end that can be tended toward and sought on many different levels by humans (and by other existing things). The sort of union that Aquinas intends as the *highest* end for a human is the continuous activity of perfectly knowing and loving that which is perfectly knowable and lovable.[79] On the basis of one's natural powers, one can conceive the perfection of one's powers and tend toward this perfection as such, without special divine aid. Specifically, one can seek the perfection of one's powers through the exercise of intellectual and moral virtue.[80] Yet a human is destined for more than this, in Aquinas's view. Faith and other divine gifts allow one to become oriented toward a higher end, namely, the continuous activity of knowing and loving *God*, not simply as the distant cause of one's being and perfection (as accessible to reason), but directly and intimately.[81] A person of faith has extended capabilities to know and to love, and one tends toward the perfect actualization of *these* capabilities through the exercise of supernatural (theological and infused) virtues.[82]

A degree of this actualization is possible in the present life. Yet perfect actualization is possible only in the life to come, when what remains of the soul is no longer limited by the material body.[83]

THE HUMAN GOOD AS FINAL OR INTERMEDIATE END

To say that an object is good for a human being is to say, in general, that it is something with which it is perfective of a human to unite—or it is a union toward which it is suitable for a human to tend. It is something that a human is permitted to pursue or ought to pursue as determined, in a given case, by the exercise of virtue: "This is the first precept of law, that good is to be done and pursued, and evil is to be avoided."[84] To be more specific, an object is suitable for *deliberate* human tending if the object (or union) constitutes the final end of one's life or it stands in a productive relationship to one's final end. With respect to everything short of God, an object is suitable inasmuch as uniting with it serves as a proximate or intermediate end or as a means to the attainment of one's final end, such that in tending toward the intermediate end one just does tend toward the final end.[85]

Consider, for example, an object that takes the form of a *situation* that provides one with an opportunity to exercise virtue. In uniting with the object *qua* end—that is, in thinking, feeling, or acting in a virtuous way—one perfects, to some extent, one's natural or supernaturally extended powers. One perfects the powers whose exercise contributes to true human happiness. Ordinarily, in doing anything that supports the daily work of virtue—such as eating appropriate amounts of nourishing food, making an honest living, cultivating character-friendships, and having wholesome fun—one does something that also contributes, in some way and to some extent, to the realization of one's "perfect and crowning good."[86] To say, then, that a finite object is good for a human being is to say that it is capable of serving as an intermediate end in this sense.

The intellect is a power that allows one to apprehend that a given object is "capable of perfecting [one] after the manner of an end."[87] In conjunction with the power of the will, the intellect makes it possible for one to tend toward that end by choice and thus to think, feel, and act for the sake of attaining it. In Aquinas's view, humans always act (when we act in human ways) for the sake of attaining our highest end, if only implicitly.[88] We always act in ways that we judge, on some level, will bring us happiness. We can, of course, be ignorant of what our highest end consists in. We can fail to think about what it would take to perfectly satisfy our human appetites. We can also have beliefs about our highest end that are mistaken (thinking, for example, that this end consists simply in the enjoyment of bodily pleasure). Humans can and often do mistake intermediate ends (and dead ends) for our final end.[89] If we have the wrong final end in view, we can and probably will order our intermediate end-seeking in tragic ways. Even in cases where we get the final principle more or less right, we can be wrong in judging, in particular cases, what will contribute to that end. With respect to all of this judging, we can be misled by sensory judgments in ways that we do not fully understand. What is important for our purposes is to know that, for Aquinas, the intellect makes it possible for humans to apprehend a final end and to apprehend particular objects of experience in light of this end. However, having an intellect does not guarantee that one will exercise it well.

Aquinas maintains that there is one form of union with goodness that could completely satisfy a human's desire. Yet there is more than one way for a human to attain this end: "There are many ways of reaching the last end, and for different people different ways prove suitable."[90] Everyone must determine for himself or herself (in community with others who also seek the good) how to respond to the myriad possibilities for more or less fitting unions with intermediate ends that present themselves at any given moment and over the course of a lifetime. It is the work of virtue to make these determinations well.

It should be evident that the intellect makes possible many different acts that are involved in apprehending an object's goodness. Every such act can and typically does arouse a corresponding act of the will, and any of these coordinated acts or processes of the intellect and the will can have an impact on motions of the sensory appetite. Specifically, the intellect makes it possible for one to apprehend that goodness is to be sought.[91] It allows one also to consider the arguments of Aquinas and other intelligent people regarding the nature of goodness. The intellect thus makes it possible to apprehend that goodness, as one currently conceives it, is to be sought. It allows one to apprehend particular items or situations as opportunities or demands for seeking that goodness—as objects with which it would be suitable to unite. Once one has lighted on a particular opportunity or demand for seeking goodness, the intellect allows one to engage in additional acts of apprehension that contribute to a (sometimes extended) process of deliberation and decision making. The several intellectual acts that are involved in practical reasoning are explored in Aquinas's treatise on the final end, which opens the *prima secundae* of the *Summa theologiae*.[92]

As we proceed, we must thus think broadly and flexibly, not only about what constitutes an object of intellectual apprehension, and about the many dimensions of goodness that one can entertain as one considers an object from various points of view, but also about the many intellectual acts by which one can consider objects that enter one's mind.

INTELLECTUAL AND SENSORY APPREHENSIONS
OF GOODNESS CONJOINED

Aquinas holds that the intellect as such is concerned with "apprehending the universal."[93] With respect to the good, the intellect is a power that makes it possible to apprehend "the very idea of appetible good."[94] It is a power that allows one to think of the good generally as that which is capable of perfecting another, and as that which is to be pursued for the sake of perfection and perfect happiness.[95] Yet just as the intellect is concerned with apprehending "the universal nature existing *in* the individual,"[96] so it is concerned with apprehending the good *in* the particular. The intellect is concerned with apprehending whether and in what respects a given object is good and thus to be pursued.

One apprehends an object's goodness, via the power of the intellect, by abstracting from a phantasm of the object a universal, namely, the object's capability of serving as a suitable end for another. This implies that one who is engaged in intellectual operations with respect to an object is engaged, at the same time, in sensory operations. As one judges intellectually that an object of a certain kind is generally suitable to seek and ought generally to be sought—or one determines, in a particular case, that a union with a particular object would be good for one to seek at this time—one will likely have in mind one or more sensory images and impressions of an object. If the prospect of uniting with the object (or something related to the object) strikes one as suitable on a sensory level—as attractive or useful to one as a sensory being—then one will apprehend the object as good or appetible on more than one level at a time; one will form a layered judgment of its goodness.

Suppose one apprehends, via the intellect, that other persons generally serve as good opportunities for exercising virtue, and that a given person (in the present situation) offers one a fine opportunity to pursue a specific excellence and thus to approach one's highest end. In order to apprehend a person's goodness in this broad sense, one must first apprehend the person via one's exterior senses or otherwise have the person in one's awareness or before one's mind. Let us say that the person is available to the five senses and what Aquinas calls the common sense. If that person, *qua* sensible object, strikes a chord with one's appetite for five-sensory stimulation and pleasure, one will likely apprehend the person *as* "suitable to [the] senses for sensing,"[97] and one will be pleased in sensing the person.[98] Thus, while one con-

siders ways in which uniting with this person through the exercise of a particular virtue could allow the self and the other to achieve a measure of perfection and satisfaction, one will likely register, at the same time, how the
other appears to the eyes or the way his or her voice strikes the ears. One is
also likely to register how these five-sensory inputs make one feel. We can
leave open how consciously aware and reflective one is in regard to what one
feels.

Suppose a person whom one apprehends intellectually to be good is not
right in front of one's eyes or other exterior senses but appears instead in the
form of a sensory image that one has called to mind.[99] As one entertains this
image on a sensory level, one might call other, related objects to mind in the
form of sensory images. One might jump, within one's mind, from one image
to another, forming a series of impressions of the qualities of the objects that
are represented by these images. As one does this, one will likely imagine
what it would be like to unite with various objects in various ways. As one
entertains possible scenarios, one will likely find some of them attractive,
such that the scenarios are pleasing to entertain, and it will likely occur to
one that some of these scenarios would be pleasing to try to bring about in
the world outside the mind. Again, as one considers intellectually how one
could interact with another self so as to become more fully human, while as-
sisting the other in doing the same, one is bound to imagine on a sensory
level the forms such interactions could take, and one will notice how having
these possibilities in mind makes one feel, on a number of different levels.

As one entertains a sensory image or set of images, it is possible that one
will apprehend the person to whom those images correspond, not only as
suitable to the eyes for seeing (and pleasing to look at) as well as suitable to
the mind's eye for imagining (and pleasing to ponder mentally) but also suitable for the well being of the "one sensing." Consider, for example, the sensory impression that a given person would make a suitable companion.[100]
Such an apprehension requires the use of one's cogitative power, for companionability cannot be reduced to a five-sensory quality (although five-
sensory impressions can have an impact on higher-level sensory impressions).
Nor can companionability be considered something detectable by the intellect only, for nonhuman animals (which lack intellects, in Aquinas's view)
judge certain animals—and not others—to be companionable, if only with
respect to certain purposes, such as hunting or mating. Again, the cogitative
power is a sensory power, but some of its acts resemble acts of the intellect
and combine with intellectual acts in seamless ways.

As one exercises the cogitative power, one might go on to register and
sort through a number of additional "intentions"—other ways in which a

person might be suitable or useful in his or her particularity, in more than a five-sensory way. One might also apprehend that some other person in the present situation would also be suitable or useful in some way, and one might set the two persons side by side and form a sensory impression that one of them is more suitable than the other—or one is more suitable in one respect, but the other is more suitable in some other respect. And so on. The point is that, while one considers the other person intellectually—in respect of the idea of goodness and the apprehension that goodness is to be sought, both in general and in this case—one will have recourse to one or more phantasms, and it is likely that one will engage the person, at the same time, as a sensible object that strikes one, via the interior senses, as friendly or helpful or suitable in some other way.

In cases where one regards an object intellectually and apprehends it to be good, one has *reasons* for tending toward the object: One apprehends that the object is capable of perfecting one's being or operation in a way that will likely allow one to approach and thus anticipate the enjoyment of one's highest end. In cases where one apprehends the object also via the senses, and one apprehends it to be suitable on that level, one has, in a sense, additional reasons for tending toward the object. There are ways in which seeking and uniting with the object bodily or in imagination could bring one (further) pleasure, or in some other way benefit one as a sensory being, and one's sensory powers allow one to "sense" this, counting the sensory benefit as a kind of "sensory reason" for pursuing the union. In addition, there are often good intellectual reasons for pursuing and enjoying certain sensory pleasures. Often reasons of the intellect and "sensory reasons" reinforce each other. One would expect as much, given that humans are sensory *and* intellectual beings who tend toward what we apprehend on both sensory and intellectual levels to be good for ourselves and for other selves (at least, when we are in reasonably good working order).

Sometimes these different "reasons" reinforce each other, and sometimes they work at cross purposes. For example, one might judge intellectually that a particular person brings out the best in one as a moral agent, and one might judge also, on a sensory level, that it would be suitable and pleasing for one to engage this person as a companion. In such a case, the sensory pleasure that one enjoys in the person's company will likely strike one intellectually as an added reason for spending time with him or her, or as a welcome bonus—for it is a good thing to be pleased on every level by what is in fact good for one as a human being.[101] However, one might instead judge, on a sensory level, that it would be suitable and pleasing to engage a person as a companion, while judging intellectually that one's final end would be better approached by spending time alone or, in a different situation, attending to the child who is searching frantically for his or her mother. In either case, it is the power of the intellect that allows one to consider forms of union with sensible objects as intermediate ends with respect to one's highest end.

LAYERING AND INFLUENCE IN BOTH DIRECTIONS

What we have said about the way in which intellectual judgments become layered with sensory judgments applies in the reverse direction as well. We need not trace this process in detail. We need only recognize that when we begin with sensory apprehensions of an object's attractiveness or suitability, we tend as intellectual beings to intellectualize our apprehensions and consider whether or not various forms of union with this object are or could be good for us in a more-than-sensory way. Wanting to be happy, most of us realize that pleasing interactions with objects that appear fitting on a sensory level do not necessarily contribute to our complete happiness or improve the overall quality of our lives. Thus, we often wonder, in some form, about whether a given sensible union and the pleasure associated with that union are really beneficial for us, as we entertain pleasing sensory impressions of that union.

It is common for us, as humans, to judge intellectually that enjoying this or that union on a sensory level is consistent with seeking our final end. Sometimes this judgment is on target, and sometimes it is not. Aquinas makes the critical point that a pleasing motion of the sensory appetite can sometimes undermine the very operations of the intellect on which one relies to make good judgments about intermediate ends. He says, for example, that sometimes "according as [one] is affected by a passion, something seems to him fitting, which does not seem so when he is not so affected: thus that seems good to a man when angered, which does not seem good when he is calm."[102] Indeed, extreme sensory-appetitive motions can paralyze our intellectual powers so that we do not even try to ascertain whether a prospective union is conducive to our highest good.[103] Yet there are many acts of the sensory appetite and related pleasures that are consistent with the best operations of the human intellect, according to Aquinas.[104] For example, the sensory love of a friend's company, which attends the impression of his or her companionability, is often compatible with exercising good judgment in his or her regard.

The flow of influence between the intellect and the senses goes in both directions. What is important from Aquinas's ethical perspective is that the intellect take the lead in determining what is good for us.[105] Our intellect is not perfectly reliable in guiding us to complete happiness, even if it is extended by a special gift of grace. Yet it is a more reliable guide than our senses, for our senses regard only particulars; they cannot provide us with the ability to deliberate about and judge particulars in light of a reflective ideal. At the same time, it is important to consider that our senses often give us valuable information about what is good for us on a sensory level. Our senses are part of our evolutionary inheritance; they are part of the wherewithal that has made it possible for us to survive as animals and as a species. Sometimes humans try, through the power of our intellects, to deny certain features of our animality, such as our need for intimacy or for aggressive forms of play, but neglecting these features can put ourselves and our kin in peril.

Given the close connection between the intellectual and interior sensory powers of apprehension, it is to be expected that humans will ordinarily exercise both powers at the same time in assessing the significance of various objects. When we apprehend an object to be good on an intellectual level, we will ordinarily apprehend it (or an image or impression of it or something related to it) to be good on a sensory level as well, and vice versa. Appreciating this connection prepares us to understand the influence that the intellect, working in conjunction with the interior sensory powers, can have on motions of the sensory appetite. Rather than tracking the impact of the intellect in isolation from the will, however, it would be best to introduce the will and consider briefly its relationship to the intellect.

NOTES

1. Again, Aquinas recognizes that humans have introduced and continue to introduce a tremendous amount of disorder and destruction into the processes of cosmic creativity. Yet he holds that this disorder is intelligible to the Divine mind, and it is contained within a fundamental tending of creation toward perfection (i.e., Love). He chooses to focus on the possibility of goodness, as do I in this project.

2. For many people today, "human" is defined biologically or genetically. For Aquinas, "human" is defined with reference to the form of rational animality. In his view, this form is not present in the early embryo or fetus. It is "infused" by God only when the fetus has undergone sufficient physiological development to support (primitive forms of) distinctively human activities (*ST* I 118.2 and *SCG*, bk. 3a, chap. 22). For a brief discussion of the theory of delayed hominization in Aquinas, see Joseph Donceel, "A Liberal Catholic's View," in *The Problem of Abortion*, 2nd ed., ed. Joel Feinberg (Belmont, Calif.: Wadsworth, 1984), 15–20.

3. Aquinas says that "the will regards good according to the common notion of good, and therefore in the will, which is the intellectual appetite, there is no differentiation of appetitive powers, so that there be in the intellectual appetite an irascible

power distinct from a concupiscible power" (*ST* I 82.5; see also I 59.4). However, acts of the will such as love of friendship and hope cannot be distinguished without some reference to the concept of difficulty (*ST* II-II 17).

4. An emotion is distinctively human if it occurs in a being whose intellect and intellectual appetite influence how he or she relates to objects of sensory experience. Aquinas would say that the more one's sensory-appetitive motions are governed by virtue, the *more human* the appetitive motions are.

5. *ST* I 79.10.

6. Misunderstanding can occur particularly in cases where one "joins and divides concepts by affirmation or denial" (*Truth* 14.1).

7. *ST* I-II 8.1.

8. *ST* I 79.12.

9. Pasnau, *Thomas Aquinas on Human Nature*, 307.

10. *ST* I 86.2, 84.7.

11. *ST* I 84.7.

12. *ST* I 85.1.

13. *SCG*, bk. 2, chap. 73. In the human, memory includes the power of reminiscence, but for the sake of simplicity, I will refer to memory only (*ST* I 78.4).

14. See chapters 3 and 5.

15. *ST* I 79.4, 85.1 *ad* 1.

16. *ST* I 84.6.

17. *ST* I 85.5.

18. Here, "rational" simply means "*capable* of engaging in intellectual acts, including acts of reasoning."

19. Today, all of these forms or categories are subject to deconstruction within academia. For our purposes, it is important to leave open the possibility that such categories can be an aid to understanding, even as they can also mislead those who use them, in ways that serve to reinforce particular arrangements of social power.

20. *ST* I 85.5. Note that, for Aquinas, the intellect (the power of intellectual apprehension) makes a variety of intellectual acts possible; *understanding* is one of these, *reasoning* is another.

21. *ST* I 85.3, 58.4.

22. *ST* I 79.9. Aquinas quotes Augustine, "*De Trinitate*" xii. 4.

23. *ST* I-II 62–63.

24. *ST* II-II 2.3.

25. *ST* I 84.7, including *ad* 3; 85.1; 79.9.

26. *ST* I 84.7 (my emphasis). Aquinas refers to Aristotle, "*De Anima*" 431a14.

27. *ST* I 84.7.

28. Ibid.

29. The very act of turning to one's experience for evidence involves appealing to images and impressions of one's life and world, which proves Aquinas's point.

30. *ST* I 84.7.

31. Ibid.

32. *ST* I 84.7 *ad* 3.

33. Ibid.

34. *ST* II-II 2.3, including *ad* 3, 8.7.

35. *Truth* 19.1.

36. *ST* I 1.8 *ad* 2.

37. *ST* I 84.7 *ad* 3.

38. There are times when this does not happen, as when one apprehends a medicine as good for health, but awful to the taste.

39. I referred in chapter 2 to the way in which James Gustafson wishes to capture the unity of human experience. Here is an example of where Aquinas allows us to do the same, but by first teasing apart various dimensions of experience and then considering how they function in relation to each other.

40. *ST* I 86.1 *ad* 4.

41. *ST* I 84.1, 85.2.

42. This is most evident in his discussion of the soul in *ST* I 75.2, 76.1, 77.1.

43. *Truth* 14.1 *ad* 9; *ST* I 77.7.

44. *SCG*, bk. 2, chap. 60.

45. *Truth* 24.2.

46. See Pasnau, *Thomas Aquinas on Human Nature*, sect. 9.2.

47. *Truth* 10.5.

48. Ibid.

49. Ibid.

50. Ibid..

51. *Truth* 14.1 ad 9.

52. *ST* I 81.3; see also I-II 17.7.

53. *ST* I 81.3 *ad* 2.

54. *ST* I 78.4 *ad* 5, 81.3.

55. *ST* I 78.4 *ad* 5.

56. *ST* I 81.3 *ad* 2.

57. *ST* I-II 46.

58. On a sensory level, it makes a kind of "sense" that, after being treated as if one were negligible, one would want to regain one's standing by asserting one's power, including one's power to cause reciprocal injury to the other. Yet it seems that what one wants most in anger is to make the other take one seriously as a person and this end cannot necessarily be attained by causing the other injury. See Diana Fritz Cates, "Taking Women's Experience Seriously: Thomas Aquinas and Audre Lorde on Anger," in *Aquinas and Empowerment: Classical Ethics for Ordinary Lives*, ed. G. Simon Harak (Washington, DC: Georgetown University Press, 1996), 47–88. Note that anger is an emotion that not only reflects but also functions to assert and uphold a particular (hierarchical) social order in which some persons are permitted to be offended by insult and injury, and others are not. Daniel Gross makes this point in *The Secret History of Emotion*. Unfortunately he works with an extreme version of social constructionism

and neglects the animal dimension of human anger (its relationship to mechanisms for self-defense and the defense of one's kin).

59. *ST* I-II 46.4.

60. *Truth* 25.1.

61. *ST* I 85.5.

62. Aquinas uses the term "being" (*ens*) broadly: "That which is not a being in nature, is considered as a being in the reason, wherefore negations and privations are said to be *beings of reason*. In this way, too, future things, in so far as they are apprehended, are beings" (*ST* I-II 8.1 *ad* 3).

63. *Truth* 21.1 (my emphasis).

64. Ibid.

65. *SCG*, bk. 3b, chap. 107.

66. As we have seen, "uniting" is an open category; it can refer to anything from seeing—to eating—to learning—to knowing—to playing—and more.

67. *ST* I-II 28.1.

68. For a more in-depth discussion of the way in which the self is composed partly through the activities of friendship, see Cates, *Choosing to Feel: Virtue, Friendship, and Compassion for Friends* (Notre Dame, Ind.: University of Notre Dame, 1997).

69. *ST* I-II 26.4, 28.2.

70. *ST* I-II 28.1 *ad* 2.

71. *Truth* 22.1.

72. *ST* I 3.2.

73. *ST* I-II 1.5.

74. *ST* I 12.12 (my emphasis).

75. *ST* II-II 1.1, 1.4, 2.3. Keep in mind that, for Aquinas, faith ordinarily functions in tandem with other gifts of grace, such as love; it ordinarily causes related effects, such as reverence; and it ordinarily finds certain forms of outward expression, such as worship. Although faith is technically a perfection of the intellect, it is misleading to think of it as "merely intellectual" (*ST* II-II 6.2, 7.1, 7.2).

76. *ST* I 12.13, including *ad* 1.

77. *ST* I 13 *ad* 1.

78. *ST* I-II 62.1.

79. *ST* I-II 3.2 *ad* 4.

80. *ST* I-II 4.5.

81. *ST* I-II 62.1, 62.2, 62.3.

82. *ST* I-II 5.5, 3.8, 62.1. In Aquinas's highly intelligible universe, the natural and the supernatural are in continuity with each other. One does not cease to be a rational animal (essentially human) when one becomes a person of Christian faith; one simply becomes a rational animal who is capable of grasping truths that take one beyond the limits of natural reason, even as one grasps other truths that are accessible to natural reason. In addition, no mere human is in fact perfect: Extended capacities are still, in significant respects, limited by finitude and corrupted by sin.

83. Aquinas holds that after the resurrection, the beatified soul will operate with an incorruptible spiritual body, and the perfection of one's intellectual nature will redound upon this body (*ST* III 57.3). He does not have a lot to say about how the glorified body will work.

84. *ST* I-II 94.2.

85. *ST* I-II 8.2.

86. *ST* I-II 1.5.

87. *Truth* 21.1.

88. *ST* I-II 1.6 *ad* 3, 5.8.

89. *ST* I-II 1.7 *ad* 1.

90. *Truth* 22.6.

91. *ST* I-II 94.2.

92. For a discussion of the various acts of the intellect and related acts of the will that compose the decision-making process, see Sherwin, *By Knowledge and By Love.*

93. *Truth* 22.4.

94. *ST* I 82.3.

95. *ST* I-II 94.2.

96. *ST* I 84.7 (my emphasis).

97. *Truth* 25.1.

98. It appears that, in Aquinas's scheme, this sort of sensory apprehension already engages the imagination to some extent. I do not know that Aquinas says this explicitly. He does say that one can understand an object only by means of a phantasm, and that forming a phantasm requires the use of the imagination. It must be, then, that one can understand even what is right in front of one only by means of a phantasm and thus via the power of one's imagination. The idea seems to be that the sensory image of the object, which one is later able to call to mind in the object's absence, is present in one's mind as one apprehends the object with one's exterior senses. See Aquinas, *Commentary on Aristotle's "De Anima,"* sects. 838–39.

99. It could be important for someone who is attracted to Aquinas's account of the emotions to consider whether and how persons who are congenitally blind form phantasms or mental images. See Markus Knauff and Elisabeth May, "Mental Imagery, Reasoning, and Blindness," *Quarterly Journal of Experimental Psychology* 59, no. 1 (2006): 161–77.

100. *Truth* 25.1.

101. *ST* I-II 24.3.

102. *ST* I-II 9.2.

103. *ST* I-II 10.3.

104. *ST* I-II 24.3.

105. *ST* I-II 10.3 *ad* 1.

CHAPTER EIGHT

Approaching the Human Sensory Appetite from Above (II)

◆

The powers of intellectual and sensory apprehension make it possible to understand and assess aspects of one's world that bear on one's happiness. The connection between the intellect and the cogitative power, in particular, makes it possible to judge an object, on an intellectual level, to be an object of a certain kind with which one could unite in a way that contributes to one's flourishing, even as one judges the same object, on a sensory level, to be useful, helpful, friendly, or the like. The connection between the intellect and the cogitative power makes it possible also to engage in well-integrated intellectual-sensory modes of reasoning about what is beneficial for oneself or for others in a given situation. The cogitative power operates with the cooperation of memory and imagination, which make it possible to hold in mind events that are now past, and to project future scenarios.

Just as the powers of intellectual and sensory apprehension work in conjunction with each other, so do the powers of intellectual apprehension (intellect) and appetite (will), although the latter conjunction is different in kind. The intellect makes it possible to understand an object and its relationship to one's well-being, but the act of understanding an object presupposes a prior appetitive motion, a motion of the will. It presupposes, for example, an appetite or wish to understand one's world, and a wish to understand a particular object as a part of one's world. If one understands an object, and part of what one understands is the object's goodness, then it is likely that one will also undergo a subsequent motion of the will in relation to the object. One will recognize and consent to the object's goodness. One might also wish to unite with the object or its goodness in a further way.

Borne by this wish, one might apply one's intellect to the work of determining the best strategy for attaining the union one desires. And so the interaction continues.

I now consider what Aquinas takes the will to be, and how he construes
its relationship to the intellect. As with the intellect, I attend to the will only
to the extent that I must, in order to elucidate Aquinas's account of the emotions. I leave to others a thorough analysis of the will as such. This chapter
will prepare us to consider, in the following chapter, some of the contributions that the intellect and the will, operating together, can make to the formation of human emotions. It will also allow us to explore the influence that
emotions can have on the intellect and the will. Apprehending this reciprocal flow of influence within a typical human being allows us to understand
emotions *as* motions of the sensory appetite while appreciating how they
arise and unfold under the impact of, and in combination with, other interior acts.

THE INTELLECTUAL APPETITE

The human will (*voluntas*) is the power to tend toward (or away from) what
one apprehends, by the power of one's intellect, to be good (or bad). It includes the power to tend toward what one judges intellectually to be one's
highest end. It includes also the power to tend toward what one judges, in
general or in particular situations, to be intermediate ends relative to one's
highest end.[1]

When Aquinas speaks of the will, he usually emphasizes that the will, like
its partner the intellect, operates within the realm of the universal and the abstract. Just as the proper object of the intellect is "universal *being* and *truth*," so
the proper object of the will is universal goodness or appetibility.[2] In this account, "the proper object of the will is good itself taken absolutely"[3] or "good
in the abstract"[4] or "good in general, which has the nature of an end."[5] However, the main function of the will in a human being is to enable one to tend
toward the good as it appears in—or with reference to—particular objects.[6]
The main function of the will is to enable one to make one's way in the world
as a moral agent by engaging daily situations in ways that contribute to one's
own or others' complete happiness, as one understands that.[7]

What is it to *tend*, by the power of the will, toward human happiness, and
toward what appears to contribute to happiness? It can be helpful to consider
intellectual-appetitive tending in light of what we know about sensory-
appetitive tending. These two forms of tending resemble each other in certain respects. For example, both are object-oriented. An act of the will cannot

be identified or specified without reference to its object any more than an act of the sensory appetite can. In addition, both forms of tending involve interior motion and (on some level of awareness) the experience of such motion, where "motion" can be directional or it can simply involve "motion in place," as when one resonates with or one consents to a good that is already present.

More specifically, both forms of tending exhibit a similar three-fold structure. Whether intellectual or sensory, an appetitive motion includes one or more of the following: (1) an initial moment in which one recognizes and is pleased by an object's suitability (or one recognizes and is displeased by its unsuitability); (2) a subsequent moment in which one approaches the object interiorly and also, perhaps, exteriorly (or one withdraws from it) to attain a further sort of union with the object (or to avoid further interaction); and (3) a final moment in which one enjoys (or suffers) that further union. A motion of the appetite might also involve rising to a challenge or tending to overcoming an obstacle that stands in the way of one's attaining (or avoiding) what appears to be suitable (or unsuitable). This is a formal way of representing experiences that are often complex, in which one relates to several different dimensions of a situation at the same time. In chapter 6, working with this structure allowed us to identify eleven basic motions of the sensory appetite, most of which are known by familiar emotion terms. This same structure allows us to identify similar motions on the intellectual level, which Aquinas calls motions of the intellectual appetite, simple acts of the will or, more specifically, affections.

Acts of intellectual-appetitive tending also differ from acts of sensory-appetitive tending. Acts of the will are caused formally by acts of the intellect, whereas emotions are caused formally by acts of sensory apprehension. Thus, with respect to the central moment in a process of tending, one reaches out by an act of intellectual desire toward an object (or union with an object) in respect of its intelligible goodness (namely, the way in which it appears to contribute to one's own or another's flourishing), whereas one reaches out or, more precisely, one is drawn by an act of sensory desire toward an object (often the same object) in respect of its sensible goodness (namely, the way in which it appears to be attractive or useful on a sensory level).

In addition, Aquinas holds that intellectual-appetitive acts are not mediated directly by changes in the body, although they depend in the present life on the cooperation of the sensory powers. By contrast, sensory-appetitive acts are performed directly by means of bodily organs or organ systems.[8] Thus, an emotion is usually experienced as an object-oriented interior motion with a noticeable (if also subtle) material correlate, whereas an affection, which is an act of the will, is experienced as a mode of interior tending, but not one that registers directly in the body. Aquinas says that "love, concupiscence, and the like can be understood in two ways. Sometimes they are taken as passions—arising, that is, with a certain commotion of the soul. And thus they are commonly understood, and in this sense, they are only in the sensitive appetite. They may, however, be taken in another way, as far as they are simple affections without passion or commotion of the soul, and thus they are acts of the will."[9] Aquinas does acknowledge that affections can be "intense," such that they cause a corresponding motion of the sensory appetite and thus register *indirectly* in the body.[10] We will explore this effect later in this chapter and in the following chapter.

Another difference between acts of the intellectual appetite and those of the sensory appetite is that the former have an active dimension, a dimension of self-motion, whereas the latter are only passive (even though they often *feel* active to the subject of the emotion).[11] The intellectual appetite does include the power to *be moved*. Specifically, it includes the power to be moved by acts of one's own intellect. It includes the power to receive, as an object of one's appetite, the goodness that one abstracts intellectually from an object. For example, it includes the power to receive as an object of one's appetite the prospect of uniting with a fellow human being in the form of exercising virtue in his or her regard. That is, it includes the power to have as an object of one's appetite the prospect of one's own and another's flourishing. The intellectual appetite includes also the power to *move oneself* relative to an object that one has in mind.[12] It includes the power to relate directly to another human being in respect of his or her goodness, say, as someone who excels in some respect or allows one to excel in relation to him or her.[13] It includes the power to unite or interact with another in ways that express the best in oneself and thus benefit both self and other. The sensory appetite, by contrast, is a power to *be moved* by what strikes one's exterior or interior senses as attractive or repulsive, helpful or hurtful, friendly or threatening. The sensory appetite allows one to be acted upon, reoriented interiorly, and changed bodily by perceived or imagined sensible objects and their properties.

MODES OF TENDING: INTELLECTUAL DESIRE

We can elucidate the will further by examining particular acts of the will. Given that we are most interested in acts of the intellectual appetite as they relate to acts of the sensory appetite, it is helpful to examine more closely the three moments that characterize a typical process of being moved by—

and moving oneself in relation to—an intelligible good. As on the sensory level, so also on the intellectual level, each of these moments has its own name: love, desire, and delight, or joy.

Let us begin with the central moment of the triad, as we did in chapter 6. The will is a power that allows one to *desire* an object (or union with an object) in respect of its goodness, which includes the object's ability to be perfective of those who unite with it. One can speak of the will as the power to *will* (*velle*) a fitting union with another, as long as one keeps in mind that "willing" usually means "desiring, by the power of one's will," but it can also mean "exercising one's will," which can take additional forms. Ordinarily, one is said to desire an object or good with which one is not already united. Paradigmatically, one desires a union that goes beyond merely having an object's goodness in mind and being pleased with the way that goodness is already present to the self.[14] By an act of desire, one reaches out interiorly and also, perhaps, exteriorly toward a further, more tangible, way of interacting with the goodness of the object. One might wish to actualize oneself by uniting with the object's perfective power—by interacting with the other in a way that allows one to become more fully actual. One might wish to extend the object's perfective power for its own sake—by acting on the other in a way that allows the other, in turn, to become more fully actual.

Intellectual desire is a principle or cause of voluntary action. It is, in part, a cause of *exterior* action. Suppose one has a desire to bring out the best in a colleague—to see him or her thrive as a human being. Motivated by this desire, one might choose to say encouraging things. Intellectual desire is also a cause of (additional) *interior* acts and processes. Countless acts of desire drive, from within, the processes by which one calls to mind a valuable goal, one regards the present situation as an opportunity to pursue that goal, one deliberates about how one can be most successful in realizing one's goal, one takes all viable options seriously, and one chooses from among them what appears to be the best option. Aquinas says, "the will moves the other powers of the soul to their acts, for we make use of the other powers when we will. For the end and perfection of every other power is included under the object of the will as some particular good."[15]

By the power of one's will, one is able to act interiorly and exteriorly for an end. More specifically, one is able to act *for a reason*. One is able to desire something and seek it through a deliberate course of action because one judges that in doing so one will benefit oneself or another as a human being who has important potential waiting to be realized.[16] Of course, the will can be misdirected: One can fail to think well about what is beneficial for humans. One can move oneself, accordingly, to seek for oneself or for another a state of being or an activity that does not, in fact, contribute to human flourishing. The will can also be weak or corrupt: one can think well, at times, about what is good for humans, but fail to move oneself consistently in light of this understanding. One can be driven by sensory desires that have not been vetted by the power of reason and may resist the vetting process, as when one judges that it would be inappropriate to say anything encouraging to a colleague, and one avoids constructive interactions, because the colleague "doesn't deserve my good will," when what one is really doing is acting on envy. Having the capacity to desire something for a reason and to express that desire in action does not guarantee that one's desires or actions will express virtue. It does not guarantee that one's reasons will be good reasons.

In the *secunda secundae* of the *Summa theologiae*, Aquinas treats hope as an example of an intellectual desire. Actually, he treats hope as a virtue, and more specifically as a theological virtue. Considered as a *virtue*, hope is a habit of the intellectual appetite, a stable disposition of the will that causes one to desire rightly what pertains to one's highest end.[17] Considered as a *theological* virtue, hope is a habit infused by God, which causes the power of one's intellectual appetite to be healed to some extent of inherited and acquired disorders, and extended in its ability to orient one toward what lies beyond one's understanding.[18] Hope is a virtue, but it is known by its *act*. The interior act of hope is a motion of the appetite, "since its object is a good."[19] In chapter 6, we saw that hope can name a motion of the *sensory* appetite inasmuch as the object of one's appetite is something that one judges, by the power of one's interior senses, to be good, future, and difficult, but possible to attain.[20] Here we see that hope can also, by extension, name a motion of the *intellectual* appetite inasmuch as the object of one's appetite is something that one judges, by the power of one's intellect and thus "in general," to be good, future, and difficult, but possible to attain.[21] In addition, hope can name a motion of the intellectual appetite inasmuch as the object is something "more than intelligible," namely, something whose goodness one can grasp only by the added power of faith. The central act of *theological* hope is the desire for a perfectly enjoyable union with the God of faith, along with a desire for God's help in realizing this end.[22] This is a union that reason alone might suggest is impossible or undeserved, and even to the person of faith appears remarkable, way beyond one's ordinary capabilities.[23]

Aquinas focuses on hope as a form of self-motion that is made possible by a gift of grace, but there are many forms of intellectual hope that are possible for humans on the basis of their natural powers alone. For example, anyone can hope for a just resolution to an old, stubborn conflict. Anyone can hope for a friend's recovery from a chronic illness. Indeed, anyone can, through the use of natural human powers, hope in the possibility that something of who one is will survive the dissolution of one's body. One can hope that something good (which could be left open or specified in different ways, in terms of different religious or philosophical paths) will happen to whatever remains of oneself. One can hope for these and other goods without Christian faith, although it could be that such hope requires some other sort of faith, or it requires going beyond reason in some sense, but we are not concerned here with the rationality of hope. The point is simply that Christian hope is only one form of intellectual hope.

Moreover, intellectual hope is only one form of intellectual desire. Hope is a desire for a future good that seems difficult but not impossible to attain. Clearly, one can also desire a good that seems close at hand and not beyond one's ordinary abilities. For example, one can desire intellectually to bring out the best in a colleague, and one can do so without being constrained by envy. Motivated by benevolence, one can deliberate and decide that the best strategy, in a given situation, is simply to say something encouraging. One might determine, instead, that doing something more substantial is required. In any case, one reaches out interiorly toward the prospect of benefiting the other. If one discerns that the other is struggling with profound self-doubt, which makes it difficult for him or her to receive help from others in becoming more fully alive and confident in his or her gifts, then one's desire might have to give way to hope. As noted in chapter 6, this is a matter of assessing the level of difficulty in bringing about the end desired. One's assessment of this difficulty can shift over the course of ongoing interactions.

INTELLECTUAL LOVE

The will is a power that enables one also to *love* an object of intellectual apprehension, where love is construed partly as a principle or cause of intellectual desire. As noted with regard to the sensory appetite, love, for Aquinas, does *not* denote a motion whereby "the appetite moves towards the realization of the appetible object" in the mode of being drawn or (in a more active voice) reaching out toward union interiorly;[24] this is the central motion of desire. Rather, love denotes a prior appetitive motion that is presupposed by desire—a motion "whereby the appetite is [simply] changed by the appetible object, so as to have complacency therein."[25] With respect to the sensory appetite, undergoing the motion of love involves having a sensory impression that one stands in a well-ordered relationship to an object (which makes it possible for one to tend toward a further union with the object), and resting with pleasure in this impression.

Much the same applies with respect to the intellectual appetite, except that an act of the will proceeds, in a unique way, from the person himself or herself. Intellectual love, like intellectual desire, involves a form of self-motion.[26] It involves apprehending that one stands in a fitting relationship to an object that is characterized by goodness and *consenting* to that goodness—opening oneself to it and holding it, with pleasure, in one's appetitive field.[27] Frederick Crowe puts it this way: "The will, before being the faculty of appetite, of process to a term, is the faculty of affective consent, of acceptance of what is good, of concord with the universe of being."[28]

Intellectual love is not an active, directional tending, but it is nevertheless appropriate to regard it as a mode of tending. It is the activation of a natural tendency to attend to, recognize as familiar, welcome, and take pleasure in the way one stands in relation to goodness or particular good things, namely, things that promote human well-being, as one conceives that.[29] Intellectual love is a readiness to "go out from oneself," if one desires, in the direction of an object whose goodness appears as an invitation to actualize one's own goodness—or an invitation to contribute to the good of another—in a way that contributes to the perfection of some larger whole.[30]

After examining faith and hope in the *Summa theologiae*, Aquinas examines the theological virtue of charity (*caritas*). Like hope, charity is an infused habit that heals and extends (into a higher dimension, for the sake of a supernatural end) the power of one's natural intellectual appetite.[31] One of the principal *acts* of charity is intellectual love.[32] Charity is partly a change in one's appetite that becomes possible when one apprehends (by faith) that one stands in a fitting relationship to God and to all that God loves. It is a change that becomes possible when one realizes that one has been granted by God, a special capacity to relate to God, not only as the first cause of one's being and goodness (as evident to natural reason) but as an intimate Friend with whom one shares one's life,[33] and one has been granted the capacity to relate to one's fellow human beings (even one's enemies) as friends of this Friend.[34] Charity is partly the act of consenting to the goodness of the way in which every human being (by virtue of being a friend or child of God) is "another oneself" whose well-being is of significance to the self.[35] Charity is partly the act of opening oneself to a full appreciation of the notion that one is "fit" to partake in the "fellowship of the spiritual life" whereby humans seek the perfect enjoyment of God's goodness as their common end.[36]

In Aquinas's scheme, charity ordinarily includes more than an initial act of intellectual love; it includes also an act of intellectual desire or benevolence, which is commonly expressed in acts of beneficence.[37] Charity involves desiring and seeking, as circumstances allow, to promote the perfection of all things in relation to God as their highest end, to the glory of God.[38] In particular, charity includes wishing oneself well, partly for one's own sake, and wishing others well, partly for their own sake, where one appreciates, in love, how one's own good is connected to the good of others.[39] We noted with regard to sensory love that Aquinas sometimes speaks of love broadly, as including not only the initial moment of complacency but also the subsequent moment of desire. Yet he insists that complacency is the more basic appetitive motion. Similarly, charity includes an act of good will or benevolence, but such acts of benevolence are predicated on prior acts of intellectual love.[40]

Intellectual love can take many different objects (as many objects as there are objects of desire), and there are many examples of intellectual love that do not appear to depend on infused virtue. Generally speaking, intellectual love is simply "the aptitude of the . . . will to some [intelligible] good, that is to say, its very complacency in good."[41] More specifically, intellectual love is the act of accepting and taking pleasure in the way an object appears to have the capacity to be perfective of the self, and one thus has the capacity to become more fully human and more fully oneself in relating to that object. It could be that few of us are explicitly aware of the way in which countless objects in our world enable us to actualize our potential by interacting with them. We seldom look around us and say, "all of this . . . is truly wonderful. I fully appreciate it. I consent to all of this goodness." Yet what Aquinas allows us to do is to say just this, if we wish. He allows us to identify and characterize an experience that might go unnoticed by many of us, or might be left largely implicit, namely, the experience of relishing the fact that we exist—as intellectual beings, sensory beings, living things, and material entities who have our existence in dynamic relation to other existing things, in relation to a principle of order that somehow holds everything together. Many of us do not have the religious language that allows us to ponder the underlying nature of things. Aquinas gives us some language with which to start.

INTELLECTUAL JOY

The third moment in a typical process of tending toward an intelligible good is *joy* (*gaudium*). As noted in chapter 6, Aquinas calls this moment "delight" (*delectatio*) when it occurs primarily on a sensory level, in relation to a perceived sensible good. Delight and joy are both forms of coming to rest and being pleased when one attains a desired union with what one apprehends to be a suitable object, and one is aware of this attainment.[42] Aquinas reserves the name "joy" for what occurs when one attains an object that one judges intellectually to be good for oneself or for "another oneself." He specifies that "we take delight both in those things which we desire naturally, when we get them, and in those things which we desire as a result of reason. But we do not speak of joy except when delight follows reason."[43]

Aquinas indicates that "joy is compared to desire, as rest to movement."[44] In a sense, then, joy is without motion: It is without active, directional motion, for it is a way of relating to a good that one previously desired and sought, but one has now attained. Yet in another sense joy is an appetitive motion. Aquinas characterizes it explicitly as a motion of the will (*motus voluntatis*).[45] By the power of one's intellectual appetite, one is actually conjoined with an intelligible good, and one acquiesces in that conjunction—one resonates with pleasure in the perfective power of that union.[46] The pleasure that Aquinas associates with joy can be "sober and moderate,[47] but it can also be so full and expansive that one's "inward joy breaks forth from its bounds" and finds expression in "exterior signs."[48] It is common for intellectual joy to register, indirectly, in one's body.[49]

Again, in the *secunda secundae* of the *Summa theologiae*, after a discussion of faith, hope, and love, Aquinas considers Christian joy as a motion of a supernaturally extended intellectual appetite. This sort of joy takes God and union with God—especially the union that is effected in charity—as its object.[50] This joy involves being at ease and pleased in the awareness that one has been perfected, in some respect, by the indwelling presence of the divine Friend.[51] Aquinas describes the perfect joy of the life to come, when one finally "sees" God "face to face," as a state in which one is completely at rest in the sense that one attains—and one knows one has attained—all that one had (worthily) desired and even more than one had been able to desire.[52] At the same time, Aquinas describes perfect human happiness (*beatitudo*) as an operation—as the continual, everlasting act of perfectly knowing and loving that which is perfectly knowable and lovable.[53] Perfect joy is thus a moment of completion *and* complete actuality.

There are many forms of joy, not simply those that take the God of Christian faith as their object. One example of a natural intellectual joy is the appetitive motion of resonating with pleasure in the good of finally understanding something that one has long sought to understand.[54] Another example is the motion of taking pleasure in the observation that a loved one, whom one has long wished well, is thriving. Aquinas says that "joy is caused by love, either through the presence of the thing loved, or because the proper good of the thing loved exists and endures in it; and the latter is the case chiefly in the love of benevolence, whereby [one] rejoices in the well-being of his friend, though [the friend] be absent."[55] Aquinas connects joy, in this passage, with complacency and with desire (or well-wishing), suggesting that joy is incipient in the initial consent to the way in which one stands in relation to an intelligible good, and also in the desire by which one tends toward a further form of union with that good. Yet joy is more specifically the act of embracing and affirming the good attained.

THE INTELLECTUAL APPETITE AND THE SENSORY

Aquinas characterizes joy as "nothing but [a] mere movement of the will."[56] He would characterize intellectual love and desire in the same way. Because the will, like the intellect, is a power of the immaterial intellectual soul, in his view, motions of the will, considered in themselves, are unaccompanied by "bodily transmutation."[57] It might therefore seem odd to hear him refer to the pleasure that attends the apprehension that one has attained a suitable union with an intelligible good[58]—or to hear me refer to complacency, with respect to the will, as a pleasing resonance that occurs when one apprehends that one stands in suitable relationship to some object—a relationship that makes a perfective union with the object possible. It might also seem strange to hear Aquinas refer to the "intensity" of the will—as when he says that motions of the will can be so intense that they "break forth" in signs of celebration or "overflow" into the lower powers of the soul.[59] In what sense can purely intellectual acts be considered intense and a source of intense pleasure? Indeed, how are we even to think about "purely intellectual acts"? As I interpret Aquinas, such notions can make sense to us only because acts of the intellect and the will are bound up with sensory experience in one way or another.

First, consider the intellect and the will as potentially intelligible objects in their own right, which we seek now to understand. Just as purely intellectual beings (such as angels) can be understood (to some extent) only by way of "remotion," by abstracting from our own experience as intellectual *and* sensory beings, so simple acts of the intellect and the will in humans can be understood only by beginning with acts that engage the sensory powers, and trying to reason from these to other sorts of interior acts that concern universals and do not engage the body directly. For example, an act of the will might be understood partly by considering an object to which one is attracted, by considering other objects that one finds similarly attractive, by identifying a formal property that the objects share, particularly a property that bears on human well-being, and by considering that one is attracted to this property, and one wishes to unite with it, wherever it appears. An act of the will might be understood also by beginning with a presumption that there is a close relationship between consciousness and the brain, in a living human being, and then trying to project a dimension of consciousness, along with a cause of self-motion, that is not reducible to material causes, whether inside or outside the brain. An act of the will might be understood as intense and pleasurable inasmuch as some of its *effects* are intense and pleasurable, as when one observes that one has the ability to put many hours a day into one's studies, and one gets a physical rush from studying, so one reasons that one must have an intense intellectual desire to understand.

Second, what many of us call "intellectual pleasure" is an experience known to humans whose intellectual powers function in coordination with our sensory powers. Humans rarely wish simply and abstractly to unite with goodness as such. Usually we wish to unite with particular objects in respect of their goodness. In tending toward good things, we tend toward possibilities for ourselves or for others that we cannot help but imagine, in some form, with reference to phantasms, examples, or experiences. If a way of uniting with a prospective good strikes us as significant for our well-being, partly through the use of our interior sensory powers, then our sensory appetite is likely to become engaged. Inasmuch as we succeed in uniting with our prospective good, we will experience delight as well as joy. That is, our experience of being perfected in relation to an intelligible good will be accompanied by noticeable bodily changes, such as a heightening of our energy level, a lessening of our awareness of physical discomfort, or a relaxation response. Thus, the intellectual pleasure of studying Aquinas registers on a sensory level because such studying involves trying to relate Aquinas's thoughts about the nature of reality to the world as we experience it, which involves noticing all sorts of things about our world and holding these things in mind by means of mental images. It also involves being moved by some of these images.

THE INTELLECTUAL APPETITE AND EVIL

The will enables one to tend *toward* objects *qua* good, in light of one's conception or vision of the good. It enables one also to tend *away from* objects *qua* bad or evil, in light of the same conception.[60] For Aquinas, good is a (relative) perfection of being. A particular good is the actualization of what is proper to a being, which makes possible certain fitting and perfecting relations among beings. Evil, by contrast, is a privation of good. A particular evil is an imperfection, a lack of what is proper to a being, a failure of actualization, a dysfunction, or the like, which tends to cause disrelation (and further failure and dysfunction) among beings.[61] To say that evil is a privation is not to deny that it can be a powerful force for destruction. It is simply to recognize that evil gains its power to destroy, particularly in a human being, in the absence of countervailing forces—in the absence of critical reflection on the content of human happiness, in the absence of a deliberate consent to the goodness of human life, and in the absence of a sincere intention to cultivate virtue.

To apprehend an object as evil in relation to oneself is to apprehend that one stands in an unfitting relationship to the object. It is to judge that the object is poised to diminish or destroy the self or another being who is important to the self. By the power of the will, one tends away from an object that one apprehends in these terms. One wishes to be apart from the object; one wishes to be rid of its destructive power. Or one tends toward the object in the mode of wishing to limit or destroy its ability to unite with others in ways that injure them. When one wishes to injure an object's power to injure others, one typically does so with the understanding that causing the object a particular injury is necessary for protecting the good. The underlying interior motion is toward a perceived good and away from the possibility of its loss or destruction.[62]

The same three-fold structure that is present in the act of tending toward a good is present in the act of tending away from an evil; at least, there are strong similarities. The same three moments of hatred, aversion, and sorrow that can arise in the course of a sensory-appetitive motion can arise also in the course of an intellectual-appetitive motion, in respect of a perceived good. Aquinas does not have a lot to say about hatred, aversion, or sorrow as simple acts of the will, and what he does say about them is concerned primarily with vicious versions of these acts (for example, hatred of God, sorrow over the flourishing of others, and sorrow over a spiritual good that requires changing one's pleasing relationship to the sensible world).[63] It suits our purposes simply to construct intellectual hatred, aversion, and sorrow, in bare outline, as parallel to the sensory versions of the same interior motions, noting again that motions of the intellectual appetite are unique in that they concern evils that one apprehends by the power of one's intellect, and they are forms of moving oneself, rather than simply being moved by the apprehension of a sensible object.

Hatred is an interior motion of dissonance and discomfort with respect to what one judges, on some level, to be hurtful. As a motion of the will, in particular, hatred is a refusal to welcome or tolerate what one judges to be contrary to human well-being. Whereas intellectual love involves an initial motion of consenting to an object in respect of its capacity to be perfective

of others, intellectual hatred involves the initial motion of dissenting or refusing to consent to an object in respect of its capacity to diminish or destroy
what is good.[64] Aquinas sometimes conflates hatred with the subsequent moment of aversion, just as he sometimes conflates love with the subsequent
moment of desire, but we can distinguish hatred from aversion by saying that
intellectual hatred is the prior act of noticing that an object is poised to harm
one's own or another's well-being and refusing to accept that harm as good
or tolerable, refusing to acquiesce to it.

With the subsequent motion of aversion, one actively turns away from
what one judges to be hurtful.[65] One does so interiorly; one might also do
so in the form of exterior motion or action. It is instructive to consider the
parallel between desire (in respect of good) and aversion (in respect of evil).
Intellectual desire can appear as a reaching out toward something in order
to unite with its goodness (as when one desires to spend time with a kind
person in order to benefit from his or her kindness). Intellectual desire can
appear also in the form of benevolence (as when one wishes to assist another
in becoming kind, simply because it is good for him or her to be kind). By
implication, intellectual aversion can appear as a turning away from something in order to avoid uniting with its power to injure (as when one turns
from another's aggression, which has grown monstrous in the absence of
basic kindness).[66] Yet aversion can appear also in the form of malevolence (as
when one wishes to limit or destroy the other's capacity to be so aggressive).[67] Note that one can easily be mistaken in thinking that one's own
good—or the good of another—is served by wishing the other evil, in any
respect. In addition, malevolence in respect of a particular property can easily become malevolence toward a person as such, which is never acceptable
in Aquinas's view.[68]

If a hurtful union occurs, one is conjoined with a debilitating lack of
goodness, or with a power of disregard or destruction that has come to the
fore in the absence of goodness. One is inhibited or damaged, to some extent, in one's ability to function well as a human being. If one is aware of this
damage, one sorrows. Presumably there is an active element in intellectual
sorrow—an element of self-motion—as there is with every other motion of
the will. I do not know that Aquinas brings this element out explicitly, but
just as intellectual joy involves a pleasing opening to, and an embracing of, a
benefit that one has gained in uniting with an intelligible good, so intellectual sorrow would seem to involve a painful closing down in the presence of
an object that has done one damage. This act of closing down resembles the
act of hatred, but hatred is a response to the *prospect* of an injurious union,
and it has more the quality of refusal or rejection. Sorrow is a response to the

reality of such a union that one had wished to avoid, and sought to avoid, but was unable to avoid. It seems to have more the quality of shutting down.

The intellectual-appetitive motions of hatred, aversion, and sorrow can arise as motions of the natural intellectual appetite. They can arise also under the influence of faith, hope, and charity. That is, they can occur as motions of an intellectual appetite that has been healed and extended by God so that one is able to tend (albeit still imperfectly) toward the highest end of eternal life in the presence of God. Assured that one is already living in the presence of God, one might hate, wish to avoid, wish to destroy, or sorrow over anything that injures the self or others in their ability to thrive in the company of God. Ordinarily, a person of theological virtue moves himself or herself, not so much to attack head-on what is evil, but to strengthen the good, in the absence of which a particular evil has emerged. In relation to a person who appears evil in some respect, one loves the other's capacity to love, to desire the good, and to enjoy what is good, and one wishes to promote these capacities in creative ways, more than one hates the other's incapacities and wishes to destroy them directly.[69]

Aquinas seems prepared to replicate all of the eleven basic sensory-appetitive motions, which we identified in chapter 6, on the intellectual level, although he discusses only a few of these explicitly, and only briefly. He acknowledges that he is extending the use of *passio*-terms when he moves from the sensory to the intellectual and also from the natural to the supernatural. I do not wish to examine on the intellectual and superintellectual levels all of the motions that we delineated on the sensory level. Others are free to do so, making use of the category of affections and, more specifically, religious affections. I want to focus on familiar motions of the sensory appetite or emotions, while extending our appreciation for the way in which our emotions are informed by our intellectual powers, including our power to think and wonder about the underlying nature of reality, and our power to care about what is most important in life. I continue to think of the religious as having to do with what lies—or might lie—beyond, beneath, or at the heart of sensory experience, but cannot be separated from such experience, at least in the present life, if it is to make any sense to our finite human minds.

INTELLECTUAL APPREHENSION AND APPETITE CONJOINED

Now that we have a basic understanding of Aquinas's concept of the will, we can examine more closely the relationship between the intellect and the will. Understanding the relationship between these powers (in light of the

relationship between the intellectual and the sensory) will enable us, in the
next chapter, to draw some conclusions about the kinds of influence the intellect and the will can and typically do have on human emotions.

The intellect and the will are always implicated in each other's acts: "In
a way the intellect moves the will, and in a way the will moves the intellect
and the other powers" of the soul.[70] The intellect moves the will in the manner of a formal cause, by providing intentional content for particular acts of
the will. As we have seen, one is able to tend by the power of one's will in
relation to what one apprehends as an intelligible end. This statement implies, however, that one is able to tend via the will only in relation to what
one first apprehends as an intelligible end—and what one continues to have
in mind, on some level of awareness, as an object of one's tending.[71] One
can have a will that is not at a given moment in act, but one cannot have an
act of the will that is without specification. Every act of the will is about
something. It is for the sake of achieving, enjoying or, by extension, avoiding
something. One can have an act of the will only in relation to something that
one apprehends intellectually as fittingly loved (or hated) and perhaps also
sought (or avoided) *because* it is good in itself and perfective of other things,
most notably humans (or, in the case of an evil, because it is destructive of
human life and well-being). Aquinas says that "the intellect moves the will in
the way in which an end is said to move—by conceiving beforehand the reason for acting and proposing it to the will."[72]

In this sense, the intellect or, more specifically, a particular act of the intellect is the formal cause of *every* act of the will. For example, the intellect
specifies the act by which one takes complacency in goodness as such. It
specifies the act by which one desires one's own good, where one's good is
understood in relation to the good of others who are part of oneself.[73] The
intellect specifies the act by which one tends toward a particular object *as* an
opportunity for seeking one's good.[74] It specifies the act by which one consents to various possible ways of interacting with that object.[75] It specifies the
act by which one chooses the best of these ways.[76] It specifies the act by
which one enjoys the good that one seeks and attains. In short, the intellect
is a partial cause of intellectual-appetitive motion all the way down.

While the intellect moves the will by way of formal causation, the will
moves the intellect and other amenable powers of the soul, as well as itself,
by way of a different sort of causation, namely, efficient or agent causation.[77]
Consider first the way in which the will moves itself. The will is an interior
principle that makes it possible for one to tend toward what one apprehends,
via an act of the intellect, to be good. The power to consent to an intelligible good, to desire it, to seek it in exterior action, and to enjoy it when at-

tained is given to one by the First and Final Mover. It derives from the power one has to exist as a human and thus to tend in ways that are characteristic of humans.[78] Yet the will is a power whose particular acts are subject to one's own command:[79] "The will is the mistress of its own act, and to it belongs to will and not to will."[80]

Aquinas holds that a nonhuman animal cannot help but be moved by what sensory apprehension presents to it as appetible: "An animal is not able at the sight of something attractive not to crave it, because animals do not themselves have the mastery over their own inclination. Hence 'they do not act but are rather acted upon,' as Damascene says. This is because the sensuous appetitive power has a bodily organ and so is nearly in the condition of matter and of corporeal things so as rather to be moved than to move."[81] A human animal is like a nonhuman animal in that one does not have the power to keep motions of the sensory appetite or "concupiscence" from arising in response to certain sensory apprehensions. However, "it is in the power of the will," after such motions have been aroused, "not to desire, or not to consent to concupiscence."[82] More specifically, it is in the power of the intellect for a human being to consider a sensory-appetitive motion and its object intellectually, and determine whether and to what extent this motion contributes to one's complete happiness. Accordingly, it is "in the power of the will" to tend or not tend toward one's own sensory-appetitive motion in the sense of affirming it as good and permitting it to continue in its current course.[83] For example, one might not be able to help getting angry at a family member's action, but as soon as one's anger is aroused, one has the (limited) power to observe one's anger and the situation that provoked it, and judge whether feeling the anger one feels is really appropriate to the situation and thus consistent with virtue. One has the (limited) power either to consent or not to consent to one's anger *as* an intermediate end relative to one's highest end.

In Aquinas's view, there is no intentional content, short of the direct vision of God, that necessitates a motion of the will in relation to that content. The direct vision of God is possible for humans only in the life to come. In this life, what humans can have in mind as their highest end is but a pale reflection of what God is in Godself. Thus, there are various ways to conceive God and union with God, and none of them compels consent. Beyond the Christian context, there are additional ways to conceive one's final end and there will be various intermediate ends that present themselves, in a given moment, relative to one's final end. One is free to select from among these options. With respect to a particular option, one is free to think about it or not; one is free to think about that option differently, focusing on its more or less attractive features; and one is free to turn one's attention to other options. Aquinas says that "even concerning a determined object [the will] can perform its act or not perform it when it wishes. It can pass or not pass into the act of willing with regard to anything at all."[84]

The will is a power that is both moved (by the intellect) and mover. It is a mover of itself; it is also a mover of the intellect. Aquinas explains: "Now the object of the will is the good and the end in general, and each power is directed to some suitable good proper to it, as sight is directed to the perception of color, and the intellect to the knowledge of truth. Therefore the will as an agent moves all the powers of the soul to their respective acts, except the natural powers of the vegetative part, which are not subject to our will."[85] As hinted at previously, the will is a partial cause of every act of the intellect.[86] It is because one desires to know, that one engages in intellectual inquiry.[87] It is because one desires to know how to live that one seeks to apprehend the moral law, including the law of one's own rational nature. It is because one wishes to live well that one notices opportunities or demands for pursuing the good, and one is motivated to undertake decision-making processes.[88] It is because one wishes to flourish that one seeks counsel, in particular cases, in order to reach the best possible judgment about what is worth pursuing.[89] It is because one wishes to be a fine moral agent that one acts in light of what one apprehends to be required by prudence. And so on.

NATURAL AND SUPERNATURAL

Finally, the intellect and the will can act on each other with or without supernatural aid. Aquinas thinks that when the intellect is extended in its power by Christian faith, one can engage in intellectual-appetitive acts that are directed toward God or toward other things in relation to God, as apprehended by the light of faith. When the will is extended in its power by hope and charity, one can function as the proximate efficient cause of one's own tending toward the divine.[90]

Aquinas regards faith, hope, and charity as gifts, but they are gifts that come in the form of interior principles, so that it is the *self* that apprehends God in faith, and it is the *self* that seeks and begins proleptically to enjoy a perfect union with God. It is the same self that continues to exercise reason in regard to that which is accessible to reason. If it were not really "myself" who relates to God in faith, hope, and charity, then there would be no ground for the hope that "I" will one day attain complete happiness in the perfect exercise of "my" intellectual powers. Aquinas holds that humans are created for such supernatural elevation. We are made for "a kind of participation in the Godhead."[91] It is our nature to be receptive of supernatural gifts. Hence, when we engage in intellectual and intellectual-appetitive acts that are made possible by these gifts, we do so in a way that is proper to us as humans.

Whether the intellect is considered as a natural capacity or as a capacity that has been supernaturally extended, it is still the power by which certain objects are apprehended as intelligible goods or evils. It is still the power by which these objects are presented to the will as possible objects of intellectual-appetitive tending. Similarly, whether the will is considered as a natural capacity or as a capacity that has been supernaturally extended, it is still the power by which one tends (in one way or another) in relation to objects that one apprehends by the power of one's intellect. In treating Aquinas's theory of emotion, we can therefore speak generally about the impact that the intellect and the will can have on acts of the sensory appetite, without needing to specify at every point whether we are talking about these powers as natural capacities that have been more or less perfected by the cultivation of virtue—or as capacities that have been more or less extended by grace (and by the cultivation of one's supernatural gifts).

Intellectual acts can and typically do occur in conjunction with sensory acts, both within the realm of apprehension and within the realm of appetite. We have seen that some appetitive acts are caused by sensible objects that are apprehended simply (or mostly) as sensible; some appetitive acts are caused by the same sensible objects, but where the objects are apprehended also (or more so) with respect to their intelligible goodness; and some appetitive acts are caused primarily by intelligible goods, but where this goodness is apprehended, to an extent, with reference to sensory images and impressions. One would expect most appetitive motions to be caused by multifaceted sensory and intellectual apprehensions of an object and its appetibility. Accordingly, one would expect most appetitive motions to involve being moved (sensorily and by the power of one's intellect) and also, at the same time, moving oneself (in relation to what one apprehends intellectually).

Whatever we say regarding the relationship between acts of the intellect and the will on the one hand, and acts of the sensory appetite on the other, we have to say in the awareness that few if any of these acts occur in the absence of the others. It is the task of philosophical reflection to distinguish these acts in thought and to analyze their structured relationships; but it is the broader task of moral psychology and philosophy to use these conceptual resources to illuminate experiences—particularly experiences that engage the whole person and are continually changing (beginning, unfolding, intensifying, weakening, shifting direction, quieting, ending, or rising again in different forms).

NOTES

1. *ST* I 80.2; *Truth* 22.4.

2. *ST* I-II 9.1, including *ad* 2.

3. *Truth* 25.1.

4. *ST* I 59.1 *ad* 1.

5. *ST* I-II 9.1.

6. *ST* I 84.7; *Truth* 22.4 *ad* 2. See chapter 7.

7. *ST* I-II 1.5, 4.8, 28.1, 28.2. For Aquinas, a morally good will tends toward a particular good (e.g., one's own happiness) as it contributes to the common good, which ultimately extends to the good of the entire universe (*ST* I-II 19.10, 90.2).

8. *ST* I-II 22.3.

9. *ST* I 82.5 *ad* 1.

10. *ST* I-II 24.3 *ad* 1.

11. Recall that, in Aquinas's system, "acts" (reductions from potentiality to act) include both cases of acting and cases of being acted upon.

12. *ST* I-II 9.3.

13. *ST* I 27.4, 82.3.

14. *ST* I-II 25.2 *ad* 2, 28.1 *ad* 2.

15. *ST* I-II 9.1.

16. *ST* I 60.3.

17. *ST* II-II 17.1.

18. *ST* II-II 17.5; I-II 62.1.

19. *ST* II-II 18.1.

20. *ST* I-II 40.1.

21. *ST* II-II 17.1.

22. *ST* II-II 17.4. As soon as this becomes a desire for one's own union with God, and a hope that God will assist one in a specific way, and as soon as the imagination becomes engaged in trying to "picture" this union and assistance, say, by turning to an example of an earthly parent, ruler, or friend, one is more in the realm of the sensory and thus the realm of hope *qua* emotion.

23. *ST* II-II 17.3, 17.5 *ad* 4.

24. *ST* I-II 26.2 *ad* 3.

25. Ibid.; see also 27.4 *ad* 2.

26. *ST* II-II 28.4; I-II 26.3.

27. *ST* I-II 26.1, 27.4, including *ad* 1, 15.1; *ST* II-II 17.6.

28. Crowe, "Complacency and Concern in the Thought of St. Thomas," 4.

29. *ST* I-II 27.3.

30. *ST* I-II 28.3.

31. By contrast, faith is a habit of the intellect, that is, the power of intellectual apprehension (*ST* II-II 4.2).

32. *ST* I-II 26.3. Sometimes Aquinas refers to this act as *amor* and sometimes as *dilectio*. Sometimes he equates *dilectio* with intellectual love (the first moment in the triad) and sometimes with intellectual desire (the second moment). See *ST* II-II 27.2.

33. Inasmuch as God appears, in hope, as a helper who is already in a sense present to one, hope reveals the more fundamental motion of love (*ST* II-II 17.1).

34. *ST* II-II 23.1 *ad* 2.

35. I take this to be an implication of *ST* I-II 28.1 and 28.2.

36. *ST* II-II 25.2 *ad* 2.

37. *ST* II-II 27.2.

38. *ST* II-II 27.3.

39. *ST* I-II 26.4; II-II 23.1, including *ad* 2.

40. Aquinas says that "love, which is in the intellective appetite, . . . denotes a certain union of affections between the lover and the beloved, in as much as the lover deems the beloved as somewhat united to him, or belonging to him, and so tends toward him. On the other hand, goodwill is a simple act of the will, whereby we wish a person well, even without presupposing the aforesaid union of the affections with him" (*ST* II-II 27.2). He clarifies that an act of benevolence that expresses *charity* presupposes a prior act of love, but in the above passage he seems to suggest that an act of *natural* benevolence does not necessarily presuppose an act of love. I think this is a mistake. I would argue that every act of benevolence, properly so called, must presuppose an act of intellectual love, namely, a simple recognition of and consent to the goodness of an object. After all, it is in respect of another's potential or actual goodness that one seeks to unite with him or her in the mode of promoting that goodness.

41. *ST* I-II 26.1.

42. *ST* I-II 31.1.

43. *ST* I-II 31.3.

44. *ST* II-II 28.3.

45. *ST* I-II 31.4

46. *ST* I-II 33.1, including *ad* 1 and *ad* 2.

47. *ST* I-II 31.5 *ad* 3.

48. *ST* I-II 31.3 *ad* 3.

49. *ST* I-II 31.5, 24.3.

50. *ST* II-II 28.2.

51. *ST* II-II 28.1.

52. *ST* II-II 28.3.

53. *ST* I-II 3.2, 4.1 *ad* 3

54. *ST* I-II 31.5.

55. *ST* II-II 28.1.

56. *ST* I-II 31.4.

57. *ST* I-II 31.4 *ad* 2.

58. *ST* I-II 32.1.

59. *ST* I-II 3.3 *ad* 3, 24.3, 31.3 *ad* 3, 59.5; *Truth* 26.6.

60. *ST* I-II 8.1 *ad* 1.

61. *ST* I 5.5 *ad* 3; see also St. Thomas Aquinas, *The De Malo of Thomas Aquinas*, trans. Richard Regan, ed. Brian Davies (New York: Oxford University Press, 2001) (hereafter *De Malo*), 1.1–1.2.

62. This is not to say that there are not human beings who wish to destroy other human beings simply for the sake of destroying them, and find destruction as such good and pleasing, but for Aquinas this impulse would have to be a reflection of profound irrationality and perhaps even pathology.

63. *ST* II-II 34–36.

64. *ST* II-II 34.2, 34.6.

65. *ST* II-II 34.6.

66. *ST* II-II 34.2.

67. *ST* II-II 34.3 *ad* 3.

68. *ST* I-II 46.6; II-II 34.3; *De Malo* 12.4.

69. *ST* I 21.3.

70. *Truth* 22.12.

71. *ST* I-II 9.1, including *ad* 2.

72. *Truth* 22.12.

73. *ST* I-II 1.7.

74. *ST* I-II 12.1.

75. *ST* I-II 15.1, 15.3, including *ad* 3.

76. *ST* I-II 12.4 *ad* 3, 13.1, 16.4.

77. *Truth* 22.12.

78. *Truth* 22.1, 22.2.

79. *Truth* 22.6.

80. *ST* I-II 9.3.

81. *Truth* 22.4.

82. *ST* I-II 10.3 *ad* 1.

83. *Truth* 22.4.

84. *Truth* 22.6.

85. *ST* I 82.4.

86. *ST* I 83.4 *ad* 3.

87. *SCG*, bk. 3a, chap. 25.

88. *ST* I-II 8.1.

89. *ST* I-II 14.1, 14.2, 13.1 *ad* 2, 13.3.

90. *ST* II-II 23.2.

91. *ST* I-II 62.1.

CHAPTER NINE

The Formation of
Distinctively Human Emotions

◆

The power of *intellectual apprehension* (the intellect) makes it possible to apprehend the intelligible goodness of various objects—their likely contributions to one's distinctively human happiness. The *intellectual appetite* (the will) makes it possible to tend toward this goodness or toward objects in respect of their intelligible goodness. At the same time, the power of *sensory apprehension* makes it possible to apprehend the sensible goodness of particulars—their attractive five-sensory qualities and, with higher-level operations of the interior senses, the objects' contributions to one's well-being as a sensory being. The *sensory appetite* makes it possible to tend toward particulars that one apprehends as basically useful, helpful, friendly, companionable, or the like.

A layering ordinarily occurs with acts of *intellectual and sensory apprehension*. As a human, one naturally desires to understand one's world, and thus one usually seeks to find sensible objects and their goodness intelligible, even as they strike one as sensible. If one has a religious imagination, one seeks also to discern the religious significance of certain objects that appear, on a sensory level, to bear on one's well-being.[1] A similar layering occurs with motions of the *intellectual and sensory appetites*. Motions of the intellectual appetite are dependent on acts of intellectual apprehension, for one tends toward what one apprehends as good; acts of intellectual apprehension go hand in hand with acts of sensory apprehension, for one abstracts the intelligible goodness *from* a phantasm; and apprehensions of an object in respect of its *sensible* goodness often elicit motions of the sensory appetite. Moreover, in a situation that one apprehends to be significant for one's sensory well-being, one typically tends toward more than a sensible union with a particular good. One wishes, at the same time, to unite with the causes or constituents of human flourishing as such, and with particular objects in respect of their intelligible goodness.[2] Inasmuch as one possesses good habits or virtues, one tends, on a sensory level, in ways that are consistent with tending, on an intellectual level, toward one's highest end.

In this chapter, I consider further some of the causal relations that obtain between these layers. I consider how, for Aquinas, the intellect (in relation to the will) and the will (in relation to the intellect) can influence the sensory powers, most notably motions of the sensory appetite or emotions. I consider also how motions of the sensory appetite can, in turn, influence acts of the intellect and the will. As I interpret Aquinas, human emotions are best construed as motions of the sensory appetite that are caused by acts of sensory apprehension, but the object-orientedness of these appetitive motions virtually guarantees that they will reveal the influence of the intellect. To the extent that emotions reveal the influence of the intellect, they also reveal the influence of the will, which is the motive power by which one seeks to understand and reason about what contributes to human well-being.

Ideally, for Aquinas, emotions reveal the power of the intellect and the will in another way as well. Well-ordered emotions reveal the power one has to be an *observer* of one's own functioning and a *determiner* of some of that functioning.[3] As a rational animal, one has the power to examine one's emotional response to a situation—or one's lack of emotion. One has some power to arouse an emotion where one judges that it is important to do so.[4] Where an emotion is already under way, one has some power to make that emotion an object of reflection, even as one is feeling it, and one has some power to alter the emotion's content, intensity, and duration, as needed, according to the light of reason and, perhaps, according to insight that comes from beyond the limits of reason. One has the capacity, in turn, to monitor the effects of one's efforts to change an emotion—partly in feeling the emotion and partly in reflecting upon what one is feeling—and one has the capacity to adjust one's efforts accordingly.

INFLUENCE OF THE INTELLECT ON EMOTION: PARTICIPATION

The principal way in which one can influence the shape of an emotion is by using one's intellect. The intellect operates in conjunction with the will, but I want to consider the intellect and the will separately because this is a helpful strategy for discerning the relevant detail of Aquinas's account. By the power of one's intellect, one can interpret and (if one wishes) alter one's interpretation of the way in which an object bears on one's own or another's flourishing. In the process, one can sometimes alter one's emotional state. The way this works is that, by the exercise of one's intellect, one influences the acts of sensory apprehension that serve as the formal causes of—and thus provide the intentional content for—one's emotion.

Following Aristotle, Aquinas says that "even the lower appetitive powers are called rational, in so far as they *participate in reason in some way* [*participant aliqualiter rationem*] (*Ethic.* i. 13)."[5] Here, "reason" appears as a power of the intellect—most notably, the power to apprehend, by a process of inquiry and discovery, what will likely contribute to human well-being in a given situation.[6] A motion of the sensory appetite "participates" in reason by virtue of the way the cognitive content of the motion is formed. An emotion whose content is formed by an act of the cogitative power has, by that very fact, "some slight participation in reason" because the cogitative power "[comes] into contact at its highest level of activity with reason at its lowest."[7] The same is true of an emotion that forms, in a human, around high-level activities of memory or imagination.[8] Activities of the cogitative power, or "particular reason," are rational inasmuch as they operate like—and also combine in seamless ways with—the activities of "universal reason," most notably the activities of understanding and practical reasoning. Activities of particular reason are rational also in that they are "naturally guided and moved according to the universal reason."[9] Some of this guiding and moving is deliberate on the part of the self, as we will see shortly, but some of it occurs simply as a matter of course. As one thinks, and as one thinks about a particular situation, one's thinking just does, to an extent, affect the way the situation appears on a sensory level. For example, one is more likely to apprehend a particular comment as hurtful and a cause for anger if one believes that the person who made it is one's friend (rather than a mere acquaintance), and the friend could have known the comment would expose a painful vulnerability.

INFLUENCE OF THE INTELLECT ON EMOTION: PERSUASION

Emotions can be influenced by the intellect or reason in another way as well. Here "reason" refers not only to the power to judge, in a particular situation, how one can best realize a desired end. It refers also to the power to *direct* other powers of the self to agree with the judgments one has made. Often, in Aquinas's writing, the power of reason seems to refer to what lies behind reason, namely, the intellectual soul or the principle of the self as a whole. We cannot sort through the philosophical complexities regarding the relationship between the powers of the intellectual soul and the intellectual soul itself.[11] For our purposes, it is enough to appreciate that reason is a power or capability of the self, but it often appears in Aquinas's discourse as an agent in its own right who can direct and command what is going on in the rest of the self.

By the power of one's intellect, especially the power of reason, one is able to step back, as it were, and reflect upon the sensory impressions that currently occupy one's attention, and the impressions that *could* occupy one's attention if one were to shift one's point of view. One is able to reflect upon the appetitive motions that one is currently undergoing, and the motions that one *could* undergo if one were to focus on different impressions. By reflecting upon the way in which a sensible object currently appears, by noticing that it is possible to look at that object from a different perspective, and by *directing* oneself to look at the object from a new perspective, turning one's interior sensory powers toward different features of the object, one is sometimes able to alter one's emotional state. One is able (to some extent) to quiet or dispel a state that one judges to be contrary to virtue. By the same token, one is able (to some extent) to arouse a state that one judges to be appropriate to the situation.[12]

Aquinas explains that "the same [sensible object] considered under different conditions can be made either pleasurable or repulsive."[13] A person can use the power of reason to "[lay] a particular thing before sensuality under the aspect of the pleasurable or the disagreeable as it appears to reason; and so sensuality is moved to joy or to sorrow. The Philosopher accordingly says that reason *persuades* 'to the best.'"[14] In our example of the hurtful comment, one might judge intellectually that it is contrary to virtue to take offense at human finitude. One might consider the possibility that one's friend is simply tired or frustrated with another aspect of his or her life. One might look for and attend to visible signs of tiredness or recollect what the other said about his or her job over the last few weeks. Recognizing that one has a similar propensity, when tired or frustrated, to say things one does not really mean, one might choose to bring a sense of humor to the situation, or to focus with compassion on how the friend is struggling. In effect, reason persuades the sensory appetite to let go of anger or move beyond anger, but it does so by directing the interior senses to present or re-present sensible particulars in ways that are likely to cause a shift in one's appetitive motion.

In a similar vein, Aquinas remarks that "from the apprehension of something by the intellect there can follow a passion in the lower appetite . . . in so far as that which is understood by the intellect in a universal way is represented in the imagination in particular, thus moving the lower appetite."[15]

He provides an interesting example of his own: "When . . . the intellect of a believer assents intellectually to future punishment and forms phantasms of the pains, imagining the fire burning and worm gnawing and the like, the passion of fear follows in the sensitive appetite."[16] Let us make this example active by considering the way in which one might *use* the power of reason (and will) to *arouse* the fear of hell in oneself—by directing oneself to form and focus on mental images of "the fire burning and worm gnawing."

Suppose one believes in hell. One wishes, generally, to avoid wrongdoing partly in order to avoid going to hell. Yet one is driven, periodically, by a strong desire to do something that one finds pleasing but knows to be wrong. At least, one has been *taught* that the action is wrong, and there *appear* to be good reasons for believing it to be wrong. Thus enters an element of doubt, which can be a sign of intelligence but can also be born of self-deception: Maybe what I have thought to be wrong is not so bad after all; what could it really hurt if I did it just this once?[17]

In a quieter moment, after the impetuous desire is spent, and the reasons for judging one's behavior wrong appear more compelling, one might direct one's imagination to form image after image of the horrors of hell in order to get at the source of one's motivation, namely, the desire to enjoy a particular pleasure. When one imagines something terrible that will happen if one indulges this desire, one causes the object of one's desire to appear less attractive. The object now appears as something that is pleasing in some respects but also threatening and ultimately painful to unite with. The idea/image of hell functions in much the same way as the idea/image of other negative consequences for one's actions, such as punishment by human law, which one might picture as being arrested and thrown in jail, or rejection by others, which one might picture as a look of disgust in a loved one's face. An object whose attainment appears to carry painful penalties is less attractive for most humans than an object that promises simple and resounding pleasure. But sometimes in order to appreciate negative consequences, one must represent those consequences in tangible ways, in the form of fearful images, for the tendency in a state of sensory pleasure (or its anticipation) is to focus on what is most colorful and delightful in the object of one's pleasure, and to neglect its troublesome features.

By conjuring up images of hell, one might fill one's sensory awareness with these images to the point that they crowd out the images that provide intentional content for the unwanted sensory desire. In this way, one might inhibit (for a time) the reemergence of that desire. By Aquinas's account, however, this would not suffice as a strategy for managing one's desire, for the power of one's reason will soon be needed for other purposes, one's imagination will drift and play, the object (or something like it) will eventually reappear, and the desire will once again arise. Once it arises, it will likely cause the object to appear more attractive than it really is, potentially undermining one's judgment.[18]

What is necessary for successful self-determination is to get to a point that, when the object reappears, it appears *as* troubling or (better yet) simply unattractive, for one is not disposed to ignore or dismiss its negative qualities. This is part of the work of virtue (in cases where uniting with the object is, indeed, unsuitable). More than this, what is necessary is to direct the imagination and other sensory powers to entertain objects that are actually *good* for one. A human being cannot live, let alone thrive, while remaining focused on the *absence* of good. The strategy is to entertain images—for example, images of something else with which one might unite, or something else that one might do—which cause sensory-appetitive motions and suggest related actions that are consistent with one's well-being and are also quite pleasing.

THE FEAR OF HELL AS A RELIGIOUS EMOTION

The fear of hell is an example of a religious emotion. It takes as its object a future state of being that one apprehends as terribly painful and nearly impossible to avert (without special asistance)—a state from which one recoils, but which one feels powerless to avoid or escape. Typically, the object of such fear is something that one projects as a possibility beyond the present life, but it is something that one projects on the basis of one's experiences and observations in this life.

The object of this fear can become increasingly abstract as one moves, say, from the image of being burned in a fire (a Christian might refer to *Matthew* 18:8–9)—to the image of a God (or Devil) who ensures that one's body is not consumed by the fire, so that one will *keep* burning forever (*Mark* 9:43–48)[19]—to the thought that this image of God (or the Devil) and torture is but a way of trying to imagine what it would it be like to live in the complete absence of goodness, unable to unite in a pleasing way with what is suitable for oneself—to the thought that repeated acts of wrongdoing give rise to habits that destroy one's capacity to function well as a human and destroy one's capacity even to recognize that this destruction is taking place. Yet whether one interprets hell literally or figuratively, the fear of hell is fundamentally sensory, in Aquinas's view. It is high-level sensory inasmuch as it is caused by imagining horrible places, situations, or states of being that resemble but also (for most people) go beyond what one has encountered in one's life.[20] It is likely that humans alone, among the animals, are able to conjure images of (what they interpret to be) hell, which suggests that this conjuring (and interpreting) is dependent on the intellect; yet acts of the intellect or, more specifically, acts of reason, do not themselves generate such fear. The thought of evil or the thought that moral evil is its own punishment, apart from any sensory representation of the same, does not cause a human to recoil, tremble, freeze, or panic.

The fear of hell can be caused by a sensory apprehension over which one lays higher forms of judgment, speculation, or wonder. It can be caused, for example, by noticing the look on a loved one's face when he or she finds out that one has done something terrible—by recollecting that face repeatedly, rehearsing in one's mind what one did, and reflecting over time on the fact that one can never take that mistake back; indeed (one might reason), one has committed mistake upon mistake, and for that one will surely have to pay. The fear of hell can also be caused, so to speak, in the other direction. It can be caused, indirectly, by the apprehension of an intelligible evil, such as the idea of self-destructive moral decline, but where this idea is understood with reference to examples from one's own life or the life of a loved one. In other words, it can be caused by sensory images or impressions that are already informed by reason—images or impressions that occur to one, and take the forms they do, partly by virtue of the way one thinks.

With Aquinas's account, we are free to speak of the object of an emotion with flexibility, as a sensible appearance that one finds meaningful (or incomprehensible) in various respects; as a situation that one entertains, perhaps in the form of mental pictures or a set of impressions, and about which one speculates or wonders; as a particular item that one apprehends as a window or a vehicle to what lies beyond the ordinary; or what have you. As humans, we typically engage in countless, coordinated acts of the intellect or reason as we apprehend sensible objects that appear to affect our well-being. Aquinas holds that, technically, the object of an emotion is something that one registers by the power of one's interior senses, rather than something that one registers via the interior senses and the intellect considered as a pair.[21] Yet we have seen that the interior senses have a remarkable range in a human being; they participate in reason, and their acts can be influenced, in additional ways, by the power of reason. As I interpret Aquinas, the object of an emotion includes many of the contributions that reason makes to a sensible appearance. We need not worry about abstracting from a complex, emotion-laden experience of a situation the features of the situation that reason allows one to apprehend, in order to isolate the features that the interior senses allow one to apprehend (the features that compose the formal object of the emotion). We need only acknowledge that acts of reason, considered apart from all sensory images or impressions, cannot and do not give rise to emotions.

Ideas and images of future suffering—and corresponding modes of appetitive tending—take Christian forms inasmuch as their intentional content is informed by Christian teachings, including visual and literary representations of those teachings. Yet the world is populated by millions of people who participate in other traditions—and people with religious imaginations who do not participate in established traditions but find it difficult (or do not wish) to dismiss some of the traditional teachings that permeate their cultures. These people, too, can experience a religious emotion of fear at the complex sensory apprehension of what could happen to them after death, when they will be unable to do much about their situation—or, perhaps, what could happen to them in *this* life if they surrender to their worst tendencies.[22] One hears a Tibetan Buddhist nun say, for example, that her greatest fear, when she is tempted to neglect her duties, is that she will reincarnate as a lower form of life, such as an insect.[23] Or one hears a recovering alcoholic refer to alcohol as a "demon" and to states of being lost to the power of addiction as "being in hell."

INTELLECTUAL INFLUENCE AND ITS LIMITS

Claudia E. Murphy writes, "Aquinas describes two broad ways in which passions are capable of being affected by reason and will: externally—when a passion is already occurring, it can be affected by reason and will—and internally—when reason's or will's activity gives rise to a passion."[24] I would put the point somewhat differently. The intellect and, more specifically, the power of reason can influence an emotion *either in the emotion's initial formation or in the form it takes over time* by virtue of two factors, namely, (1) the way in which reason informs and interacts with the cogitative and other interior sensory powers—the way in which the interior senses *participate* in reason—and (2) the way in which reason can *persuade* other powers of the self to follow its lead, particularly in cases where the other powers are sluggish in their operations, or they seem (from the perspective of reason) to be affecting the self in ways that are contrary to good human functioning. In other words, because one is an intellectual being or a rational animal, one's sensory powers are informed by the thinking one does, even when one is not thinking *about* one's sensory operations. In addition, one has the power to think about the latter and try to alter them in order to ensure that all of one's operations and actions accord, as far as possible, with one's judgment concerning what contributes to human flourishing.

With regard to both modes of influence, the power of reason is limited. Sensory images and impressions often come to mind unbidden; sometimes these images and impressions are distorted and misleading; sometimes we judge that they are misleading and wish to correct them, but they resist our mental manipulations; indeed, sometimes they manipulate us mentally, as we will explore later in the chapter.[25] Inasmuch as sensory images fail to reflect the influence of reason, or they resist our efforts to alter them, the sensory-appetitive motions that are caused by these images are difficult to alter as well.

Aquinas characterizes the relationship between reason and emotion as something *less* than "despotic." He draws a classic analogy between forms of political rule (with respect to whole communities) and forms of rational self-rule: "For a power is called despotic [*despoticus*] whereby [one] rules over his slaves, who have not the [ability] to resist in any way the orders of the one that commands them, since they have nothing of their own. But that power is called politic [*politicus*] and royal [*regalis*] by which [one] rules over free subjects, who, though subject to the government of the ruler, have nevertheless something of their own, by reason of which they can resist the order of him who commands."[26] Reason is said to govern motions of the sensory appetite by a politic and royal power "because the sensitive appetite has something of its own, by virtue whereof it can resist the commands of reason. For the sensitive appetite is naturally moved, not only by the estimative power in other animals, and in [a human being] by the cogitative power which the universal reason guides, but also by the imagination and sense. Whence it is that we experience that the irascible and concupiscible powers do resist reason, inasmuch as we sense or imagine something pleasant, which reason forbids, or unpleasant, which reason commands."[27] One's power to influence the (rest of the) content of one's consciousness via the use of one's imagination is limited, but it is significant. It is often possible to call to mind, reconstruct, or banish images and impressions for the sake of eliciting, increasing, or diminishing sensory appetitive motions, in order to realize a desired end: "reason is [thus] able to move sensuality to different objects."[28]

In summary, whether we are concerned with the original composition of an emotion, the composition of an emotion over time (which must occur as long as the emotion lasts, for an emotion is an intentional state), or about its recomposition into a somewhat different form of the same emotion or a different emotion, we can exercise our intellectual powers, including the power of reason, in ways that influence how sensible objects appear to us and thus how they affect us. We can also *undermine* reason's influence on our ways of apprehending and being moved. Ethically, it is important to cultivate the ability to observe and influence the interior conflicts that arise within us, even as aspects of ourselves seem to identify to some extent with the different parties to these conflicts.

THE INTELLECT AND "A KIND OF OVERFLOW"

Aquinas says that the intellect can influence an emotion "in so far as the higher appetite is moved by the intellectual apprehension, with the result that the lower appetite also is stirred up by the higher through a kind of overflow or through a command."[29] One could consider this statement with respect to the influence that the higher appetite, or the will, can have on an emotion, but I want to highlight the intellect's role in the generation of appetitive "overflow."

It is initially unclear what Aquinas intends by the images of "stirring up" and "overflowing." At his clearest, he holds that motions of the sensory appetite in humans are caused directly by acts of sensory apprehension, not by acts of the intellect or motions of the will. As we have seen, acts of the intellect *can* cause emotions indirectly by instructing the interior sensory powers to form new sensory images or impressions that provide intentional content for corresponding emotions. As we will see shortly, acts of the *will* can cause emotions in the sense that, once an emotion has been aroused and one makes an assessment of its suitability, one can consent to the emotion, giving it more of the energy of the self—or one can withhold one's consent, causing the emotion to dissipate. But in order to form in the first place, an emotion must be given formal cause by a sensory apprehension that an object bears in a significant way on one's well-being. Hence, any "stirring up" of or "overflowing onto" the "lower appetite" must take place through the medium of sensory apprehension.

Keep in mind that the will, like the intellect, is an immaterial power in Aquinas's view. A motion of the will cannot be thought of as a material motion or vibration that extends from one dimension of the self to another when it reaches a particular level of intensity. Nor is it the case that one can "will" oneself to feel an emotion straightaway. What one can do, however, is "will" oneself to engage in intellectual acts that influence how a sensible object appears and how it speaks to one's concerns. One can choose to reimagine an emotion-laden situation and its significance for oneself, anticipating that by making certain changes in one's way of apprehending the situation one will cause corresponding changes in one's emotional response. Note that the mysterious connection between the immaterial powers of the soul—and the body-mediated powers of the same human soul—is made by Aquinas where practical and particular reason meet. It is here, where the two modes of apprehension overlap, interact, and somehow concur, that it becomes possible to conceive the object of an intellectually influenced motion of the sensory appetite.

In discussing the morality of emotion, Aquinas says that an emotion can follow from a "judgment of reason . . . by way of redundance: because . . . when the higher part of the soul is intensely moved to anything, the lower part also follows that movement; and thus the passion that results in consequence, in the sensitive appetitive, is a sign of the intensity of the will, and so indicates greater moral goodness."[30] My understanding is that a motion of the will (in relation to something good) is "intense" when it is caused by a judgment concerning the remarkable value that an object has for one's own or another's life. Engaging in an intense motion of the will involves consenting to the value of such an object, and wishing, perhaps, to unite with that value further. Typically, while one considers an object's value, one considers related images or impressions of sensible goodness, so that the object one has in mind appears to be good on intellectual and sensory levels at the same time. Judging an object to be attractive in both respects, one experiences a motion of the will and a motion of the sensory appetite at the same time. In this way, a motion of the will can be *accompanied* by a notable bodily resonance.

Again, Aquinas's account allows us to be flexible with respect to the object of an emotion. In cases where one's intellectual and sensory judgments concur, it makes sense to identify the object of one's emotion as "the situation *as* one apprehends it," without trying to separate what one apprehends by virtue of one's interior senses from what one apprehends by virtue of one's intellect. Yet in cases where one's intellectual and sensory judgments are at odds—in cases where one tends, on a sensory level, toward a union that reason forbids, or one tends away from a union that reason enjoins—it can be helpful to say that the object of the emotion is, more specifically, the "situation *as* one apprehends it *by the power of one's interior senses.*" It is *this* form of apprehension that gives rise directly to a body-resonant emotion. Still, as one undergoes the emotion, one will ordinarily reconsider "the situation" from a larger perspective, through the use of one's intellectual powers, and this reconsideration might influence sensory judgments in a way that causes a shift in the course of the emotion.

RESONANT JOY

In chapter 8 we considered a motion of the intellectual appetite that Aquinas calls "joy"—the "motion in place" of resonating with pleasure in the attainment of an intelligible good. Such joy can be so "intense" that it causes, indirectly, a felt change in the sensory appetite and the body.[31] Aquinas refers to the joy of a Christian who believes that he or she has attained some sort of union with the source of his or her happiness. He quotes *Psalm* 83.3: "*My heart and my flesh have rejoiced in the living God*: where by *heart* we are to understand the intellectual appetite, and by *flesh* the sensitive appetite."[32] Setting aside the possibility of direct, supernatural causation, we can say that, by Aquinas's account, a Christian's joy in God is caused by the intellectual apprehension that he or she has attained a desired union with God. Yet if this joy is to be something more than a "mere movement of the will"[33]—if it is to be a movement that *feels* like opening, expanding, or being elevated, in a way that is attended by bodily sensations of relaxation, warmth, or increased energy—the Christian must apprehend God, or his or her pleasing union with God, with reference to sensory images or impressions of some kind. It is natural for a Christian to apprehend God, in any case, with reference to sensible reality, while taking care not to confuse God with the sensible. As noted in chapter 2, Aquinas would agree with James Gustafson that "the ultimate power that sustains us and bears down upon us is experienced through the particular objects, events, and powers that sustain us, threaten our interests, create conditions for human action, or evoke awe and respect."[34] It is when a Christian has such objects, events, and powers in mind, even as he or she reflects on their deeper significance by the power of reason and faith, that he or she is likely to undergo sensory-appetitive motions.

A Christian's joy might include, for example, reference to an image of Jesus that is brought to life through Bible stories and religious art—where Jesus appears, say, as a man wearing a robe and sandals, looking radiant and welcoming. A Christian's joy will not be contained by any *one* image of Jesus. Moreover, it is not just *any* man fitting this description who will evoke the joy; it is the image of a man whose welcoming presence signifies, to the Christian, the extraordinary love of God. The human intellect makes it possible to apprehend remarkable significance in the image of a sensible figure; indeed, Aquinas would argue that it is the intellect *qua* extended by the theological virtue of faith that makes it possible for a Christian to apprehend the reality of God in Jesus. Yet without an interior sensory image or impression of some kind, even if it is only a vague impression of light, warmth, inclusion, embrace, or the like, one will not experience joy in the "flesh."

From the perspective of religious ethics, one could construe certain motions of joy as religious emotions. A religious emotion of joy would involve thoughts, intuitions, or questions concerning one's relationship to what lies beyond, beneath, or at the heart of ordinary reality, but it would involve thoughts, intuitions, or questions that come to mind *as* one appeals—ineluctably—to interior sensory images or impressions. From a Buddhist perspective, one might ponder the nature of reality as "dependent-arising" with the aid of a visual representation such as "the wheel of cyclic existence," which allows one to make illuminating connections to one's own experience.[35] It could be that the more one penetrates to the heart of reality, including one's own, everyday reality, and the more one is aware of doing so, the more flexible, capable, and energized one becomes in one's interactions with sensible objects. It could be that one experiences more frequent and vibrant joy in the ordinary activities of one's life.

To take another example, joy might involve an encounter with a person whom one believes to be a spirit medium. Let us say that one approaches the medium because one wishes to make contact with a deceased relative with whom one has an unresolved conflict. One does so with the hope of somehow resolving the conflict and alleviating one's emotional pain. One might begin with abstract thoughts or questions about what is ultimately real (is it even possible to communicate with the dead?); yet most of one's awareness is likely to be occupied with painful memories, images of the relative's unhappy face, images of oneself continuing to suffer, and vague impressions of being cut off from something important or being in a dark and threatening place. One might entertain thoughts about what mediums are, how they do what they do, and how one can know if they are trustworthy; yet one's awareness is likely to be occupied much more with the person in front of one, as one waits to see what happens. As one listens to the medium's words, the tone with which they are spoken, the facial expressions that accompany the words, and so on, one might have a sensory impression that one is in the presence of something or someone more than the medium. One might hear that one has already been forgiven by the relative, and these words might feel like a rush of wind that generates an unexpected desire to laugh. As one receives the sensory impression of a relaxed and happy relationship, one might experience a resonant joy.

One could think of other examples, working with other religious contexts. The point is that it is possible to experience intense joy at the apprehension that one has realized a desired union with an intelligible good (a power, a truth, or the like) that lies, in some sense, beyond the ordinary world or beneath the surface of ordinary reality; however, this intensity will register as an interior motion of resonating, opening, or rising, which has a pleasing material correlate, only inasmuch as one's apprehension is, in part, an interior sensory apprehension. If one wishes to arouse or encourage a motion of joy, it is not enough to think abstract thoughts about what is highest and best; one must form and entertain relevant sensory images and impressions.

INFLUENCE OF THE WILL ON EMOTION: CONSENT

Focusing more directly on the power of the will, Aquinas says that one can exert an influence on one's sensory appetite in at least three ways. First, as we saw in chapter 8, an act of the will is the cause of a sensory-appetitive motion in a specific sense. As an intellectual being or a rational animal, one naturally tends toward what one apprehends (rightly or wrongly, clearly or vaguely, explicitly or implicitly) as something that is capable of contributing to one's happiness. When one is moved by an object of sensory apprehension, one naturally considers that very movement intellectually in light of *its* contribution to one's happiness. In other words, one naturally considers whether one's emotional response is appropriate to the circumstance. Again, one might do this well or poorly. Many humans do not get much perspective on their emotions as they feel them, and what perspective they do get is informed by a confused conception of happiness. Other humans are better observers of their emotions but are sometimes caught off guard by unusually intense emotions. In any case, Aquinas's view is that, if an emotion continues for more than a few moments to qualify one's interior life, this is because one is allowing it to do so; one is effectively consenting to the emotion, and for this one is, to some extent, responsible.[36]

As we have seen, the will is a power that allows one to move oneself with respect to a range of one's own, interior operations. To consider a previously quoted passage in its larger textual context, Aquinas says,

> wherever we have order among a number of active powers, that power which regards the universal end moves the powers which regard particular ends. And we may observe this both in nature and in things politic. For the heaven, which aims at the universal preservation of things subject to generation and corruption, moves all inferior bodies, each of which aims at the preservation of its own species or of the individual. The king also, who aims at the common good of the whole kingdom, by his rule moves all the governors of cities, each of whom rules over his own particular city. Now the object of the will is good and the end in general, and each power is directed to some suitable good proper to it, as sight is directed to the perception of color, and the intellect to the knowledge of truth. Therefore the will as agent moves all the powers of the soul to their respective acts, except the natural powers of the vegetative part, which are not subject to our will.[37]

Here the will, like the intellect, appears as an "agent" close to the core of the self. Whereas the intellect or reason appears as the power to *inform* and *persuade* other powers within the self, the will appears as the power to *move* or *motivate* other powers (including the intellect) to carry out their operations. The "will as agent" moves the sensory appetite, in particular, by allowing particular sensory-appetitive motions to continue in their initial form, by allowing those motions to continue in some other form, as directed by reason, or by disallowing their continuation, such that one tries to stop them in their course. As noted, "the will cannot prevent the movement of concupiscence from arising . . . ; yet it is in the power of the will not to will to desire, or not to consent to concupiscence."[38] Ideally, one exercises one's will in a conscious manner, in light of a well-considered vision of the good.

Consent is a form of intellectual love. When one consents to one's emotion, one apprehends it intellectually as an object with which it is suitable to unite. One considers the emotion as an object in light of the object *of* one's emotion, in order to assess whether the emotion is appropriate to the circumstance—but let us keep things simpler here. When one consents to one's own emotion, one apprehends its intelligible goodness, namely, its contribution to one's good human functioning, and one rests with pleasure in this goodness. Often, one also judges that it would be good to unite with the emotion further in the sense of allowing it to continue in its present course or directing that course in a suitable way by the power of reason, and one desires the continuation of one's emotion. In a sense, one wishes the emotion well, or one wishes oneself well with respect to one's emotional state.

When one refuses to consent to an emotion, one effectively hates it intellectually: One judges that feeling the emotion as one currently feels it is contrary to one's proper functioning and one rejects it. One refuses to welcome the emotion and give it any more of one's energy, namely, the energy of one's will, which is the motive power that is closest to the core of the self, in Aquinas's view. One might also turn away from the emotion in a subsequent motion of aversion. Indeed, one might do any number of things: One might wish the emotion a crushing defeat, in the mode of malevolence; one might fear the emotion in its power to control one's mental state; one might get angry with the emotion and wish it evil for the sake of restoring a balance of power within the self. However, these sorts of responses, which focus on the emotion as a problem, are likely to invest the emotion with *more* of the self's energy, and grant it a longer life, than a simple refusal to welcome the emotion and follow its lead, or a turning of oneself in another direction.

THE WILL AND "A [DELIBERATE] KIND OF DISTRACTION"

One can sometimes undermine a problematic emotion by withholding one's consent from it. One can sometimes avoid or overcome an unwanted emotion also by investing one's energy in some other object—by "willing" oneself to think about or otherwise occupy oneself with something else, such that one's chosen activity keeps one from dwelling on the sensory images and impressions that cause the undesired sensory-appetitive motion. Aquinas explains that "since all the soul's powers are rooted in the one essence of the soul, it follows of necessity that, when one power is intent in its act, another power becomes remiss, or is even altogether impeded, in its act, both because all energy [*virtus*] is weakened through being divided, so that, on the contrary through being centered on one thing, it is less able to be directed to several; and because, in the operations of the soul, a certain attention is requisite, and if this be closely fixed on one thing, less attention is given to another."[39] Aquinas offers what I have just quoted as an explanation for the way in which, "by a kind of distraction," motions of the rational appetite can be impeded by motions of the sensory appetite, but the same principle applies in the other direction as well.

Deliberate distraction can be a useful strategy in managing an unwanted emotion. One can sometimes make oneself forget what one is feeling—that is, one can cease to feel it and manage not to revert to it any time soon—by turning to another object or activity, especially an object or activity that one knows, from experience, will fill one's sensory awareness with captivating images or impressions and thus elicit different sensory-appetitive motions. For example, one can often alleviate lingering and debilitating sorrow by listening to upbeat music, going for a walk, or watching a funny movie. However, this sort of strategy is best accompanied by a complementary effort to alter the unwanted emotion at its intentional roots, if it has negotiable roots. For as long as one is disposed to apprehend certain objects in certain ways, those objects—when they reenter one's awareness—will likely cause one to be moved in the same, troubling way. As suggested earlier in this chapter, undermining a bad habit of emotion requires getting to a point where certain objects cease to appear through the same, familiar lens or in a certain guise, namely, with sensible accoutrements that virtually guarantee a corresponding emotional reaction.

By the power of one's will, one can sometimes influence an emotion also by altering the exterior motions—the actions—that are motivated or driven by that emotion. Just as the will includes the power to consent or not consent to a given emotion, so it includes the power to act or not act on an emotion to which one has given one's consent. Thus Aquinas says that

> just as in an army the advance to the battle depends upon the command of the general, so in us the motive power moves the members only at the command of that which rules in us, namely reason, whatever sort of move-

ment may occur in the lower powers. Reason therefore holds the irascible and the concupiscible powers in check lest they proceed to an external act. . . . Thus it is clear that the irascible and the concupiscible powers are subject to reason, and likewise sensuality, though the name sensuality does not refer to these powers according to their participation in reason but according to the nature of the sensitive part of the soul.[40]

Inasmuch as acting on an emotion gives life to the emotion—or instead releases it, causing it to dissipate—acting on the emotion can affect the course of the emotion itself. Hence, the will can influence motions of the sensory appetite by influencing whether and how one acts on them or chooses to express them.

In summary, by the power of one's intellect and one's will, one can exercise *limited* influence over one's emotions and, by implication, over the felt quality of one's life. One can influence one's emotions, so to speak, *before* they arise, by seeking to cultivate thoughtful ways of apprehending certain features of sensible reality—by training oneself to (re)describe certain situations in ways that are likely, consistently, to evoke what one judges to be fitting emotional responses. One can influence one's emotions also *as* they arise—for an emotion arises in response to interior sensory apprehensions that participate in reason and are amenable to reason's direction or persuasion. Moreover, one can, to a limited extent, re-form emotions that have already been aroused. With problematic emotions, one can seek to reconstitute their intentional content or withdraw from them one's consent. One can refuse to let one's consciousness be occupied with a consideration of the interior sensory apprehensions that cause unwanted emotions, or one can deliberately occupy one's awareness with competing apprehensions. Finally, one can choose not to act on emotions in ways that are likely to reinforce them.

RECIPROCAL INFLUENCES OF EMOTION ON THE WILL (AND THE INTELLECT)

Just as the intellect and the will can exercise an influence on the formation and course of sensory-appetitive motions, so the latter can exert an influence on the intellect and the will so that, for example, sometimes a judgment or piece of reasoning by which one seeks to shape a given emotion has already been shaped by that emotion and ends up functioning in the emotion's service. Indeed, one should expect this sort of reciprocal influencing, given that humans are both rational and animal. One is continually apprehending and having to respond on both intellectual and sensory levels to features of reality that bear on one's well-being. Sometimes one's intellectual judgments and motions predominate, so that one is able to exercise a more or less rational governance over one's sensory operations, and sometimes one's sensory judgments and motions predominate. If a given sensory-appetitive motion is contrary to good judgment and unresponsive to reason's directives—especially if the motion is subversive of reason's very ability to provide directives and have them heard—such a motion undermines the exercise of one's moral agency. If, however, an emotion arises and persists in a manner that one judges rightly to be appropriate to the situation, and one therefore gives it one's consent, it enhances one's agency and perfects one morally.[41]

Aquinas identifies two main ways in which emotions can influence operations of the will, focusing primarily on emotions that undermine one's rational self-command. Let us reconsider a passage from the *Summa theologiae* that I quoted earlier. Aquinas argues that an emotion cannot affect the will directly, but it can do so indirectly:

> First, by a kind of *distraction*: because, since all the soul's powers are rooted in the one essence of the soul, it follows of necessity that, when one power is intent in its act, another power becomes remiss, or is even altogether impeded, in its act, both because all energy is weakened through being divided, so that, on the contrary, through being centered on one thing, it is less able to be directed to several; and because, in the operations of the soul, a certain attention is requisite, and if this be closely fixed on one thing, less attention is given to another. In this way, by a kind of distraction, when the movement of the sensitive appetite is enforced [*fortificatur*] in respect of any passion whatever,[42] the proper movement of the rational appetite or will must, of necessity, become remiss or altogether impeded.[43]

We have considered some of the ways in which one can undermine the course of an unwanted emotion. Many of these strategies involve a kind of deliberate distraction—a turning of one's attention away from the object of the emotion, and toward something else, or a reconsideration of the emotion's formal causes through the use of one's interior sensory powers. Here we note that if the emotion gets the upper hand within the dynamics of the self, *it* can become the agent of distraction. An emotion can so consume one's awareness that one's world simply becomes the world as defined by one's emotion. The emotion-evoking situation is all one can see, and it is all that matters. This sort of collapse of the interior space of one's moral agency can occur with many emotions, but Aquinas thinks it occurs most often with pleasing sensory-appetitive motions that have a strong material component, for "we attend much to that which pleases us." He notes that "if [a] bodily pleasure be great, either it entirely hinders the use of reason, by concentrating the mind's attention on itself; or else it hinders it considerably."[44] Aquinas is not saying that falling into the immediacy of one's emotion is unavoidable and is thus excusable. It is the responsibility of every moral agent to shape his or her character in such a way that this crucial interior space, and the prominence of the power of reason within this space, are well maintained.[45]

Second, an emotion can influence the will by way of "the will's object, which is good apprehended by reason."[46] Under this description, Aquinas highlights the way in which "the judgment and apprehension of reason is impeded on account of a vehement and inordinate apprehension of the imagination," with the result that one misjudges the intelligible goodness of an object, and one thereby conceives a misguided motion of the will.[47] To begin with, Aquinas holds that even a well-ordered emotion can alter the way one apprehends a sensible object.[48] It can do so in a way that supports, rather than undermines, the exercise of virtue. To take a rather simple example, the sensory judgments that cause the emotion of love can, on occasion, assume a prominent place in one's awareness, and one can be moved accordingly. Pleased by the way this movement feels, and by the way one's emotion seems to highlight the attractive qualities of the object of one's emotion, the object can appear even more attractive, on a sensory level, than it did before one was moved. Consider the way a parent's love for a child can cause the child to appear especially beautiful and wonderful, and it can make it easier for the parent to do the daily work of caring for that child.

Generally speaking, a problem arises only when an object appears (on a sensory level) to be *highly* attractive, repulsive, or threatening, and one tends with *vehemence* in relation to the object.[49] In such a situation, the intensity of one's reaction can further focus and reinforce one's sensory impressions of the object's high value or disvalue, or its immense significance for one's well-being, which can ramp up one's emotional response to the object in a way that escapes the judgment of reason. What happens, in effect, is that one fails to ask the question of whether this emotion is appropriate to the circumstance; one fails to ask whether the object of one's emotion is really as significant as it seems. One takes the powerful sensible attractiveness or repulsiveness of the object to constitute, in itself, a sufficient reason for tending toward or away from the object on an intellectual level. In other words, one is moved in a powerful way by certain sensory images or impressions; the reasoning part of oneself is captivated by this movement, quickly convinced that it is on target; and one moves oneself accordingly. This is partly the result of distraction: one becomes so preoccupied with a sensory experience that one fails to exercise one's intellectual powers as one ought. Yet this is also the result of an intellectual mistake: One takes a sensory judgment to be sufficient for determining one's rational judgment and thus the motion of one's will.

In short, Aquinas holds that when one is in the grip of an inordinate emotion, one "[does] not easily turn [one's] imagination from the object of the emotion, the result being that the judgment of the reason often follows the passion of the sensitive appetite, and consequently the will's movement follows it also, since it has a natural inclination always to follow the judgment of the reason."[50] This is why it is crucial to cultivate virtuous habits of emotion, so that one's emotions arise and persist in ways that are inherently reasonable or consistent with good judgment, and one retains the ability to transcend, examine critically, and affect deliberately the pull that a given object has on one's sensory appetite, even as one might continue, to some extent, to be subject to that pull.

RECIPROCAL INFLUENCES OF EMOTION ON THE INTELLECT (AND THE WILL)

Aquinas elucidates the impact that unruly emotions can have on one's moral agency by considering emotions' impact not only on the will but also on the intellect. Just as (from above) the will influences emotions primarily via acts of the intellect and *their* relationship to acts of sensory apprehension, which provide sensory-appetitive motions with their formal objects, so (from below) emotions influence the will primarily via acts of sensory apprehension and *their* relationship to acts of the intellect, which provide intellectual-appetitive motions with their objects. Some of what Aquinas says with respect to emotions' influence on the will thus shows up also under the category of emotions' influence on the intellect.

In the exercise of practical reasoning, one proceeds (schematically) from a general intellectual desire for happiness, and a more specific desire to enjoy some happiness in the present situation—to a judgment that uniting with this or that object will likely contribute (and contribute best, out of the available options) to one's happiness—to a conclusion that involves tending toward a particular union as suitable (or tending, by extension, away from a union that one judges unsuitable).[51] One could construct the practical syllogism also as a process of reasoning from the universal that "such and such should be done"—to the particular judgment that "*this* thing is *such*, and . . . *I am such*"—to the act of doing what one ought, therefore, to do.[52] In any case, a key to the exercise of sound practical reasoning is the ability to apprehend particulars clearly, as they stand under relevant universals, so that one can judge truthfully the contributions that uniting with a given object, in any manner, has made, is now making, or will likely make to the attainment of one's highest end—or to the doing of what is morally right.

Aquinas argues that emotions can inhibit one in making these sorts of judgments well, particularly when the emotions are intense. He is most concerned with individuals who have a reasonably good grasp of the content of happiness and basically know right from wrong. He is most concerned with people who, when they are not intensely emotionally charged, can rather easily place a given object under the relevant universal and make a proper judgment. Regarding such people, Aquinas says that sometimes an emotional engagement with a sensible object can cause one to fail to consider explicitly what one knows implicitly to be true—what one knows to be true in general and also in particular, when one is not caught up in a strong appetitive motion. The result is that one forms a mistaken judgment concerning the value (for one's happiness) of uniting with a particular object, and one draws the wrong practical conclusion.[53]

Aquinas provides a classic example. One might believe that "fornication" is bad or wrong, and one might ordinarily be able to judge well, in the abstract, whether this or that sort of sexual act counts as an act of fornication and is thus to be shunned. Yet one can be so gripped by a particular sexual appetite that one fails to consider or make mentally explicit that "*this* would be a case of fornication, " and "committing this act would be wrong."[54] It could be that one simply fails to admit such a judgment into one's consciousness, so that later on, after the moment of passion has passed, one realizes that one held the correct judgment all along but it failed to make any difference to one's choice about what to do. It could be that this judgment intrudes into one's consciousness, but a part of oneself—the part that identifies more with the desire for sensory pleasure—drives it back out. It could be that the judgment comes to mind and one holds it in mind, but one disregards its significance, as when one knows that a particular act is wrong, but in the experience of anticipated pleasure, one does not care.[55]

Noting, but moving beyond, the general category of "distraction," Aquinas argues that a person who is under the spell of an intense emotion can be misled also "by way of opposition."[56] Due to the power of one's attraction, which follows from and in turn reinforces one's sensory judgment of the object's amazing value, one actually drums up *reasons* for judging the object to be good intellectually, just as one judges it to be good on a sensory level. One comes up with reasons for judging a desired union with this object to be good, right, or justifiable. One does so for the purpose of justifying to oneself and to others what one knows—or at least ought to know—to be wrong. These reasons can become so compelling that long into an illicit affair one can continue to believe that one is entitled to enjoy another person's partner sexually and that this enjoyment is critical for one's happiness.

Aquinas explains further: "He that has knowledge in a universal, is [sometimes] hindered, on account of a passion, from reasoning about that universal, so as to draw the conclusion: but he reasons about another universal proposition suggested by the inclination of the passion, and draws his conclusion accordingly."[57] Aquinas references Aristotle, interpreting Aristotle to hold that "the syllogism of an incontinent [person] has four propositions, two particular and two universal."[58] Clearly, many more "premises" are at work in most decision-making processes, but this is a helpful formal representation. Roughly, the intemperate person judges, first, that "fornication is (morally) unlawful." He or she is *poised* to judge that "this act, in particular, would be a case of fornication, and it would therefore be unlawful." Practically speaking, the person is *poised* to forgo the act. Yet the person also judges, second, that "pleasure is to be pursued." He or she judges that "this act, in particular, would be pleasurable, and it ought therefore to be committed." Practically speaking, the person concludes by performing the (unlawful, but) pleasurable act. In effect, the prospect of intense sensory pleasure "fetters the reason, and hinders it from arguing and concluding under the first proposition; so that while the passion lasts, the reason argues and concludes under the second."[59]

A virtuous person values sensory pleasure but wishes to enjoy only those forms of sensible union that are consistent with the pursuit of moral goodness and thus contribute to true human happiness. Note that, for Aquinas, the pursuit of moral goodness is itself a source of intellectual pleasure that ordinarily resounds (through the coordinated engagement of the senses) throughout the whole of the person.

Finally, an intense emotion can hinder one in making good practical judgments partly "by way of bodily transmutation." The power of reason can be "fettered so as not to exercise its act freely; even as sleep or drunkenness, on account of some change wrought on the body, fetters the use of reason. That this takes place in the passions is evident from the fact that sometimes, when the passions are very intense, [a] man loses the use of reason altogether: for many have gone out of their minds through excess of love or anger. It is in this way that passion draws the reason to judge in particular, against the knowledge which it has in general."[60] In Aquinas's view, sensory-appetitive motions take place by means of changes in the heart and circulatory system, and they are caused (and defined) by acts of interior sensory apprehension, which also have a material element, namely, changes in the brain and nervous system. Aquinas does not say much about the relationship between the heart, the brain, and the related organ systems. The basic idea, however, is that an intense disturbance in one part (or system) of the body can cause a disturbance in a related part (or system) of the body. For example, a sudden surge in heart rate and blood flow (the material component of certain emotions) can affect what happens in the part of one's brain by which one carries out acts of imagination. It can thus affect one's ability to make rational judgments *about* the predicament in which one imagines oneself to be. Aquinas's best explanations are "mental," rather than directly physiological, but it is important to keep the materiality of emotions in view.

On a positive note, Aquinas says that emotions can affect the will by making it easier and more pleasant for the will to carry out certain of its operations. He says, for example, that

> when by a judgment of reason the will chooses anything, it does so more promptly and easily if in addition a passion is aroused in the lower part, since the lower appetitive power is closely connected with changes in the body. Thus Augustine says: "The movement of pity is of service to reason when pity is shown in such a way that justice is preserved." And this is what the philosopher also says, bringing in the verse of Homer: "Stir up your courage and rage," because when a man is virtuous with the virtue of courage the passion of anger following upon the choice of virtue makes for greater alacrity in the act.[61]

Certain virtuous passions provide this sort of help primarily because they cause changes in the body that help the person literally to move—and to move more energetically—as needed to meet the challenges of the situation.

EMOTIONS AS MOTIONS OF THE SENSORY APPETITE, REVISITED

We have approached motions of the human sensory appetite partly from below, noting some of the ways in which they resemble the appetitive motions that occur in other sorts of entities, especially other animals. Approaching emotions from below helps us to avoid overintellectualizing them. It reduces the temptation to think of emotions as forms of judgment while neglecting to make explicit the many kinds of judgment (from the most intellectual and abstract to the most sensory and particular) of which humans are capable. Keeping this range of human capabilities in view is important if we wish to account for the interplay and, sometimes, the painful competition that erupts between judgments of various kinds that influence the intentional content of a given emotion, at a given moment, and might also influence how one thinks and feels about the emotion that has come, with its object, to one's attention.

Approaching emotions from below helps us also to take seriously the way in which emotions do not simply occupy our awareness; they also *move* us interiorly, physically, and sometimes also exteriorly, in the form of behavior or action, relative to objects that we represent to ourselves through the use of our interior sensory powers. It helps us to appreciate the structural similarity between emotions and various animal appetites, such as the appetite for food or sexual pleasure, the appetite to flee a perceived danger, or the appetite to defend oneself against an attacker, especially if we interpret the concept of appetite broadly, as including one or more moments in the typical unfolding of an object-oriented appetitive motion. Approaching emotions from below helps us to acknowledge that, inasmuch as emotions are aspects of our animality, they are not completely amenable to reason.

We have also approached motions of the human sensory appetite from above. From this direction, we can appreciate that emotions are naturally and normally influenced by the intellect in the formation of their original content and in the courses they take over time, particularly if and as one subjects one's emotions to reflection. Emotions are caused by sensory impressions, but humans almost never entertain sensory impressions in the absence of thought, and thinking can affect sensory appearances in many ways. Emotions are naturally and normally influenced also by the will in that one has a stable desire to be happy (however one understands that), and this desire motivates one to engage in acts of understanding and reasoning that influence the content of one's emotions and thus the emotional tenor of one's life. Moreover, if one understands that happiness is attained primarily through the exercise of virtue, one will choose to invest one's energy in (or withhold it from) emotions that one judges to be appropriate (or inappropriate) to the circumstances. One will choose to feel one's emotions in ways that reflect well on one morally.

Approaching emotions from above allows us to appreciate that any act of the sensory appetite can be informed by intellectual judgments, so that while undergoing a given emotion, one has in mind a complex object of experience that is both sensible and intelligible, and one responds appetitively in a way that engages both the sensory and the intellectual dimensions of one's appetitive power. If the acts of one's sensory and intellectual appetite concur, the result can be a resounding act of the will that is indistinguishable experientially from a vibrant, intellectually informed emotion.

Given the ways in which the intellect and the will can and often do influence motions of the sensory appetite, particularly via the intellect's influence on the cogitative and other interior sensory powers, it is not surprising that motions of the sensory appetite can and often do, in turn, influence operations of the intellect and the will. Aquinas tends to emphasize the ways in which extreme emotions can *distort* one's intellectual judgments and thus one's reasoning about whether a particular (union with a) sensible object would really contribute to one's happiness. He tends to focus on the ways in which distortions or mistakes of judgment cause one to conceive misguided motions of the will, which can yield regrettable choices. Yet it is an important part of his ethic that *well-ordered* emotions are a reflection of goodness. They also motivate the further cultivation of goodness.

It is in the midst of all of this dynamic, reciprocal, causal activity that emotions are best located. Emotions are well construed as features of our sensory or animal nature, yet as humans our animal nature is informed by an intellectual principle, which means that we typically respond to sensible particulars in ways that are both like and unlike the ways in which wolves, sheep, and other animals appear to respond to what matters to them. Indeed, humans are highly advanced intellectual beings who can register and respond to what we believe to be beyond all sensory experience. Yet even when we relate to the transcendent, to the underlying nature of reality, or to the principle of that reality, as we conceive it, we must retain some reference points; we must rely on symbols, images, or examples to make our understanding real, even as we intuit that what we understand in this way is a far cry from the "really real" itself. As long as we are embodied beings, we live through the engagement of our sensory powers. Yet because we are intellectual beings, we are free and responsible, to some extent, for the rational management of these sensory powers.

NOTES

1. It is important to be flexible in our use of the term "religious imagination" (my term, not Aquinas's). An act of the religious imagination might be chiefly an act of the intellect; it might involve questioning, probing, analyzing, or believing something quite general and abstract about the truth of reality, and reflecting on what is possible for humans, given the way things are. When one engages in this sort of intellectual activity, one does so with reference to images and impressions that are produced via the interior senses. An act of the religious imagination might be more an act of sensory apprehension; it might involve constructing images and possible scenarios upon which one goes on to reflect critically and metaphorically. When one engages in this sort of sensory activity, one does so necessarily with the aid of one's intellectual powers.

2. As noted previously, Aquinas holds that all humans, by nature, seek happiness as their end, but many do so only implicitly and with only a vague and sometimes poor idea of the *content* of happiness in mind.

3. *ST* I 87.1, 87.3, 87.4.

4. For Aquinas, as for Aristotle, a failure to become emotionally engaged in a situation can amount to a moral failure, as when one sees innocent people suffering, and one is not the least bit moved to compassion, or one sees a child laughing and wanting to share his or her delight, and one is not at all moved to delight. Virtue does not make one unemotional; it makes one respond to situations with appropriate emotion, where what is appropriate is determined in light of the particulars of the situation, but generally falls between the extremes of too much and too little. There is much to be debated here, in another context, regarding how one determines what is right with respect to particular emotions.

5. *ST* I-II 24.1 *ad* 2 (my translation).

6. Sometimes Aquinas equates intellect and reason, and sometimes he distinguishes them (*ST* I 79.8, 81.3). As noted previously, I use "intellect" and "intellectual apprehension" to cover all operations of the soul that concern the registering and processing of intelligible information. We have focused on (1) the power to *understand* what an object is, and how the object can serve, in principle, as an intermediate end relative to one's final end, and (2) the power to *reason* about how best to use the means at one's disposal, in a given situation, to bring about an end that one judges to be good or required (usually a way of acting and feeling). As we will see, practical reason in Aquinas includes not only the power to judge what is good or what ought to be done; it includes also the (limited) power to "persuade" other powers or parts of the self to "concur" with what one has judged, by the power of reason, to be good or required. Given Aquinas's flexibility, we too can be flexible in our use of the terms "intellect" and "reason."

7. *Truth* 25.2.

8. *ST* I 82.1 *ad* 2.

9. *ST* I 81.3.

10. *ST* I-II 47.2 *ad* 3.

11. *ST* I 79.1. See Pasnau, *Thomas Aquinas on Human Nature*, chap. 5.

12. *ST* I-II 24.3.

13. *Truth* 25.4.

14. Ibid., (my emphasis).

15. *Truth* 26.3 *ad* 13.

16. Ibid.

17. The philosophical literature on self-deception and its relationship to *akrasia* or weakness of will is large, and the issues are endlessly complex. I must leave it to others to consider the full implications of Aquinas's theory of emotion for understanding the causes of these phenomena.

18. *ST* I-II 9.2.

19. In *Contesting Justice: Women, Islam, Law, and Society* (New York: State University of New York Press, 2008), Ahmed Souaiaia notes that, in the *Quran*, a Muslim learns that the "fires of hell" will burn one's skin from one's flesh, but one will continue to grow new skin so that one can continue to suffer the horrifying pain of having it burned away (40).

20. Recall the example of the golden mountain, an object that only a human animal is able to apprehend, in Aquinas's view (*ST* I 78.4).

21. *ST* I 80.2; I-II 22.3.

22. If one is concerned about the ethical formation of one's emotions, it is important to reflect upon and try to assess the epistemological status of acts of religious imagination that shape one's emotions, for virtue requires that one be moved consistently in ways that accord with "the way things really are." However, it is beyond the scope of this project to specify the conditions under which a judgment of any kind may be regarded as true, and in what sense.

23. See the excellent film produced and directed by Bari Pearlman, *Daughters of Wisdom* (Los Angeles: Seventh Art Releasing, 2007).

24. Murphy, "Aquinas on Our Responsibility for Our Emotions," 175.

25. *ST* I 81.3 *ad* 2.

26. Ibid.

27. Ibid.

28. *Truth* 25.4 *ad* 4; see also 26.6.

29. *Truth* 26.3 *ad* 13; see also *ST* I II 24.3.

30. *ST* I-II 24.3 *ad* 1.

31. *ST* I-II 24.3, including *ad* 1.

32. *ST* I-II 24.3.

33. *ST* I-II 31.4.

34. Gustafson, *Ethics from a Theocentric Perspective*, 208–9.

35. See Dalai Lama, *The Meaning of Life: Buddhist Perspectives on Cause and Effect*, trans. Jeffrey Hopkins (Boston: Wisdom, 2000).

36. There are many qualifications that could be introduced concerning the conditions under which—and the degree to which—one can reasonably be held responsible for an emotion that consumes one's awareness and causes one to say or do something contrary to reason, but exploring these would take us too far from our central concern. See, for example, *ST* I-II 6.6, 6.7, 7.2, 10.3, 77.7.

37. *ST* I 82.4.

38. *ST* I-II 10.3 *ad* 1. The will *can* keep some sensory-appetitive motions from arising in the first place, in Aquinas's scheme, by powering acts of the intellect by which one trains oneself to construc certain aspects of one's world differently (see *ST* I-II 9.2 and 17.7). This is an implication of Aquinas's theory of virtue, which is evident especially in his mature account of temperance.

39. *ST* I-II 77.1.

40. *Truth* 25.4.

41. For a monograph devoted to this topic see Baker, *The Thomistic Theory of the Passions and Their Influence upon the Will.*

42. Aquinas must mean any passion that is not itself consistent with the exercise of virtue; by definition, a well-ordered emotion is consistent with, rather than an impediment to, the proper exercise of the will.

43. *ST* I-II 77.1 (my emphasis).

44. *ST* I-II 33.3.

45. Aquinas does suggest that this space collapses, and unavoidably so, during experiences of orgasm (*ST* II-II 153.2 *ad* 2).

46. *ST* I-II 77.1.

47. Ibid.

48. *ST* I-II 9.2, 24.3.

49. *ST* I-II 77.1.

50. Ibid.

51. This is a simplification of the moments in a decision-making process discussed in *ST* I-II 8–17.

52. Thomas Aquinas, *In Aristotelis Librum De Anima* (Turin: Marietti, 1936), III, 16n845, as translated and quoted by Baker, *The Thomistic Theory of the Passions and Their Influence upon the Will*, 110. See also *ST* I-II 77.2.

53. *ST* I-II 77.2.

54. Recall that, for Aquinas, sexual desire counts as an emotion when one experiences it in relation to a particular "object" that one apprehends to be attractive.

55. In Aquinas's scheme, when one does something that one knows is wrong, one does so under the impression that committing this act will somehow contribute to one's happiness. Usually, the problem is that one does not fully understand the relationship between sensory pleasure and the enjoyment of a distinctively human happiness, nor does one fully understand the relationship between virtue and happiness. Or one understands these things quite well, intellectually, but this understanding has not informed one's sensory appetites, which have a "mind" of their own (namely, the power of sensory apprehension).

56. *ST* I-II 77.2.

57. Ibid.

58. *ST* I-II 77.2 *ad* 4. Aquinas references *NE* vii. 3, but the exact passage he has in mind is not clear to me.

59. *ST* I-II 77.2 *ad* 4. See also *ST* I-II 33.3.

60. *ST* I-II 77.2.

61. *Truth* 26.7.

CHAPTER TEN

The Religious-Ethical
Study of Emotion

✦

Thomas Aquinas's account of the structure of emotion is partly what Robert Roberts (in describing his own account) calls "mentalist."[1] Aquinas construes emotions as embodied states of mind or awareness, and he analyzes them from the perspective of the subjects who experience them. Yet Aquinas analyzes the structure of emotion relative to what he takes to be the structure of reality as such. In this chapter I present a summary of Aquinas's account, recollecting some of its metaphysical depth and making explicit the way in which, in his view, certain principles or laws at work in the universe and in humans themselves determine, to some extent, the forms that emotions can take, how emotions can and do behave, and how (in formal terms) humans do *well* to feel emotions. I also highlight some practical ethical benefits of this sort of inquiry, indicating how religious-ethical reflection on our emotions, aided by the study of Aquinas and others, can help us to gain perspective on what is going on within us and around us, and can thereby enhance our freedom to make desirable changes in our lives.

ORDER WITHIN THE UNIVERSE

Aquinas thinks that everything has a built-in appetite or tendency to be the sort of thing it is and to realize its defining potential in relation to other things, which have their own tendencies.[2] Everything has an appetite to unite with itself—with its own actuality. Moreover, everything stands in relation to other things with which it *can* in principle unite and *must* unite if it is to actualize its potential and contribute to the actualization of the larger wholes of which it is a part. Objects move into and out of various unions, some of which are relatively stable (such as the union of the elements that compose a stone), and some of which are relatively fleeting (such as the union that occurs between a person and a blooming lilac bush, through the person's sense of smell).

Aquinas observes patterns of motion or interaction in nature, and with the science of his day he infers laws that help to account for these patterns. For example, he observes that iron filings are attracted to a magnet.[3] They "love" the magnet in that they have properties that allow them to unite with the magnet, which has its own related properties. When the magnet is brought within a certain distance of the filings, the filings "desire" and "seek" the magnet and come to relative "rest" on the magnet. From this and other observations, Aquinas infers that the heavenly bodies have something to do with the relationship between iron and magnets. In effect, he looks to the other planets and the stars, in relation to the earth and the material bodies *on* the earth, for comprehensive laws that determine how various bodies behave relative to other bodies. Indeed, as a theologian, he looks all the way to the first principle of the universe for the most complete explanation of how things can exist at all, how they operate in relation to other existing things, and what purpose all of this relating serves.

When Aquinas turns from the relationship between iron and magnets to the relationship between humans and objects of human experience, he observes similar patterns.[4] He observes, for example, that human bodies, like many other entities, are "attracted" to the earth. Human bodies have properties that make them well suited to "seek" the earth and "cling" to its surface. Looking to a higher level of complexity within the human, he observes that human bodies are also "attracted," as living organisms, to the nutrients and water that are essential for life and proper functioning. Human organisms are capable of "uniting" with these elements through natural processes of nutrition and hydration. Today, we might think of events that occur inside cells as "drawing" certain molecules into the cells, where the molecules can "seek" (or "be sought") and "unite" (or "be united") with other molecules in the form of biochemical reactions.[5]

Looking to an even higher level of complexity, Aquinas observes that hungry humans are drawn toward items of food as if toward magnets. Yet humans enter into relationships with food through the use of sensory powers, by entertaining real or imagined food items as objects of apprehension and appetite. To be sure, humans enter into relationships with food through the use of other powers as well: Intellectual powers are engaged when we judge that a food item is healthful and we choose to eat it for that reason, and vegetative powers are engaged when we digest the food we eat. But hunger is best understood as an appetitive motion that we undergo when (under certain conditions) we apprehend something as suitable for eating. It is a sensory-appetitive motion that implies a prior act of sensory apprehension.

Looking to a higher level still, Aquinas observes that humans are attracted to other humans whom we apprehend to be good for ourselves.[6] Commonly, we are attracted to others who are, in turn, attracted to us. Certain humans are drawn to each other as if each of them were oppositely charged, magnetically, but through the medium of consciousness. Finally, Aquinas observes that some humans are explicitly attracted to God as their highest end. These humans seek whatever else they seek in life in ways that they trust will allow them to be drawn into the heart of God and come to rest—or complete actuality—there.

ORDER WITHIN HUMAN NATURE

Aquinas infers from these and countless other observations that there are some general laws that govern the "behavior" of humans, just as there are laws that govern the "behavior" of iron and magnets.[7] Some laws that govern human behavior *connect* us with other elements of the natural world. We ordinarily tend (with other material entities) toward the surface of the earth; we tend (with other living beings) toward what preserves life; and we tend (with other sensory beings) toward what we apprehend via our sensory powers to be good for ourselves and our kin. Other laws that govern human behavior *distinguish* us from other sensible things. We tend toward objects that we apprehend intellectually, as well as sensorily, to be suitable for ourselves and for others within our range of concern.[8]

Because humans have a characteristic form of operation, one can often bring about predictable changes in a human's behavior by working with his or her intellectual and sensory powers in particular ways. For example, one can place in a person's hand a picture of his or her child and ask the person to "look at this sweet picture I found!" Let us say that the child appears in the picture to be happy, and the person who now holds the picture is generally happy with the child. Barring unusual causes or conditions, one can predict that the person will look at the picture, smile, and tend emotionally toward the child who appears in the picture. The person will tend toward the child in love, desire, or delight. This sort of regularity and predictability in human behavior is part of what makes psychology and other social sciences possible.

In Aquinas's view, human nature as such determines that humans have certain powers and, to some extent, we exercise these powers.[9] Most notably, the form of rational animality determines that humans have the power of intellect or reason and, to some extent, we exercise this power (or its developmental bases, as with an infant) unless something is amiss (as with certain forms of brain damage). One can, of course, exercise the power of reason well or poorly. Within the realm of deliberation and decision making, one can be relatively active or inactive. One's reasoning can be skillful or unskillful. In addition, it can be morally on target or off. For Aquinas, functioning well as a rational animal is partly a matter of reasoning *effectively* to bring about desired ends, but it is also a matter of reasoning *rightly* to bring about ends that are worth bringing about—ends that contribute to human flourishing. The form of rational animality does not determine that one will exercise the power of reason with excellence. It determines only that one has (or can acquire) this power, and one can, in principle, improve one's ability to exercise this power, up to a point. It determines, further, that one *must* exercise and cultivate this power if one is to flourish as a rational animal.[10]

Whether one reasons well or poorly, reason functions as a kind of interior principle or law. Practical reason, in particular, determines to some extent how a situation appears to one (most notably, as bearing—or not bearing—on one's own or another's flourishing). It also provides direction (and sometimes misdirection) regarding the moral principles that are applicable to the situation, the responses that are possible on one's part, the effects that various responses are likely to have, and the ways in which these effects are likely to honor one's moral commitments and promote other important goods. As such, reason is a power that makes moral deliberation and decision making possible. Aquinas thinks that reason is a reflection of the eternal law, which is a principle of order at work in the universe—a principle that has its origin in the divine mind or "Divine Reason."[11] This does not mean that every human being's power of reason is such that its exercise provides good guidance. It does mean that a typical human being can, under certain conditions, develop this power to the point that reason becomes a relatively reliable guide for behavior that contributes, in fact, to human well-being. It also means that, if one fails to develop this power, one fails to become an excellent example of the human kind—one fails to flourish. If one is well-habituated, one "hears" the "voice" of *right* reason reminding or persuading one to "do good and avoid evil."[12] One hears right reason (often in relation to other interior voices, such as sensory judgments that are linked to emotions) directing one to unite (or avoid union) with particular objects in order to approach one's proper end or promote human well being more generally.[13]

Just as the voice of reason, if nurtured within the context of truthful communities, can serve as a relatively reliable guide for indicating how one ought to act, reason can also guide the operation of one's interior sensory powers, so that these, too, are put in the service of directing one to pursue suitable unions.[14] Through the exercise of right reason, one can cultivate habits that allow particular sensory-appetitive motions to arise and find expression in ways that reflect the governance of reason over the whole of one's person. Virtuous emotions—namely, emotions that are appropriate to the situation and to which one consents because one judges them appropriate—often guide one differently than appetitive motions that are more a function of one's animality, although the latter do not necessarily mislead. Again, the form of rational animality does not determine that one will use the power of reason to habituate oneself to be moved in ways that are morally fine. It determines only that, in principle, one has *some* power to shape the exercise of one's sensory powers, and it determines that one can *thrive* as a rational animal only inasmuch as one *does* engage in this sort of ethical formation.

The form of rational animality determines that humans can and ordinarily do exercise reason and other powers that are informed by reason, and that we must do so relatively well if we are to be in good and satisfying working order. Aquinas holds further that humans can and do, under certain circumstances, undergo changes to our nature that alter, to some extent, what is possible for us and how we are directed interiorly (or how we direct ourselves) to be and to behave. Through a gift of grace, God can add to one's wherewithal certain higher-order virtues.[15] In receiving and consenting to these virtues, one is healed of some of the distortions to which one has become accustomed through the misuse of one's powers, although one is still finite and prone to moral failure and sin.[16] Moreover, one undergoes an elevation or extension of one's powers, so that one is able to tend toward God, not only as God is apprehended through the exercise of natural reason, as a first and final cause of being, but also as God is apprehended through faith, as Friend.[17] In addition, one is able to tend toward (or away from) whatever else one apprehends as good (or evil) in light of this friendship with God.[18]

In effect, Aquinas holds that human nature is such that God can bestow on a human a "new law" that is added to the other laws (most notably the law of reason) that guide the human from within.[19] The new law does not destroy or replace the other interior principles, but it qualifies them. Persons of natural reason alone are limited to the ability to construe situations as bearing on their (or a loved one's) natural happiness. They are limited to directing themselves to seek or promote natural happiness through well-chosen means. Persons of faith—who are also persons of reason, but persons whose intellectual powers have been extended somewhat—are able to construe situations as bearing *also* on humans' eternal blessedness and the glory of God. Persons of faith are able to direct themselves to seek natural happiness while tending also toward a perfect union with the source of all goodness in a life to come. Once again, simply because one receives a new law, this does not mean that one will make good use of it.[20] It does mean, however, that one can, in principle, make use of it. It also means that one can *flourish* as a child of God only inasmuch as one *does* make good use of it, even as one makes good use of reason and one's other, well-ordered interior principles.

Aquinas apprehends that there is a kind of lawfulness at the heart of reality. There is a lawfulness within human nature, in particular, which determines in a general way not only what is (and is not) possible for humans, and how humans typically and predictably behave under various circumstances, but also what is profitable or good (and unprofitable or bad) for humans, given the sorts of beings we are, and given what we have to work with, individually and collectively. "The order of love" (*ordo amoris*) is a phrase that Aquinas uses to specify the ways in which we naturally and suitably privilege some objects over others in extending our limited affection and benevolence.[21] In the spirit of Aquinas, I sometimes use the phrase more broadly to refer to the way in which every existing thing has existence, exists as a particular sort of thing with particular properties, and behaves in relatively well-ordered ways in relation to everything else. I use the phrase to refer to the way everything is ordered—by a principle of goodness, by a power that makes suitable unions of all kinds possible—to tend toward its own being and perfection; toward goods beyond itself; and toward some sort of comprehensive good in which humans can believe or trust, in the abstract, but the details of which transcend the ability of the human mind to understand. "The order of love" can refer more specifically to the ways in which humans *must* behave (in the exercise of virtue) if we are to be—and help each other to be—excellent examples of our kind.

CONCERNS, BRIEFLY NOTED

Many people eschew metaphysical or theological interpretations of reality, for various reasons. Some people reject such interpretations because they are not interested in speculating about what, if anything, lies beyond the limits of scientific reason or physics. They find such speculation silly, ignorant, or confused, reflecting a mind-set that has evidently not comprehended the insights of the European Enlightenment or modern science.[22] Some people reject such interpretations because the interpretations are often misrepresented *as* matters of science.[23] Critics point, for example, to the way in which some Christians think "intelligent design" competes with "evolution" as a scientific explanation for how things work, and "creation" is on par with "the big bang" as a scientific explanation for the origin of the cosmos. Some people reject theological interpretations because such interpretations have been used by people with considerable social power to legitimate their unequal access to power and the subjugation of other people, as when general accounts of the orderliness or lawfulness of the universe open up into specific accounts which assert that certain humans are, by nature, fit to rule over other humans (white over black, one tribe over another, male over female, those born with high social status over those born at the bottom of the social ladder). Aquinas himself perpetuates some of these mistakes.[24]

Indeed, there are many reasons to be suspicious of and reject (in part or in whole) particular theological interpretations and their uses for particular purposes. However, it would be misguided simply to reject religious thinking as such without considering the quality of a person's thinking, how his or her religious thinking stands in relation to other sorts of thinking in which he or she engages or ought to engage, and the impact that the person's thinking has on his or her life and community. There is much religious thinking that has contributed to the well-being of humans and the development of civilizations. A form of religious thinking, namely, an insatiable curiosity to dig deeper and deeper into the "nature of nature," has been basic to the advancement of science. In any case, if one is to appreciate Aquinas's account of emotion—and any other account that has a similar metaphysical depth—one must investigate this depth. In order to do that, one must surrender to at least some religious curiosity and concern. One must imagine how an intelligent human being could see the world in such terms. One must think with flexibility and generosity of mind about what a given thinker is even saying, particularly when it comes to the use of religious symbols such as "God," which contain many layers of meaning.[25]

Most humans, I take it, have thoughts or intuitions, or conceive questions once in a while, about whether there is or might be more to reality than meets the eye. Moreover, most of us—from the religiously most doctrinaire and traditional to the most skeptical and antitraditional—have experiences in which we are blown away by the intricacy, the complexity, the power, and the beauty of the universe, and we naturally pronounce and *feel* that "it is good." Indeed, the universe is unbelievably, incomprehensibly wonderful, even as it contains so much that people fittingly regard as chaotic, ugly, destructive, and downright evil. In my view, it is natural and appropriate, when we do experience a love for life and for all that we regard as good in life, to *wonder* (in whatever terms are available to us) whether there is a cause of all this goodness—and whether part of our reason for being is to find a way to live well in relation to this cause. It is, in principle, good for humans in their diverse social contexts to ask these and other questions of themselves and each other as we search for ways to go on in the face of life's difficulties. I have sought to interpret Aquinas in a way that honors this broadly religious impulse in him and in his (and my) readers, trying not to get tangled in concerns about particular doctrines, for there are countless doctrines, countless ways of explicating these doctrines and, yes, countless concerns.

EMOTIONS AND THE ORDER OF LOVE

Aquinas sets his account of emotion within the context of a rich and provocative account of the nature of reality. He thinks that emotions, like everything else in our universe, exhibit certain patterns and follow certain laws. Emotions (as he defines them) have a formal structure, and they exhibit a kind of logic. One can experience an emotion only in relation to an object of sensory apprehension (albeit an object that one commonly seeks to find intelligible as well as sensible) or an object of intellectual apprehension that one entertains in relation to a sensory image or impression. In addition, one can experience an emotion only in relation to an object that one apprehends as bearing on one's own or another's well-being.[26] One experiences an emotion only in relation to what becomes an object of one's sensory *appetite* (where acts of the sensory appetite are often joined with related acts of the intellectual appetite). Moreover, specific sensory-appetitive motions can be caused by only certain apprehensions. One can feel sorrow, for example, only at the apprehension that one is united with an object that is unsuitable for one's being (or one is *not* united with an object that is suitable or desirable).[27] Commonly, one experiences sorrow at the perceived absence or loss of a good. One cannot feel sorrow over the presence of a good unless one interprets that good as related, in some way, to a loss (as when one sorrows in the presence of a beloved, knowing that love is impermanent).

Emotions have a certain structure, and this structure is part of what makes them intelligible. It is also part of what makes it possible to relate emotions to other phenomena, especially phenomena that are capable of being apprehended by humans (and are thus capable of becoming mental causes). Aristotle is able in the *Rhetoric* to explain, in general terms, the strategies that successful orators employ in order to evoke and manipulate emotions in their audiences.[28] Aristotle pays particular attention to anger, recognizing that this emotion can "so change [people] as to affect their judge-ments."[29] He analyzes "(1) what the state of mind of angry people is, (2) who the people are with whom they usually get angry, and (3) on what grounds they get angry with them."[30] Armed with this information, a skilled orator—say, a prosecutor—can alter many people's interpretations of the significance of events. For example, a prosecutor can ask members of the jury to picture themselves or a loved one in a similar situation of victimization, and he can point to the defendant and say things that make the defendant appear both contemptible and contemptuous. Some of the sensory images introduced by the orator become images in the minds of the jurors, and some of these im-ages become objects of the juror's own emotions. In feeling anger toward the defendant and pity toward the victim[31] jurors are more likely to appreciate the gravity of the crime committed, and more likely to want to punish the defendant—unless the defense attorney works a counterspell, making use of the same information about how emotions work.[32] In any case, the fact that humans can sometimes cause specific emotional reactions in themselves and in others—and they can, to some extent, predict what humans will do under the influence of these emotions—shows that emotions are, in certain re-spects, law-like in their behavior.

Just as there are laws that determine the forms that emotions can take, and laws that determine the ways in which emotions can and typically do re-late to other phenomena, there are also laws that determine (in general terms) how emotions *must* behave—that is, how humans must undergo their emotions—if humans are basically to be in good working order. The form of rational animality determines that certain emotions, felt in certain ways, are consistent with good human functioning, and the same or different emo-tions, felt in different ways, are inconsistent with good human functioning.[33] Functioning well as a human includes experiencing (and being motivated partly by) emotions that are important for survival and certain social rela-tions. Yet it includes experiencing these and other emotions (and their ef-fects) in ways that are influenced by well-habituated intellectual powers. Much of Aquinas's ethic of virtue is intended to help people cultivate excel-lences of character that dispose them to undergo emotions (and make choices concerning their emotions) in ways that are reason-governed, wherever pos-sible. Virtuous people are consistently moved, emotionally, with respect to "the right things, with the right persons, and moreover in the right way, at the right time, and for the right interval."[34]

The interior laws that determine what is fitting with respect to emotion include certain laws of nature (including various "natural inclinations") and certain laws of right reason (including the descriptive law that everything acts for an end, and the normative law that one ought to act for ends that are morally fine).[35] Emotions are themselves natural inclinations *and* acts or modes of tending that are, to some extent, informed by reason. For some humans, the interior laws that determine what is fitting with respect to emotion include also the "new law."[36] Aquinas holds that this new law comes as a supernatural gift, but it becomes a principle of operation in a particular human in the exercise of faith, hope, and charity. Whereas a general principle of love is at work in every facet of the cosmos, causing every existing thing to tend toward what is suitable for it, and this principle is at work in humans, causing humans to tend, additionally and more specifically, toward what they *apprehend* intellectually and sensorily to be suitable for them, Aquinas thinks that a further, more comprehensive principle of love is at work in people of living faith, causing them also to tend explicitly toward God as their highest end, and toward (or away from) everything else in light of its relationship to God.[37]

This higher order of love (*ordo caritatis*, broadly speaking) determines some of what is possible for a human. It also determines, in a general way, what a human is likely to do in the exercise of his or her new principles, although humans who receive the gifts of faith, hope, and charity make use of these gifts imperfectly and as beings who confront different situational demands.[38] A Christian whose life is governed by charity, as well as by other interior principles, believes certain things about what is really happening and what is most important, and these beliefs affect, to some extent, how sensible goods (and evils) appear to him or her.[39] Some of the Christian's religious beliefs thus influence the content of certain sensory-appetitive states; some beliefs influence the ways these states unfold over time; and some beliefs influence how the Christian responds to his or her own appetitive states.

The order of charity determines, formally, that some of a Christian's emotional states, and some of his or her second-order responses to his or her emotional states, contribute to the well-being of the Christian, while others do not, or do so to a lesser extent. Viewed from below, sensory-appetitive motions that support the maintenance of human life, support the exercise of reason and the formation of habits that reflect the governance of reason, support the maintenance of just and peaceful human communities, and support the pursuit and enjoyment of the highest human good—all generally contribute to the flourishing of a Christian. Viewed from above, sensory-appetitive motions that amount to an "overflow" or an appetitive resonance that occurs with the apprehension of a religious "object" (such as God) and an appetitive motion toward that object (where the divine is conceived with reference to a sensory image, such as an image of Jesus or light) also contribute, in principle, to the Christian's well-being.[40] One must exercise virtue in order to determine in particular cases which emotions, felt in which ways, are consistent with tending toward what is truly worthwhile. The order of charity determines only that the cultivation of supernatural virtue is required if one is consistently to make these determinations well.

Aquinas's account of emotion is thus woven rather seamlessly into the rest of his worldview. This does not entail that one must agree with the whole of his worldview in order to make use of any or all parts of his account of emotion. For example, one could agree with certain aspects of Aquinas's natural theology, appreciating what this theology indicates about the lawfulness of emotion (as part of nature and of rational human nature, in particular), while questioning or rejecting what he says about certain laws that are revealed in the Bible, about the authority of such laws, about the meaning of Christ as a symbol, about the notion that certain virtues are "infused . . . by God" and are infused into some people only, and so on.[41] One could judge that Aquinas's way of interpreting reality has much going for it, and it makes possible an interesting way of construing emotions—yet one could think that there are other interpretations of reality that give rise to different ways of construing emotions—ways that are also interesting. One could wonder whether there is any way, finally, to determine the truth or truthfulness of competing accounts. The main point is that, if one wishes to understand Aquinas's analysis of the emotions, one must consider the religious worldview within which it is set. The better one understands the relationship between his account of emotion and his account of the rest of reality, the better one is able to think through what would happen to either one of these accounts if adjustments were made to the other.

EMOTIONS, RELIGION, AND MORALITY

Emotions are ways in which we are moved interiorly and also bodily relative to objects that we apprehend to be suitable or unsuitable, friendly or unfriendly, helpful or harmful, attractive or repulsive. As noted, our emotions are partly a function of our animality; they are ways in which we, like other animals, typically respond to certain sensory inputs, with implications for the preservation of life and species. *In* their sensory dimension, considered apart from all intellectual influences, emotions are not well construed as elements of morality—not if we think that morality concerns matters relative to which we have some choice, over which we can exercise some influence, and for which we can hold ourselves and one another accountable. Yet there is no reason to consider emotions, *qua* motions of the sensory appetite, irrespective of the ways in which they can be and ordinarily are in-fluenced by the intellectual powers that inform our sensory operations.[42] At least, there is no reason to consider emotions in this way if we are interested in analyzing them ethically and religiously.

Sensible objects and the ways they affect our well-being are things that we *sense*, but they are also things about which we ordinarily *think*, in the ab-stract and in particular cases. It is common for a human being to wonder whether wanting, seeking, or enjoying this or that good (say, a third glass of wine, a particular sexual encounter, the revenge that we currently crave, or the erasure of a hateful person from the face of the earth) will really promote our well-being or be of benefit to other humans whose well-being is tied to our own. It is a function of most moralities or moral traditions to get peo-ple to think about such things so they do not go through life in a state of vir-tual immediacy, simply following their noses to the trough or falling into predicaments that promise to be pleasing or satisfying but actually diminish them and others. Many people who participate in moralities reflect on what and how they are doing as humans in light of teachings that are connected, in one way or another, to religious musings, questions, symbols, and images.

When we sense, think, judge, question, and wonder about an object (or union with that object) and its immediate and deeper significance for us—when we engage in such acts of apprehension all, more or less, at the same time—we tend to be moved in multiple and mutually influential ways. Aquinas distinguishes sensory and intellectual-appetitive motions, holding that the former are directed toward goods or evils *qua* sensible, while the lat-ter are directed toward goods or evils *qua* intelligible, but things are more complex than this formal distinction suggests. We often tend toward a sen-sible good about which we have made a high-level sensory judgment that ap-proximates a judgment of practical reason, such that the object-oriented sensory-appetitive motion that is caused by our sensory judgment is diffi-cult to distinguish from related acts of the will (particularly when the latter "overflow," as discussed in chapter 9, "onto" our sensory operations). In ad-dition, the object toward which we tend is sometimes a sensible good that we seek to find intelligible (as well as sensible), about which we make moral judgments, become curious, or think religiously, all of which can elicit lay-ered motions of the intellectual appetite. Again, the latter motions can have an impact (most notably via the intellect and its relationship to the interior sensory powers) on related sensory-appetitive motions.

Our emotions are sensory, for Aquinas, but the sensory is a broad cate-gory. Acts of sensory apprehension, which provide the objects of our emo-tions, include the sorts of cognitive acts that one finds in other, nonhuman animals *plus* more. In addition, our sensory-appetitive motions are subject to intellectual input at every point in their unfolding. They are subject to intellectual influence in their pre-formation (in the ways we judge the significance of certain features of reality and in the ways we direct ourselves to attend, from one angle or another, to emotion-evoking objects). Our emotions are subject to intellectual influence also in their ongoing formation and the directions they take over time (in the ways we choose to hold sensible objects in mind and perhaps turn them around in our minds, monitoring the effects of our considering and our reconsidering). Our emotions are subject to intellectual influence also with respect to the reactions that we have to our emotions (in the ways we indulge them, repress them, deny them, punish them, relax with them, create space around them, collapse into them, act on them, or what have you). Given the fact that most of our emotions are, to some extent, intellectually penetrable and thus amenable to deliberate formation and re-formation, in light of our understanding of (or our wondering about) the final end of human life, emotions are fitting subjects for ethical reflection.[43]

Culture, upbringing, and life experience (as well as biology) have a huge impact on how we apprehend the world around us, what we notice and take to be important in that world, and how we are moved by what we apprehend. For example, some of us are raised to "see" a wide range of acts as insults, and we habitually judge insults to be good occasions for anger. We not only *think* of anger as noble; we *feel* righteous and bold in being angry, and we consider people who do not experience anger in the face of insult to be weak and self-denigrating. Others of us are raised to "see" insult less often, and to regard it more as an occasion for caution. We not only *think* of anger as ugly and ignoble; we *feel* diminished in giving way to anger, and we regard people who do so as foolish and lacking in self-control.[44] Indeed, some of us are raised with both perspectives, and we are sometimes torn intellectually in ways that affect our sensory judgments and thus influence the extent to which we feel anger—and the ways in which we feel it, when it does arise.

For many of us, an element of culture, upbringing, and experience that tends to have a powerful impact on how we apprehend reality—and how we are moved by what we see—is religion (whether it be our participation in an organized religion, our effort to separate from the influence of a religion, or our effort to pursue a more individual path). Consider, for example, a Christian who is confused about the role of anger in a good human life. He or she might turn to Jesus as the truth of life and a paragon of virtue. On the one hand, the person might look to the Jesus who is represented in the Gospel of John as being "consumed" with "zeal" as he overturns the tables of the money-changers and asserts that these people will *not* make his Father's house "a house of trade" (2:14–17).[45] The person might look also to Jesus as a second Moses who emboldens people who identify with the Israelites (people who regard themselves as similarly oppressed) to fight for what is rightfully theirs. On the other hand, the person might look to the Jesus of Matthew's "Sermon on the Mount," who says, "Do not resist one who is evil. But if any one strikes you on the right cheek, turn to him the other also" (5:39). The person might hear Jesus saying, "Blessed are the meek," and "Blessed are you when men revile you and persecute you and utter all kinds of evil against you falsely on my account. Rejoice and be glad, for your reward is great in heaven" (Matthew 5:5 and 5:11). As a result of such an exploration, the Christian might wonder if his or her very confusion about anger has roots in the narrative world in which he or she was raised—a world that lurks in the background as the person composes and elaborates the intentional objects of his or her emotions. From here the person could go in countless directions in search of more of the truth about anger.

It is a task of religious ethics to help people of various traditions and paths to step out of their immersion in particular habits of emotion, to think about how they acquired those habits, and to make assessments of whether they wish—whether they ought—to continue to fall into those habits or whether they ought, instead, to alter their habits in some way. It is a task of religious ethics also to determine what is, indeed, good or right, and how one's thinking about goodness can and should (or should not) be informed by thinking about the underlying nature of reality. However, our main concern has been to get to a point where we are more likely to ask such questions for ourselves and take responsibility for investigating the questions, rather than simply believing and doing as we are told. Religious influences are multiple and extremely complex, and they are only some of the innumerable social influences that bear down upon us from the moment we are born, but one has to start somewhere. Becoming aware of and giving deliberate shape to one's habitual ways of being moved is a central task of moral virtue. It is a task of religious ethics to provide resources for engaging in the practice of virtue.

BENEFITS OF THIS SORT OF INQUIRY: LEARNING A USEFUL GRAMMAR

Some of us have been socialized to operate within a particular worldview as if that worldview just were "the world." We have never really entertained the possibility that there are other ways of interpreting what is going on in our world and our lives. In addition, some of us have been raised, within particular cultural and familial contexts, in ways that make us prone to collapse into the immediacy of our emotions, and it is difficult for us even to imagine opening up a space of reflection and freedom around our emotions. I do not want to overstate the power we have to (learn how to) affect the composition and recomposition of our own emotional states. Yet I also do not want to underestimate this power and its ethical significance. At some point in our development, most of us realize that we are capable of self-reflection (even if the one who engages in reflection and the self upon whom one reflects are regarded primarily as part of a community). We realize that we can and must take some responsibility for the ways in which we interpret what is happening around us, between ourselves and others, and within us. More specifically, we must take some responsibility for the ordinary judgments we make about the ways in which situations bear on our well-being: Is this person *really* trying to hurt me, or am I perhaps imagining it? How much of what I apprehend coming at me from other people is a projection of my own mind or a result of broader cultural scapegoating? Accordingly, we must take some responsibility for our modes of tending in relation to what we "see"—for our ways of resonating, desiring, enjoying, dissonating, recoiling, rising, attacking, and suffering interiorly in relation to objects of concern. All such appetitive motions reflect on us morally, to some extent, especially when we add the power of our will to them by consenting to them. How we undergo our emotions reflects the moral quality of our lives, even when we do not act on those emotions.

Studying Aquinas's account of emotion can enhance our ability to take greater responsibility for the quality of our lives. First, his account provides us with a way of highlighting certain dimensions of our experience so that these dimensions can become objects for reflection and conversation. Starting with experiences of what many of us call "emotions" (experiences that we commonly refer to, in English, as love, fear, anger, hatred, despair, sadness, and the like), he proposes a way of construing these experiences. He proposes that emotions are well construed as forms of appetitive motion. Emotions ought not, he says, to be construed as cognitive acts or judgments, for judgments alone do not move us to bodily acts, nor do judgments alone compose action-motivating interior motions. Yet emotions are inseparable from judgments. An appetitive motion cannot *be* an emotion without being *about* something, and it is an act of judgment that specifies what an emotion is about.

Aquinas holds, more specifically, that emotions are motions of the sensory appetite that presuppose prior acts of sensory apprehension. Holding this position requires that he distinguish between the intellectual and the sensory, both with respect to apprehension and with respect to appetite. He opens the category of sensory apprehension up widely to include all sorts of judgments, including judgments of "value," but where an object's "value" is not (on the sensory level as such) intellectualized in terms of a universal, such as "contributes to specifically human happiness." Aquinas's emphasis on the sensory dimension of our humanity reflects the insight that, while mature humans have the capacity to consider sensible objects in light of a reflective understanding of complete happiness or a vision of the good, we can and often do fail to exercise this capacity. We behave more like nonrational animals than like the rational animals we are. At the same time, Aquinas indicates many ways in which emotions can come under the influence of the intellect, and he argues that they must be brought under this influence if we are to flourish as rational animals.

Aquinas distinguishes several forms of sensory-appetitive motion in terms of their objects (usually situations *as* one apprehends them)—good or evil, suitable or unsuitable; present (having already occurred) or future (having not yet occurred); simple or arduous; and in some cases mixtures of each. He distinguishes forms of sensory-appetitive motion further in terms of direction of tending (approach or withdrawal or both, in respect of different aspects of an object), and various moments in the process of tending in one direction or another. He opens up the category of interior motion to include not only the motion of desire or aversion but also the principle of desire (on the front side) and the completion of desire (on the other side), both of which involve a kind of resonance or dissonance—an opening or a closing down. Making these formal distinctions allows Aquinas to specify eleven basic forms of sensory-appetitive motion or emotions and to argue that other emotions can be specified with reference to these.

Even if one does not, in the end, find this particular grammar more useful than others in identifying, naming, and helping one to understand important features of one's life—even if one has philosophical objections to it, or one cannot see how this grammar could be made to cohere with certain findings of science, or there are parts of one's experience that are not illuminated or are obscured by this account—the act of learning this grammar in all of its detail is likely to be fruitful. Indeed, learning *any* grammar that has this kind of detail and depth—especially one that encourages the free and critical exercise of religious imagination—is likely to be fruitful. It gives one a place to stand as one considers and compares other possibilities. It could be that one already has another, excellent place to stand (say, in an Aristotelian, Stoic, or Buddhist account)—or it could be that, as one investigates other accounts, one of them will appear more capable than Aquinas's of explaining and even enriching one's experience (increasing one's sense of well-being, decreasing one's experience of being a mere victim of one's emotions, or the like). In that case, one would still in principle have benefited from having Aquinas's account in mind. Aquinas leads one to ask important questions of any account that one might not otherwise think to ask, and the level of care with which he tries to answer these questions raises the bar for others.

BENEFITS OF THIS SORT OF INQUIRY: PUTTING A PARTICULAR GRAMMAR TO USE

Learning the language of Aquinas's account is not only intellectually informative; it has the potential to be ethically transformative as well. Suppose that I am consumed with what I take to be hatred for an enemy. Aquinas's account identifies typical judgments that compose the intentional content of hatred. In feeling what I regard as hatred, I might step back, as it were, consider the images, impressions, and judgments that are running through my mind, and compare them with the acts of apprehension that are identified by Aquinas. I might ask, for example, Does the person before my mind appear straightforwardly evil or despicable,[46] such that what I am experiencing is best described as a painful dissonance in the face of a hurtful prospect? Do I also feel an inclination to withdraw or run away from the person, so that it makes more sense to say that my dominant emotion is aversion? Do I also have an impulse to attack the person? If so, what is the more specific intentional content of this impulse? Do I want to attack the person for treating me with contempt? Do I want, in attacking the person, to somehow "get even?" If so, then what I am feeling might better be described as anger.[47] Do I want, instead, to destroy the person so that I never have to deal with him or her again? Do I basically wish him or her dead?

The desire to destroy looks somewhat like the central motion of anger, but anger paradigmatically aims at causing an offender pain for the sake of a good end—for the sake of restoring what one regards as an agreeable relationship between oneself and the offender. Perhaps in asking the last question, I realize immediately that *of course* I do not wish the person dead. I just find it difficult to accept that I cannot now—nor have I ever been able to— make this person treat me as I think I deserve. What I would like to destroy, more specifically, is the other's lack of amenability to my will. On the other hand, I might realize that, yes, I wish that I or some bad fate could remove this person from the face of the earth, in a painful manner, and I refuse to let go of this impulse. In that case, Aquinas's account would invoke the idea of the will in order to capture the active, deliberate dimension of my hatred—the deliberate rejection; the deliberate blocking of the possibility of reconciliation; and the deliberate turning of the whole self to face the other in the mode of malevolence.[48] Aquinas's account would encourage me to reflect further on hatred as a sensory-appetitive motion and consider whether my hatred is essentially a perversion of anger—anger that has come "unhinged from justice."[49] Another option is to think of my hatred as a simple, albeit intense, motion of dissonance and discomfort, but one that has become disconnected from the love of self that partially caused it. I might be under the impression that destroying another person would make me happy, only to find out that, in fact, nothing makes me happy anymore because my preoccupation with destroying life has quashed my very love for life. Finally, many emotional states are complex mixtures of simpler emotions; maybe what I feel is a mixture of envy, anger, and hatred.

If I am not utterly consumed by my hatred, I might ask myself whether it is *good* for me to feel the hatred I am feeling now. I have not attended in detail to the morality of emotions. Aquinas offers some formal guidance on this score. However, as I have indicated, to understand his guidance and to apply it to oneself, as a unique individual who faces what are in many respects unique situations, one would need to understand his theory of virtue, as well as his theory of natural (and related forms of) law, in light of his Christian theology. He does make clear that, in principle, it is wrong to wish another human being evil for the sake of evil.[50] But he does not rule out wishing someone evil for the sake of good, for example, hating the sin as part and parcel of one's intellectual love for the sinner—or hating the hostility that someone shows toward oneself and one's kin.[51] He clearly thinks that the simple appetitive motion of hatred—dissonance at the sensory apprehension of something that is unsuitable for the self—is often fitting. It is part of the way in which one registers, as an embodied being, that one is in the presence of something that is capable of causing one injury and pain. There is much here that is worth sorting out further. The point is that Aquinas's account gives someone like me, in the present example, a foothold in the effort to figure out how I am really tending in relation to this person whom I say, at first blush, I hate.

Let us say that I judge my hatred to be inappropriate. The vehemence of my impulse to destroy the other is out of proportion to his or her offense, if the other has even committed an offense. My hatred has caused me to forget all that is good in my life and to become fixed on what is bad, and it is "eating me up alive," causing me to become physically ill. I might choose, then, to reject my hatred and try to alter it. What Aquinas's account allows me to do is to judge where, in a complex flow of causal factors, I could most effectively step in—as if into a river—to bring about changes in my experience, immediately or further downstream. If I want to alter my hatred, it will not be enough to chastise myself in formal terms for my immorality. I will have to change the content of my imagination and my sensory judgments with respect to the person in question. I will have to change the way the other appears to me, the way he or she appears to bear on my well-being, or both. I might begin with intellectual judgments, including religious convictions, but I must relate those judgments to sensory images or impressions if I hope to dispel or otherwise change my sensory-appetitive motion. In particular, I must change the scenario or the narrative in which the other appears as the particular object of my hatred, by conjuring up other images that qualify or displace the images that formally cause my hatred.[52] I must, for example, picture the other at his or her best, playing with a child or taking care of an ailing parent. I must monitor the appetitive effects of my attempts to conjure up various alternatives and adjust my efforts accordingly. I must also be aware that, at any point, the image of the other "with horns" or the image of myself as a pitiful victim of the other's nastiness could reassert itself, thwart my efforts, and even undermine my ability to care about the fact that my efforts have been thwarted, such that once again I am nearly consumed with the wish to make the other go away.[53]

Part of what is so exciting about Aquinas's account is that it can spur one to uncover and seek to articulate some of the deepest mental causes of one's emotional reactions and habits, including assumptions that one makes about what is ultimately real and really important in life. Studying Aquinas might cause me, for example, to realize that a prominent cause of my hatred for a particular individual is an assumption I make about the way the world is supposed to be or ought ideally to be, namely, ordered in such a way that I always get my way. Making such an assumption explicit gives me the opportunity to question it. In questioning it, I might realize many important things—for example, that it is not so much the other whom I hate, but the other has become a scapegoat for my growing hatred concerning "the way things are" in the world or in my life, so that hating the other, in particular, allows me to feel rational and justified in feeling hatred almost all of the time. Making this hatred explicit will likely cause a shock, as it will quickly become clear that I have a much bigger problem than simply dealing with a difficult person. The very act of becoming curious about my hatred and its causes is likely to alter my hatred, partly because this curiosity involves making my hatred the central object of my apprehension, which takes some of the focus off of the original object of the hatred and gives me the opportunity to reconceive that object. Repeated acts of curiosity and concern regarding one's own emotional states are likely to increase one's emotional flexibility generally so that one is less dominated by opaque habits of being moved.

There are many other potential benefits of learning and putting to use a well-developed grammar of emotion, including additional benefits to one's relationships with others. Learning such a grammar can support the practice of virtuous communication regarding the dynamics of one's own and others' interior lives; it can thus support more discerning and responsible human interactions. It could be that my hatred for one person is causing me to be disagreeable at home, to the point that I say thoughtless things to my partner or child, causing him or her to become angry with me, and me to become resentful in turn. I am at a great advantage, and my relationships, too, are at an advantage, if I can discern that something like this is happening, confess it to my loved one in a way that is meaningful to him or her, and ask him or her to help me make a change. Rather than indulging my hatred, the other can help me do the work of constantly reimagining the person whom I am prone to hate. It helps if people share a common grammar, a common way of conceiving and talking about the logic of each other's emotional lives. Few of us are likely to "talk Aquinas" in our personal relationships, with people who are not academics, but it is quite easy, once one understands Aquinas, to translate central elements of his view into terms that will make sense to friends, family members, colleagues, and such.[54]

It must be noted that all of the information and tools that Aquinas's account provides people can be used well or poorly. They can be used for good or for ill. Notably, these tools can be used to manipulate others emotionally in ways that one might judge to be good, but in ways that inhibit human flourishing. Most of us are familiar with the way in which various media manipulate the emotions of consumers and political agents, in ways that go tragically unexamined and have devastating, long-term effects. Nevertheless, one way to arm ourselves and others against emotional manipulation is to learn for ourselves and to encourage others to learn for themselves a relatively sophisticated grammar of emotion—particularly one that allows us to think critically about that very grammar and use it with flexibility—so that we can consider carefully the impact that various exterior and interior forms of instruction have on our patterns of perception and inclination.

Finally, I want to make explicit that adopting or considering (for the sake of argument) Aquinas's account of the structure of emotion is likely to alter how one apprehends one's own emotions as objects. It can cause one to pay more attention to how one's emotions are composed and recomposed over time. This, in turn, can cause one to reexamine how one construes certain objects and the significance one takes those objects to have for one's happiness. If one experiments with Aquinas's account, with an explicit awareness of its metaphysical dimensions, one could come to see the world or aspects of it differently. One could become more reflective about the content of one's happiness. All of this could change, further, the impact that certain sensible goods and evils have on one's sensory appetite. In the end, one has to ascertain whether these changes are good, whether they improve the quality of one's life and one's relationships. It cannot be denied that one takes risks in engaging in this sort of inquiry—most notably in that the ground on which one decides such questions can itself shift. If one comes to be moved in a different way by a particular object, this could effect changes in one's intellectual judgments and acts of one's will, which could, in turn, reinforce one's sensory impressions and appetitive motions. One is constrained to make choices about emotions while being, at least some of the time, under the influence of emotions. The more virtuous one's habits of emotion, the more that influence is likely not only to be helpful but also to be partly constitutive of one's well-being. It is not a simple thing, however, to cultivate virtuous emotions.

FINAL THOUGHTS

I have offered an interpretation of Aquinas on the emotions—one that I find compelling, but not without problems, and not without need for supplementation. I have not sought to *defend* this account in all of its metaphysical depth. Virtually every feature of his account stands in relation to one or more lines of philosophical and theological inquiry, many of which relate to investigations in the natural and social sciences. Nearly every one of these lines extends in front of, through, *and* in the wake of Aquinas's thought, in ways that could not be described, let alone assessed or defended, without writing a history (indeed, multiple histories, with respect to different issues) of Western philosophical and religious thought. If one were to explore even a few relevant puzzles in depth (for example, the relationship between consciousness and the brain, or the relationship between what a human apprehends and what is "there" in the world to be apprehended) one would have to postpone indefinitely saying much about the emotions.

I have also not sought to defend Aquinas's account of the emotions in relation to other, competing accounts. I did set Aquinas's account up in relation to the work of James Gustafson (with reference to Jonathan Edwards) and Martha Nussbaum (with reference primarily to the Stoics). However, I am as interested in highlighting what is good and provocative in these and other alternatives as I am in showing how Aquinas improves on them. As I have argued, there is good reason not to settle too quickly, narrowly, and defensively into a single account when there is so much of value that one can glean from alternative perspectives. I have concentrated on trying to make Aquinas's account intelligible or available to a relatively wide range of contemporary readers who might find it illuminating and perhaps useful, in some ways, for self-reflection and ethical formation. I have not done much to relate Aquinas's account to other sorts of descriptive and explanatory accounts, of which there are many—neurobiological, evolutionary-biological, cross-cultural anthropological, experimental psychological, and so on. I have referred to these accounts, and I have tried to anticipate some of the objections they might bring to Aquinas; but to deal with these other sorts of accounts adequately, one has to place them within the context of their own disciplinary histories, methodological complexities, and relevant controversies, and this makes it difficult to draw them into a meaningful conversation with Aquinas. Much of Aquinas's account of the emotions (minus his thesis concerning the immateriality of the soul) is consistent, for example, with Antonio Damasio's scientifically based philosophical account of emotions and feelings, but there is no simple way to represent Damasio's perspective without placing it in conversation with competing views of its own kind, and it is clear how complicated this can be.[55] There are disagreements concerning how to interpret the scientific evidence, some of which are rooted in philosophical disagreements that are not likely, any time soon, to be resolved.

To compare Aquinas's analysis with the analysis of a worthy competitor, particularly a conceptual account that has significant metaphysical underpinnings, would require treating the other with the same seriousness and care. Only then could one hope to draw comparisons that are interesting and fair. It would be especially interesting, I think, to compare Aquinas's account with a competing account that is set explicitly within a different metaphysical frame, such as a neo-Stoic or a Buddhist worldview. Yet I have explored these possibilities enough to realize that analyzing well what even one great Stoic or Buddhist thinker has to say about emotions and related concepts would require another book of this sort. Comparing Aquinas to such a thinker would require comparing worlds of meaning, each of which is open to different interpretations, and each of which can thus offer different objects of comparison, some of which draw out similarities, and some of which draw out differences. Comparative religious ethical inquiry is difficult to do well without getting stalled in the mode of methodological reflection, but it is an important thing to attempt, and I encourage colleagues in this area of study to proceed, drawing on each other's strengths.

One must read Aquinas on the emotions in relation to other kinds of accounts, and in relation to accounts that are rooted in other worldviews, if one hopes to appreciate what is at issue in his or anyone else's account. Yet one must start somewhere. Aquinas's thought is a worthwhile place to start, particularly for those who care to know, or at least to wonder, about how we can best find our way in the face of so much that we do not—and may never—fully understand.

NOTES

1. Roberts, *Emotions*, sect. 1.5.

2. *ST* I 80.1; I-II 109.3.

3. In this paragraph, I am reading various comments of Aquinas concerning the causes of physical motion, such as *SCG* bk. 3b, chap. 92, in light of *ST* I-II 109.3 and 26.2.

4. I am calling to mind, here, the general move that Aquinas makes from natural love to higher forms of love, as explicated in earlier chapters.

5. I am mindful of the feminist philosophy of science, which has called attention to the ways in which biological "motions" tend to be described by scientists in ways that are gendered. See, for example, Emily Martin, "The Egg and the Sperm: How Science Has Constructed a Romance Based on Stereotypical Male—Female Roles," *Signs: Journal of Women in Culture and Society* 16, no. 3 (1991): 485–501.

6. For Aquinas, this sort of tending, the central moment of which is "concupiscence," is only one way that humans tend toward other humans in love. Another way is "friendship," which includes (on the part of each friend) the act of wishing the other well for his or her own sake. See *ST* I-II 26.4.

7. *ST* I-II 91.2 and 94.2. I use the term "behavior" to include operations over which an entity has no control as well as conscious operations over which a being has some choice.

8. In this chapter, I am connecting "love" with "law," but it is beyond my scope here to engage seriously the tradition of Thomistic natural law theology and ethics. I have been most influenced in my thinking about Aquinas and natural law by Jean Porter's excellent scholarship and by a desire to square Aquinas on natural law with what I understand to be his eudaimonistic ethic of virtue. See Jean Porter, *Natural and Divine Law: Reclaiming the Tradition for Christian Ethics (Grand Rapids, Mich.: Eerdmans, 2000) and Nature as Reason: A Thomistic Theory of the Natural Law* (Grand Rapids, Mich.: Eerdmans, 2005).

9. In cases where a human fails to exercise these powers at all, he or she dies, unless another human exercises these powers on his or her behalf. In addition, questions arise as to whether the first human is indeed human.

10. *ST* I-II 3.5.

11. *ST* I-II 91.1, 93.1, and 93.2. The eternal law (*lex aeterna*) differs from the divine law (*lex divina*) in that the latter is a rule for (outer and inner) behavior that is promulgated by God and recorded in Christian scripture in the form of the Old and the New Testaments (*ST* I-II 91.4, 91.5).

12. *ST* I-II 90.4 *ad* 2, 91.2, and 94.2.

13. *ST* I-II 57.5.

14. *ST* I-II 59.2.

15. *ST* I-II 109.2, 109.3 (including *ad* 1), and 110.2. See also Aquinas's discussion of the theological and infused virtues, *ST* I-II 62.1, 63.3.

16. On the relationship between moral failure and sin see *ST* I-II 71.6.

17. *ST* II-II 23, 24.

18. *ST* II-II 25, 26.

19. *ST* I-II 106.1. The "new law" is a symbol that encompasses many things, including the New Testament, the person of Christ, the Christian love command, and the grace of the Holy Spirit that is instilled in a person who believes in Christ, which allows the Christian to hear the law of love *as* the demand and delight of his or her own being. For further reflection on the relationship between the law of human reason and the laws that are promulgated in scripture, see Porter, *Nature as Reason*.

20. *ST* I-II 106.2 *ad* 2.

21. See Stephen J. Pope, *The Evolution of Altruism and the Ordering of Love* (Washington, DC: Georgetown University Press, 1994).

22. See, for example, Stephen J. Pope's review of Jean Porter's *Natural and Divine Law*, in the *Journal of Law and Religion* 16, no. 2 (2001): 685–87.

23. See Pope, *Human Evolution and Christian Ethics*.

24. See, for example, *ST* I 92.1, including *ad* 1 and *ad* 2.

25. Without this sort of curious and concerned engagement, one will likely be "tone deaf" with respect to religious ideas, and one's criticisms of them will likely be "flat."

26. Aquinas thinks that a "self" who is functioning *well* apprehends that "its own" interests are tied up with the interests of "other selves." He agrees with Aristotle that complete happiness is "self-sufficient," yet "what we count as self-sufficient is not what suffices for a solitary person by himself, living an isolated life, but what suffices also for parents, children, wife and in general for friends and fellow-citizens, since a human being is a naturally political [animal]" (*Nicomachean Ethics* 1097b7). Aquinas agrees with Aristotle that one fittingly loves a friend, in particular, as "another oneself," whose well-being is included in one's own, extended well-being (*ST* I-II 28.1). One of the functions of grace, in Aquinas's view, is to make it possible for one to experience "love of friendship" (charity) toward one's fellow humans as such, even as one enjoys special affection for certain humans in one's life (*ST* II-II 23.1, including *ad* 2). See Cates, *Choosing to Feel*. See also Stephen J. Pope, "'Equal Regard' versus 'Special Relations'? Reaffirming the Inclusiveness of Agape," *Journal of Religion* 77, no. 3 (1997): 353–79.

27. Aquinas defines sorrow as a painful "conjunction with some evil (which is [evil insofar as] it deprives one of some good), and perception of this conjunction" (*ST* I-II 35.1).

28. *Rhetoric*, trans. W. Rhys Roberts, in *The Basic Works of Aristotle*, ed. Richard McKeon (New York: Random House, 1941), 1317–1451.

29. *Rhetoric* 1378a20. This is part of the definition of emotion that Aristotle puts forward in the *Rhetoric*: "The Emotions are all those feelings [*pathê*] that so change [humans] as to affect their judgements, and that are also attended by pain or pleasure."

30. *Rhetoric* 1378a23.

31. *Rhetoric* 1385b12–1386b8.

32. For example, there is a section in the *Rhetoric* on how to calm people's anger, beginning at 1380a5.

33. *ST* I-II 24.3, 24.4, including *ad* 1, 56.4.

34. Aquinas, *Commentary on Aristotle's "The Nicomachean Ethics"* (1964), bk. 4, lect. 13.

35. *ST* I-II 94.2.

36. *ST* I-II 106.1, 108.3. What Aquinas says about the ordering of intellectual-appetitive motions applies also to the ordering of sensory-appetitive motions that are amenable to reason.

37. See Aquinas's discussion of the object and the order of charity in *ST* II-II 25–26.

38. *ST* II-II 24.8, 24.9; *Truth* 22.6.

39. See, for example, *ST* I-II 69.3, 61.5, 64.1 *ad* 3. For further discussion of the impact of theological and infused virtue on emotion, see Cates, *Choosing to Feel*, 42–48.

40. *ST* II-II 25.5; I-II 24.3.

41. *ST* I-II 62.2.

42. *ST* I-II 24.4.

43. For an excellent discussion of the ways in which Thomistic emotions are "cognitively penetrable," see King, "Aquinas on the Passions," 126–32.

44. See Seneca's brilliant treatment of anger in *De Ira*, in *Seneca: Moral Essays*, vol. 1, trans. John W. Basore (Cambridge, Mass.: Harvard University Press, 2003), 106–355.

45. Compare J. Giles Milhaven, *Good Anger* (Kansas City, Mo.: Sheed and Ward, 1989), and E. P. Sanders, *Jesus and Judaism* (Philadelphia: Fortress, 1985).

46. It is valuable to distinguish hatred from its close cousin, disgust. See Martha Craven Nussbaum, *Hiding from Humanity: Disgust, Shame, and the Law* (Princeton, N.J.: Princeton University Press, 2004).

47. Many people think that in being angry and expressing their anger they can *make* a person who has slighted them show them the regard they are due. In thinking this, people are often mistaken. Many expressions of anger simply scare people or cause them to become angry in response. However, if what one wants is simple to assert one's power and make someone suffer the force of one's power—because feeling one's power is pleasing in the wake of having been treated as "small" and feeling "small"—then anger can be an effective means to this end. If one keeps in mind that anger is a motion of the sensory appetite that is more *or less* informed by judgments of reason, one can treat it with due flexibility. See Cates, "Taking Women's Experience Seriously."

48. Aquinas treats hatred briefly, both in his discussion of the passions or emotions (*ST* I-II 29) and in his discussion of intellectual appetites or affections (*ST* II-II 34).

49. This is Keith Green's apt phrase (personal conversation). For further discussion of Aquinas on hatred, see Keith Green, "Aquinas on Attachment, Envy, and Hatred in the *Summa Theologica*," *Journal of Religious Ethics* 35, no. 3 (2007): 403–28.

50. *ST* II-II 34.3.

51. *ST* II-II 34.3 *ad* 3.

52. Aquinas's account leads us to anticipate that "cognitive therapies" are likely to be most effective when they are associated with the deliberate use of images, symbols, and other more sensory inputs. Consider, for example, the archetypal approach of Carl Jung and contemporary interpreters, such as James Hillman, Caroline Myss, or Clarissa Pinkola Estés.

53. Even this very basic use of Aquinas allows one to apprehend that it is precisely one's hatred that keeps the other from going away because it keeps him or her present to one's mind even when he or she is physically absent.

54. A good way to begin familiarizing oneself with Aquinas's account of the emotion is to read his treatise on the passions (*ST* I-II 22–48).

55. See the works by Damasio that are included in the bibliography.

APPENDIX

Aquinas on the Powers or Capabilities of a Human Being (Relevant Selections)

✦

INTELLECTUAL POWERS

Intellectual apprehension (INTELLECT)
>   divinely infused principle that can influence intellectual apprehension: faith
>   understanding, practical reasoning, and other acts of the intellect involved in decision-
>   making processes; self-awareness and self-direction

Intellectual appetite (WILL)
>   divinely infused principles that can influence the intellectual appetite: hope and charity
>   modes of tending in relation to goods or evils that one apprehends via the powers of in-
>   tellectual apprehension: simple acts of the will, affections, and other acts of the will
>   involved in decision-making processes; self-movement

SENSORY POWERS

Sensory apprehension
>   interior senses: cogitative power (particular reason), memory, imagination, common sense
>   exterior senses: sight, hearing, smell, taste, touch
Sensory appetite
>   modes of tending in relation to goods or evils that one apprehends via the powers of
>   sensory apprehension (under the influence of the intellect and will, usually through
>   the medium of the cogitative power).
>   irascible emotions: hope and despair; daring and fear; anger
>   concupiscible emotions: love and hatred (first moment); desire and aversion (second mo-
>   ment); delight and sorrow (third moment)

VEGETATIVE POWERS

Apprehension on the part of God
>   internal principles of order that make good human functioning possible on the level of
>   living organism
>   *Natural appetite*
>   nutrition, growth, generation

Bibliography

Angelou, Maya. *I Know Why the Caged Bird Sings*. New York: Random House, 1969.

Aquinas, Thomas. *Commentary on Aristotle's "De Anima."* Translated by Kenelm Foster and Silvester Humphries. Notre Dame, Ind: Dumb Ox, 1994.

————. *Commentary on Aristotle's "Metaphysics."* Translated by John P. Rowan. Notre Dame, Ind: Dumb Ox, 1961.

————. *Commentary on Aristotle's "Nicomachean Ethics."* Translated by C. I. Litzinger. Notre Dame, Ind: Dumb Ox, 1964.

————. *The De Malo of Thomas Aquinas.* Translated by Richard Regan. Edited by Brian Davies. New York: Oxford University Press, 2001.

————. *Summa contra Gentiles.* Translated by English Dominicans. London: Burns, Oates, and Washbourne, 1924. Electronic access via *The Collected Works of St. Thomas Aquinas.* http://library.nlx.com/display.cfm?&clientID=79640633&depth=2&infobase=pmaquinas.nfo&softpage=GetClient42&titleCategory=0&view=browse.

————. *Summa Theologica.* Translated by Fathers of the English Dominican Province. Westminster, Md.: Christian Classics, 1981.

————. *Truth.* Vol. 2. Translated by James V. McGlynn. Indianapolis, Ind: Hackett, 1994.

————. *Truth.* Vol. 3. Translated by Robert W. Schmidt. Indianapolis, Ind: Hackett, 1994.

————. *Summa theologiae.* Edited by Petri Caramello. Rome: Marietti, 1950.

Aquinatis, S. Thomae. *Quaestiones disputatae de veritate.* Edited by Raymundi Spiazzi. Rome: Marietti, 1949.

de Aquino, S. Thomae. Sentencia libri De anima. *Opera Omnia.* Fundación Tomás de Aquino, 2006. http://www.corpusthomisticum.org/iopera.html.

————. *Sententia libri Ethicorum. Opera Omnia.* Fundación Tomás de Aquino, 2006. www.corpusthomisticum.org/iopera.html.

————. *Sententia libri Metaphysicae. Opera Omnia.* Fundación Tomás de Aquino, 2006. www.corpusthomisticum.org/iopera.html.

————. *Summa contra Gentiles. Opera Omnia.* Fundación Tomás de Aquino, 2006. www.corpusthomisticum.org/iopera.html.

Aristotle. *De Anima.* Translated by J. A. Smith. In *The Basic Works of Aristotle*, edited by Richard McKeon, 534–603. New York: Random House, 1941.

————. *Metaphysics.* Translated by W. D. Ross. In *The Basic Works of Aristotle*, edited by Richard McKeon, 682–926. New York: Random House, 1941.

————. *Nicomachean Ethics.* Translated by Terence Irwin. Indianapolis, Ind: Hackett, 1985.

————. *Rhetoric.* Translated by W. Rhys Roberts. In *The Basic Works of Aristotle*, edited by Richard McKeon, 1317–1451. New York: Random House, 1941.

Baker, Richard R. *The Thomistic Theory of the Passions and Their Influence upon the Will*. PhD diss., University of Notre Dame, 1941.

Blum, Lawrence. *Friendship, Altruism and Morality*. London: Routledge and Kegan Paul, 1980.

Cahill, Lisa Sowle. *Theological Bioethics: Participation, Justice, and Change*. Washington, DC: Georgetown University Press, 2005.

Calhoun, Cheshire, and Robert C. Solomon, eds. *What Is an Emotion?: Classic Readings in Philosophical Psychology*. New York: Oxford University Press, 1984.

Cates, Diana Fritz. *Choosing to Feel: Virtue, Friendship, and Compassion for Friends*. Notre Dame, Ind.: University of Notre Dame, 1997.

————. "Conceiving Emotions: Martha Nussbaum's *Upheavals of Thought*." *Journal of Religious Ethics* 31, no. 2 (2003): 325–43.

————. "The Religious Dimension of Ordinary Human Emotions." *Journal of the Society of Christian Ethics* 25, no. 1 (2005): 35–53.

————. "Taking Women's Experience Seriously: Thomas Aquinas and Audre Lorde on Anger." In *Aquinas and Empowerment: Classical Ethics for Ordinary Lives*, edited by G. Simon Harak, 47–88. Washington, DC: Georgetown University Press, 1996.

————. "Thomas Aquinas on Intimacy and Emotional Integrity." *Studies in Spirituality* 16 (2006): 111–30.

————. "The Virtue of Temperance." In *The Ethics of Aquinas*, edited by Stephen J. Pope, 321–39. Washington, DC: Georgetown University Press, 2002.

Cooper, John M. "An Aristotelian Theory of the Emotions." In *Essays on Aristotle's Rhetoric*, edited by Amélie Oksenberg Rorty, 238–57. Berkeley: University of California Press, 1996.

————. *Reason and Emotion: Essays on Ancient Moral Psychology and Ethical Theory*. Princeton, N.J.: Princeton University Press, 1999.

Corrigan, John, ed. *The Oxford Handbook of Religion and Emotion*. Oxford: Oxford University Press, 2008.

Crowe, Frederick. "Complacency and Concern in the Thought of St. Thomas." *Theological Studies* 20 (1959): 1–39, 198–230, 343–95. Reprinted in *Three Thomist Studies* (Supplementary Issue of Lonergan Workshop, Vol. 16), Boston College, 2000.

Dalai Lama. *Healing Anger: The Power of Patience from a Buddhist Perspective*. Translated by Geshe Thupten Jinpa. Ithaca, N.Y.: Snow Lion, 1997.

————. *The Meaning of Life: Buddhist Perspectives on Cause and Effect*. Translated by Jeffrey Hopkins. Boston: Wisdom, 2000.

Damasio, Antonio R. *Descartes' Error: Emotion, Reason, and the Human Brain*. New York: Avon, 1994.

————. *The Feeling of What Happens: Body and Emotion in the Making of Consciousness*. New York: Harcourt Brace, 1999.

————. *Looking for Spinoza: Joy, Sorrow, and the Feeling Brain*. Orlando, Fla.: Harcourt, 2003.

De Sousa, Ronald. *The Rationality of Emotion*. Cambridge, Mass.: MIT Press, 1987.

Donceel, Joseph. "A Liberal Catholic's View." In *The Problem of Abortion*, edited by Joel Feinberg, 15–20. Belmont, Calif.: Wadsworth, 1984.

Drost, Mark P. "In the Realm of the Senses: St. Thomas Aquinas on Sensory Love, Desire, and Delight." *The Thomist* 59, no. 1 (1995): 47–58.

Eberl, Jason T. "Aquinas's Account of Human Embryogenesis and Recent Interpretations." *Journal of Medicine and Philosophy* 30, no. 4 (2005): 379–94.

————. "The Beginning of Personhood: A Thomistic Biological Analysis." *Bioethics* 14, no. 2 (2000): 134–57.

Edwards, Jonathan, "A Dissertation Concerning the Nature of True Virtue." In *The Works of Jonathan Edwards*, Vol. 1, revised and corrected by Edward Hickman, 122–142. Avon, U.K.: Bath, 1992.

————. "A Treatise Concerning Religious Affections." In *The Works of Jonathan Edwards*. Vol. 1, 234–343. Avon, U.K.: Bath, 1992.

Ekman, Paul. "Facial Expressions of Emotion: New Findings, New Questions." *Psychological Science* 3, no. 1 (1992): 34–38.

Fasching, Darrell. *Narrative Theology after Auschwitz: From Alienation to Ethics*. Minneapolis, Minn.: Fortress, 1992.

Floyd, Shawn D. "Aquinas on Emotion: A Response to Some Recent Interpretations." *History of Philosophy Quarterly* 15, no. 2 (1998): 161–75.

Frankenberry, Nancy K., and Hans H. Penner. "Clifford Geertz's Long-Lasting Moods, Motivations, and Metaphysical Conceptions." *Journal of Religion* 79, no. 4 (1999): 617–40.

Gadamer, Hans-Georg. *Truth and Method*. Translated by Joel Weinsheimer and D. G. Marshall. 2nd ed. New York: Crossroads, 1992.

Geertz, Clifford. "Religion as a Cultural System." Reprinted in *The Interpretation of Cultures: Selected Essays*. New York: Basic Books, 1973.

Gereboff, Joel. "Judaism." In *The Oxford Handbook of Religion and Emotion*, edited by John Corrigan, 95–110. Oxford: Oxford University Press, 2008.

Gereboff, Joel, Keith Green, Diana Fritz Cates, and Maria Heim, "The Nature of the Beast: Hatred in Cross-Traditional Religious and Philosophical Perspective." *Journal of the Society of Christian Ethics* 29, no. 2 (2009).

Green, Keith. "Aquinas on Attachment, Envy, and Hatred in the *Summa Theologica*." *Journal of Religious Ethics* 35, no. 3 (2007): 403–28.

Griffiths, Paul E. *What Emotions Really Are: The Problem of Psychological Categories*. Chicago: University of Chicago Press, 1997.

Gross, Daniel M. *The Secret History of Emotion: From Aristotle's Rhetoric to Modern Brain Science*. Chicago: University of Chicago Press, 2006.

Gustafson, James M. *Can Ethics Be Christian?* Chicago: University of Chicago Press, 1975.

————. *Ethics from a Theocentric Perspective, Volume One: Theology and Ethics*. Chicago: University of Chicago Press, 1981.

————. "Retrospective Interpretation of American Religious Ethics, 1948–1998." *Journal of Religious Ethics* 25, no. 3 (1998): 2–22.

Harak, G. Simon. *Virtuous Passions: The Formation of Christian Character*. Mahwah, N.J.:
    Paulist, 1993.
Hardman, Charlotte E. *Other Worlds: Notions of Self and Emotion among the Lohorung Rai*.
    Oxford: Berg, 2000.
Hatzimoysis, Anthony, ed. *Philosophy and the Emotions*. Cambridge: Cambridge Uni-
    versity Press, 2003.
Hauerwas, Stanley. *Truthfulness and Tragedy: Further Investigations in Christian Ethics*. Notre
    Dame, Ind: University of Notre Dame Press, 1977.
Heim, Maria. "Buddhism." In *The Oxford Handbook of Religion and Emotion*, edited by
    John Corrigan, 17–34. Oxford: Oxford University Press, 2008.
Inwood, Brad. *Ethics and Human Action in Early Stoicism*. Oxford: Clarendon, 1985.
Irwin, Terence H. "Who Discovered the Will?" *Philosophical Perspectives* 6 (1992): 453–73.
James, William. *The Principles of Psychology*. Vol. 2. New York: Dover, 1950.
———. *The Varieties of Religious Experience*. New York: Macmillan, 1961.
Jenkins, Willis. "Biodiversity and Salvation: Thomistic Roots for Environmental Ethics."
    Journal of Religion 83, no. 3 (2003): 401–20.
Johann, Robert. *The Meaning of Love: An Essay towards the Metaphysics of Intersubjectivity*.
    Glen Rock, N.J.: Paulist, 1966.
Keenan, James F. *Goodness and Rightness in Thomas Aquinas's* Summa theologiae. Wash-
    ington, DC: Georgetown University Press, 1992.
King, Peter. "Aquinas on the Passions." In *Aquinas's Moral Theory: Essays in Honor of Nor-
    man Kretzmann*, edited by Scott MacDonald and Eleonore Stump, 101–32. Ithaca,
    N.Y.: Cornell University Press, 1999.
Kloos, John. "Constructionism and Its Critics." In *The Oxford Handbook of Religion and
    Emotion*, edited by John Corrigan, 474–89. Oxford: Oxford University Press,
    2008.
Knauff, Markus, and Elisabeth May. "Mental Imagery, Reasoning, and Blindness." *Quar-
    terly Journal of Experimental Psychology* 59, no. 1 (2006): 161–77.
Lauritzen, Paul. "Emotion and Religious Ethics." *Journal of Religious Ethics* 16, no. 2
    (1988): 307–24.
———. *Religious Belief and Emotional Transformation: A Light in the Heart*. Lewisburg,
    Pa.: Bucknell University Press, 1992.
———. "The Self and Its Discontents: Recent Work on Morality and the Self." *Jour-
    nal of Religious Ethics* 22, no. 1 (1994): 189–210.
Leget, Carlo. "Martha Nussbaum and Thomas Aquinas on the Emotions." *Theological
    Studies* 64, no. 3 (2003): 558–81.
Leighton, Stephen R. "Aristotle and the Emotions." In *Essays on Aristotle's "Rhetoric,"* ed-
    ited by Amélie Oksenberg Rorty, 206–37. Berkeley: University of California Press,
    1996.
Little, David, and Sumner B. Twiss. *Comparative Religious Ethics: A New Method*. San Fran-
    cisco: Harper & Row, 1961.
Lovin, Robin W., and Frank E. Reynolds. "In the Beginning." In *Cosmogony and Ethical
    Order: New Studies in Comparative Ethics*, edited by Robin W. Lovin and Frank E.
    Reynolds, 1–35. Chicago: University of Chicago Press, 1985.

Lutz, Catherine A. *Unnatural Emotions: Everyday Sentiments on a Micronesian Atoll and Their Challenge to Western Theory*. Chicago: University of Chicago Press, 1998.

Lyons, William. *Emotion*. Cambridge: Cambridge University Press, 1980.

MacDonald, Scott C., and Eleonore Stump, eds. *Aquinas's Moral Theory: Essays in Honor of Norman Kretzmann*. Ithaca, N.Y.: Cornell University Press, 1998.

MacIntyre, Alasdair. *Dependent Rational Animals: Why Human Beings Need the Virtues*. Chicago: Open Court, 1999.

Martin, Emily. "The Egg and the Sperm: How Science Has Constructed a Romance Based on Stereotypical Male–Female Roles." *Signs: Journal of Women in Culture and Society* 16, no. 3 (1991): 485–501.

McDaniel, June. "Hinduism." In *The Oxford Handbook of Religion and Emotion*, edited by John Corrigan, 51–72. Oxford: Oxford University Press, 2008.

McDonough, William. "Etty Hillesum's Learning to Live and Preparing to Die: *Complacentia Boni* as the Beginning of Acquired and Infused Virtue." *Journal of the Society of Christian Ethics* 25, no. 2 (2005): 179–202.

Midgley, Mary. *Beast and Man: The Roots of Human Nature*. London: Routledge, 1995.

———. *Wickedness: A Philosophical Essay*. London: Ark Paperbacks, Routledge and Kegan Paul, 1986.

Milhaven, J. Giles. *Good Anger*. Kansas City, Mo.: Sheed and Ward, 1989.

Murdoch, Iris. *The Sovereignty of Good*. London: Routledge and Kegan Paul, 1985.

Murphy, Claudia E. "Aquinas on Our Responsibility for Our Emotions." *Medieval Philosophy and Theology* 8 (1999): 163–205.

Murphy, Nancey. *Bodies and Souls, or Spirited Bodies?* Cambridge: Cambridge University Press, 2006.

Nelkin, Dorothy, and M. Susan Lindee. *The DNA Mystique: The Gene as a Cultural Icon*. New York: W. H. Freeman, 1995.

Nussbaum, Martha Craven. *Hiding from Humanity: Disgust, Shame, and the Law*. Princeton, N.J.: Princeton University Press, 2004.

———. *The Therapy of Desire: Theory and Practice in Hellenistic Ethics*. Princeton, N.J.: Princeton University Press, 1994.

———. *Upheavals of Thought: The Intelligence of Emotions*. Cambridge: Cambridge University Press, 2001.

———. "Virtue Ethics: A Misleading Category?" *The Journal of Ethics* 3 (1999): 162–201.

Oakley, Justin. *Morality and the Emotions*. London: Routledge, 1992.

Otto, Rudolf. *The Idea of the Holy*. New York: Oxford University Press, 1982.

Pasnau, Robert. *Thomas Aquinas on Human Nature*. Cambridge: Cambridge University Press, 2002.

Pearlman, Bari, producer and director. *Daughters of Wisdom*. Los Angeles: Seventh Art Releasing, 2007.

Pope, Stephen J. "'Equal Regard' versus 'Special Relations'? Reaffirming the Inclusiveness of Agape." *The Journal of Religion* 77, no. 3 (1997): 353–79.

———. *The Evolution of Altruism and the Ordering of Love*. Washington, DC: Georgetown University Press, 1994.

————. *Human Evolution and Christian Ethics*. Cambridge: Cambridge University Press, 2007.

————. Review of Jean Porter, *Natural and Divine Law: Reclaiming the Tradition for Christian Ethics. Journal of Law and Religion* 16, no. 2 (2001): 679–88.

Porter, Jean. "Desire for God: Ground of the Moral Life in Aquinas." Theological Studies 47, no. 1 (1986): 48–68.

————. "Mere History: The Place of Historical Studies in Theological Ethics." *Journal of Religious Ethics* 25, no. 3 (1998): 103–26.

————. *Natural and Divine Law: Reclaiming the Tradition for Christian Ethics*. Grand Rapids, Mich.: Eerdmans, 2000.

————. *Nature as Reason: A Thomistic Theory of the Natural Law*. Grand Rapids, Mich.: Eerdmans, 2005.

Potts, Michael. "Sensory Experiences in Near Death Experiences and the Thomistic View of the Soul." *International Journal for Philosophy of Religion* 49 (2001): 85–100.

President's Council on Bioethics. "Neuroimaging and Antisocial Personality Disorder Case Study." Session Five: Neuroscience, Brain, and Behavior, IV: Brain Imaging (Case Study), 2004. www.bioethics.gov/transcripts/june04/session5.html (accessed March 7, 2006).

Proudfoot, Wayne. *Religious Experience*. Berkeley: University of California Press, 1985.

Raboteau, Albert J. *Slave Religion: The "Invisible Institution" in the Antebellum South*. New York: Oxford University Press, 1978.

Reeder, John P., Jr. "Religion and Morality." In *Oxford Handbook of the Sociology of Religion*, edited by Peter Clarke, 336–59. Oxford: Oxford University Press, 2009.

————. *Source, Sanction, and Salvation: Religion and Morality in Judaic and Christian Traditions*. Englewood Cliffs, N.J.: Prentice Hall, 1988.

————. "What Is a Religious Ethic?" *Journal of Religious Ethics* 25, no. 3 (1998): 157–81.

————. "Why Are We So Confused about Religion?" James C. Spalding Memorial Lecture, The University of Iowa, 2002.

Reynolds, Thomas E. "Toward the Other: Christianity and Buddhism on Desire." *Journal of Ecumenical Studies* 39 (Summer/Fall 2002): 325–39.

Roberts, Robert C. *Emotions: An Essay in Aid of Moral Psychology*. Cambridge: Cambridge University Press, 2003.

————. "Emotions among the Virtues of the Christian Life." *Journal of Religious Ethics* 20 (Spring 1992): 37–68.

————. "Emotions Research and Religious Experience." In *The Oxford Handbook of Religion and Emotion*, edited by John Corrigan, 490–506. Oxford: Oxford University Press, 2008.

————. "Thomas Aquinas on the Morality of Emotions." *History of Philosophy Quarterly* 9, no. 3 (1992): 287–305.

Rosaldo, Michelle Z. *Knowledge and Passion: Ilongot Notions of Self and Social Life*. Cambridge: Cambridge University Press, 1980.

Ryan, Thomas. "Revisiting Affective Knowledge and Connaturality in Aquinas." *Theological Studies* 66 (2005): 49–68.

Saliers, Don E. *The Soul in Paraphrase: Prayer and the Religious Affections.* New York: Seabury, 1980.

Sanders, E. P. *Jesus and Judaism.* Philadelphia: Fortress, 1985.

Sarot, Marcel. "God, Emotion, and Corporeality: A Thomist Perspective." *The Thomist* 58 (January 1994): 61–92.

Schofer, Jonathan Wyn. *The Making of a Sage: A Study in Rabbinic Ethics.* Madison: University of Wisconsin Press, 2005.

Seneca. "On Anger." In *Seneca: Moral Essays.* Vol. 1. Translated by John W. Basore, 106–355. Cambridge, Mass.: Harvard University Press, 2003.

———. "On Providence." In *Seneca: Moral Essays.* Vol. 1. Translated by John W. Basore, 2–47. Cambridge, Mass: Harvard University Press, 2003.

Sherman, Nancy. *The Fabric of Character: Aristotle's Theory of Virtue.* New York: Oxford University Press, 1989.

Sherwin, Michael S. *By Knowledge and By Love: Charity and Knowledge in the Moral Theology of St. Thomas Aquinas.* Washington, DC: Catholic University of America Press, 2005.

Smith, John E. *Experience and God.* New York: Newman, 1971.

Solomon, Robert C. *The Passions: The Myth and Nature of Human Emotion.* Notre Dame, Ind.: University of Notre Dame Press, 1976.

Sorabji, Richard. *Emotion and Peace of Mind: From Stoic Agitation to Christian Temptation.* Oxford: Oxford University Press, 2000.

Souaiaia, Ahmed E. *Contesting Justice: Women, Islam, Law, and Society.* New York: State University of New York Press, 2008.

Spohn, William C. "Passions and Principles" (Notes in Moral Theology: 1990). *Theological Studies* 52 (1991): 69–87.

———. "Spirituality and Ethics: Exploring the Connections." *Theological Studies* 58 (1997): 109–23.

———. "Spirituality and Its Discontents: Practices in Jonathan Edwards's *Charity and Its Fruits.*" *Journal of Religious Ethics* 31, no. 2 (2003): 253–76.

Stalnaker, Aaron. *Overcoming Our Evil: Human Nature and Spiritual Exercises in Xunzi and Augustine.* Washington, DC: Georgetown University Press, 2006.

Stark, Susan. "A Change of Heart: Moral Emotions, Transformation, and Moral Virtue." *Journal of Moral Philosophy* 1, no. 1 (2004): 31–50.

Stendahl, Krister. "The Apostle Paul and the Introspective Conscience of the West." In *The Writings of St. Paul*, edited by Wayne A. Meeks, 422–34. New York: W. W. Norton, 1972.

Stout, Jeffrey. "Commitments and Traditions in the Study of Religious Ethics." *Journal of Religious Ethics* 25, no. 3 (1998): 23–56.

———. *Democracy and Tradition.* Princeton, N.J.: Princeton University Press, 2004.

Tallon, Andrew. *Head and Heart: Affection, Cognition, Volition as Triune Consciousness.* New York: Fordham University Press, 1997.

Taylor, Charles. *Sources of the Self: The Making of the Modern Identity.* Cambridge, Mass.: Harvard University Press, 1989.

Taylor, Gabriele. "Justifying the Emotions." *Mind* 84 (1975): 390–402.

Tillich, Paul. *Systematic Theology, Volume One: Reason and Revelation, Being and God.* Chicago: University of Chicago Press, 1951.

Trungpa, Chögyam. *The Myth of Freedom and the Way of Meditation.* Boston: Shambhala, 1988.

Uffenheimer-Lippens, Elisabeth. "Rationalized Passion and Passionate Rationality: Thomas Aquinas on the Relation between Reason and the Passions." *Review of Metaphysics* 56 (2003): 525–58.

Vacek, Edward Collins. "The Eclipse of Love for God." *America* 174 (8). http://web.ebscohost.com/ehost/detail?vid=1&hid=9&sid=2d619fe1–8f14–4965-913f-3aa8e2e246a1%40sessionmgr2 (accessed May 26, 2008).

———. *Love, Human and Divine: The Heart of Christian Ethics.* Washington, DC: Georgetown University Press, 1994.

Wallace, William A. "St. Thomas on the Beginning and Ending of Human Life." In *Autori Vari, Sanctus Thomas de Aquino Doctor Hodiernae Humanitatis. Studi Tomistici 58* Vatican City: Libreria Editrice Vaticana, 1995, 394–407. http://www2.nd.edu/Departments//Maritain/ti/wallace3.htm (accessed November 11, 2005).

Westberg, Daniel. "Emotion and God: A Reply to Marcel Sarot." *The Thomist* 60 (January 1996): 109–21.

———. *Right Practical Reason: Aristotle, Action, and Prudence in Aquinas.* New York: Clarendon, 1994.

White, Kevin. "The Passions of the Soul." In *The Ethics of Aquinas*, edited by Stephen J. Pope, 103–15. Washington, DC: Georgetown University Press, 2002.

White, Lynn, Jr. "The Historical Roots of our Ecological Crisis." *Science* 155 (March 10, 1969), 1203–7.

Yeager, D. M. "Passion and Suspicion: Religious Affections in 'The Will to Believe.'" *The Journal of Religion* 69, no. 4 (1989): 467–83.

Yearley, Lee H. *Mencius and Aquinas: Theories of Virtue and Conceptions of Courage.* Albany: State University of New York Press, 1990.

———. "New Religious Virtues and the Study of Religion." Reprinted in *Ways of Being Religious*, edited by Gary E. Kessler, 7–16. Mountain View, Calif.: Mayfield, 2000.

———. "Selves, Virtues, Odd Genres, and Alien Guides." *Journal of Religious Ethics* 25, no. 3 (1998): 127–55.

Zukov, Gary. *The Dancing Wu Li Masters: An Overview of the New Physics.* New York: Bantam, 1980.

Index

Abrams, Nancy Ellis, 123n10
abstracting universals from phantasms, 87,
    167–69, 173, 176, 182, 194, 213
act
    for an end, 135, 143–44, 195, 249–50
    concept of, 66, 75–76n2, 122n7, 130–
        32, 210n11
    interior (or interior motion), 67–70,
        127n88, 195
    simple, of the will, 8, 45, 91, 93–96,
        193–94, 211n40, 267
affections. *See also* intellectual appetite
    Aquinas on, 8–9, 17, 46, 88, 91, 93–94,
        96, 194, 205, 266n48, 267
    Edwards on, 8, 42, 44–45
    emotions, distinguished from, 7–9, 95–
        96, 193–94
    Gustafson on, 42, 43–47, 58
    religious, 8, 14, 42, 45–47. *See also*
        religious emotions
African American slaves, Exodus story for,
    41
akrasia (weakness of will), 70, 74, 79n69,
    238n17
Angelou, Maya, 58n3
angels, 35n14, 88, 91, 92, 93, 103–4,
    105, 201
anger
    Aquinas on, 61n72, 82–83, 122–23n9,
        152–54, 156–57
    Aristotle on rhetorical use of, 248–49
    bodily changes and, 83–84
    disgust and, 265n46
    ethical reflection on, 253–54
    goal of, 162n83, 188n58, 257, 265n47
    of God, 94–95
    hatred, relation to, 162n83, 257–58
    mental causes or objects of, 47–48, 54–
        57, 65, 82–83, 122n9, 175–76,
        188n58, 215–16, 253, 257

morality of, 55–56, 185, 207, 253–54
Nussbaum on, 54–57
the self, involving thoughts of, 54–56,
    188–89n58, 265n47
animals. *See* nonhuman animals
appetite
    apprehension, relation to, 14, 48n46,
        65–74, 78n43, 78n46, 80, 85,
        100n38, 110–11, 127n88, 129–30,
        164–65, 205–8, 213–18, 232–35,
        248, 267
    defined, 66, 80
    emotion as form of appetitive motion,
        62–63, 67–68, 93, 95, 235–37
    intellectual. *See* intellectual appetite
    natural. *See* natural appetite
    sensory. *See* entries at sensory appetite
apprehension
    appetite, relation to, 14, 48n46, 65–74,
        78n43, 78n46, 80, 85, 100n38,
        110–11, 127n88, 129–30, 164–65,
        205–8, 213–18, 232–35, 248, 267
    defined, 65–68, 80
    of goodness, 176–78
    intellectual. *See* intellectual
        apprehension
    sensory. *See* sensory apprehension
Aquinas on the emotions, 14–18
    affections, 8–9, 17, 46
    appetitive motion, emotion as form of,
        62–63, 67–68, 93, 95, 235–37
    Aristotelian-Thomistic framework, 5–6,
        27, 33, 36–37n21, 43
    concupiscible emotions, 118–20, 133–
        34. *See also* aversion; delight;
        desire; hatred; love; sorrow
    emergence of emotions, order of,
        163n24
    emotional engagement, importance of,
        238n4

sensory appetite (*continued*)
  emotions as motions of, 62–63, 67–68,
      93, 95, 235–37
sensory appetite from above, 16, 164–
    212
  desire, intellectual, 194–97
  goodness. *See* goodness
  guidance of sensory emotions by
      intellectual powers, 165–66
  intellect. *See* intellectual apprehension
  intellectual appetite (will), relation to,
      129–30, 193–94, 201–2
  intellectual emotions, 194–205. *See also*
      under specific emotions
  interplay of emotions and intellectual
      powers, 235–37
  natural and supernatural, 189n82, 208–
      9
  relationship between will and intellect,
      17, 191–92, 201–2, 205–8
  scale of being, 15–16, 164–65
  theological virtues, role of, 196, 198–
      99, 205, 208
sensory appetite from below, 15, 103–63
  cogitative power, 114–20, 128n97
  conclusions regarding, 157–58
  concupiscible sensory emotions, 133–
      39. *See also* aversion; delight;
      desire; hatred; love; sorrow
  emotions and cogitative power, 117–20
  estimative power, 113–15, 117, 128n97
  humans and nonhuman animals
      compared, 155–58
  interplay of emotions and intellectual
      powers, 235–37
  irascible sensory emotions, 149–53. *See
      also* anger; daring; despair; fear;
      hope
  memorative power, 116–17
  natural appetite. *See* natural appetite
  nonhuman animals. *See* nonhuman
      animals
  object-oriented nature of emotions,
      130–31
  plants and other living things, 108–10

poised between intellectual and natural
    appetite, 129–30
range and flexibility of phenomena
    analyzed by Aquinas, 120–22
relationships between basic sensory
    emotions, 153–55
scale of being, 15–16, 103–5
sensory apprehension, 111–13, 117
stones and other existing things, 105–
    8
tending, emotion as mode of, 131–34
sensory apprehension, 66, 67, 82
  cogitative power and, 117–20
  defined, 267
  of fear of hell, 219
  intellectual apprehension (intellect) and.
      See under intellectual apprehension
  in nonhuman animals, 111–13, 207
  "overflow," Thomistic concept of, 222–
      23
  range and flexibility of, 120–21
sensory soul of nonhuman animals, 111,
    124n29
sensus communis (common sense), 77n34,
    112–13, 117–19, 182
sexual desire
  as appetite, 10, 127n88
  as emotion, 127n88, 240n54
  judgment influenced by, 233–34
Sherman, Nancy, 78n43
Sherwin, Michael S., 78n43, 79n69,
    160n50, 190n92
situational emotions, 51
slaves, African American, Exodus story for,
    41
Smith, Adam, 77n30
Smith, John E., 46
Solomon, Robert C., 20n15
Sorabji, Richard, 20n15
sorrow
  defined, 264n27
  hatred, relation to, 147
  intellectual, 204–5
  Nussbaum on, 52, 53
  object-oriented nature of, 248